International Criminal Justice Series

Volume 25

The series aims to create a platform for publications covering the entire field of international criminal justice. It therefore deals with issues relating, among others, to:

- the work of international criminal courts and tribunals;
- transitional justice approaches in different countries;
- international anti-corruption and anti-money laundering initiatives;
- the history of international criminal law.

It is peer-reviewed and seeks to publish high-quality works emanating from excellent scholars.

More information about this series at http://www.springer.com/series/13470

Marian Yankson-Mensah

Transitional Justice in Ghana

An Appraisal of the National Reconciliation Commission

ASSER PRESS

Springer

Marian Yankson-Mensah
International Nuremberg
Principles Academy
Nuremberg, Germany

ISSN 2352-6718 ISSN 2352-6726 (electronic)
International Criminal Justice Series
ISBN 978-94-6265-378-8 ISBN 978-94-6265-379-5 (eBook)
https://doi.org/10.1007/978-94-6265-379-5

Published by T.M.C. ASSER PRESS, The Hague, The Netherlands www.asserpress.nl
Produced and distributed for T.M.C. ASSER PRESS by Springer-Verlag Berlin Heidelberg

This T.M.C. ASSER PRESS imprint is published by the registered company Springer-Verlag GmbH, DE part of Springer Nature.
The registered company address is: Heidelberger Platz 3, 14197 Berlin, Germany

To my daughters, Naa Dromo Mensah (may she rest in peace) and Evette Ama Kumah Mensah

Foreword

Marian Yankson-Mensah's study of the Ghanaian National Reconciliation Commission (NRC) provides a reminder of the recurring nexus between time, place, ideas and values in the quest for national as well as international justice. No community, nation, region or continent is an island unto itself—especially not in the age of global media. Each nation is directly and indirectly influenced by the trends, ideas, lessons and ideologies of others, as well as the wish of all people in every part of the world to be free from oppression, exploitation and dictatorship.

The book provides a lucid and exemplary study of the African struggle for accountability and the endeavours in Ghana for political stability—within the parameters of the scholarly debate on the continuity between norms of international justice and the pursuit of peace. It traces this debate from the escalation of democracy in African and Latin American nations in the 1980s, which gave rise to the proliferation of truth commissions in global politics.

No one model or size fits all. The debate on which comes first, justice or peace, and the inevitable quest for a balance between the two, requires careful contextual analysis and realistic choices, grounded in an ethic of responsibility rather than abstract forms of idealism. It involves a realistic commitment to international law, which requires a process of prosecutions for gross violations of human rights and a commitment to 'ultimate ends' that serve the emotional and material needs of victims. This aspires to the restoration of the basic principles and praxis of social justice by seeking to redress losses suffered by victims of past abuses as well as the creation of institutional structures that minimise the repetition of atrocities.

In a formative essay on the study of transitional justice written in the wake of the Chilean National Commission on Truth and Reconciliation, José Zalaquett argues that the ultimate goal of transitional justice involves the creation of a policy that furthers two overall objectives: the prevention of the recurrence of past abuses, and to the extent that this is possible, reparations for the damage caused by these atrocities. Allowing for the pursuit of these ideals to be exercised with different levels of severity or prudence, Zalaquett insists that this discretion needs to reflect the sovereign will of a nation. It is at the same time pertinent to recognize that the Rome Statute of the International Criminal Court (ICC), ratified on 1 July 2002, states that the four core crimes under international law: genocide, crimes against humanity, war crimes, and the crime of aggression 'shall not be subject to any statute of limitations'. Where states are 'unable' or 'unwilling' to investigate and prosecute such crimes, the ICC has jurisdiction to do so, provided such crimes are committed in the territory of a state party or by a national of a state party. In addition, the ICC may exercise its jurisdiction with respect to cases committed in the territory of or by a national of a non-state party where such a case is referred to the prosecutor by the United Nations Security Council.

Important, not least in the African situation, where presidents often endeavour to be 'presidents for life', Article 27(1) of the Rome Statute applies jurisdiction 'equally to all persons without any distinction based on official capacity'. A head of state or a government official, serving in an official capacity, shall not be exempted from criminal responsibility. Article 27(2), in turn, states that 'Immunities or special procedural rules which may attach to the official capacity of a person, whether under national or international law, shall not prevent the ICC from exercising its jurisdiction over such a person'.

The African Union and some of its member states, together with scholars elsewhere in the world, have frequently resisted the investigation of heads of state as well as other government officials investigated in pre-trial structures of the ICC. Some African states have, in turn, threatened to withdraw from the ICC in protest against the threat of such investigations. Other reasons for resistance to the court by African states include its apparent reluctance to prosecute the alleged atrocities of major powers and permanent members of the United Nations Security Council. African nations have further objected to what is perceived as an undue focus by the ICC on African states.

However, international legal norms have not been consistently applied as seen in transitional justice processes in Ghana, South Africa and other parts of the world. Written within the context of this debate, Yankson-Mensah provides a pertinent case-study on the Ghanaian NRC, which suggests that prosecution of perpetrators was not realistically possible. Unlike the South African Truth and Reconciliation Commission, it did not make allowance for perpetrators to apply for amnesty as an incentive to uncover past atrocities and did not name individual perpetrators in its final report.

The formal discussion on 'The Role of Truth Commissions and Prosecutions', organised by the Ghana Centre for Democratic Development, after the presentation of the NRC report to President John Agyekum Kufuor, is representative of the enduring tensions concerning the possibility of future prosecutions of past human rights abuses in Ghana. The president is reported to have neither anticipated nor eliminated the possibility of prosecutions. This, it appears, will be left to the discretion of the judicial and political leadership, the will of the people through democratic and civil processes.

The focus and subsequent response to the NRC in Ghanaian civil society, political debate and scholarly circles is primarily focused on the objectives, methodology and praxis of the commission, its impact on the pursuit of national reconciliation and the right of victims to reparations as well as the need for institutional reforms. Yankson-Mensah provides a penetrating legal and contextual analysis of these and related objectives in her concluding chapters, providing an important assessment of the NRC and possible future developments in the pursuit of human rights in Ghana—and by implication in other African countries. Her study makes a pertinent contribution to the global transitional justice debate.

Cape Town, South Africa
2019

Prof. Charles Villa-Vicencio
Former National Research Director
South African Truth and Reconciliation Commission
Visiting Professor in Conflict Resolution
Georgetown University
Washington, DC, USA

Professor Emeritus
University of Cape Town
Cape Town, South Africa

Acknowledgements

The study that led to this book was conducted with funding from the Deutscher Akademischer Austauschdienst (DAAD) through the South African-German Centre for Transnational Criminal Justice, a former DAAD Centre of Excellence in Africa. I therefore wish to extend my sincerest appreciation to the DAAD and the South African-German Centre for Transnational Criminal Justice, for equipping me with the financial means, the needed research materials and for providing me with a supportive research environment in Berlin and Cape Town to enable me to complete this research.

I am immensely grateful to my supervisors, Prof. Dr. Moritz Vormbaum and Prof. Dr. Gerhard Werle for their invaluable guidance and support in the course of undertaking this study. I deeply appreciate their patience and their encouragement, especially during my maternity break. Their support gave me the courage to work harder, and I am truly thankful to them for believing in my abilities throughout my studies. I am also very grateful to Prof. Lovell Fernandez of the University of the Western Cape, for his encouragement, constructive guidance and proofreading at the beginning of this book.

I would also like to say a big thank you to all the experts and respondents who participated in the surveys that led to the writing of this book. I am especially grateful to Prof. Kumi Ansah-Koi, Department of Political Science, University of Ghana; Prof. Kwame Boafo-Arthur, Department of Political Science, University of Ghana; Dr. Franklin Oduro, deputy director, Ghana Centre for Democratic Development; and Dr. Isaac L Annan, director and chief investigator, Commission on Human Rights Administrative Justice. Undoubtedly, your invaluable responses contributed immensely to the depth and richness of this book.

My sincere thanks goes to the staff of the South African-German Centre for Transnational Criminal Justice in Cape Town and Berlin, especially Frau Anja Schepke, Miss Anna Krey, Dr. Leonie Steinl and Dr. Aziz Epik for their diverse administrative roles that made my study life comfortable and successful.

I greatly appreciate the love and support I received from my family and friends in Ghana, Berlin and Cape Town. I am particularly grateful to my partner, Dr. Daniel K. A. Mensah, for his support and encouragement during this study. I thank my sweet daughter, Evette, who had to forgo important childhood moments to enable me to complete this book. I am also grateful to my brother, Dr. Eric Yankson, for his input, particularly with respect to editing and proofreading my draft. My greatest appreciation goes to my dear parents, Anthony Kobina Yankson and Grace Yankson, and my siblings, Cynthia, Ernest, Eric and Anthony, for their constant prayers, encouragement and support in the course of this research. I also say a big thank you to my dear friends, Dr. Seada Adem Hussein, Philippa Bogere, Franziska Tolksdorf, Dr. Marshet Tadesse Tessema, Victoria Ojo Adewuyi, Kennedy Paschal Anaba, Ellen Lordina Serwaa Mireku, Papa Yaw Owusu-Ankomah, Nana Adwoa Gyanoah Ansah and all my classmates in my master's class at the University of the Western Cape. You have all inspired me in different ways, and I owe this achievement to you all.

Finally yet importantly, I am eternally grateful to the Almighty God, in whom I live and have my being. His grace has brought me thus far and I am forever grateful.

Nuremberg, Germany Marian Yankson-Mensah

Contents

1 Introduction 1
1.1 Background to the Study 2
1.1.1 Defining Transitional Justice 3
1.1.2 Tracing the Roots of Transitional Justice 4
1.1.3 Transitional Justice and Truth Commissions 6
1.1.4 The Origin of Truth Commissions 7
1.1.5 The Right to Truth 9
1.1.6 Benefits and Shortcomings of Truth Commissions 12
1.2 Objectives and Methodology 13
1.2.1 Historical Review 15
1.2.2 Normative Analysis 15
1.2.3 Comparative Analysis 16
1.2.4 Empirical Analysis 17
1.3 Structure of the Book 20
References 21

2 Historical Background to the Establishment of the National Reconciliation Commission 27
2.1 Introductory Remarks 28
2.2 Early Signs of Social Division in Ghana 29
2.2.1 Nkrumah and the United Gold Coast Convention 29
2.2.2 The National Liberation Movement 30
2.2.3 The Togoland Factor 31
2.3 Ghana's First Republican Regime (6 March 1957 to 24 February 1966) 31
2.4 The Genesis of Military Rule: The National Liberation Council (24 February 1966 to 1 October 1969) 36
2.5 A Second Venture into Constitutional Democracy: The Government of the Progress Party (1 October 1969 to 13 January 1972) 37

2.6 The Return to Military Rule (1972–1979) 39
2.6.1 The National Redemption Council and the First Supreme Military Council (13 January 1972 to 5 July 1978) 39
2.6.2 The Second Supreme Military Council (5 July 1978 to 4 June 1979) 41
2.6.3 The Armed Forces Revolutionary Council (4 June 1979 to 24 September 1979) 41
2.7 The Third Republic: Peoples' National Party (24 September 1979 to 31 December 1981) 43
2.8 The Second Coming of Rawlings: The Provisional National Defence Council (31 December 1981 to 7 January 1993) 45
2.9 Transition to Democracy and the National Reconciliation Commission 49
2.10 Chapter Summary 53
References 53

3 The Legal Framework of the National Reconciliation Commission 57
3.1 Introductory Remarks 58
3.2 Reasons for the Establishment of the National Reconciliation Commission 60
3.2.1 The Amnesty Provisions Under the 1992 Constitution . . . 60
3.2.2 Complexities with Amending the Amnesty Provisions . . . 61
3.2.3 Absence of a Transitional Justice Policy for the Country 62
3.2.4 The Principle of Legality *(Nullum Crimen, Nulla Poena Sine Lege)* 63
3.2.5 Other Factors 65
3.3 The Features of the National Reconciliation Commission 66
3.3.1 Time Frame for Operation 69
3.3.2 Membership and Staffing 70
3.3.3 Independence of the National Reconciliation Commission 75
3.3.4 Confidentiality of Information 77
3.3.5 Objects and Mandate of the National Reconciliation Commission 79
3.3.6 Powers of the National Reconciliation Commission 84
3.3.7 Funds of the National Reconciliation Commission 94
3.3.8 Provisions on the Report 95
3.3.9 Offences and Penalties 97
3.4 Chapter Summary 98
References 98

4 The National Reconciliation Commission in Practice 103
4.1 Introductory Remarks 104
4.2 The Work of the National Reconciliation Commission 104
4.2.1 Interpretation and Implementation of the Mandate 105
4.2.2 Structures and Offices 106
4.2.3 Statement Taking and Processing 109
4.2.4 Conduct of Investigations 110
4.2.5 Hearings 111
4.2.6 Assistance of Witnesses 112
4.3 Challenges 113
4.3.1 Inadequacy of Funds and Logistics 114
4.3.2 Weak Investigative Capacity 115
4.3.3 Condemnation of and Resistance to the Commission's Work 116
4.3.4 Political Resistance to the Commission's Work 119
4.3.5 Difficulty in Engaging Perpetrators 121
4.4 Outcome of the Commission's Work 124
4.4.1 Overview of the Report 124
4.4.2 Interim Analysis of the Commission's Report and Recommendations 132
4.4.3 Publicity of the Report 137
4.4.4 Implementation of the Report 139
4.5 Chapter Summary 142
References 142

5 The National Reconciliation Commission in Hindsight: An Evaluation of Impact 145
5.1 Introductory Remarks 146
5.2 The Concepts of 'Impact' and 'Success' 147
5.3 The Assessment Criteria 148
5.4 The Impact of the National Reconciliation Commission on Truth 152
5.4.1 Overview of the Goal of Truth 152
5.4.2 Perceptions of the National Reconciliation Commission's Impact on the Establishment of Truth 153
5.4.3 Discussion 157
5.5 The Impact of the National Reconciliation Commission on Justice 160
5.5.1 The National Reconciliation Commission and the Pursuit of Victims' Rights to Remedies 161
5.5.2 Preventing the Recurrence of Human Rights Violations 167
5.5.3 Summary 173

5.6 The Impact of the Commission on National Reconciliation 173
5.6.1 Perceptions of the Commission's Impact on National Reconciliation 175
5.6.2 Discussion 178
5.7 The Impact of the National Reconciliation Commission on Peace 180
5.7.1 Perceptions of the National Reconciliation Commission's Impact on Peace 181
5.7.2 Discussion 183
5.8 Chapter Summary 185
References 186

6 After the National Reconciliation Commission: The Way Ahead 191
6.1 Introductory Remarks 192
6.2 Issues Related to the Duty to Prosecute 193
6.2.1 The Scope of the Duty to Prosecute 193
6.2.2 Discussion 197
6.3 Issues Related to the Amnesty Provisions in the 1992 Constitution 202
6.3.1 The Legality of Amnesties under International Law 202
6.3.2 Ghana's Amnesty Law Under International Law 206
6.4 Issues Related to the Right to Reparations 209
6.4.1 The Scope of the Right to Reparations 209
6.4.2 Has Ghana Fulfilled Victims' Rights to Reparations? 210
6.5 Institutional Reforms 213
6.5.1 The Basis and Scope of Institutional Reform 213
6.5.2 Gaps in Institutional Reform 215
6.6 Chapter Summary 216
References 217

7 Conclusion 221
7.1 Research Summary and Findings 221
7.2 Recommendations 224
7.3 Final Thoughts 226
References 227

Appendix A: Qualitative Survey Questions 229

Appendix B: Quantitative Survey Questions 231

Appendix C: Demographic Details of Respondents 243

Index 245

Abbreviations and Acronyms

NRC	National Reconciliation Commission
TRC	Truth and Reconciliation Commission

List of Figures

Fig. 4.1 Organisational structure of the NRC (*Source* The author 2018) 107
Fig. 5.1 Perceptions of the Commission's Impact on Establishing Truth: What reasons explain your points of view in statements **a** and **b** above? (Please select all that apply) (*Source* The author 2018) 155
Fig. 5.2 Perceptions of the Commission's Impact on the Right of Victims to Remedies: What reasons explain your points of view in the statement above? (Please select all that apply) (*Source* The author 2018) 163
Fig. 5.3 Perceptions of the Commission's Impact on Preventing the Recurrence of Human Rights Violations: What reasons explain your points of view in the statement above? (Please select all that apply) (*Source* The author 2018) 169
Fig. 5.4 Perceptions of the Commission's Impact on Reconciliation: What reasons explain your points of view in the statement above? (Please select all that apply) (*Source* The author 2018) 176
Fig. 5.5 Perceptions of the Commission's Impact on Peace: What reasons explain your points of view in the statement above? (Please select all that apply) (*Source* The author 2018) 182

List of Tables

Table 5.1 Perceptions of the Commission's Impact on Establishing Truth: What are your opinions regarding the following statements? 154

Table 5.2 Perceptions of the Commission's Impact on the Right of Victims to Remedies: What are your opinions regarding the following statements? 162

Table 5.3 Perceptions of the Commission's Impact on Preventing the Recurrence of Human Rights Violations: What is your opinion regarding the following statement? 168

Table 5.4 Perceptions of the Commission's Impact on Reconciliation: What is your opinion regarding the following statement? 175

Table 5.5 Perceptions of the Commission's Impact on Peace: What is your opinion regarding the following statement? 181

Chapter 1
Introduction

Contents

1.1 Background to the Study ... 2
 1.1.1 Defining Transitional Justice ... 3
 1.1.2 Tracing the Roots of Transitional Justice ... 4
 1.1.3 Transitional Justice and Truth Commissions ... 6
 1.1.4 The Origin of Truth Commissions ... 7
 1.1.5 The Right to Truth ... 9
 1.1.6 Benefits and Shortcomings of Truth Commissions ... 12
1.2 Objectives and Methodology ... 13
 1.2.1 Historical Review ... 15
 1.2.2 Normative Analysis ... 15
 1.2.3 Comparative Analysis ... 16
 1.2.4 Empirical Analysis ... 17
1.3 Structure of the Book ... 20
References ... 21

Abstract In 2002, a transitional justice process was initiated in Ghana through the establishment of the National Reconciliation Commission. In order to situate the Ghanaian transitional justice process within the context of international human rights principles for post-conflict and post-dictatorship state reconstruction, this chapter elucidates the subject of transitional justice by highlighting its scope, sketching its origins and identifying the underlying factors for development of the subject. It also focuses on the topic of truth commissions by examining their history, benefits and shortcomings. In addition, the chapter reflects on the contemporary legal basis for establishment of truth commissions by providing an overview of the right to truth. It concludes with an outline of the research objectives as well as the methodology and structure of the book.

M. Yankson-Mensah, *Transitional Justice in Ghana*, International Criminal Justice Series 25, https://doi.org/10.1007/978-94-6265-379-5_1

Keywords Ghana · Transitional Justice · Truth Commissions · Right to Truth · Transitions · Origins of Transitional Justice · History of Truth Commissions · Benefits and Shortcomings of Truth Commissions

1.1 Background to the Study

Sited in a subregion that is notoriously known for civil wars, political dictatorship and massive human rights violations,[1] Ghana has earned a reputation as a model of peace and political stability within West Africa. The country has been described as 'a model for Africa' in relation to democracy,[2] and 'one of Africa's stars of democracy'.[3] Yet Ghana has not always enjoyed this reputation. Like its counterparts in West Africa, the country has had to confront human rights violations perpetrated during decades of political instability.

Following independence from British colonial rule in 1957, much of Ghana's first three and half decades were marred by political instability on account of military disruptions of constitutional government. The nation has experienced four republican regimes and five military regimes. The current (fourth) republican regime, which started on 7 January 1993, marked the third transition to constitutional rule after independence and was the first transitional era in which steps were taken to address human rights violations perpetrated by past regimes. The main transitional justice mechanism that was utilised during Ghana's transition to democracy was the National Reconciliation Commission (NRC), which was established in 2002 and completed its work in 2004.

---

[1]For instance, West Africa is believed to have witnessed the highest number of military putsches in the world: see Kandeh 2004, p. 1. Also, the subregion has been plagued by civil wars in Sierra Leone (1991–2002), Liberia (1989–1997, 1999–2003), Mali (2012 to date), and Côte d'Ivoire (civil war from 2002 to 2007 and election crisis from 2010 to 2011) as well as devastating terrorist activities by the Boko Haram group in Nigeria (2002 to date). These civil wars and terrorist activities have visited untold human rights violations on West Africa.

[2]This description was made by the former President of the United States, Barack Obama during his speech to Ghana's Parliament when he visited the country in 2009: see Slack 2012. https://www.whitehouse.gov/blog/2012/06/14/archives-president-obamas-trip-ghana. Accessed 7 October 2019.

[3]See Kermeliotis 2014. http://edition.cnn.com/2014/02/26/world/africa/ghana-history-overview-on-the-road/index.html. Accessed 5 August 2019.

1.1.1 Defining Transitional Justice

The word 'transition' originates from the Latin word '*transire*', which means to 'go across'.[4,5] In transitional justice, the notion of transition connotes a change that brings about a form of liberation, which is usually a change from a dictatorial or conflicted political regime to a democratic one.[6] Societies in transition engage in a form of self-assessment, given that even key state actors, such as the relevant adjudicating authorities, may have been complicit in past atrocities.[7] A primary question that runs through most transitions is how to deal with perpetrators of past human rights abuses. Transitional justice thus reflects the different methods available to transitional societies in this regard.[8] The United Nations has defined the term as 'the full range of processes and mechanisms associated with a society's attempts to come to terms with a legacy of large-scale past abuses, in order to ensure accountability, serve justice and achieve reconciliation'.[9] The five main mechanisms that are utilised by transitional societies are prosecutions, truth commissions, amnesties, reparations and institutional reform.[10]

[4]Oxford Learners Dictionary 2019. http://www.oxfordlearnersdictionaries.com/definition/english/transition_1?q=transition. Accessed 14 October 2019.

[5]Ibid.

[6]Regarding the subject of change, Ambos 2009, pp. 21–22, has conceptualised instances in which the concept of transitional justice could apply in the absence of a regime change. An example is where negotiations for peace occur in the time of a conflict that is still in progress. See also Teitel 2000, p. 5, who writes that different factors have been used to ascertain the end of a transition, such as the holding of elections and the acceptance of principles of rule of law in the country.

[7]Elster 1998, p. 14.

[8]Arthur 2009, pp. 328–329.

[9]See United Nations Security Council 2004, para 8. For further explanation of the concept, see also Teitel 2000, p. 6, who conceptualises the terminology in terms of the role of law during transition; and Roht-Arriaza 2006, pp. 1–2.

[10]See Roht-Arriaza 2006, p. 2, where she states that these four mechanisms put together make up a narrower meaning of transitional justice. See also Ambos 2009, pp. 21–22; and Bonacker and Buckley-Zistel 2013, p. 5. In addition to the above-mentioned mechanisms which are common, other mechanisms of transitional justice are occasionally identified, such as memorialisation and national consultation: see for instance Freeman 2006, pp. 5–6; International Centre for Transitional Justice. https://www.ictj.org/about/transitional-justice. Accessed 1 April 2019; and the United Nations 2010, p. 2.

1.1.2 Tracing the Roots of Transitional Justice

Views differ on when the field of transitional justice began to emerge. Elster compares modern transitions to those that occurred in the fifth century,[11] whilst Arthur argues that the field began to emerge in the late 1980s.[12] Teitel, however, writes that the development of transitional justice can be traced to the aftermath of the First World War.[13] According to Teitel, the Treaty of Versailles, which ended the war, required Germany to accept responsibility for the war and prosecuted German perpetrators,[14] setting the stage for the subject's further internationalisation through later trials to punish war criminals.[15] Prominent amongst the trials used to hold perpetrators accountable were the Nuremberg Trial of 1945–1946 and the 1946 Tokyo Trial.[16]

Following these trials, the subject of transitional justice took further shape in 1979, when the Woodrow Wilson International Center for Scholars launched a 'Transitions' project.[17] Pursuant to this project, a four-volume series, *Transitions from Authoritarian Rule*, was published in 1986.[18] Hayner believes that these books helped to shape the subject further by highlighting and putting into proper perspective the predicaments that transitional societies in Latin America faced regarding how to deal with perpetrators and members of past regimes.[19]

The parameters of transitional justice gained further crystallisation after the Cold War, a period that witnessed an increase in political transitions worldwide.[20] It was not until 1992 that the term 'transitional justice' was first used to refer to justice in

[11]See Elster 2004, pp. 3–4, 21, who writes that as early as the 5th Century, democratic transitions occurred in Athens, when there was a defeat of a democratic regime by an oligarchy, and a subsequent return of democracy. According to him, each of these transitions occasioned some means for dealing with the oligarchs, and the Athenians were confronted with several questions that are similar to the very questions that modern societies in transition have had to answer. Another notable historical example is the trial and execution of Louis XVI, during the French Revolution of the 18th Century, because of the offence of treason. On this example, see Allen 1999, p. 318; and Benomar 1995, p. 32.

[12]Arthur 2009, pp. 321–367.

[13]See Teitel 2003, pp. 70, 72–74, who calls this the post-war phase.

[14]See Trueman 2015. https://www.historylearningsite.co.uk/modern-world-history-1918-to-1980/the-treaty-of-versailles/. Accessed 12 April 2018; and Teitel 2000, p. 39.

[15]See Teitel 2003, pp. 70, 72–74.

[16]For details of these trials, see Werle and Jessberger 2014, pp. 5–11.

[17]The Woodrow Wilson International Center for Scholars is a memorial of America's former President Woodrow Wilson, where research is undertaken on issues of global and national concern. See Wilson Center. https://www.wilsoncenter.org/about-the-wilson-center. Accessed 21 October 2019.

[18]See Lowenthal 1986, pp. vii–viii.

[19]Hayner 2011, p. 7. See also O'Donnell and Schmitter 1986.

[20]See Teitel 2003, pp. 71, 75–78, who refers to this phase as post-cold war transitional justice.

times of transition from a repressive regime to democracy.[21] The term gained further popularity as a result of the 1995 publication of Neil Kritz's four volumes on the subject.[22] By then, the subject had become well known to the extent that the various mechanisms of transitional justice were firmly established.[23] Today, transitional justice has become more recognised, with nongovernmental organisations having emerged to assist transitional societies in diverse ways.[24] Nonetheless, the concept remains very broad and sometimes unclear regarding its actual scope. Key international organisations, such as the United Nations, the African Union and the European Union, have drafted guidelines and policies on the subject.[25] In addition, a number of United Nations soft law documents have expounded principles applicable to mechanisms of transitional justice, thereby throwing light on how they can be implemented in states.[26] Although these guidelines and policies have no binding effect, they constitute a guidance framework for societies in transition.

[21]According to Arthur 2009, p. 329; and Leebaw 2008, p. 100, the term was first used in an article in the Boston Herald, which talked about a conference which was scheduled to be held in Salzburg, Austria about 'Justice in Times of Transition'. The conference, which was organised by the Charter 77 Foundation, New York was supposed to help the rulers in Eastern Europe take some lessons from how some Latin American countries had dealt with past human rights violations. Prior to the said conference, the term was used severally by the coordinators and their consultants, which included Ruti Teitel and Herman Schwartz. In that same year (1992), the co-ordinators of the conference started 'the Project on Justice in Times of Transition', an organisation which helps divided societies who are in the process of bringing out change in their society. This organisation is now known as 'Beyond Conflict'. For further details about the Salzburg Conference, see Kritz 1995, pp. xix–xxx. See also Teitel 2003, pp. 71, 89–92.

[22]See Kritz 1995. See also Arthur 2009, pp. 329–331.

[23]See Arthur 2009, pp. 329–331.

[24]Chiefly amongst the organisations that deal with transitional justice are the International Centre for Transitional Justice, the United States Institute of Peace's Rule of Law Centre and the Institute of Justice and Reconciliation in South Africa. These bodies provide assistance to transition al societies by undertaking research on transitional justice, providing advice on policy making and collaborating with victim support groups, nongovernmental organisations and civil society bodies: see the International Centre for Transitional Justice. https://www.ictj.org/about. Accessed 30 June 2019; Institute of Justice and Reconciliation. http://www.ijr.org.za/. Accessed 30 October 2019; and United States Institute of Peace http://www.usip.org/centers/rule-of-law-glas. Accessed 30 October 2019.

[25]See for instance, African Union 2019. https://au.int/sites/default/files/documents/36541-doc-au_tj_policy_eng_web.pdf. Accessed 2 November 2019; European Union. http://eeas.europa.eu/archives/docs/top_stories/pdf/the_eus_policy_framework_on_support_to_transitional_justice.pdf. Accessed 22 January 2019; and United Nations 2010.

[26]Examples of such soft law documents are the United Nations Basic Principles and Guidelines on the Right to a Remedy and Reparation for Victims of Gross Violations of International Human Rights Law and Serious Violations of International Humanitarian Law, 2005 and the United Nations Commission on Human Rights Updated Set of Principles for the Protection and Promotion of Human Rights through Action to Combat Impunity, 2005.

1.1.3 Transitional Justice and Truth Commissions

Truth commissions are recognised as one of the main mechanisms of transitional justice. Yet, like other terminologies in the field of transitional justice, there are diverse definitions of the term.[27] According to the United Nations, truth commissions are 'non-judicial or quasi-judicial investigative bodies, which map patterns of past violence, and unearth the causes and consequences of these destructive events'.[28]

Truth commissions constitute an institutional means of dealing with past human rights violations, without subjecting perpetrators to trial. Truth commissions are therefore distinguishable from courts in many ways. Unlike courts, the underlying focus of truth commissions is to establish historical truth by providing an account of past human rights violations to form part of the country's historical records.[29] Moreover, truth commissions are more victim-centred in comparison with courts. In court trials, victims may be called to provide testimony for the sole purpose of ascertaining the guilt of a perpetrator (and the testimony may be vehemently opposed by the defence), whereas truth commissions pay attention to victims' stories and also hear from perpetrators when necessary, with a central focus on the healing of victims. Therefore, truth commissions do not normally utilise judicial methods like cross-examinations, which may cause trauma to the victims.[30] Unlike courts, truth commissions have the capacity to deal with a large number of cases over a short period of time[31] and are therefore practicable in instances where a significant part of the society might have been involved in the crimes in question.[32] In addition, the proceedings and outcomes of truth commissions differ significantly from those of courts. For instance, the proceedings of truth commissions cannot establish individual criminal responsibility, although they produce a record of the crimes committed. Moreover, they cannot give sentences to perpetrators.[33]

---

[27]For examples of truth commission features, see Freeman 2006, pp. 14–18; Hayner 2011, pp. 11–12; Lund 1998, p. 282; and Mncwabe 2013, pp. 98–99.

[28]United Nations 2010, p. 8.

[29]See Lund 1998, p. 282.

[30]See for instance González and Varney 2013, p. 11. https://www.ictj.org/sites/default/files/ICTJ-Book-Truth-Seeking-2013-English.pdf. Accessed 2 November 2019, who write on the victim friendliness of East Timor's Truth, Reception and Reconciliation Commission, which utilised a large number of staff to facilitate the provision of funds to enable people who were displaced go back to their homes. For further explanation and instances of the victim-centredness of truth commissions, see also: Aldana 2006, p. 111; and Hayner 2011, p. 22.

[31]See Buergenthal 2006–2007, p. 222, who calls this the 'macro fact-finding' function of truth commissions. In contrast, courts undertake 'micro fact finding' for specific criminal cases. For a detailed discussion of the difference between truth commissions and courts, see also Freeman 2006, pp. 10, 72.

[32]See Tomuschat 2001, pp. 236–237.

[33]See González and Varney 2013, p. 10. https://www.ictj.org/sites/default/files/ICTJ-Book-Truth-Seeking-2013-English.pdf. Accessed 2 November 2019.

1.1.4 The Origin of Truth Commissions

Historically, trials were the usual recourse for addressing atrocities perpetrated during past political regimes. Scharf, however, considers the first instance of a truth commission, in the beginning of the 20th century: the establishment of a commission to conduct enquiries into war crimes that occurred during the Balkan Wars of 1912 and 1913.[34] According to Scharf, subsequent to this was the Commission des Responsabilités des Auteurs de la Guerre et Sanctions, which was created after the First World War by the 1919 preliminary Paris Peace Conference to determine the originators of the war and the violations committed by Germany and its allies during the war.[35] During the Second World War, the Allied powers established the United Nations War Crimes Commission (in 1943) to investigate German war crimes.[36] In 1944, the Far Eastern and Pacific Sub-Commission (a subcommission of the United Nations War Crimes Commission) was established to investigate Japanese war crimes.[37] In 1971, a truth commission was set up in Uganda by former president Idi Amin Dada to investigate disappearances that occurred during the initial stages of his government.[38]

Truth commissions eventually gained widespread use in the 1980s. There were many reasons for the popularity of truth commissions at that time. A key factor is globalisation and its attendant effects, such as enhanced dissemination of human rights–related information and increased maturity of human rights advocacy.[39] Nevertheless, the most cited factor is the so-called third wave of democratisation, which occurred from the 1970s through the 1980s and early 1990s.[40] In Europe, Latin America and Africa, approximately 30 countries transitioned during this

[34]See Scharf 1997, p. 377. See also the International Commission to Inquire into the Causes and Conduct of the Balkan Wars 1914. http://www.pollitecon.com/html/ebooks/Carnegie-Report-on-the-Balkan-Wars.pdf. Accessed 6 October 2019.

[35]Scharf 1997, p. 377. According to him, this commission's findings formed the groundwork for the establishment of an international tribunal to try the German Kaiser. About this commission, see also Werle and Jessberger 2014, pp. 2–3.

[36]Ibid. See also the United Nations War Crimes Commission 1948, pp. 2–3.

[37]See Schoepfel 2016, p. 113.

[38]See Hayner 1994, pp. 611–613. According to her, the outcome of this commission was short-lived. Subsequent to submission of the commission's report to the President, the members of the commission suffered various ill treatments from the state. One member was dismissed from his employment while another member was sentenced to death after institution of some murder charges against him. Eventually, a third member escaped being arrested by fleeing the country. It should be noted that it is still debatable whether these commissions can be regarded as truth commissions. However, Hayner 2011, pp. 239–240 regards the Ugandan commission of enquiry as a truth commission. See also Scharf 1997, p. 377, who describes the Commission des Responsabilités des Auteurs de la Guerre et Sanctions, the United Nations War Crimes Commission, and the Far Eastern Commission as truth commissions.

[39]See Heine 2007, pp. 70–71.

[40]Ibid., p. 67. See also Reilly 1998, p. 135.

period from dictatorial, repressive regimes to democracy.[41] Moreover, the collapse of the Soviet Union played a major role,[42] through the consequences of the end of the Cold War in 1989, which in turn led to the cessation of deep-seated conflicts and dictatorial regimes.[43] With these transitions, the states in question were confronted with the recurring questions faced by transitional societies. For instance, transitions give rise to the need to prevent the recurrence of past human rights violations and also to satisfy the rights of victims.[44] Furthermore, the nature of human rights violations that characterise repressive and conflicted regimes give rise to many unanswered questions and leave several facts undisclosed, hence leading to calls for 'truth' during transition.[45] These needs of transitional societies could not be effectively and exclusively catered to by prosecutions.[46] It may be argued that if the judiciary was present throughout the period when massive human rights violations were committed, then it was somehow 'complicit' in the commission of those atrocities.[47] Hence, it is not recommendable to use that same channel to investigate abuses, when it has not yet been reformed.[48]

Truth commissions thus became an alternative means for dealing with past human rights violations. Unlike prosecutions, truth commissions find a middle

---

[41]See Huntington 1991a, p. 12, who has outlined five underlying causes of the third wave: (1) the heightened issues of 'legitimacy' that were associated with repressive regimes, at a time when the values of democracy had become widely accepted, coupled with the economic and energy crisis of the 1970s; (2) the increase in worldwide population of the urban middle class in the 1960s as a result of worldwide 'economic growth', improved standards of living and increase in education; (3) transformation in some of the doctrinal values of the catholic church in 1963, which led the church into advocacy for social, political and economic changes and opposition of repressive rule; (4) general attitudinal change of western 'external actors', such as the European Community and the United States, towards advocacy for protection of democracy and human rights; and (5) the new democratic societies provided inspiration for other societies to adopt democracy, which sparked off a 'snowball effect'. See also Huntington 1991b, pp. 45–46.

[42]See Goldstone 1996, p. 485.

[43]See Bloomfield and Reilly 1998, p. 13; Hayner 2011, p. 3; and Heine 2007, pp. 70–71.

[44]See Hayner 2011, p. 3; Heine 2007, p. 67; and Reilly 1998, p. 135.

[45]For instance, although a greater part of the society might be aware of the occurrence of human rights violations in general, the nature of some of these violations, such as disappearances, involves a large amount of secrecy. See Popkin and Roht-Arriaza 1995, p. 81. See also Roht-Arriaza 2006, p. 3, where she uses the example of Eastern Europe to explain this point.

[46]See Hayner 2011, pp. 7–8, who asserts that when trials are used, the state in question will not be able to establish the underlying causes of the human rights violations nor put in place mechanisms to effect institutional reform in the police, military and the judiciary to prevent future occurrences of a similar nature. Moreover, she asserts that strained relationships amongst different sections of the society may remain unhealed.

[47]See Popkin and Roht-Arriaza 1995, p. 82.

[48]Ibid. In this regard, it may take a long time after transition to create a new, effective and independent judiciary and bring about reform in the state's law enforcement mechanisms. For further details on the strengths of truth commissions, as against prosecutions, see Freeman 2006, pp. 10, 72; Verdeja 2009, pp. 100, 102; Gitau 2010, p. 148. See also Kritz 1995, p. xxii, who writes that using prosecutions to deal with perpetrators of past human rights violations may be contrary to the principles of 'nullum crimen sine lege' and 'nulla poena sine lege'.

ground between criminal justice and societal healing by increasing a society's comprehension of its past, without merely focusing on bringing perpetrators to book.[49]

In Latin America, the first truth commission was established in Bolivia in 1982.[50] This was followed by Argentina's Comisión Nacional sobre la Desaparición de Personas in 1983.[51] Other truth commissions were subsequently established in Chile (1990), El Salvador (1992) and Guatemala (1994).[52] With the establishment of the South African Truth and Reconciliation Commission (TRC) in 1994, truth commissions received more international attention.[53] Unlike earlier truth commissions, the South African TRC's enabling law gave it a large mandate and massive investigative powers, including the power to grant amnesties, conduct search and seizures and issue subpoenas.[54] The South African TRC thus set the precedent for several other transitional societies to establish truth commissions.[55]

As of August 2019, 58 truth commissions were listed on the website of the Transitional Justice Database Project, which was started by the University of Wisconsin.[56] Of this number, 19 truth commissions were in Africa, 17 in the Americas, 16 in Asia and six in Europe.[57]

1.1.5 The Right to Truth

As observed above, one of the factors that led to the emergence of truth commissions as a mechanism of transitional justice is the need for 'truth' about past human rights violations during transitions from repressive regimes to democracy.[58] The establishment of truth commissions is recognised as a means of fulfilling the right to truth.

The right to truth entails the entitlement of victims, their next of kin and representatives to the facts relating to the causes and conditions of breaches of international human rights law and serious violations of international humanitarian

---

[49]See Allen 1999, p. 320; and Hayner 2011, pp. 11–12.

[50]See Hayner 2011, pp. 240–241.

[51]See Freeman 2006, pp. 25–26; Hayner 1994, pp. 614–615, 2011, p. 10.

[52]For more information about these truth commissions, see Fuentes and Collins 2013, pp. 295–299; Collins 2013, pp. 156–157; and Isa 2013, pp. 322–325.

[53]See Wiebelhaus-Brahm 2010, p. 3; Freeman 2006, pp. 25–26; and Hayner 2011, p. 4.

[54]See Hayner 2011, pp. 27–31.

[55]See Wiebelhaus-Brahm 2010, p. 3; Freeman 2006, pp. 25–26; and Hayner 2011, p. 4.

[56]See Transitional Justice Database Project. http://www.tjdbproject.com/index.php?page=1&&mtype%3A%3A2=Truth+Commission&startyear=&endyear=. Accessed 31 August 2019.

[57]Ibid.

[58]See Sect. 1.1.4 in the present chapter of this book.

law.[59] For instance, Additional Protocol I to the Geneva Conventions of 12 August 1949 entitles relatives of disappeared individuals to know the 'fate' of the disappeared.[60] Also, parties to armed conflicts have an obligation to trace the whereabouts of missing individuals when circumstances permit them to do so.[61] The International Convention for the Protection of All Persons from Enforced Disappearances sets out the right of the relations of disappeared individuals to know the factors that led to the disappearance, the whereabouts of their relatives and the progress of any enquiries being made regarding their disappeared relatives, and obliges states parties to take the necessary steps to trace such individuals.[62]

The right to truth can be realised through judicial and non-judicial mechanisms to conduct 'effective, prompt, thorough and impartial' investigations of past human rights violations, and where appropriate, 'to take action against those allegedly responsible in accordance with domestic and international law'.[63] For example, Article 2 of the International Covenant on Civil and Political Rights—which requires states parties to respect and ensure' realisation of the rights in the Convention and to utilise any needed legislation or mechanisms to give effect to' the rights in the treaty—gives rise to a duty to investigate the truth.[64] Thus, failure by a state to conduct investigations into violations of the rights in the International Covenant on Civil and Political Rights constitutes a breach of the 'ensure and respect' provisions.[65] In addition, the duty of states to provide remedies for

[59]See the United Nations General Assembly 2006, paras 11(c), 24; and United Nations Commission on Human Rights 2005, paras 2 and 4. See also United Nations General Assembly and Human Rights Council 2009, paras 3–6; and United Nations General Assembly 2014, paras 3–6, 10. Also, some regional bodies such as the Organisation of American States, the Council of Europe and the European Union have variously encouraged states parties to disclose information about human rights violations to the victims and their families. See Organisation of American States General Assembly 2008a, paras 1–8; Organisation of American States General Assembly 2008b, para 6; Council of Europe Parliamentary Assembly 1987, p. 17.2; and Council of Europe 2011, para v.

[60]Protocol Additional to the Geneva Conventions of 12 August 1949 and relating to the Protection of Victims of International Armed Conflicts, opened for signature 12 December 1977, 1125 UNTS 3 (entered into force 7 December 1978) (Additional Protocol 1), Articles 32 and 33.

[61]See Additional Protocol 1, above n 60, Articles 32 and 33.

[62]See the International Convention for the Protection of All Persons from Enforced Disappearance, 20 December 2006, Article 24(2).

[63]See United Nations Commission on Human Rights 2005, para 5; and United Nations General Assembly 2006, para 3(b); Convention against Torture and Other Cruel, Inhuman or Degrading Treatment or Punishment, opened for signature 10 December 1984 (entered into force 26 June 1987) (Torture Convention), Article 12; and United Nations Economic and Social Council 1989, para 9.

[64]International Covenant on Civil and Political Rights, opened for signature 16 December 1966 (entered into force 23 March 1976) (Covenant on Civil and Political Rights), Articles 2(1), 2(2); and United Nations General Assembly 2006, para 3(b).

[65]See United Nations Human Rights Committee 2004, para 8; and United Nations General Assembly 2006, para 3(b).

violations under the International Covenant on Civil and Political Rights and the Universal Declaration of Human Rights includes an obligation by the state to investigate the truth.[66]

As regards the contents of the right to truth, victims of human rights violations and their relatives as well as the society as a whole are entitled to know the 'full and complete truth' about past human rights violations.[67] Specifically, they deserve information about the basis for commission of those violations, the status of investigations with regards to the human rights violations and the 'fate and whereabouts of victims' in cases of death and enforced disappearances.[68] Where non-judicial mechanisms are used, their recommendations must be implemented.[69] The right to truth also involves an obligation on the part of states to preserve the memory of the information revealed to victims and their families, promote knowledge of such information and prevent it from being lost.[70] This includes an obligation to prevent absolute destruction of the state's history or alteration of the facts relating to past human rights violations. The state must foster knowledge of its past by creating and protecting records and erecting memorials in relation to its history.[71] In addition, the state must provide guarantees for the protection of the individual's right to truth. This involves laying down the appropriate institutional and administrative frameworks to protect and enhance assertion of this right, such as a well-functioning judiciary and non-judicial means, including the establishment of commissions of enquiry.[72]

[66]See Covenant on Civil and Political Rights, above n 64, Article 2(3); Universal Declaration of Human Rights, adopted 10 December 1948, 217 A (III) (Universal Declaration), Article 8; Roht-Arriaza 1990, p. 483; and the United Nations Human Rights Committee 2004, para 15. See also Inter-American Court of Human Rights, *Velásquez-Rodríguez v Honduras*, Judgment of 29 July 1988, Ser. C. No. 4 (Velásquez-Rodríguez 1988), para 174, where the court outlined the duty to prosecute and held that states owe an obligation to investigate human rights violations that occur within their jurisdiction, to find out the perpetrators and mete out the requisite punishment and compensate victims.

[67]United Nations Commission on Human Rights 2006, paras 3, 4.

[68]Ibid., p. 11, paras 38, 39. According to the report, the question of whether the right entails knowing the perpetrators of human rights violations is still debatable.

[69]United Nations General Assembly 2014, paras 2, 3; and United Nations Human Rights Council 2012, paras 2, 3.

[70]See United Nations Commission on Human Rights 2005, paras 3, 5, 14, 15.

[71]See United Nations Commission on Human Rights 2005, para 3. See also Office of the United Nations High Commissioner for Human Rights 2015, pp. 3, 4; United Nations General Assembly 2014, para 10; United Nations Human Rights Council 2012, para 10; and United Nations General Assembly 2006, para 24.

[72]See United Nations Commission on Human Rights, para 5.

1.1.6 Benefits and Shortcomings of Truth Commissions

Over the years, several benefits have been ascribed to truth commissions. For instance, it is claimed that they serve the psychological and emotional needs of victims, establish an accurate record of a country's past, provide explanations for the occurrence of a dictatorial or violent political regime, ensure acknowledgement of past wrongs by the state, provide a means for rehabilitation of perpetrators, renew trust amongst members of the society, prevent similar episodes of human rights violations in the future, bring about a renewal of national identity, promote justice and rule of law and ensure lasting peace in the society.[73] It is also believed that truth commissions can have some elements of retribution and deterrence,[74] whilst at the same time making perpetrators part of the nation-building process.[75] Truth commissions have also been greatly credited with helping to achieve reconciliation and democracy.[76]

However, truth commissions have also been vastly criticised on different footings. Opponents have asserted, contrary to popular belief, that truth-telling may not necessarily lead to forgiveness or provide psychological and emotional restoration for victims. Rather, it may open old wounds and put more psychological strain on victims,[77] and may lay the groundwork for divisions in society.[78] Some critics see truth commissions as what Heine calls a 'witch-hunting' expedition, geared towards exposing the bad deeds of past political regimes and discrediting them in the eyes of the entire society.[79] Other studies allege that truth commissions may not necessarily impact positively on human rights. Olsen, Payne, Reiter and Wiebelhaus-Brahm,

[73]For different perspectives of the perceived impacts of truth commissions, see: Aldana 2006, p. 109; Gitau 2010, p. 148; Goldstone 1996, pp. 488–489; González 2014, p. 1; Gready 2011, p. 21; Teitel 2000, pp. 88, 90–91; Heine 2007, p. 72; Landsman 1996, pp. 88–89; Office of the United Nations High Commissioner for Human Rights 2006, pp. 1–2; Villa-Vicencio 2004, p. 93; and Wiebelhaus-Brahm 2010, p. 4.

[74]Trejo et al. 2018, pp. 796–797, for instance argue that truth commissions can bring about a reduction in the rate of murders. See Weiner 2005, p. 130, who asserts that truth commissions can result in retribution. However, Landsman 1996, p. 89, is of the opinion that the retributive value of truth commissions is very little as compared to trials. Also, the deterrent capabilities of non-judicial mechanisms is still debatable. See also Méndez 1997, p. 266, where he cites the example of Haiti's recurrent disruptions of democracy as a factor to prove that amnesties for instance could rather result in more impunity.

[75]See Villa-Vicencio 2000, p. 209.

[76]See Gibson 2004, p. 216.

[77]For instance, a study conducted by Kaminer 2001, pp. 373–377, revealed that some victims who had appeared before the South African TRC had not been either emotionally healed or forgiven perpetrators. See also Hamber and Wilson 2002, p. 50.

[78]See for instance Lundy 2010, p. 104.

[79]See Heine 2007, p. 77.

for instance, have conducted a study that suggests that when truth commissions are not accompanied by trials and amnesties, human rights violations will not be reduced in the society.[80] Hence, they assert that the ability of truth commissions to enhance the protection of human rights in a society depends on the presence of other transitional justice mechanisms.[81] Other criticisms of truth commissions express concern over the fact that any mechanism that does not provide full retribution and accountability through trials downplays efforts by the international community to ensure that grave crimes of international concern are punished.[82] In addition, it has been argued that the records produced by truth commissions may be a merged version resulting from a collection of stories, which becomes a nationally accepted truth.[83] This deprives victims of the facts they believe in and may even cause ethnic divisions in societies.[84] Other writers have asserted that truth commissions may not actually bring out the truth, as perpetrators may lie or twist certain facts to protect their social image.[85]

1.2 Objectives and Methodology

This book is one of the first and most comprehensive efforts to situate discussions about Ghana's NRC within the context of the impact of transitional justice mechanisms. It does so by undertaking a holistic assessment of the NRC's historical and legal foundations, its work and its aftermath. Even though the NRC's establishment marked a distinct step in the history of Ghana, there is little literature devoted to it. In fact, no author has extensively examined the commission's impact. Moreover, there seems to be a perception that the commission was merely an instrument for fulfilling the selfish political interests of the then ruling party and was

---

[80]Olsen et al. 2010, pp. 458, 464–465.

[81]Ibid. See also Theissen 1999, p. 51, who also asserts that the South African TRC failed to change the dominant perceptions amongst the general populace of the people who were behind the apartheid regime and instil a sense of 'collective responsibility' in South Africans for the past human rights violations. See also Bachmann 2010, pp. 72–73, where he describes the performance of truth commissions so far as 'patchy'.

[82]See Villa-Vicencio 2000, 2004, p. 90, where this criticism is mentioned.

[83]See Waldorf 2009, p. 112.

[84]For instance, Shaw 2007, p. 202, writes that, in Sierra Leone, a widow who was one of the victims of the civil war felt that the Sierra Leonean TRC had replaced her voice with the commission's 'model of redemptive memory'. On the possibility of causing ethnic divisions, see also Nwogu 2010, p. 279.

[85]See Waldorf 2009, p. 112, who grounds this assertion in the fact that truth commissions do not use the strict rules of evidence that are used during trials, hence making them susceptible to bringing out twisted facts. See also Chapman and Ball 2001, p. 23.

adjudged to be inappropriate for Ghana's transition.[86] Thus, as a means of increasing knowledge of the commission's work and outcome, whilst enriching the depth of scholarship on truth commissions, the core aims of this book are to:

- explore the underlying reasons for Ghana's recourse to the NRC as a mechanism of transitional justice;
- evaluate the key features, mandate and competences of the NRC;
- analyse how the work of the NRC turned out in practice;
- ascertain the appropriate criteria for assessing the effectiveness of the NRC;
- assess, based on the established criteria, whether the NRC was effective;
- identify the loopholes in Ghana's transitional justice process and reflect on the country's way forward in light of international legal standards for dealing with past human rights violations.

The first objective, regarding why Ghana opted for the NRC as a mechanism of transitional justice, relates to a review of the historical, social and legal factors underlying the establishment of the commission. The second objective, on the features, mandate and competences of the NRC, is addressed through an examination of the commission's legal framework, entailing the law through which the NRC was established as well as other applicable laws in Ghana. The third objective, on the how the NRC turned out in practice, is pursued through an analysis of the NRC's work considering its actual experiences. As regards the fourth objective, concerning the plausible approach for examining the impact of the NRC, the book derives the criteria for assessing the NRC's impact by analysing existing literature. The fifth objective, on the effectiveness of the NRC, is arrived at by utilising the established criteria in light of empirical data to explore the impact of the commission. Finally, regarding the sixth objective, the book examines the Ghanaian context against the backdrop of other transitional justice mechanisms—namely, prosecutions, amnesties, reparations and institutional reform, taking into account international human rights standards, to arrive at the gaps in Ghana's transitional justice process.

Given the multidimensional nature of the above objectives, different methods are employed in this undertaking, comprising a review of the NRC's historical background, a normative and comparative assessment of the features, work and aftermath of the NRC, and an empirical analysis of its impact.

[86] See for instance Mncwabe 2013, p. 102, where she cites the NRC as an example of how truth commissions can be used for political manipulation. See also Wain 2003, p. 8, where she mentions this criticism.

1.2.1 Historical Review

The relevance of history in transitional justice cannot be understated, owing to its potential to create a better understanding of the context within which the mechanism in question was initiated. Moreover, transitional justice, according to Teitel, is both 'backward-looking' and 'forward-looking', since it relies on the past as a way of safeguarding the future.[87] A historical background therefore serves as a foundation for subsequent analysis.

The following discussion of the NRC's historical context in Chap. 2 comprises a review of the political and social occurrences in Ghana prior to the NRC. It also unearths the impact of these occurrences and the factors that necessitated the establishment of the NRC, in order to examine why Ghana opted for the NRC as a mechanism of transitional justice.

1.2.2 Normative Analysis

The normative analysis in this book covers aspects of the first and second objectives, regarding why the NRC was established and its features, mandate and competences. It also addresses the sixth objective, on the loopholes in Ghana's transitional justice process. The normative analyses entail an assessment of the NRC in light of applicable Ghanaian laws and relevant international human rights principles. As regards Ghanaian laws, the major sources utilised are the enabling law of the NRC and the 1992 Constitution of Ghana. The key paradigms to be discussed are the commission's object, features, functions and mandate as contained in the enabling law. The analysis also includes the commission's report and recommendations. The informative value of these sources is however limited because, according to Ainley, assessing a body solely on the basis of its mandate is to agree to its make-up and goals from the very outset. In her view, this is problematic because the terms of reference are creations of politics, rather than ethics.[88]

Hence, this study also factors in principles of international human rights law.[89] This entails the obligations that states must fulfil when massive human rights

[87]Teitel 2000, p. 6.

[88]See Ainley 2015, p. 247. According to Sikkink 2012, p. 29, this kind of assessment can be referred to as 'a comparison with the ideal', which entails comparisons with certain standards of the course or manner which justice is supposed to take.

[89]See Andreu-Guzmán 2013, p. 1; and the United Nations 2010, p. 3. https://www.un.org/ruleoflaw/files/TJ_Guidance_Note_March_2010FINAL.pdf, where it is stated that whatever mechanisms that are utilized by the state to deal with past human rights violations should conform to the standards of international human rights law as well as international humanitarian law, where applicable. Accessed 12 October 2019.

violations occur on their territories as well as the rights of victims of human rights violations.[90] International human rights law is particularly helpful as a point of reference in the Ghanaian context because Ghana's Constitution after transition did not contain a well carved out policy to deal with past human rights violations. However, since the preamble of the Constitution expresses unqualified support for human rights protection,[91] relying on international principles to assess the NRC is in order.

1.2.3 Comparative Analysis

This book utilises comparative analysis to examine the features, mandate and competencies of the NRC as well as how it turned out in practice. The comparative analysis can be justified in two main ways. First, a comparative analysis proves to be beneficial, as it will draw on the practices in other countries to provide better understanding of the Ghanaian context and of the appropriateness or otherwise of the NRC's features.[92] Second, comparisons add to the knowledge base of truth commissions and transitional justice in general.[93] Although no two transitional processes are the same, it is only by comparing transitional experiences that formulations on appropriate practices can be made. Indeed, it has been asserted that truth commissions may fail if they are established without initially learning some lessons from other truth commissions.[94] A comparison of truth commissions can, therefore, expose their benefits and weaknesses as compared to other mechanisms of transitional justice and throw light on alternative practices for future transitional processes.[95]

The comparisons consist of references to different truth commissions, where they bear significance to a point of discussion. In particular, the study refers to the Brazilian Comissão Nacional da Verdade, the Nigerian Human Rights Violations Investigation Commission (Oputa Panel) and the Liberian TRC. These truth commissions were chosen in light of their significant features. The Brazilian Comissão

[90]The obligations owed by states and the rights of victims are expressions of customary international human rights law, as well as emerging international jurisprudence. See Méndez 1997, p. 259.

[91]See Republic of Ghana, Constitution of the Republic of Ghana, 1992 (1992 Constitution), preamble.

[92]On the aims and advantages of comparative law, see Eberle 2009, pp. 471–472; and Zajtay 1974, p. 322.

[93]See Oettler 2014, pp. 18, 19 where she writes on the potential benefits and limitations of using comparisons for transitional justice research. See also Ragin and Rubinson 2009, p. 15.

[94]See González 2014, p. 2. https://www.ictj.org/sites/default/files/subsites/challenging-conventional-truth-commissions-peace/docs/ICTJ-Report-KAF-TruthCommPeace-2014.pdf. Accessed 2 November 2019.

[95]See Backer 2009, p. 24.

Nacional da Verdade shares many similarities with the NRC in terms of the kind of regime that it was established to investigate (i.e., a military junta). Moreover, the Comissão Nacional da Verdade was similarly established several years after the country's transition to democracy and operated alongside an amnesty law that prevented prosecution of people involved in the military regime. The Oputa Panel of Nigeria also shares similarities with the NRC.[96] Beyond being in West Africa, the Oputa Panel was established to investigate past military regimes. Moreover, the Oputa Panel, like the NRC, was made up of only nationals of the country.

There is also the need to incorporate into the analyses a truth commission that shares significant differences with the NRC in order to highlight variant perspectives on how truth commissions function. The Liberian TRC was chosen for comparison for this reason. Unlike the NRC, it was established to investigate a period of civil war. Moreover, whereas the NRC was established by an act of parliament, the Liberian TRC was established through a peace accord between the government of Liberia and two rebel groups. In addition, the commission's membership included both Liberian nationals and non-nationals.[97]

The above-mentioned truth commissions were also chosen because of the dearth of literature analysing their features and mandate. Hence, a comparison of the NRC with these truth commissions is also a contribution to the knowledge base on these truth commissions.

1.2.4 Empirical Analysis

It has been asserted that studies which suggest the expected outcomes of truth commissions, without empirical basis, have narrowed the knowledge of the actual impact of truth commissions on transitional societies.[98] As Hirsch, MacKenzie and Sesay have rightly observed, the general tendency in the past has been to mix 'advocacy with scholarship'.[99] Thus, the very advocacy organisations, non-governmental organisations and individuals involved in the work of truth commissions end up writing about them.[100] Even though these bodies and individuals have generated informative reviews, there is the need for analyses that link the expected outcomes with the actual performance of truth commissions to assess their

[96]For further information about the Nigerian truth commission, see Hayner 2011, pp. 249–250.

[97]About the Liberian TRC, see Long 2008, pp. 1–14.

[98]For further discussions on the need for literature on the impact of transitional justice, see Kritz 2009, p. 17; Van Der Merwe et al. 2009, p. 4; and Wiebelhaus-Brahm 2010, p. 22. See also Hirsch et al. 2012, pp. 387, 391–392; Lundy 2010, p. 105; and Thoms et al. 2010, p. 330.

[99]Hirsch et al. 2012, p. 391.

[100]Ibid.

legitimacy and their impact.[101] Utilising empirical data in assessing the NRC is therefore practical, since empirical methods rely on evidence rather than mere descriptions.[102] Moreover, an empirical assessment offers more precise conclusions and has capabilities of throwing light on different reactions to transitional justice mechanisms within the society.[103]

In view of the forgoing, Chap. 6 of this book complements the normative and comparative analyses with assessment of both qualitative and quantitative data on the NRC's impact. The quantitative data was obtained from 130 respondents through both online and personally administered questionnaires. The online and hard copies of the questionnaires were administered concurrently from 15 April to 20 June 2018. Overall, 70 questionnaires were administered personally, whilst 60 were administered online.

Regarding the personally administered questionnaires, the research combined purposive sampling with simple random sampling. Purposive sampling was used to identify the communities where the research was conducted, whilst simple random sampling was used to identify the potential respondents. With the aim of sampling respondents with different demographic backgrounds, the research was conducted in Accra, because of its cosmopolitan nature. The questionnaires were administered in four of the Greater Accra Region's 16 districts. The specific communities polled were Legon, East Legon, Burma Camp, Labone, Abossey-Okai, Makola, Teshie and Madina Zongo.

The online survey was conducted to augment fieldwork data and to enable a wider reach of audience in a short span of time. Snowball sampling was used for the online survey. The link to the survey was widely disseminated on social media pages.

In both online and personally administered questionnaires, the main factors that guided the random sampling were the respondents' age, gender, educational background, home region, knowledge of the commission's work and whether they were victims of the human rights violations that were investigated by the commission.

A qualitative survey was also conducted as a means of triangulation, to confirm or debunk the findings of the quantitative survey. The qualitative survey involved structured interviews conducted between 6 August 2016 and 28 August 2016. Four

---

[101]Ibid. See also Landsman 1996, pp. 82–83, where he mentions the need for truth commissions to be assessed to determine whether they meet the expectations of dealing with past human rights violations.

[102]See Pham and Vinck 2007, pp. 231–248; and Van Der Merwe et al. 2009, p. 4. Indeed, a number of instances of literature on truth commissions disclose a preference for empirical methods in conducting either qualitative or quantitative analysis. See for instance Ferrara 2015; Gibson 2004, pp. 201–217; Millar 2010, pp. 477–496; Pozen et al. 2014, pp. 31–52; and Wiebelhaus-Brahm 2010, p. 17.

[103]Van Der Merwe et al. 2009, p. 4; and Pham and Vinck 2007, pp. 231–248.

experts who have significant knowledge of the NRC's work were interviewed in person to obtain information regarding the NRC's impact.[104]

In addition to the surveys conducted in this study, quantitative data from independent surveys were also used to highlight reactions to the work of the NRC. Two surveys conducted by the Ghana Centre for Democratic Development in March 2006 and April 2005 on 102 and 98 victims, respectively, were referred to regularly in the analysis.[105]

The findings of the empirical analysis in this book are subject to possible limitations. The sample size for the author's quantitative survey has a confidence interval (margin of error) of 8.6%.[106] A higher sample size would have produced more reliable results. However, attempts to obtain a higher sample size were hampered by resource constraints and considerable challenges with finding respondents for the survey. Specifically, a significant number of people refused to participate because of their lack of knowledge about the NRC or their general reservations about commenting on the commission's work.

Nevertheless, the author has included the survey outcomes in this book for a number of reasons. First, the quantitative survey with 130 respondents currently constitutes the most comprehensive empirical study on the impact of the NRC. At the time of writing, the only known surveys related to the NRC were conducted by the Ghana Centre for Democratic Development, involving no more than 102 respondents, a study by a political scientist at the University of Ghana, involving 100 respondents, and an independent survey involving four female victims.[107] These surveys did not, however, relate to the impact of the NRC in Ghana. Second, since random samples are considered to better reflect the entire population, the partial use of random sampling in the survey eliminates the risks of sampling bias in terms of age, gender, level of education and the nature of respondents' relationship with the NRC (i.e., whether or not they are victims of the human rights violations that were investigated by the NRC). Third, survey experts tend to disregard the size

---

[104]The consideration of expert views in this study is in reliance on the major 'components for understanding a commission's impact', as stated by Van Der Merwe et al. 2009, pp. 4–5. According to them, these include perceptions or opinions regarding objectivity, fairness and the appropriateness of the commission's processes.

[105]See the Ghana Centre for Democratic Development 2006, pp. 3–4. In total, 41% of the respondents were from the then Northern Region (currently the Savannah, North-East and Northern Regions), 20% from the Ashanti Region, 19% from the Greater Accra Region, 16% from the then Western Region (currently Western-North and Western Regions) and 4% from the Central Region of Ghana.

[106]For details on how the sample size and error margin can be calculated, see the Survey System. https://www.surveysystem.com/sscalc.htm#one. Accessed 16 August 2019. See also Singh and Masuku 2014, p. 11, where they provide examples of published tables, which provide the sample sizes for each given population size as well as the error of margin.

[107]See Baiden 2019, pp. 22–35; Boafo-Arthur 2006, p. 149; and the Ghana Centre for Democratic Development 2006, pp. 3–4.

of the population when calculating sample sizes.[108] Arguably, a sample of 130 people with inclusion from all regions in the country does provide a fairly useful representation of views. In statistical terms, a sample size of 100 could be as relevant as a sample of 400 in explaining the views of extremely large populations, on the basis of probability. Hence the population size of Ghana (approximately 30 million) does not affect the level of representation of the sample used for the survey. Fourth, the possible limitations posed by the sample size are addressed by augmenting the quantitative data with qualitative data and data from independent surveys. This ensures proper saturation of views regarding the impact of the NRC. Fifth, the intention of this book is not to imply that the empirical analysis points conclusively to the impact of the NRC or truth commissions in general. Rather, the core aim is to provide insight into current perceptions about the NRC, in order to illustrate how the impact of the NRC and other truth commissions can be assessed and to encourage more empirical research on the work of the NRC and truth commissions in general.

1.3 Structure of the Book

This book is made up of seven chapters. This first chapter has provided an introduction, including the research background, objectives and methodology. Chapter 2 gives an overview of Ghana's history and the events that culminated in the establishment of the NRC. This, in particular, includes outlines and discussions of the military coup d'états and human rights violations that occurred between the period of Ghana's independence and its transition to democracy. Chapter 3 gives an outline of the legal framework for establishment of the NRC. This includes the legal basis for the commission's establishment as well as the law that was used to establish it. The chapter also examines the NRC's features and scope and compares them with those of other truth commissions. Chapter 4 discusses the work of the NRC in practice, the challenges it faced and the means by which it overcame those challenges. The chapter also compares the work of the NRC and its experiences with that of other countries. In addition, the chapter discusses the final report and recommendations of the NRC, the country's general reaction to the report and the major steps that were taken to implement the NRC's recommendations. Chapter 5 reflects on plausible avenues for assessing the impact of transitional justice mechanisms and defines criteria for assessing the NRC's impact. Based on the established criteria, the chapter analyses the impact of the commission using empirical data. Chapter 6 discusses the work of the NRC against the backdrop of international legal standards for post-dictatorship and post-conflict reconstruction. Taking into account the principles related to prosecutions, amnesties, reparations

[108]See Singh and Masuku 2014, p. 11; the Survey System. https://www.surveysystem.com/sscalc.htm#one. Accessed 16 August 2019; and Tortora 1978, pp. 100–102.

and institutional reform, the chapter unearths the loopholes in Ghana's transitional process and assesses the way forward. Chapter 7 concludes this book by summarising its findings. The chapter also makes recommendations for future transitional justice practice.

References

African Union (2019) Transitional justice policy. https://au.int/sites/default/files/documents/36541-doc-au_tj_policy_eng_web.pdf. Accessed 22 November 2019.

Ainley K (2015) Evaluating the success of transitional justice in Sierra Leone and beyond. In: Ainley K et al (eds) Evaluating transitional justice accountability and peacebuilding in post-conflict Sierra Leone. Palgrave Macmillan, New York and London, pp 241–264.

Aldana R (2006) A victim-centered reflection on truth commissions and prosecutions as a response to mass atrocities. Journal of Human Rights 5:107–126.

Allen J (1999) Balancing justice and social unity: Political theory and the idea of a truth and reconciliation commission. University of Toronto Law Journal 49(3):315–353.

Ambos K (2009) The legal framework of transitional justice: A systematic study with a special focus on the role of the ICC. In: Ambos K et al (eds) Building a future on peace and justice: Studies on transitional justice, peace and development – The Nuremberg Declaration on Peace and Justice. Springer, Berlin, pp 19–103.

Andreu-Guzmán F (2013) Peace processes and international law. https://www.files.ethz.ch/isn/164673/80ed6b7fa08ff1e0620fe297f85f63f0.pdf. Accessed 1 November 2019.

Arthur P (2009) How "transitions" reshaped human rights: A conceptual history of transitional justice. Human Rights Quarterly 31(2): 321–367.

Bachmann K (2010) Do truth commissions make a difference? When and how truth commissions contribute to reconciliation. Review of International Affairs LXI (1138–1139): 71–100.

Backer D (2009) Cross-national comparative analysis. In: Van Der Merwe et al (eds) Assessing the impact of transitional justice: Challenges for empirical research. United States Institute of Peace, Washington DC, pp 23–90.

Baiden RAD (2019) In the aftermath of reparations: The experiences of female beneficiaries of Ghana's reparations programme. Journal of Peacebuilding and Development 14(1):22–35.

Benomar J (1995) Justice after transitions. In: Kritz N (ed) Transitional justice: How emerging democracies reckon with former regimes, vol. I. United States Institute of Peace Press, Washington DC, pp 32–41.

Bloomfield D, Reilly B (1998) The changing nature of conflict and conflict management. In: Harris P, Reilly B (eds) Democracy and deep-rooted conflict: Options for negotiators. International Institute for Democracy and Electoral Assistance, Stockholm, pp 7–28.

Boafo-Arthur K (2006) The quest for national reconciliation in Ghana: Challenges and prospects. In: Boafo-Arthur K (ed) Voting for democracy in Ghana: The 2004 elections in perspectives. Freedom House Publishing, Accra, pp 127–155.

Bonacker T, Buckley-Zistel S (2013) Introduction: Transitions from violence – Analyzing the effects of transitional justice. International Journal of Conflict and Violence 7(1):4–9.

Buergenthal T (2006–2007) Truth commissions: Between impunity and prosecution. Case Western Reserve Journal of International Law 38:217–223.

Chapman AR, Ball P (2001) The truth of truth commissions: Comparative lessons from Haiti, South Africa, and Guatemala. Human Rights Quarterly 23(1): 1–43.

Collins C (2013) El Salvador. In: Stan L, Nedelsky N (eds) Encyclopedia of transitional justice, vol 1. Cambridge University Press, New York, pp 154–160.

Council of Europe (1987) National Refugees and Missing Persons in Cyprus, Recommendation 1056. http://assembly.coe.int/nw/xml/XRef/Xref-XML2HTML-en.asp?fileid=15090&lang=en. Accessed 22 October 2019.

Council of Europe (2011) Eradicating impunity for serious human rights violations: Guidelines and reference texts, H/Inf (2011)7. https://rm.coe.int/1680695d6e. Accessed 22 October 2019.

Eberle EJ (2009) The method and role of comparative law. Washington University Global Studies Law Review 8(3): 451–486.

Elster J (1998) Coming to terms with the past. A framework for the study of justice in the transition to democracy. European Journal of Sociology 39(1): 7–48.

Elster J (2004) Closing the books: Transitional justice in historical perspective. Cambridge University Press, Cambridge.

European Union (2015) The EU's policy framework on support to transitional justice. http://eeas.europa.eu/archives/docs/top_stories/pdf/the_eus_policy_framework_on_support_to_transitional_justice.pdf. Accessed 22 October 2019.

Ferrara A (2015) Assessing the long-term impact of truth commissions: The Chilean Truth and Reconciliation Commission in historical perspective. Routledge, New York.

Freeman M (2006) Truth commissions and procedural fairness. Cambridge University Press, New York.

Fuentes C, Collins C (2013) National Commission on Truth and Reconciliation, the Rettig Commission/Comisión Nacional de Verdad y Reconciliación, Comisión Rettig (Chile). In: Stan L, Nedelsky N (eds) Encyclopedia of transitional justice. Cambridge University Press, New York, pp 295–300.

Ghana Centre for Democratic Development (2006) Opinions of victims of past human rights abuse in Ghana after the National Reconciliation Commission public hearings. Ghana Centre for Democratic Development, Accra.

Gibson JL (2004) Does truth lead to reconciliation? Testing the causal assumptions of the South African truth and reconciliation process. American Journal of Political Science 48(2): 201–217.

Gitau RC (2010) The price of peace, the costs of war: Addressing anti-social passions in post-conflict Liberia. The Review of International Affairs LX (1138–1139):134–152.

Goldstone RJ (1996) Justice as a tool for peace-making: Truth commissions and international criminal tribunals. New York University Journal of International Law and Politics 28: 485–503.

González E (2014) Set to fail? Assessing tendencies in truth commissions created after violent conflict. In: International Centre for Transitional Justice, Kofi Annan Foundation (eds) Challenging the conventional: Can truth commissions effectively contribute to peace processes? https://www.ictj.org/sites/default/files/subsites/challenging-conventional-truth-commissions-peace/docs/ICTJ-Report-KAF-TruthCommPeace-2014.pdf. Accessed 2 November 2019.

González E, Varney H (2013) Truth seeking: Elements of creating an effective truth commission. https://www.ictj.org/sites/default/files/ICTJ-Book-Truth-Seeking-2013-English.pdf. Accessed 2 November 2019.

Gready P (2011) The era of transitional justice. The aftermath of the Truth and Reconciliation Commission in South Africa and beyond. Routledge, Abingdon.

Hamber B, Wilson RA (2002) Symbolic closure through memory, reparation and revenge in post-conflict societies. Journal of Human Rights 1(1):35–53.

Hayner PB (1994) Fifteen truth commissions – 1974 to 1994: A comparative study. Human Rights Quarterly 16:597–655.

Hayner PB (2011) Unspeakable truths: Transitional justice and the challenge of truth commissions, 2nd edn. Routledge, London.

Heine J (2007) All the truth but only some justice? Dilemmas of dealing with the past in new democracies. In: Hughes E et al (eds) Atrocities and international accountability: Beyond transitional justice. United Nations University Press, Tokyo, New York and Paris, pp 65–80.

Hirsch MBJ et al (2012) Measuring the impacts of truth and reconciliation commissions: Placing the global 'success' of TRCs in local perspective. Cooperation and Conflict 47(3):386–403.

Huntington SP (1991) Democracy's third wave. Journal of Democracy 2(2): 12–34.

Huntington SP (1991) The third wave. Democratisation in the late Twentieth Century. University of Oklahoma Press, Norman.

International Centre for Transitional Justice. What is transitional justice. https://www.ictj.org/about/transitional-justice. Accessed 1 November 2019.

International Commission to Inquire into the Causes and Conduct of the Balkan Wars (1914) Report of the International Commission to Inquire into the Causes and Conduct of the Balkan Wars. http://www.pollitecon.com/html/ebooks/Carnegie-Report-on-the-Balkan-Wars.pdf. Accessed 6 October 2019.

Isa FG (2013) National Reconciliation Commission/Comisión Nacional de Resarcimento (Guatemala). In: Stan L, Nedelsky N (eds) Encyclopedia of transitional justice. Cambridge University Press, New York, pp 322–326.

Kaminer D et al (2001) The truth and reconciliation commission in South Africa: Relation to psychiatric status and forgiveness among survivors of human rights abuses. British Journal of Psychiatry: 373–377.

Kandeh JD (2004) Coups from below: Armed subalterns and state power in West Africa. Palgrave Macmillan, New York.

Kermeliotis T (2014) Ghana: Keeping one of Africa's stars of democracy shining. http://edition.cnn.com/2014/02/26/world/africa/ghana-history-overview-on-the-road/index.html. Accessed 5 October 2019.

Kritz N (2009) Policy implications of empirical research on transitional justice. In: Van Der Merwe et al (eds) Assessing the impact of transitional justice: Challenges for empirical research. United States Institute of Peace, Washington DC, pp 13–22.

Kritz NJ (1995) The dilemmas of transitional justice. In: Kritz N (ed) Transitional justice: How emerging democracies reckon with former regimes, vol. I. United States Institute of Peace, Washington DC, pp xix–xxx.

Landsman S (1996) Alternative responses to serious human rights abuses: of prosecution and truth commissions. Law and Contemporary Problems 59(4): 81–92.

Leebaw BA (2008) The irreconcilable goals of transitional justice. Human Rights Quarterly 30: 95–118.

Long WJ (2008) Liberia's Truth and Reconciliation Commission: An interim assessment. International Journal of Peace Studies 13(2): 1–14.

Lowenthal AF (1986) Foreword. In: O'Donnell G et al (eds.) Transitions from authoritarian rule: Comparative perspectives. Johns Hopkins University Press, London, pp vii–x.

Lund M (1998) Reckoning for past wrongs: Truth commissions and war crimes tribunals. In: Harris P, Reilly B (eds) Democracy and deep-rooted conflict: Options for negotiators. Institute for Democracy and Electoral Assistance, Stockholm, pp 281–307.

Lundy P (2010) Commissioning the past in Northern Ireland. The Review of International Affairs LX (1138–1139):101–133.

Méndez JE (1997) Accountability for past abuses. Human Rights Quarterly 19(2):255–282.

Millar G (2010) Assessing local experiences of truth-telling in Sierra Leone: Getting to 'why' through a qualitative case study analysis. International Journal of Transitional Justice 4:477–496.

Mncwabe N (2013) Truth commissions. In: Stan L, Nedelsky N (eds) Encyclopedia of transitional justice. Cambridge University Press, New York, pp 98–106.

Nwogu NV (2010) When and why it started: Deconstructing victim-centered truth commissions in the context of ethnicity-based conflict. International Journal of Transitional Justice 4:275–289.

O'Donnell G, Schmitter PC (1986) Transitions from authoritarian rule: Tentative conclusions about uncertain democracies. Johns Hopkins University Press, Baltimore.

Oettler A (2014) The scope and selectivity of comparative area studies: Transitional justice research. https://www.giga-hamburg.de/en/system/files/publications/wp246_oettler.pdf. Accessed 2 November 2019.

Office of the United Nations High Commissioner for Human Rights (2006) Rule-of-law tools for post conflict states: Truth commissions. https://www.ohchr.org/Documents/Publications/RuleoflawTruthCommissionsen.pdf. Accessed 2 November 2019.

Office of the United Nations High Commissioner for Human Rights (2015) Rule-of-law tools for post-conflict states: Archives. https://www.ohchr.org/Documents/Publications/HR_PUB_14_4_Archives_en.pdf. Accessed 4 September 2019.

Olsen TD et al (2010) When truth commissions improve human rights. The International Journal of Transitional Justice 4: 457–476.

Organisation of American States (2008) Persons who have disappeared and assistance to members of their families, AG/RES. 2416 (XXXVIII-O/08). http://www.oas.org/DIL/AG-RES_2513-2009_eng.doc. Accessed 2 November 2019.

Organisation of American States (2008) Right to the truth, AG/RES. 2406 (XXXVIII-O/08). https://www.oas.org/dil/AGRES_2406.doc. Accessed 2 November 2019.

Oxford Advanced Learners Dictionary (2019) Transition. http://www.oxfordlearnersdictionaries.com/definition/english/transition_1?q=transition. Accessed 14 August 2019.

Payne LA (2001) Collaborators and the politics of memory in Chile. Human Rights Review 2 (8):8–26.

Pham P, Vinck P (2007) Empirical research and the development and assessment of transitional justice mechanisms. International Journal of Transitional Justice 1:231–248.

Popkin M, Roht-Arriaza N (1995) Truth as justice: Investigatory commissions in Latin America. Law and Social Inquiry 20(1):79–116.

Pozen J et al (2014) Assessing the Rwanda experiment: Popular perceptions of Gacaca in its final phase. International Journal of Transitional Justice 8:31–52.

Ragin CC, Rubinson C (2009) The distinctiveness of comparative research. In: Landman T, Robinson N (eds) The Sage handbook of comparative politics. Sage, London, pp 13–34.

Reilly B (1998) Democratic levers for conflict management. In: Harris P, Reilly B (eds) Democracy and deep-rooted conflict: Options for negotiators. International Institute for Democracy and Electoral Assistance, Stockholm, pp 133–342.

Roht-Arriaza N (1990) State responsibility to investigate and prosecute grave human rights violations in international law. California Law Review 78(2): 449–513.

Roht-Arriaza N (2006) The new landscape of transitional justice. In: Roht-Arriaza N, Mariezcurrena J (eds) Transitional justice in the twenty-first century: Beyond truth versus justice. Cambridge University Press, Cambridge and New York, pp 1–16.

Scharf MP (1997) The case for a permanent international truth commission. Duke Journal of Comparative and International Law 7:375–410.

Schoepfel AS (2016) Dynamics of justice in Indochina (1944–1946): France's commitment to the rule of law and the punishment of Japanese war crimes. In: Tolliday P et al (eds) Asia-Pacific between conflict and reconciliation. Vandenhoeck and Ruprecht, Göttingen, pp 103–124.

Shaw R (2007) Memory frictions: Localizing the Truth and Reconciliation Commission in Sierra Leone. International Journal of Transitional Justice 1(2):183–207.

Sikkink K (2012) Models of accountability and the effectiveness of transitional justice. In: Popovski V, Serrano M (eds) After oppression: Transitional justice in Latin America and Eastern Europe. United Nations University Press, New York, pp 19–38.

Singh AS, Masuku MB (2014) Sampling techniques and determination of sample size in applied statistics research: An overview. International Journal of Economics, Commerce and Management II (11):1–22.

Slack M (2012) From the Archives: President Obama's Trip to Ghana. https://www.whitehouse.gov/blog/2012/06/14/archives-president-obamas-trip-ghana. Accessed 25 October 2019.

Survey System. Sample size calculator. https://www.surveysystem.com/sscalc.htm#one. Accessed 16 August 2019.

Teitel RG (2000) Transitional justice. Oxford University Press, New York.

Teitel RG (2003) Transitional justice genealogy. Harvard Human Rights Journal 16:69–94.

Theissen G (1999) Common past, divided truth: The Truth and Reconciliation Commission in South African public opinion. http://userpage.fu-berlin.de/theissen/pdf/IISL-Paper.PDF. Accessed 13 November 2019.

Thoms ONT et al (2010) State-level effects of transitional justice: What do we know? International Journal of Transitional Justice 4:329–354.

Tomuschat C (2001) Clarification Commission in Guatemala. Human Rights Quarterly 23(2): 233–258.

Tortora RD (1978) A note on sample size estimation for multinomial populations. The American Statistician 32(3):100–102.

Trejo G et al (2018) Breaking state impunity in post-authoritarian regimes: Why transitional justice processes deter criminal violence in new democracies. Journal of Peace Research 55(6): 787–809.

Trueman CN (2015) The Treaty of Versailles. https://www.historylearningsite.co.uk/modern-world-history-1918-to-1980/the-treaty-of-versailles/. Accessed 12 October 2019.

United Nations (2010) United Nations approach to transitional justice: Guidance note of the Secretary-General. http://www.unrol.org/files/TJ_Guidance_Note_March_2010FINAL.pdf. Accessed 14 October 2019.

United Nations Commission on Human Rights (2005) Promotion and protection of human rights: Impunity, Report of the independent expert to update the set of principles to combat impunity, Diane Orentlicher, Addendum – Updated set of principles for the protection and promotion of human rights through action to combat impunity, E/CN.4/2005/102/Add.1.

United Nations Commission on Human Rights (2006) Promotion and protection of human rights: Study on the right to the truth, Report of the Office of the United Nations High Commissioner for Human Rights, E/CN.4/2006/91.

United Nations Economic and Social Council (1989) Principles on the effective prevention and investigation of extra-legal, arbitrary and summary executions. https://www.ohchr.org/Documents/ProfessionalInterest/executions.pdf. Accessed 2 November 2019.

United Nations General Assembly (2006) Resolution adopted by the General Assembly on 16 December 2005: Basic Principles and Guidelines on the Right to a Remedy and Reparation for Victims of Gross Violations of International Human Rights Law and Serious Violations of International Humanitarian Law, A/RES/60/147. https://documents-dds-ny.un.org/doc/UNDOC/GEN/N05/496/42/PDF/N0549642.pdf?OpenElement. Accessed 2 November 2019.

United Nations General Assembly (2014) Resolution adopted by the General Assembly on 18 December 2013, Right to the truth, A/RES/68/165.

United Nations General Assembly, Human Rights Council (2009) Annual Report of the United Nations High Commissioner for Human Rights and Reports of the Office of the High Commissioner and the Secretary-General: Resolution adopted by the Human Rights Council, Cooperation with the United Nations, its representatives and mechanisms in the field of human rights, A/HRC/RES/12/12.

United Nations Human Rights Committee (2004) General Comment No. 31, The nature of the general legal obligation imposed on states parties to the Covenant, CCPR/C/21/Rev.1/Add. 13.

United Nations Human Rights Council (2012) Resolution 21/7 adopted by the Human Rights Council, Right to the truth, A/HRC/RES/21/7.

United Nations Security Council (2004) The rule of law and transitional justice in conflict and post-conflict societies: Report of the Secretary-General, S/2004/616.

United Nations War Crimes Commission (1948) History of the United Nations War Crimes Commission and the development of the laws of war. http://www.unwcc.org/wp-content/uploads/2017/04/UNWCC-history.pdf. Accessed 31 October 2019.

Van Der Merwe H et al (2009) Introduction. In: Van Der Merwe H et al (eds) Assessing the impact of transitional justice: Challenges for empirical research. United States Institute of Peace, Washington DC, pp 1–12.

Verdeja E (2009) Unchopping a tree: Reconciliation in the aftermath of political violence. Temple University Press, Philadelphia.

Villa-Vicencio C (2000) Why perpetrators should not always be prosecuted: Where the International Criminal Court and truth commissions meet. Emory Law Journal 49(1):205–224.
Villa-Vicencio C (2004) Truth commissions. In: Villa-Vicencio C, Doxtader E (eds) Pieces of the puzzle: Keywords on reconciliation and transitional justice. Institute for Justice and Reconciliation, Cape Town, pp 89–95.
Wain M (2003) Ghana's National Reconciliation Commission. http://peacemagazine.org/archive/v19n2p18.htm. Accessed 30 November 2019.
Waldorf L (2009) Ex-combatants and truth commissions. In: Patel AC et al (eds) Disarming the past. Transitional justice and ex-combatants. Social Science Research Council, New York, pp 108–131.
Weiner MA (2005) Defeating hatred with truth: An argument in support of a truth commission as part of the solution to the Israeli-Palestinian conflict. Connecticut Law Review 38:123–156.
Werle G, Jessberger F (2014) Principles of international criminal law. Oxford University Press, Oxford.
Wiebelhaus-Brahm E (2010) Truth commissions and transitional societies. The impact on human rights and democracy. Routledge, London and New York.
Zajtay I (1974) Aims and methods of comparative law. The Comparative and International Law Journal of Southern Africa 7(3): 321–330.

Chapter 2
Historical Background to the Establishment of the National Reconciliation Commission

Contents

2.1 Introductory Remarks 28
2.2 Early Signs of Social Division in Ghana 29
- 2.2.1 Nkrumah and the United Gold Coast Convention 29
- 2.2.2 The National Liberation Movement 30
- 2.2.3 The Togoland Factor 31

2.3 Ghana's First Republican Regime (6 March 1957 to 24 February 1966) 31
2.4 The Genesis of Military Rule: The National Liberation Council (24 February 1966 to 1 October 1969) 36
2.5 A Second Venture into Constitutional Democracy: The Government of the Progress Party (1 October 1969 to 13 January 1972) 37
2.6 The Return to Military Rule (1972–1979) 39
- 2.6.1 The National Redemption Council and the First Supreme Military Council (13 January 1972 to 5 July 1978) 39
- 2.6.2 The Second Supreme Military Council (5 July 1978 to 4 June 1979) 41
- 2.6.3 The Armed Forces Revolutionary Council (4 June 1979 to 24 September 1979) 41

2.7 The Third Republic: Peoples' National Party (24 September 1979 to 31 December 1981) 43
2.8 The Second Coming of Rawlings: The Provisional National Defence Council (31 December 1981 to 7 January 1993) 45
2.9 Transition to Democracy and the National Reconciliation Commission 49
2.10 Chapter Summary 53
References 53

Abstract The establishment of Ghana's National Reconciliation Commission was a response to gross human rights violations perpetrated under the rule of eight different civilian and military governments. Starting from the era of the Convention Peoples' Party in 1957 and continuing through the end of the military rule by the Provisional National Defence Council in 1993, this chapter delves into the historical and social context within which the National Reconciliation Commission was

M. Yankson-Mensah, *Transitional Justice in Ghana*, International Criminal Justice Series 25, https://doi.org/10.1007/978-94-6265-379-5_2

established. It also relates the recurrence of the military in Ghanaian politics during the period as well as the role of both the military and constitutional governments in perpetrating human rights violations. Tracing the factors that created political divisions in the country, the chapter asserts that pre-independence polarisation in the country disposed successive governments to opposition. The chapter also provides a description of Ghana's transition to democracy, the factors that either enhanced or disrupted the process and identifies the reasons why Ghana remained a conflicted democracy for nearly ten years after transitioning to democratic rule. The events that culminated in the creation of the National Reconciliation Commission not only provide an insight into the choices that Ghana made during its transition but also shed light on the rationale behind the commission's mandate.

Keywords Human Rights Violations · Ghana · Military Regimes · Constitutional Rule · Coups d'État · Transition · Democracy

2.1 Introductory Remarks

In transitional justice, history serves as a conduit for unearthing the underlying causes of the injustices experienced by a society. The historical context is also a relevant factor regarding the choices that a country makes to address gross human rights violations, including identifying key perpetrators of human rights violations and understanding the plight of victims. In the case of the NRC, the relevant historical antecedents to its establishment can be traced to Ghana's independence on 6 March 1957. The transition from colonial rule marked a significant point in the history of Ghana (known as the Gold Coast until 1957). The country was the first sub-Saharan African country to gain independence from British colonial rule. In fact, Ghana's independence is regarded as a turning point for Africa, as it marked a significant step towards breaking the chains of colonial rule. Yet the bliss of attaining independence was short lived, due to nearly four decades of political instability and economic hardship that the country experienced shortly after gaining independence. The nation has undergone four republican constitutional regimes (1957–1966, 1969–1972, 1979–1981, and 1993 to date) and five episodes of military rule (1966–1969, 1972–1978, 1978–1979, 1979, and 1981–1993), all of which brought untold human rights violations. This chapter provides accounts of how successive governments used laws and arbitrary acts to repress individual freedoms and liberty in the form of abductions, killings, unlawful detentions, invasion of property rights, torture and ill-treatment as well as suppression of individuals' freedom of speech and expression. It also outlines the factors that caused social divisions over the period and the reasons that eventually led to a transition to democracy.

2.2 Early Signs of Social Division in Ghana

In order to understand the underlying causes of the long era of political instability that Ghana experienced after its independence, it is necessary to consider the factors behind initial forms of political opposition in the country, which have served as a basis for different political groupings in the country, even today. The Convention Peoples' Party, which is one of the political parties that led the struggle for independence, freed Ghana from British colonial rule under the leadership of Kwame Nkrumah. Even before the government of the Convention Peoples' Party came into power, various occurrences in the Gold Coast had created polarisation, which largely affected politics and rule of law in the independent Ghana. It is necessary, therefore, to know the pre-independence incidents that generated social divisions in the country in order to understand the roots of subsequent human rights violations.

2.2.1 Nkrumah and the United Gold Coast Convention

The relationship between the United Gold Coast Convention and Ghana's first president, Kwame Nkrumah, was one primary cause of divisions in Ghanaian society. The United Gold Coast Convention was formed in the August 1947 merger of two major political parties, the Gold Coast People's League and the Gold Coast National Party, made up of affluent traders and lawyers. This elite-dominated nationalist movement was the first political movement that started advocating for independence from British colonial rule.[1] Initially, the United Gold Coast Convention was relatively sluggish in its pro-independence endeavours.[2] Things, however, took a different turn in December 1947, when party leaders invited Kwame Nkrumah to become the party's general secretary.[3] From the time of his involvement in the United Gold Coast Convention's activities, Nkrumah held significantly different views from that of the leaders. For instance, whereas Nkrumah wanted a speedy attainment of independence, party leaders did not have any timelines in their pursuit of Ghana's political freedom.[4] Moreover, the United Gold Coast Convention aimed to make Ghana a capitalist state, whilst Nkrumah was an ardent supporter of socialism. Over time, Nkrumah's relationship with the

[1]This followed the adoption of a Constitution in 1946, by the Governor of the then Gold Coast, which permitted an African majority in the legislative council. See Bourret 1960, p. 173; and McLaughlin and Owusu-Ansah 1995, pp. 25, 26.

[2]See Bourret 1960, p. 173.

[3]At the time, Nkrumah was a student in England and was actively involved in pan-Africanist activities, which had made him quite popular. See Oppong and Oppong 2003, pp. 59–60; Osei 1999, p. 38; Poe 2003, p. 90; Rooney 2007, p. 47.

[4]See Manu 1975, pp. 125–126; and Poe 2003, pp. 91–94.

party's leaders became strained, as actions he took caused their displeasure.[5] In June 1949, he broke away from the United Gold Coast Convention to establish the Convention Peoples' Party. Unlike the slow-moving United Gold Coast Convention, the Convention Peoples' Party used all forms of urgent measures in their dealings with the colonial rulers. Within a short time, it had attained a large following, due to the dominance of lower classes in the party. The United Gold Coast Convention believed that Nkrumah had selfishly benefitted from his membership in their party to gain popularity for the Convention Peoples' Party.[6] Nkrumah's split from the United Gold Coast Convention and his eventual victory in Ghana's fight for independence earned him many political enemies. It also created a rift between supporters of the Convention Peoples' Party and the United Gold Coast Convention, which lingered on for several years after Ghana's independence.

2.2.2 *The National Liberation Movement*

The National Liberation Movement, formed in 1954, was made up of people from the Ashanti tribe and a group of expelled members of the Convention Peoples' Party. The movement was formed in the wake of Ashanti farmers' frustration with the government's failure to increase cocoa prices in accordance with world prices. Having gained substantial backing from the Ashanti chiefs, the National Liberation Movement vehemently opposed key policies of the Convention Peoples' Party prior to independence. It protested against communist ideologies and cautioned Ghanaians of the communist tendencies of the Convention Peoples' Party.[7] It also campaigned strongly for a federal government whilst the Convention Peoples' Party advocated for a unitary government.[8] Although the National Liberation Movement did not consider itself a political party, its activities gave rise to violent clashes, particularly in the Ashanti region of Ghana, often involving casualties.[9] This movement continued its opposition activities even after Ghana gained

[5]For instance, he set up a youth organisation within the party that was not approved by the leaders. See Botwe-Asamoah 2005, p. 79; Bourret 1960, p. 173; Gocking 2005, pp. 92–93; Poe 2003, p. 94.

[6]See Bourret 1960, pp. 173, 188; Manu 1975, pp. 126–127; and Oppong and Oppong 2003, p. 60.

[7]See Apter 1968, pp. 337, 341; Botwe-Asamoah 2005, p. 88; Gocking 2005, pp. 104–105; Fitch and Oppenheimer 1966, p. 59; McLaughlin and Owusu-Ansah 1995, p. 29; Osei 1999, pp. 54–56; and Poe 2003, p. 101.

[8]See Bourret 1960, p. 188; Fitch and Oppenheimer 1966, pp. 59–65; Leith and Söderling 2000, p. 6; Osei 1999, pp. 54–55; Poe 2003, p. 101; Rathbone 1978, p. 23; and Williams 1984, p. 345.

[9]For details of the violence that resulted as a result of the National Liberation Movement, see Gocking 2005, pp. 106–10; and Asamoah 2014, pp. 30–34.

independence in 1957, and it regularly incited violence against the government, including attempts to assassinate Nkrumah.[10]

2.2.3 *The Togoland Factor*

The merger of the Gold Coast with the trust territory of Trans-Volta Togoland was another underlying cause of divisions within Ghanaian society. This geographical area, which was not part of Ghana prior to independence, was one of the former colonial territories taken from Germany after the end of the First World War. Following deliberations in 1955 by a United Nations Trusteeship Council in charge of this territory, it was proposed that the area should be merged with the Gold Coast upon independence. Whereas people from the northern part of the Togoland supported this idea, other factions within the territory, particularly the Togoland Congress (part of which became the Togoland Reformative Movement), aspired to an independent state. In 1956, a United Nations plebiscite resulted in the territory's merger with the Gold Coast upon its attainment of independence on 6 March 1957.[11] In this process, differences emerged between the Convention Peoples' Party and the Togoland factions who opposed merger with the independent Ghana.[12] Their disagreements erupted in severe violent clashes that caused deaths on Ghana's independence day. This disagreement persisted long after, forming the basis of divisions within the independent Ghana.[13]

2.3 Ghana's First Republican Regime (6 March 1957 to 24 February 1966)

The United Gold Coast Convention, the National Liberation Movement and the Togoland factor created polarisation in the independent Ghana, with significant ramifications for the country's subsequent political activity and for human rights and rule of law under the first republican government. To an extent, the occurrence of human rights violations during the Convention Peoples' Party era could be explained against the backdrop of the massive opposition that the government faced

[10]See Asamoah 2014, p. 31; Botwe-Asamoah 2005, pp. 88–93; Nelson and Gyamerah. http://www.conventionpeoplesparty.org/?q=node/80. Accessed 13 August 2019; and Rathbone 1978, p. 24.

[11]See Asamoah 2014, pp. 18–20; Mensah-Bonsu 2007, pp. 247–248; and Williams 1984, p. 358. About the riots caused by the Togoland Congress, see also Gocking 2005, p. 122; and Rooney 2007, p. 194.

[12]See Asamoah 2014, p. 20.

[13]About the Convention Peoples' Party and the Togoland, see Asamoah 2014, pp. 18–25.

at the time.[14] Ghana's 1960 Constitution, which was adopted after independence, did not contain provisions for the protection of fundamental human rights. Although Article 13(1) required the president to declare his adherence to some basic rights upon his assumption of office, these could not be expressly considered human rights protection provisions.[15] The absence of human rights protection clauses in the Constitution provided leeway for the Convention Peoples' Party government to promulgate laws that resulted in massive violations of fundamental rights and freedoms, such as unlawful detentions, killings and torture.[16]

In the wake of oppositional acts that threatened the security of the government through regular eruptions of violence and casualties, a number of oppressive measures were used to clip the wings of the opposition.[17] One such arbitrary act occurred when the government enacted the Avoidance of Discrimination Act, 1957. Under this law, all political parties that bore any form of religious or tribal connotation were abolished.[18] A significant number of local Ashanti tribe chiefs, who represented substantial opposition to the Convention Peoples' Party in the National Liberation Movement, were de-stooled by virtue of this law.[19]

In December 1958, an opposition plan to assassinate Nkrumah was exposed. Following this, the Convention Peoples' Party government relied on the excessive powers of Parliament to pass the Preventive Detention Act of 1958 (Act 17), which empowered the government to arrest and detain people for up to five years without any criminal charges.[20] Some of the first detainees under the law were 43 alleged accomplices in the assassination plot.[21] The Preventive Detention Act denied detained individuals the liberty to challenge their arrest and detention in court. In the few instances in which people tried to do so, the timorous judiciary at the time was unable to safeguard their rights.[22] In the 1969 case of *Re Akoto and Seven Others*, for instance, the appellants, who had been detained under Section 2 of the Preventive Detention Act and had been refused writs of habeas corpus by the High

[14]See Asamoah 2014, p. 60. See also Bourret 1960, p. 188; Leith and Söderling 2000, p. 4.

[15]The said rights included protection against 'discrimination on grounds of sex, race, tribe, religion or political belief', freedom of movement and association, 'freedom of religion and speech', and 'right of access to courts'. The Supreme Court at the time interpreted those provisions as merely being part of the President's declaration and not amounting to a bill of rights. See Supreme Court of Ghana, *Re Akoto and Seven Others*, 28 August 1961, 1961 Ghana Law Reports 1 & 2, pp. 523–535. See also Kludze 2008, p. 678; and Oquaye 1995, pp. 560–561.

[16]See Kludze 2008, p. 678.

[17]See Botwe-Asamoah 2005, p. 98.

[18]See Rooney 2007, p. 195; and Gocking 2005, p. 123.

[19]See Rooney 2007, p. 195.

[20]See Duodo 2002, p. 405; Gocking 2005, p. 123; Biney 2011, p. 84; Kludze 2008, p. 690; McLaughlin and Owusu-Ansah 1995, p. 33; and Owusu-Ansah 2014, p. 9; and Rooney 2007, p. 210.

[21]See Asamoah 2014, p. 49.

[22]See Kludze 2008, p. 690.

Court, appealed to the Supreme Court to challenge the legality of their detention.[23] Amongst other grounds, they argued that the enactment of the Preventive Detention Act exceeded the powers conferred on Parliament under the 1960 Constitution. Moreover, they argued that their detention was a breach of the president's declaration to adhere to certain basic rights upon his assumption of office, made under Article 13(1) of the 1960 Constitution. In ruling against the appeal, the Supreme Court held that the enactment of the Preventive Detention Act was not in excess of the 1960 Constitution but was within the power of Parliament. Moreover, the court decided that the president's declaration upon his assumption of office did not give rise to 'any legal obligations enforceable in a court of law'.[24] The Preventive Detention Act thus became a tyrannical tool against people who opposed the Nkrumah regime and was used arbitrarily to arrest prominent political figures and ordinary citizens, whilst others were forced to go into exile.[25] Eventually, J. B. Danquah, the lawyer who had become famous for defending people detained under the Preventive Detention Act, was arrested twice under the act. He died in detention as a result of inadequate access, despite his ill health, to medical facilities.[26] By 1961, about 400 people were under detention pursuant to this law, and this number increased to about 1,200 in 1966.[27]

In 1962, another attempt to assassinate Nkrumah resulted in one death and 56 injuries as a result of a bomb explosion.[28] Following the assassination attempt, further deaths and injuries resulted from other bomb explosions, including bomb blasts in Accra, which resulted in 15 deaths and 256 injuries.[29] In August 1962, three Convention Peoples' Party government officials, who were implicated and prosecuted for this assassination attempt, were subsequently acquitted. In reaction to the acquittal, the government passed a law empowering it to dismiss any court decisions and orders to protect the nation's interest.[30] The government then quashed the court's acquittal decision and dismissed the chief justice from his position. The three government officials were then tried again by another court, convicted and put on death row. They remained in custody until the Convention Peoples' Party regime

[23]See the case of *Re Akoto*, above n 15.

[24]See *Re Akoto*, above n 15, pp. 534–535. For a further discussion of the case, see also Atuguba 2009, pp. 1–3.

[25]For instance, Kofi Abrefa Busia, who was the leader of the United Party, formed from the former National Liberation Movement and other opposition parties, fled to London for fear of being detained under this law. See Kludze 2008, p. 690; and McLaughlin and Owusu-Ansah 1995, pp. 3–4, 33.

[26]See Kludze 2008, p. 691.

[27]See McLaughlin and Owusu-Ansah 1995, p. 33; and Rooney 2007, p. 211.

[28]See Asamoah 2014, p. 62.

[29]Ibid.

[30]Rooney 2007, p. 322.

ended in 1966. This act weakened the Ghanaian judiciary's independence and aroused criticism both domestically and internationally.[31]

To further weaken opposition, the government granted most political appointments to members of the Convention Peoples' Party, some of whom were known to be highly unqualified.[32] This intensified the level of hostility against the government and eventually resulted in the merger of opposition bodies to form the United Party.[33] In 1964, the government crippled all forms of opposition by making Ghana a one-party state through a referendum of questionable credibility.[34] Another significant tool used to weaken opposition political activities was the deportation of people alleged to be aliens, including two well-known members of the Muslim Association Party in 1957 and six university lecturers in 1964.[35]

The establishment of the Workers Brigade to educate youth on industrial and agricultural skills further increased the unpopularity of Nkrumah's government. This group, which was formed with quite modest intentions, ultimately became a vehicle for corruption and repression. In some cases, the Workers Brigade seized private farms in the name of creating state farms. Although victims of such seizures were sometimes compensated, the state farms were grossly mismanaged and unable to yield profits for the state. Members of the Workers Brigade became notorious for taking bribes in return for governmental contracts for supply of food, materials and transportation.[36]

The army was also victim to arbitrary government acts. Nkrumah interfered with promotions and some retirements.[37] He established a wing within the army known as the President's Own Guard Regiment to enhance presidential security and protect himself from the regular members of the army. This arm of the army, which later became an independent wing, ignited friction within the army, which eventually proved to be a significant factor in the overthrow of the Convention Peoples' Party government.[38] On 24 February 1966, Nkrumah was overthrown in Operation Cold Chop, a military coup d'état led by Colonel Emmanuel Kwasi Kotoka.[39]

Several reasons can be cited for the overthrow of Nkrumah. High-level divisions within Ghanaian society coupled with the high number of political enemies that the

[31]For details of this incident, see Apter 1968, p. 343; Duodo 2002. https://www.questia.com/magazine/1G1-83534325/ako-adjei-the-walking-history-of-ghana-cameron. Accessed 20 July 2019; McLaughlin and Owusu-Ansah 1995, pp. 35–36; Mensah-Bonsu 2007, p. 263; and Rooney 2007, p. 322.

[32]See Rooney 2007, pp. 195–196.

[33]Ibid., p. 196. See also Apter 1968, pp. 337, 341.

[34]See CCTV Africa, Faces of Africa—Kwame Nkrumah (Video File) published by CGTN Africa on YouTube, 9 December 2014. https://www.youtube.com/watch?v=TMY0iTcspNA. Accessed 3 September 2019. See also Kludze 2008, p. 685; and Rooney 2007, p. 323.

[35]See Asamoah 2014, pp. 53–54.

[36]See Rooney 2007, pp. 273, 274.

[37]See Dowse 1975, p. 16; and Kandeh 2004, p. 66.

[38]See Kandeh 2004, p. 66.

[39]See Gocking 2005, pp. 138–139, 147.

party had accumulated over the years, spelt doom for the Convention Peoples' Party, even before it came into power. This is evidenced by the numerous assassination attempts against Nkrumah (about seven) during his rule.[40] In addition, the government had earned a bad reputation over time for being dictatorial. In 1962 for instance, Nkrumah declared himself a 'president for life' and thereby removed all avenues for another democratically elected government to come into power.[41]

Economic factors also played a role in Nkrumah's overthrow. As a result of the numerous projects initiated by the government after Ghana's independence, the economy became extremely weak by 1966, with a slow growth rate, high rates of unemployment and inflation.[42] Whereas state farms received government support to help them develop, private cocoa farmers, who contributed a high percentage to Ghana's gross domestic product, were heavily taxed.[43] These developments led to Nkrumah's increasing unpopularity, especially amongst the people of the Ashanti tribe, who were among the country's major cocoa producers. The nation's economy took a downturn in 1965 because of a drastic fall in world cocoa prices, leading to a great loss of revenue for the country.[44] In addition, several findings of corruption were made against Nkrumah's government, later confirmed by different commissions of enquiry.[45] Nkrumah, however, took no steps to diminish corruption. Indeed, he himself is believed to have spent far in excess of his legal entitlements.[46]

In view of these factors, Nkrumah's overthrow caused no surprise.[47] Although the military coup that overthrew his government has been classified as bloodless, it resulted in some fatalities.[48] Amongst those known to have been killed are an army general who was chief of the general staff and members of the President's Own Guard Regiment who remained faithful to Nkrumah during the military coup.[49] Moreover, a number of expatriate workers from China were brutally beaten by the coup forces.[50]

[40]See Peking Review 1966, p. 11.

[41]See CCTV Africa, Faces of Africa—Kwame Nkrumah (Video File) published by CGTN Africa on YouTube, 9 December 2014. https://www.youtube.com/watch?v=TMY0iTcspNA. Accessed 3 September 2019; and Gocking 2005, p. 294.

[42]See Kandeh 2004, p. 66; and Oppong and Oppong 2003, p. 61.

[43]Oppong and Oppong 2003, p. 61.

[44]Ibid., p. 62.

[45]The corrupt practices of the government of the Convention Peoples' Party was borne out by the luxurious lifestyles of some of the governmental officials. For instance, Krobo Edusei who was then the Minister of Industries is said to have acquired 27 houses, whilst other officials had as many as 14 houses. See Asamoah 2014, pp. 65–66; and Rooney 2007, p. 270.

[46]Rooney 2007, p. 268.

[47]See Fitch and Oppenheimer 1966, p. 139.

[48]Rooney 2007, p. 340.

[49]Ibid. See also Dowse 1975, pp. 16–17.

[50]See Peking Review 1966, p. 9.

Nkrumah's overthrow caused widespread jubilation in the country, with a general perception that the nation had been freed from a repressive regime.[51] Amongst the reasons cited by originators for the coup was the fact that the Nkrumah government had brought about 'abuse of individual rights and liberty'.[52] Indeed, the coup was perceived as a corrective step by the military, to restore the country to democracy and rule of law.[53] However, the army was to become a recurrent force in Ghana's politics.

2.4 The Genesis of Military Rule: The National Liberation Council (24 February 1966 to 1 October 1969)

After Nkrumah was overthrown, a military government known as the National Liberation Council was formed. Major General Joseph Arthur Ankrah, who had been dismissed from the military by the Convention Peoples' Party government, was made chairman of the National Liberation Council, although he had not participated in the military coup.[54]

Amongst the initial steps taken by the National Liberation Council government was the release of over 500 political prisoners who had been detained under the Preventive Detention Act.[55] Determined to bury all traces of the Nkrumah government, the National Liberation Council banned the Convention Peoples' Party from operation as a political party and eliminated all party supporters from its government. Prominent members of the Convention Peoples' Party were put under imprisonment.[56] The government of the National Liberation Council also offered top political positions to opponents of the Convention Peoples' Party, antagonising Nkrumah's supporters and thereby intensifying political friction within the country.[57]

Although the National Liberation Council government had broad support after rescuing the state from repression, its popularity started to wane after a year. A coup attempt in 1967, for instance, resulted in the death of an army captain in charge of the armoury and Colonel Kotoka, the leader of the 1966 coup.[58] On 26 May 1967,

---

[51]See CCTV Africa, Faces of Africa—Kwame Nkrumah (Video File) published by CGTN Africa on YouTube, 9 December 2014. https://www.youtube.com/watch?v=TMY0iTcspNA. Accessed 3 September 2019; and Rooney 2007, pp. 343–344.

[52]The Daily Graphic 1966, cited in Ziorklui 1993, p. 129.

[53]See Austin 1975, pp. 2–3.

[54]See Gocking 2005, p. 148; Kandeh 2004, p. 67.

[55]See Dowse 1975, p. 17.

[56]Ibid.

[57]See Kandeh 2004, p. 67; and Oppong and Oppong 2003, p. 64. See also Rathbone 1978, p. 26.

[58]See Dowse 1975, pp. 25–26; and Osei 1999, p. 83.

two leaders of the attempted coup were killed by gunshots in full view of the public.[59]

Furthermore, a major corruption scandal gave rise to increased opposition against the government. The chairman of the National Liberation Council, General Ankrah, confessed to taking bribes and resigned from his position on 2 April 1969. Amidst these incidents, the National Liberation Council felt pressured to hand over power to a constitutional government.[60] In 1969, after the promulgation of a new national Constitution, new presidential elections were held. The Progress Party, which had its roots in the pre-independence United Gold Coast Convention, emerged victorious under the leadership of Kofi Abrefa Busia and was elected to lead Ghana's Second Republic.[61]

2.5 A Second Venture into Constitutional Democracy: The Government of the Progress Party (1 October 1969 to 13 January 1972)

The 1969 Constitution of Ghana came into force on 1 October 1969. Due to the massive human rights violations that had occurred under the Nkrumah regime, the 1969 Constitution sought to promote human rights by making ample provisions for that purpose.[62] Nevertheless, large-scale human rights violations continued to persist under the Progress Party government, which turned out to be equally dictatorial, contrary to its democratic image. The new government suppressed labour strikes and student demonstrations and arrested opponents using the military.[63]

One of the Progress Party government's initial acts of oppression was the expulsion of over 150,000 foreign nationals from Ghana between December 1969 and April 1970. Under the Aliens Compliance Order, illegal foreign nationals were given a 14-day notice to leave the country. This act seriously infringed on the property rights of foreign nationals, as their properties were confiscated by the state and distributed amongst supporters of the Busia government. Foreign nationals who remained in the country were also barred from engaging in specific local businesses and were therefore placed in very difficult economic positions.[64]

---

[59]The two officers who were killed were Lieutenant Arthur and Lieutenant Yeboah. See Dowse 1975, p. 26; and The Daily Graphic 1967, cited in Ziorklui 1993, p. 187.

[60]See Osei 1999, p. 83.

[61]See Gocking 2005, p. 155; Goldschmidt 1980, p. 43; and Oppong and Oppong 2003, pp. 64–65.

[62]See Goldschmidt 1980, p. 43.

[63]See Darkwa et al. 2006, p. 21. http://www.civicus.org/media/CSI_Ghana_Executive_Summary.pdf. Accessed 4 September 2019.

[64]See Akinwumi 2003, pp. 680–681; Leith and Söderling 2000, p. 27; Owusu-Ansah 2014, p. 10; and McLaughlin and Owusu-Ansah 1995, p. 39; and Rathbone 1978, pp. 28–29.

The Progress Party government's dismissal of about 568 public officials in 1970 also led to widespread criticism.[65] Executed on the basis of a clause in the Second Republican Constitution of Ghana, the dismissal was considered discriminatory, as most of the dismissed people were members of the opposition and none belonged to the president's tribe, the Akan tribe.[66] Several lawsuits were filed in protest. One such lawsuit was the case of *Sallah v Attorney General*,[67] in which a dismissed public servant challenged his dismissal in court. When the court, in a three-to-one majority, decided in favour of the plaintiff, President Busia was deeply enraged. In a public address to the nation, he condemned the decision and declared that he could not be obliged by any court to reinstate any of the dismissed public officials, an act that undermined the rule of law and made him deeply unpopular.[68] Furthermore, Busia used his powers to recruit more people from his own tribe into the military and dismiss members of the military who opposed his government. Again, the government was accused of tribal bias against members of the military.[69]

In order to curtail opposition, the Progress Party government promulgated a law that banned all public displays and acts that directly or indirectly portrayed a 'revival of the Convention Peoples' Party'.[70] Gradually, these actions created an impetus for the second military coup in Ghana's history.[71] On 13 January 1972, the government of the Progress Party was overthrown in a military coup d'état, led by Colonel Ignatius Kutu Acheampong.[72] The numerous human rights violations perpetrated by the coup forces led to the arrest of prominent members of the military who were supporters of the Progress Party government. This action weakened the command structure of the military, which was already frail on account of past dismissals and retirements by earlier governments.[73]

---

[65]See Buah 1980, p. 199; Leith and Söderling 2000, p. 27; Owusu-Ansah 2014, p. 10; and Rathbone 1978, p. 28.

[66]See Leith and Söderling 2000, p. 27.

[67]See the Supreme Court of Ghana, *Sallah v Attorney General*, 20 April 1970, 1970 Ghana Law Report, p. 55.

[68]See Gocking 2005, pp. 158–159; and Rathbone 1978, p. 29.

[69]See Kandeh 2004, p. 68.

[70]Republic of Ghana, Criminal Code (Amendment No. 2) Act, 1971, Act 380. See also Mensah-Bonsu 2007, pp. 266–267; Osei 1999, p. 86.

[71]See Kandeh 2004, p. 68.

[72]See Darkwa et al. 2006, p. 22. http://www.civicus.org/media/CSI_Ghana_Executive_Summary.pdf. Accessed 4 September 2019; and McGowan and Johnson 1984, p. 664.

[73]See Kandeh 2004, p. 68.

2.6 The Return to Military Rule (1972–1979)

2.6.1 The National Redemption Council and the First Supreme Military Council (13 January 1972 to 5 July 1978)

Explaining the rationale for the 1972 military coup d'état, Austin writes that it marked the beginning of a wrestle for power by the army. In his view, this is because, unlike the 1966 coup that was justifiable as the only means of restoring the country to multiparty democracy, there was no such justification in 1972, other than the persistently unpopular actions of the Progress Party.[74]

The National Redemption Council, chaired by Colonel Ignatius Kutu Acheampong, was established to handle the governance of the country. Under the National Redemption Council (Establishment) Proclamation of 1972, all members of the Progress Party cabinet were removed from their positions.[75] The government of the National Redemption Council gave little indication that it would relinquish power to a democratically elected government, on the grounds that the economy must be revitalised before restoring the country to democracy.[76] Over time, government decrees inflicted greater oppression, making it no different from previous governments.

For instance, the National Redemption Council passed the Price Control Decree of 1974, under which the hoarding of consumer goods were prohibited.[77] Under this law, members of the military engaged in extortion, seizure of goods and forced sales because the law did not define a threshold for 'determination of hoarding', thereby providing leeway for military officials to apply the law in an arbitrary manner.[78] Another decree, the Newspaper Licensing Decree, 1973, was used by the government to curtail press freedom. Some privately owned newspapers were banned, whilst state-owned media was used to further the interests of the government.[79]

Following a reorganisation of the National Redemption Council government in 1975, the National Redemption Council was renamed as the Supreme Military Council and various members of the National Redemption Council were given new managerial government appointments. Despite this reshuffling, the level of corruption amongst governmental officials remained high.[80] In 1977, the Supreme Military Council government started to promote a governmental reform called the

[74]See Austin 1975, pp. 4–5.

[75]See Goldschmidt 1980, p. 43.

[76]See Kandeh 2004, p. 68.

[77]Alidu 2014, p. 59.

[78]Ibid.

[79]See Goldschmidt 1980, pp. 18, 44.

[80]See Kandeh 2004, p. 69.

Union Government. Under this proposed government, there would be power sharing in the government between some appointed members of the military, the police and elected civilians (without involvement of any political parties).[81]

At this same time, opposition to the government was on the ascendency for various reasons.[82] First, the National Redemption Council had not been able to fulfil any of the promises that it made, upon coming into power. Moreover, human rights violations continued to thrive in the country and the economy was deteriorating at a high rate. Opposition forces began to emerge, and there were protests across the country, requesting the government to fix the nation's economy. In its bid to curtail these protests, the Supreme Military Council committed further atrocities. Between 1975 and 1978, a number of political trials took place under the Subversion Decree.[83] This law mainly covered offences that were previously defined under treason and sedition. However, the broad definitions of the offences under this law provided an opportunity for the military to oppress anyone who opposed the government. In addition, the competence of the nation's judiciary at the time was gravely compromised, as a result of continuous use of military tribunals rather than the regular courts for trials. These tribunals did not follow due process of the law in their trials, and the rights of accused persons were grossly disregarded.[84]

As the level of opposition to the government continued to increase, the Ghana Bar Association and other bodies called for the restoration of democratic rule. Nevertheless, the government continued to advocate for a Union Government. On 30 March 1978, a referendum was held on the adoption of the Union Government, in which voter turnout was less than 50% of registered voters. The outcome indicated only 56% support for the Union Government, a figure far below the number required for the Union Government to enter into force. In the aftermath of the referendum, the officer in charge of the elections disappeared under mysterious circumstances and the government took steps to re-collate the referendum results by retrospectively amending the required procedure for collation. Meanwhile, the government disregarded the initial declared results of the referendum, thereby arousing intense criticisms and protests. In the government's efforts to curtail these protests, people who did not support the Union Government idea were intimidated through arbitrary arrests and detentions.[85] About 300 individuals were arrested for opposing the Union Government.[86]

Amidst the continuous economic and political chaos, Colonel Acheampong was overthrown in a palace coup and was forced to sign his resignation letter on 5 July

[81]Darkwa et al. 2006, p. 22. http://www.civicus.org/media/CSI_Ghana_Executive_Summary.pdf. Accessed 4 September 2019; Goldschmidt 1980, pp. 44–46; Hitchens 1979, pp. 171–172; Kandeh 2004, p. 69; and McLaughlin and Owusu-Ansah 1995, p. 44.

[82]See Darkwa et al. 2006, p. 22. http://www.civicus.org/media/CSI_Ghana_Executive_Summary.pdf. Accessed 4 September 2019; and Kandeh 2004, p. 69.

[83]See Republic of Ghana, Subversion Decree, 1972, National Redemption Council Decree No. 90.

[84]See Goldschmidt 1980, p. 44; and Mensah-Bonsu 2007, pp. 270–271.

[85]See Goldschmidt 1980, p. 46.

[86]See McLaughlin and Owusu-Ansah 1995, p. 45.

1978. His chief of defence staff, Lieutenant General Frederick William Kwasi Akuffo, replaced him as president, ushering in a second regime of the Supreme Military Council.[87]

2.6.2 *The Second Supreme Military Council (5 July 1978 to 4 June 1979)*

Although the government of the second Supreme Military Council continued with arrangements already begun to restore the country to constitutional rule, it took no steps to ensure the trial of the numerous army officials who were alleged to have engaged in corrupt practices during the first regime of the Supreme Military Council. Rather, the government tried to grant them immunity from prosecution, pending its preparation to restore the country to civilian rule.[88] Moreover, the country's economy continued to face crises, despite governmental policies to salvage the situation. In light of the severe economic hardships, student and professional groups in the country embarked on strikes and opposed the government's implementation of policies favoured by the International Monetary Fund.[89]

On 4 June 1979, only 14 days before presidential elections, Flight Lieutenant Jerry John Rawlings, who was in detention as a result of an earlier failed coup attempt, was freed from jail by his supporters in the army to lead the overthrow of the military government.[90]

2.6.3 *The Armed Forces Revolutionary Council (4 June 1979 to 24 September 1979)*

In explaining the rationale for the 1979 coup, the military group led by Rawlings cited the harsh economic conditions and the need to bring corrupt government officials to book.[91] The military group established a new military government, known as the Armed Forces Revolutionary Council. The new military regime touted itself as a radical regime that would deliver the country from corruption and repressive rulers and eliminate dishonesty from the Ghana Armed Forces. These claims earned its leader the name 'Junior Jesus'. This perception of radicalism

---

[87]See Goldschmidt 1980, pp. 46, 47; Gocking 2005, p. 178; Kandeh 2004, pp. 21, 69; and McGowan and Johnson 1984, p. 665.

[88]See Ibrahim 2003, p. 9; and Kandeh 2004, p. 21.

[89]See Kandeh 2004, pp. 69–70.

[90]See Goldschmidt 1980, pp. 51–52; Ibrahim 2003, p. 9; Leith and Söderling 2000, p. 32; McGowan and Johnson 1984, p. 665.

[91]See Kandeh 2004, p. 70.

provided the government with massive support from student groups and workers. Despite their supposed modest intentions, the Armed Forces Revolutionary Council, in pushing its radical vision was ultimately more 'punitive rather than transformative' in its short-term rule of four months.[92]

Shortly after assuming power, the Armed Forces Revolutionary Council started what it called a 'house cleaning exercise' to eradicate corruption from the country. In the process, notable personalities from previous governments were attacked, without due process of the law, and several extrajudicial killings occurred.[93] Eight senior army officials, including three ex-presidents were executed for 'crimes against the state', and other executions were carried out against people who had been charged with corruption, racketeering, stealing and other offences relating to economic extortion.[94] Military officials who had lost support within the army were severely tortured and detained, whilst key senior public officials were fired from their jobs and their properties seized.[95] In some instances, prominent top military officials had their heads shaved and were made to hold placards publicly renouncing their positions.[96] Property was also confiscated from private business owners, including foreign businessmen from Lebanon and India, some of whom were deported.[97] Market women became regular victims of the anticorruption drive. The raiding of their shops and seizure of their goods became quite common, whilst military forces looted private property. Market women were also publicly undressed and whipped for allegedly hoarding goods or selling above the permissible prices.[98]

As part of a 'holy war on corruption', the government established commissions of enquiry to investigate companies, government institutions and educational institutions for corruption.[99] Special courts (later called Peoples' Revolutionary Courts) were established to try all manner of corruption-related offences.[100] These courts, which resembled court martials, were equipped with abnormally broad powers, although they were largely manned by laymen. Specifically, four out of the five members of the court's panel were not required to have any legal background or to be qualified judges.[101] The courts were granted retrospective jurisdiction to prosecute cases from as far back as 24 February 1966. Moreover, they were empowered to give either death penalties or prison sentences ranging from 15 years

---

[92]Ibid.

[93]See Goldschmidt 1980, p. 52; Leith and Söderling 2000, p. 39; and Kandeh 2004, pp. 70–71, 73.

[94]Buah 1980, p. 206.

[95]See Goldschmidt 1980, p. 52.

[96]See Kandeh 2004, p. 74.

[97]See Goldschmidt 1980, p. 52.

[98]See Leith and Söderling 2000, p. 39; and Kandeh 2004, pp. 72–75.

[99]Rawlings gave this description to the revolution in his statement on national radio, quoted in Shillington 1992, p. 68.

[100]See Republic of Ghana, Armed Forces Revolutionary Council (Special Courts) Decree, 1979, Armed Forces Revolutionary Council Decree 3, para 3(1).

[101]See Mensah-Bonsu 2007, p. 278.

to 105 years. This provided an impetus to pronounce extraordinarily long sentences against prominent members of the National Redemption Council and Supreme Military Council who were convicted for corruption.[102] One major problem with the powers of these courts was the lack of clarification in relation to the specific offences that warranted a death sentence and those that did not. Discretion was thus left largely to the judges.[103] In addition, the decisions of these courts could not be appealed. The proceedings of the courts were held in camera, and people brought before the courts neither had access to legal representation nor the right to call witnesses. Although details of the court archives are unknown and the exact number of victims remain a mystery, it is believed that hundreds were convicted within the short rule of the Armed Forces Revolutionary Council.[104]

Despite its repressive nature, the Armed Forces Revolutionary Council did not bar political party activities. Six weeks after the party assumed power, successful presidential elections were held to transfer power to a constitutional government. However, the date of the transfer was delayed for three months to enable the Armed Forces Revolutionary Council complete its 'house cleaning exercise'.[105] On 24 September 1979, the Armed Forces Revolutionary Council handed over power to the People's National Party, led by Hilla Limann, with a stern caveat that the new government should expect other revolutions if it undermined the import of the revolution by the Armed Forces Revolutionary Council.[106]

2.7 The Third Republic: Peoples' National Party (24 September 1979 to 31 December 1981)

When the People's National Party assumed power in September 1979, there were high expectations from the government because of the revolutionary standards established during four months of rule by the Armed Forces Revolutionary Council. Some major problems that the government contended with were the transitional provisions that the Armed Forces Revolutionary Council provided in the Constitution of the Third Republic. One such clause disabled the government from reviewing or altering any of the actions taken by the Armed Forces Revolutionary Council whilst in power.[107] Nevertheless, people whose properties had been seized or who had been unjustly prosecuted by the Peoples' Revolutionary Courts under the regime of the Armed Forces Revolutionary Council tried to get redress from the

[102]Ibid., pp. 277–278. See also Kandeh 2004, pp. 72, 73.

[103]See Mensah-Bonsu 2007, p. 278.

[104]Ibid., pp. 278–279.

[105]See Kandeh 2004, p. 75.

[106]Ibid., p. 77. See also Owusu-Ansah 2014, p. 11.

[107]See Oppong and Oppong 2003, p. 69. Goldschmidt 1980, p. 53, also writes that Rawlings promised to continue the housecleaning exercise even after Limann assumed office.

courts. The government was thus faced with a difficult situation, in light of the several lawsuits that sought to challenge actions of the Armed Forces Revolutionary Council.[108]

In addition, the Armed Forces Revolutionary Council had set up another court, known as the Special Tribunal under the Armed Forces Revolutionary Council (Special Tribunal and Other Matters) Decree, 1979, prior to the third republican government's assumption of power. This tribunal was empowered under the transitional provisions in the Constitution of the Third Republic to assume responsibility for all the uncompleted cases of the special courts established by the Armed Forces Revolutionary Council.[109] As the Special Tribunal was administering justice in a manner similar to that of the regular courts and represented the interests of the Armed Forces Revolutionary Council, its existence posed further difficulties for the Limann government.[110]

The government of the Peoples' National Party also had to contend with the continuous, intimidating presence of Armed Forces Revolutionary Council members in the army. Rawlings and his compatriots in the Armed Forces Revolutionary Council formed a group known as the June 4 Movement, to scrutinise the activities of the Limann government. In view of this awkward situation, the government advised most of the members of the Armed Forces Revolutionary Council to retire from the army and funded some of them to pursue studies abroad. Rawlings, however, did not succumb to any of these invitations and was eventually forcefully retired by the government.[111]

A number of incidents made the government unpopular amongst supporters of the Armed Forces Revolutionary Council. First, the government did not continue the investigations of the commissions of enquiry that were created by the Armed Forces Revolutionary Council to probe the affairs of companies, government institutions and educational institutions for corrupt practices.[112] Moreover, corruption convictions that occurred under the regime of the Armed Forces Revolutionary Council were overturned by the high courts using procedural irregularities as grounds to override the ouster clauses in the transitional provisions.[113] Also, the country's economy continued to deteriorate seriously during the era of the Peoples' National Party, and the government failed to rein in the high inflation rate. Amidst these circumstances, corruption still remained a problem,

[108]See Mensah-Bonsu 2007, p. 280; Gocking 2005, p. 188.

[109]Ibid., p. 279.

[110]Things however took a different turn when allegations of corruption arose within the Special Tribunal, which was supposed to be fighting corruption. This incident greatly reduced people's confidence in the Special Tribunal. See Mensah-Bonsu 2007, p. 279.

[111]See McLaughlin and Owusu-Ansah 1995, p. 69.

[112]See Kandeh 2004, p. 73.

[113]See Gocking 2005, p. 188.

albeit to a lesser degree than during the governments of the National Redemption Council and Supreme Military Council.[114] Things took a turn for the worse when several top government officials were implicated in a corruption scandal.[115] Eventually, Limann's government was overthrown in a military coup staged once again by Rawlings on 31 December 1981, after barely 24 months of democratic rule.[116]

2.8 The Second Coming of Rawlings: The Provisional National Defence Council (31 December 1981 to 7 January 1993)

With the overthrow of the People's National Party, Ghana had experienced seven changes in government within 15 years after the overthrow of Nkrumah. The coup organisers established the Provisional National Defence Council and justified the coup by the need to continue the 'house cleaning exercise' started by the Armed Forces Revolutionary Council.[117] In this regard, the Provisional National Defence Council declared the start of a revolution and again waged 'a holy war on corruption'.[118] As Oquaye has noted, however, the so-called revolution traded the political rights of Ghanaians for socio-economic rights.[119] Rather than holding democratic elections immediately after coming into office, the Provisional National Defence Council abolished all political party activities and carved out a unique form of participatory government. Groups known as People's Defence Committees (later renamed the Committees for the Defence of the Revolution) and Workers' Defence Committees were established to provide a forum for grassroots individuals to participate in the government. These groups were also used to carry out corruption-related investigations, and members were supposed to report any cases of corruption that they discovered.[120]

Notable amongst the policies of the Provisional National Defence Council was the establishment of different breeds of courts to serve as engines of its revolutionary cause. Due to their nature and procedural rules, these courts inflicted many human rights violations. To cite an example, public tribunals resembling the Special Courts of the Armed Forces Revolutionary Council were established as part of the

[114]See Oppong and Oppong 2003, p. 69; Leith and Söderling 2000, p. 41.

[115]See Osei 1999, p. 95.

[116]See Kludze 2008, p. 692; McGowan and Johnson 1984, p. 666; McLaughlin and Owusu-Ansah 1995, p. 48; and Kandeh 2004, p. 61.

[117]See Kandeh 2004, pp. 8, 87; and Gocking 2005, pp. 189–190.

[118]See Lyons 1997, p. 67; and Gocking 2005, p. 189.

[119]Oquaye 1995, p. 561.

[120]See Gyimah-Boadi and Rothchild 1982, p. 64; Kandeh 2004, pp. 87, 88; and Leith and Söderling 2000, p. 42.

'holy war against corruption'.[121] The jurisdiction of the public tribunals was similar to that of the Special Courts and covered mainly anticorruption offences and treasonable offences.[122] Under the Public Tribunals Law, 1982,[123] decisions of the public tribunals could be neither reviewed nor appealed. Moreover, the public tribunals could impose death sentences for offences that were specified in writing by the Provisional National Defence Council. In practice, the Provisional National Defence Council made the final pronouncements regarding which people were to be given the death penalty.[124] The public tribunals were empowered to try people in absentia and confiscate their property, unless those people eventually appeared before the court. As Mensah-Bonsu asserts, the establishment of these courts was meant to cripple the powers of legal professionals and provide an avenue for commoners to participate in the adjudication of justice, since they constituted a majority of the Provisional National Defence Council's support.[125]

Unsurprisingly, the arbitrary nature of the public tribunals aroused deep disapproval. The Ghana Bar Association vehemently opposed these courts on account of their downgrading effect on the work of the regular courts. Members of the Ghana Bar Association refused to appear before the tribunals.[126] This resulted in the promulgation of another law,[127] which provided the public tribunals with an appellate feature and limited their jurisdiction to political and economic cases. Despite these amendments, the tribunals continued to operate separately from the normal courts, and their decisions could not be questioned.[128]

Special military tribunals were also established and given jurisdiction to prosecute both members of the military and civilians.[129] Like the Special Tribunals, they operated independently of the normal courts and their decisions were not appealable. Although the special military tribunals were ascribed powers akin to the powers of the Ghana High Court, legal training was not required for members of the tribunals' panel.[130] On 24 March 1984, a number of ex-military personnel and some civilians who plotted a military coup against the government of the Provisional National Defence Council were arrested and killed by firing squad without being tried. Following these executions, a number of amendments were made to the jurisdiction of the special military tribunals, granting them retrospective jurisdiction

---

[121]These tribunals were established under Section 9 of the Provisional National Defence Council (Establishment) Proclamation. See Kandeh 2004, p. 82.

[122]See Mensah-Bonsu 2007, pp. 282–283.

[123]Republic of Ghana, Public Tribunals Law, 1982, Provisional National Defence Council Law 24.

[124]See Mensah-Bonsu 2007, p. 284.

[125]Ibid., p. 281.

[126]See Gyimah-Boadi and Rothchild 1982, p. 65.

[127]See Republic of Ghana, Public Tribunals Law, 1984, Provisional National Defence Council Law 78.

[128]See Kandeh 2004, p. 83; and Mensah-Bonsu 2007, p. 285.

[129]These were established under the Special Military Tribunal Law, 1982, Provisional National Defence Council Law 19.

[130]See Mensah-Bonsu 2007, p. 287.

over the already carried out executions of the coup plotters. Under these amendments, all persons, whether military or civilian, could be detained or tried by a special military tribunal in camera (for offences involving security of the state) and given the death penalty with no access to the services of a lawyer.[131]

The Provisional National Defence Council also established commissions and committees that were used to carry out investigations to facilitate the work of the public tribunals.[132] Notable amongst these were the Citizens' Vetting Committees, which had extensive powers of investigation, including a duty to investigate the properties and finances of individuals with more than 50,000 cedis (the equivalent of approximately USD 16,000 at the time) in their private bank accounts. This discouraged individuals from opening bank accounts and weakened the country's banking sector.[133] The Citizens' Vetting Committees also had a duty to handle investigations relating to payment of taxes and the property of individuals implicated in corruption cases as well as prescribing the appropriate sentences for individuals found guilty.[134] Proceedings of the Citizens' Vetting Committees were held in public, and people who appeared before it could use the services of a lawyer.[135] Over time, these committees lost their credibility when some members were convicted of the very offences for which they conducted investigations.[136]

National Investigations Commissions were established to investigate corruption cases as well as the finances of individuals who were referred to it. This body could confiscate properties of individuals who were suspected of indulging in corrupt practices.[137] Under the one-man-one-house policy, no individual in the country was allowed to own more than one house or car, and a car or house in excess of the limit would be seized.[138] Wealthy people were automatically considered corrupt and were required to either prove the sources of their assets or forfeit those assets to the state.[139] As a result of this policy, breaches of property rights were perpetrated through seizure of private assets without adherence to correct legal procedures. Moreover, individuals whose assets were seized were deprived of the right to challenge the confiscations in court.[140]

The repressive acts of the government also resulted in a number of deaths and disappearances.[141] Notable amongst these was the murder of three High Court judges and one former governmental official in June 1982. These judges had

[131]Ibid., pp. 287–291.

[132]See Kandeh 2004, p. 82.

[133]Ibid., pp. 83, 84.

[134]See Gyimah-Boadi and Rothchild 1982, p. 83.

[135]Ibid., p. 64.

[136]See Kandeh 2004, p. 84.

[137]See Gyimah-Boadi and Rothchild 1982, p. 64; and Kandeh 2004, pp. 83–84.

[138]See Alidu 2014, p. 58.

[139]See Kandeh 2004, p. 82.

[140]See Kludze 2008, p. 695.

[141]Ibid., p. 693.

reversed court orders made under the era of the Armed Forces Revolutionary Council. Although four individuals were initially convicted and executed for the murder of the three judges, subsequent investigations revealed that some members of the Provisional National Defence Council were involved in the murders.[142] Furthermore, the Association of Recognised Professional Bodies, whose membership was predominantly lawyers, also revealed names of 180 people who had been killed during the initial seven months of the Provisional National Defence Council's rule.[143] Moreover, a prisoner who later went into exile during the Rawlings era provided in his chronicles a list of 208 people who were killed from January to June 1982, including the number of deaths in each of the regions of Ghana.[144] Also, a list of 200 abducted and disappeared individuals was published on 28 July 1982 by a former leader of the Ghana Bar Association, Sam Okudzeto, whilst other sources disclose that about 155 individuals were killed between 1984 and 1992 for attempting military coups d'état.[145]

A significant number of unlawful detention cases occurred during the era of the Provisional National Defence Council.[146] In 1983, a wing of the Ghana Police known as the Bureau of National Investigations was established and given extensive powers of arrest, detention and in some instances, execution'.[147] Under the Preventive Custody Law of 1982, the Bureau of National Investigations could arrest individuals without filing any charges or conducting a trial in cases where such individuals were perceived to pose a danger to the country's security. In 1983, for instance, 32 people were executed for attempted coups and armed robberies. Subsequently, about 46 people were executed between 1984 and 1989 for attempted coups. Some Ghanaians left the country in self-imposed exile, for fear of the lives.[148]

Amidst the brutalities of the government, a culture of silence gradually emerged and individuals' freedom of religion, speech, expression and association were grossly violated.[149] Under the Newspaper Licensing Decree (PNDC Law 211), the government was granted the authority to give specific media outlets the authority to work within the country. Some newspapers, such as the *Catholic Standard* and the *Free Press*, were banned as a result of their criticism of the government. Some

---

[142]Ibid. See also Kandeh 2004, p. 85; and Oquaye 1995, p. 563.

[143]See Leith and Söderling 2000, p. 42; and Kandeh 2004, p. 85.

[144]Adjei 1993, pp. 125–131.

[145]See BBC News 2002. http://news.bbc.co.uk/2/hi/africa/2235853.stm. Accessed 9 October 2019; and Myjoyonline TV, Scars of the revolution (Video File) published by Myjoyonline TV on YouTube, 12 December 2019. https://www.youtube.com/watch?v=p2BC4LNhnIE. Accessed 3 January 2020.

[146]See Kludze 2008, p. 693.

[147]See Kandeh 2004, p. 86.

[148]Perhaps this action of the government was due to the high number of attempted coups during the period. According to Owusu-Ansah 2014, p. 12, there were about 13 coup attempts between 1981 and 1992. See also Kandeh 2004, pp. 84, 86.

[149]See Lyons 1997, p. 68.

journalists were imprisoned for expressing opposition to actions of the Provisional National Defence Council.[150] Religious bodies were also affected. Some members of churches were tortured by soldiers, whilst strict registration requirements were put in place for religious bodies. At least four religious groups were prohibited from practising, and the assets of a number of churches were frozen.[151]

Towards the mid-1980s, the Provisional National Defence Council's anticorruption efforts became futile, as the level of corruption in the country started to increase again. Despite the government's perceived non-involvement in these corrupt practices, its failure to address the problem effectively diminished the public's interest in the Provisional National Defence Council's revolution. Moreover, the nation's economy did not fare well in the period, and Rawlings had to resort to an economic recovery programme that sought assistance from the World Bank and ultimately created harsher economic conditions for Ghanaians.[152] Gradually, resistance to the Provisional National Defence Council's rule began to take shape and laid the groundwork for Ghana's transition to its fourth constitutional democracy.

2.9 Transition to Democracy and the National Reconciliation Commission

As early as 1982, the government of the Provisional National Defence Council had established the National Commission for Democracy to serve as a body in charge of promoting democracy. This body organised workshops and discussions to ascertain the form of government suitable for Ghana.[153] Yet it has been argued that this move by the Provisional National Defence Council was not meant to restore Ghana to multiparty democracy, as political party activities remained prohibited in the country until 1992.[154] The intent was to create a non-party decentralised government through district, regional and national assemblies, with the National Assembly acting as the supreme legislative body of the country.[155] Indeed, the Provisional National Defence Council created district assemblies throughout the country, pursuant to a suggestion by the National Commission for Democracy in 1988.[156] For unknown reasons, however, these initial plans did not materialise, and in March

---

[150]See Gyimah-Boadi 1994, p. 77; and Kandeh 2004, p. 86.

[151]See Oquaye 1995, pp. 565–566; Kandeh 2004, p. 86.

[152]See Lyons 1997, p. 68.

[153]See Yayoh 2006–2007, p. 128.

[154]Ibid., p. 129.

[155]Ibid. See also Jeffries and Thomas 1993, p. 335.

[156]See McLaughlin and Owusu-Ansah 1995, p. 54.

1991, Rawlings accepted the suggestions of the National Commission for Democracy to restore a multiparty democracy.[157]

Opposition forces also contributed partly to the transitional process. The notable form of opposition that emerged was the Movement for Freedom and Justice, which used advocacy and educational posters to educate people on the need to restore the country to democratic rule.[158] Having failed to make significant impact during the initial stages of the Provisional National Defence Council's rule, this movement eventually gained ground and provided a strong voice for change during the later 1980s.[159]

The requirement for democratic practices by the World Bank and International Monetary Fund as a condition for aid also furthered democratisation, since the country's economy was in a critical state and foreign aid was urgently needed. Moreover, the transition to democracy was influenced by the worldwide wave of democracy in the 1980s.[160] Democratisation in nearby countries such as Benin, coupled with the end of the Cold War and the fall of the Berlin Wall, increased pressure on the government to restore democracy to the country.[161]

However, despite the existence of pro-democracy groups such as the Movement for Freedom and Justice, the ideas promoted in the transitional process were largely dominated by the views of the Provisional National Defence Council. For instance, although the Movement for Freedom and Justice and the Ghana Bar Association suggested the establishment of a constituent assembly (with elected members from all constituencies in Ghana) to handle the adoption of a new Constitution, their views were disregarded, and rather, a consultative assembly was created in August of 1991.[162] The consultative assembly was comprised mostly of Provisional National Defence Council members who had participated in the human rights

[157]See Abdulai 1992, p. 66; Kandeh 2004, p. 90; Lyons 1997, p. 69; and Yayoh 2006–2007, p. 132.

[158]This body was formed out of a collaboration of past political groups that existed before the banning of political activities in the country. See Darkwa et al. 2006, p. 23. http://www.civicus.org/media/CSI_Ghana_Executive_Summary.pdf. Accessed 4 September 2019. The opposition activities of this group were positively influenced by its leader, Prof. Adu-Boahen, a notable scholar in the country, through a number of lectures he gave to challenge 'the culture of silence that was in existence at the time'. See Handley and Mills 2001, p. 20. https://www.clingendael.org/sites/default/files/pdfs/20011100_cru_working_paper_2.pdf. Accessed 15 October 2019.

[159]See Addulai 2009, pp. 3–4.

[160]See Sect. 1.1.4 in Chap. 1 of this book. See also Yayoh 2006–2007, pp. 125–126.

[161]See Gyimah-Boadi 1994, pp. 83–84; and Handley and Mills 2001, p. 19. https://www.clingendael.org/sites/default/files/pdfs/20011100_cru_working_paper_2.pdf. Accessed 15 May 2019.

[162]According to Yayoh 2006–2007, pp. 132, 135, the consultative assembly could perform only advisory roles. Unlike a constituent assembly, it did not have powers to adopt the Constitution. See also Jeffries and Thomas 1993, p. 337; and Kandeh 2004, p. 90.

violations perpetrated by the group.[163] In view of this, the Ghana Bar Association, for example, did not accept the representation slot given to it.[164]

On 28 April 1992, a referendum was held to decide the fate of a draft national Constitution for Ghana's fourth republic. Despite initial disagreements about the inclusion of certain indemnity clauses in the Constitution at the final stages of its drafting, the referendum yielded 93% positive votes, which met the requirements for adoption.

In the period leading to restoration of democracy, most Ghanaians were in the dark about whether Rawlings would be a candidate in the presidential elections. Rawlings' candidature was announced on 30 September 1992. He established a new political party, the National Democratic Congress, which was made up of supporters of the Provisional National Defence Council, and in November 1992 the government lifted the ban on political party activities.[165] Presidential elections were eventually held on 3 November 1992.[166] It turned out, however, that the four opposition parties that contested the elections did not have enough support. Thus, Rawlings emerged victorious with 58% of the votes, whilst the New Patriotic Party,[167] the largest opposition party, obtained 30% of the votes.[168]

As Lyons has argued, however, the National Democratic Congress's victory in the 1992 elections was not credibly attained.[169] First, the voting process itself was believed to have been prone to manipulation, as a result of the discrepancies in the voters' register.[170] Abdulai also asserts that the collation of the voters' register prior to the election was done speedily.[171] In his view, other factors, such as Rawlings' massive influence over the media and the limitations placed on monetary donations to political parties weakened the campaigning capacity of the opposition political parties.[172] He argues that, aside from these factors, the opposition was at a disadvantage as a result of the ban on political party activities, which was not lifted until

[163]See Gyimah-Boadi 1994, p. 78; and Oquaye 1995, p. 568.

[164]See Kludze 2008, p. 684; and Yayoh 2006–2007, pp. 133–134.

[165]See Kandeh 2004, pp. 90–91; and Whitfield 2009, p. 622.

[166]On this election, see Lyons 1997, p. 69; and Owusu 1992, p. 385.

[167]This party was linked to the ideals of the second republican government and the 'anti colonialist' Joseph Boakye Danquah. See Lyons 1997, p. 69.

[168]See Kandeh 2004, p. 91; and Lyons 1997, pp. 69–70.

[169]See Lyons 1997, pp. 69–70.

[170]Regarding the allegations of discrepancies, see Abdulai 1992, p. 70; Gyimah-Boadi 1994, p. 79; Lyons 1997, pp. 69–70; and Yayoh 2006–2007, p. 139.

[171]Abdulai 1992, p. 70. See also Gyimah-Boadi 1994, p. 79; and Lyons 1997, pp. 69–70.

[172]See Abdulai 1992, p. 70. Donations to political parties could not be in excess of 200,000 cedis (which was equal to $400 at the time). This low figure crippled the opposition parties further, as they were unable to afford all the necessary logistics for their campaigns. See also Gyimah-Boadi 1994, p. 78.

six months before the elections (i.e., 18 May 1992).[173] Moreover, the electoral commissioners were appointed in a manner that was considered biased by the members of the opposition.[174] The opposition resented Rawlings' victory and cited instances of election fraud, causing violence and rioting in some parts of the country.[175] Despite these issues, an observer group from the Commonwealth declared that the electoral process was relatively credible,[176] and Ghana's fourth republican government was ushered into office on 7 January 1993.

With Rawlings' continued leadership, Ghana's transition initially proved to be a shallow process, which resulted in little change in the country's actual political atmosphere.[177] Most prominent government officials of the Provisional National Defence Council were again given positions in the new government of the National Democratic Congress.[178] Moreover, Rawlings won the presidential elections in 1996, although the major opposition party, the New Patriotic Party, was able to win one-third of the parliamentary seats in that election.[179] In 2000, Rawlings was unable to contest in the presidential elections, due to the constitutional limit of two terms for each president. The opposition New Patriotic Party finally emerged victorious in the 2000 presidential elections, representing Ghana's first real change in leadership under its 1992 Constitution (the Fourth Republican Constitution).[180]

Upon assuming office in January 2001, the New Patriotic Party, under the leadership of John Agyekum Kufuor, was faced with the challenge of resolving the deep-seated social and political divisions that had emerged in the country over the long period of repressive rule.[181] There were calls for perpetrators of past human rights violations to be prosecuted, since the Rawlings regime had taken no steps in that regard.[182] Moreover, the New Patriotic Party had made national reconciliation a major component of its campaign of positive change, which earned it victory in

---

[173]Meanwhile, it was alleged that the national Democratic Congress commenced its campaigns long before the ban was lifted, thus giving it undue advantage over the opposition. See Abdulai 1992, pp. 67, 69–70; Lyons 1997, pp. 69–70; and Yayoh 2006–2007, p. 136.

[174]See Abdulai 1992, p. 70; Gyimah-Boadi 1994, p. 79; and Lyons 1997, pp. 69–70.

[175]In a detailed write-up by the opposition titled the "Stolen Verdict", the opposition outlined the various irregularities in the electoral process. See Yayoh 2006–2007, pp. 139, 140. In Kumasi, there were riots in protest of the elections, and a curfew was imposed on the city. In Accra, there were reports that Rawlings' house was attacked causing some damage to the property. See Abdulai 1992, pp. 67, 69; Gyimah-Boadi 1994, p. 79; Lyons 1997, p. 70; and Whitfield 2009, p. 622.

[176]See Abdulai 1992, p. 67.

[177]See Lyons 1997, p. 70.

[178]Boafo-Arthur K., Department of Political Science, University of Ghana, Personal Interview (18 August 2016). See also Kandeh 2004, p. 92; Lyons 1997, p. 70; and Whitfield 2009, p. 622.

[179]See Lyons 1997, p. 65.

[180]Having obtained only 48.2% votes in the first round of the elections (a figure which is below the constitutionally required percentage for becoming President), the New Patriotic Party was able to win after a second round with 56.9% votes. See Anebo 2001, p. 71; Smith 2002, p. 522; and Whitfield 2009, p. 622; Yayoh 2006–2007, pp. 142–143.

[181]Gadzekpo 2001, p. 272.

[182]Ibid., pp. 271–272.

the 2000 elections. In the circumstances, the Parliament enacted the National Reconciliation Commission Act of 2002, pursuant to which the NRC was established in 2002.

2.10 Chapter Summary

This chapter has provided the trail of events that set the stage for massive human rights violations to be committed in Ghana. It has also indicated that the NRC was established as a result of decades of political stability and abuse of political power, which had resulted in massive human rights violations in the form of breached property rights, unlawful detentions and abuse of accused persons' rights. Although some critics have argued that the magnitude of human rights violations in the country was small and did not warrant the establishment of a truth commission, this chapter has provided insight into social divisions in the country that indicated the need to foster a spirit of unity.[183] Furthermore, Ghana's democracy at the time was 'conflicted', as the existing social divisions were not addressed during the initial years of transition to democracy.[184] The country's experience of prolonged political instability thus needed to be addressed in order to strengthen the new democracy. In summary, the NRC constituted a practical way of dealing with the country's unsettled scores to enable Ghanaians to forge ahead as one people.

References

Abdulai D (1992) Rawlings "wins" Ghana's presidential elections: Establishing a new constitutional order. Africa Today, Africa and Human Rights in the 1990s 39(4):66–71.

Addulai AG (2009) Political context study-Ghana. http://www.polis.leeds.ac.uk/assets/files/research/research-projects/abdulai-ghana-political-context-study-jan09.pdf. Accessed 12 October 2019.

Adjei M (1993) Death and pain: Rawlings' Ghana – The inside story. Black Line Publishing Ltd, London.

Akinwumi O (2003) Cold war in the sub regional level: Ghana and Nigeria 1957–1983. In: Falola T (ed) Ghana in Africa and the world: Essays in honor of Adu Boahen. Africa World Press, Trenton, pp 673–710.

Alidu SM (2014) Economic and social injustices in Ghana's military regimes: An investigation of price control policies. IOSR Journal of Humanities and Social Science 19(2): 57–65.

[183]See Wain 2003, pp. 8–9; and Valji 2006, pp. 2–3, where they make reference to the scepticism that met the establishment of the NRC.

[184]According to Aoláin and Campbell 2005, p. 176, a conflicted democracy is one in which: there exists deep-seated political polarisation owing to 'ethnic, racial, religious, class or ideological' factors and the existing polarisation and political atmosphere is so severe that it is very likely to result in violence.

Anebo FKF (2001) The Ghana 2000 elections: Voter choice and electoral decisions. African Journal of Political Science 6(1):69–88.

Aoláin FN, Campbell C (2005) The Paradox of transition in conflicted democracies. Human Rights Quarterly 27(1):172–213.

Apter DE (1968) Ghana in transition. Atheneum, New York.

Asamoah OY (2014) The political history of Ghana. The experience of a non-conformist (1950–2013). Authorhouse, Bloomington.

Atuguba RA (2009) Contemporary constitutional issues in our multiparty democracy. http://library.fes.de/pdf-files/bueros/ghana/10482.pdf. Accessed 30 October 2019.

Austin D (1975) Introduction. In: Austin D, Luckham R (eds) Politicians and soldiers in Ghana: 1966–1972. Frank Cass and Company Limited, pp 1–15.

Biney A (2011) The political and social thought of Kwame Nkrumah. Palgrave Macmillan, New York.

Botwe-Asamoah K (2005) Kwame Nkrumah's politico-cultural thought and policies: An African-centered paradigm for the second phase of the African revolution. Routledge, New York.

Bourret FM (1960) Ghana: The road to independence 1919–1957. Oxford University Press, London.

Buah FK (1980) A history of Ghana. Macmillan Education Limited, London.

Darkwa A et al (2006) Civil society in a changing Ghana. An assessment of the current state of civil society in Ghana. http://www.civicus.org/media/CSI_Ghana_Executive_Summary.pdf. Accessed 4 September 2019.

Dowse R (1975) Military and police rule. In: Austin D, Luckham R (eds) Politicians and soldiers in Ghana: 1966-1972. Frank Cass and Company Limited, pp 16-36.

Duodo C (2002) Ako Adjei – the walking history of Ghana. New African 405:42–45.

Fitch B, Oppenheimer M (1966) Ghana: The end of an illusion. Monthly Review Press, New York.

Gadzekpo A (2001) Reflections on Ghana's recent elections. Review of African Political Economy 28(88):267–273.

Gocking RS (2005) The history of Ghana. Greenwood Press, Westport.

Goldschmidt J (1980) Ghana between the second and the third republican era: Recent constitutional developments and their relation to traditional laws and institutions. African Law Studies 18:43–61.

Gyimah-Boadi E (1994) Ghana's uncertain political opening. Journal of Democracy 5(2):75–86.

Gyimah-Boadi E, Rothchild D (1982) Rawlings, populism, and the civil liberties tradition in Ghana. A Journal of Africanist Opinion XII (3/4):64–69.

Handley A, Mills G (2001) From military coups to multiparty elections: The Ghanaian military-civil transition. https://www.clingendael.org/sites/default/files/pdfs/20011100_cru_working_paper_2.pdf. Accessed 15 October 2019.

Hitchens DRM (1979) Towards political stability in Ghana: A rejoinder in the union government debate. African Studies Review 22(1):171–176.

Ibrahim J (2003) Democratic transition in anglophone West Africa. Council for the Development of Social Science Research in Africa, Dakar.

Jeffries R, Thomas C (1993) The Ghanaian elections of 1992. African Affairs 92(38):331–366.

Kandeh JD (2004) Coups from below: Armed subalterns and state power in West Africa. Palgrave Macmillan, New York.

Kludze AKP (2008) Constitutional rights and their relationship with international human rights in Ghana. Israel Law Review 41(3):677–702.

Leith JC, Söderling L (2000) Ghana: Long-term growth, atrophy, and recovery. https://www.oecd.org/countries/ghana/2674846.pdf. Accessed 11 October 2019.

Lyons T (1997) A major step forward. Journal of Democracy 8(2):65–77.

Manu Y (1975) Reflections on nationalism in the Gold Coast (Ghana) 1944–1951. Journal of the Historical Society of Nigeria 8(1):117–131.

McGowan P, Johnson TH (1984) African military coups d'état and underdevelopment: A quantitative historical analysis. The Journal of Modern African Studies 22(4): 633–666.

McLaughlin JL, Owusu-Ansah D (1995) Historical setting. In: Berry L (ed) Ghana: a country study. Federal Research Division, Library of Congress, Washington DC, pp 1–58.

Mensah-Bonsu HJAN (2007) Political crimes in the political history of Ghana: 1948–1993. In: Mensah-Bonsu HJAN et al (eds) Ghana law since independence: History, development and prospects. Black Mask Limited, Accra, pp 239–307.

Nelson E, Gyamerah M (2009) The origins and the case for preventive detention in Ghana. http://www.thepatrioticvanguard.com/the-origins-and-the-case-for-preventive-detention-in-ghana. Accessed 13 October 2019.

Oppong JR, Oppong ED (2003) Ghana. Chelsea House Publishers, Philadelphia.

Oquaye M (1995) Human rights and the transition to democracy under the PNDC in Ghana. Human Rights Quarterly 17(3):556–573.

Osei AP (1999) Ghana: Recurrence and change in a post-independence African state. Peter Lang Publishing Inc, New York.

Owusu M (1992) Democracy and Africa- A view from the village. Journal of Modern African Studies 30(3):369–396.

Owusu-Ansah D (2014) Historical dictionary of Ghana. Rowman and Littlefield, Lanham and Plymouth.

Peking Review (1966) Reactionary coup d'état in Ghana: Africa's revolutionary tide cannot be stemmed. http://www.massline.org/PekingReview/PR1966/PR1966-11-Ghana.pdf. Accessed 3 November 2019.

Poe DZ (2003) Kwame Nkrumah's contribution to pan-Africanism: An afrocentric analysis. Routledge, New York and London.

Rathbone R (1978) Ghana. In: Dunn J (ed) West African states, failure and promise: A study in comparative politics. Cambridge University Press, London and New York, pp 22–35.

Rooney D (2007) Kwame Nkrumah: Vision and tragedy. Sub-Saharan Publishers, Accra.

Shillington K (1992) Ghana and the Rawlings factor. Macmillan, London and Basingstoke.

Smith D (2002) Ghana's 2000 elections: Consolidating multiparty democracy. Notes on Recent Elections/Electoral Studies 21:519–526.

Valji N (2006) Ghana's National Reconciliation Commission: A comparative assessment. https://www.ictj.org/sites/default/files/ICTJ-Ghana-Reconciliation-Commission-2006-English_0.pdf. Accessed 24 October 2019.

Wain M (2003) Ghana's National Reconciliation Commission. http://peacemagazine.org/archive/v19n2p18.htm. Accessed 30 November 2019.

Whitfield L (2009) Change for a better Ghana: Party competition, institutionalization and alternation in Ghana's 2008 elections. African Affairs 108/433:621–641.

Williams D (1984) English-speaking West Africa. In: Crowder M (ed) The Cambridge history of Africa, vol 8: From c. 1940 to c.1975. Cambridge University Press, New York, pp 331–382.

Yayoh KW (2006–2007) Resurgence of multiparty rule in Ghana, 1990–2004: A historical review. Transactions of the Historical Society of Ghana 10:125–147.

Ziorklui ED (1993) Ghana: Nkrumah to Rawlings. Em-Zed Books Centre, Accra.

Chapter 3
The Legal Framework of the National Reconciliation Commission

Contents

3.1 Introductory Remarks 58
3.2 Reasons for the Establishment of the National Reconciliation Commission 60
  3.2.1 The Amnesty Provisions Under the 1992 Constitution 60
  3.2.2 Complexities with Amending the Amnesty Provisions 61
  3.2.3 Absence of a Transitional Justice Policy for the Country 62
  3.2.4 The Principle of Legality *(Nullum Crimen, Nulla Poena Sine Lege)* 63
  3.2.5 Other Factors 65
3.3 The Features of the National Reconciliation Commission 66
  3.3.1 Time Frame for Operation 69
  3.3.2 Membership and Staffing 70
  3.3.3 Independence of the National Reconciliation Commission 75
  3.3.4 Confidentiality of Information 77
  3.3.5 Objects and Mandate of the National Reconciliation Commission 79
  3.3.6 Powers of the National Reconciliation Commission 84
  3.3.7 Funds of the National Reconciliation Commission 94
  3.3.8 Provisions on the Report 95
  3.3.9 Offences and Penalties 97
3.4 Chapter Summary 98
References 98

Abstract The enabling laws and key features of a truth commission provide a basis for understanding its work. Hence, the absence of a comprehensive legal framework and extensive powers can translate into significant restrictions on addressing gross human rights violations. In unearthing the unique features and limitations of Ghana's National Reconciliation Commission, this chapter examines the legal foundations for its establishment. Starting from the laws that limited recourse to prosecutions, the chapter reflects on the challenges posed by the existence of a blanket amnesty under Ghana's 1992 Constitution. The chapter identifies the absence of a transitional justice policy and the principle of legality as other factors

M. Yankson-Mensah, *Transitional Justice in Ghana*, International Criminal Justice Series 25, https://doi.org/10.1007/978-94-6265-379-5_3

that hindered prosecutions during the transitional process. Using normative and comparative approaches, the chapter discusses the key features of the National Reconciliation Commission, including the nature of its membership, operational time frame, level of independence, nature of its powers and mandate. The discussion highlights the commission's massive legal powers, which make it almost akin to a court.

Keywords Transitional Provisions · Blanket Amnesty · 1992 Constitution of Ghana · Features of Truth Commissions · Mandate of Truth Commissions · Powers of Truth Commissions · Brazil · Nigeria · Liberia

3.1 Introductory Remarks

Different conceivable circumstances may inform the choice of truth commissions in favour of prosecutions.[1] In Liberia, for example, there was a breakdown of the country's judicial system as a result of prolonged war;[2] and the country's earlier attempts to attain peace through different agreements had been unsuccessful, thereby making a truth commission the best alternative to prevent recurrence of the conflict.[3] In Brazil, Law No. 6.683/79, of 1979 had created a blanket amnesty granting immunity to specific members of the Brazilian police and military with respect to human rights violations perpetrated between 2 September 1961 and 15 August 1979.[4] Pursuant to this law, the state failed to prosecute perpetrators of

[1]On this subject, Roht-Arriaza 2006, p. 3, for instance writes that the need for truth may be due to the nature of the dictatorship that a society has experienced, or may be borne by the need to kill the culture of 'silence and denial' that has been caused by a long period of dictatorship.

[2]Long 2008, p. 2.

[3]See Wiebelhaus-Brahm 2013, pp. 282, 283. It has also been asserted by, Long 2008, p. 2, that the truth-telling process in Liberia constituted a step for ensuring accountability through prosecution and other means. Thus, Section 26(g) of the Truth and Reconciliation Commission Act of Liberia limited the ability of the Liberian TRC to suggest amnesties to only cases, which did not amount to crimes against humanity or violations of international humanitarian law.

[4]Between 1964 and 1985, Brazil experienced a dictatorial military regime, under which many human rights violations were perpetrated. During this era, torture, unlawful detentions and disappearances were commissioned by representatives of the state. The said amnesty law was enacted by the Brazilian Congress during the military era in 1979 and covered all individuals who had been under imprisonment or sent into exile from 1961, with few exceptions, and reinstated some politicians to their ability to engage in politics. In 2010, the legality of the amnesty law was reaffirmed by the Brazilian Supreme Court. See Abrão and Tirekky 2012, pp. 153–154, 165, 176–177; Aljazeera America 2014. http://america.aljazeera.com/articles/2014/12/10/brazil-truth-commission.html. Accessed 19 October 2019; BBC News 2014. http://www.bbc.com/news/world-latin-america-30410741. Accessed 19 October 2019; Cavallaro and Delgado 2012, pp. 87–89, 97–99; Comparato and Sarti 2012, p. 8; Kritz 1995a, p. 432; and Mezarobba 2013, pp. 68, 69.

human rights violations who were covered by the amnesty provisions.[5] Although Brazilians still sought to know exactly what had happened under the military dictatorship, the amnesty law created an immense barrier for investigations, making a truth commission a good option for the country.[6] Indeed, Article 1 of Law No. 12.528, under which the Brazilian Comissão Nacional da Verdade was established, expressly provided that its establishment was a move towards fulfilling the individual's right to truth and facilitating national reconciliation.[7] In Chile, the government of Patricio Aylwin faced a comparable predicament on account of an amnesty law enacted by former president Augusto Pinochet regarding the offences committed by his government. Also, by virtue of constitutional amendments, Pinochet was to continue his office as commander-in-chief of the Chilean army until 1998 and afterwards as senator for life. It was amidst such limitations that Chile's National Commission on Truth and Reconciliation was established.[8]

The above examples indicate the diverse contextual factors that could inform a country's transitional choices. As a follow-up to the historical context of Ghana's transition, this chapter focuses on the legal context within which the NRC was established. The chapter discusses the legal factors underpinning the establishment of the NRC and examines the laws that established the NRC by analysing the commission's key features and mandate. The analysis involves comparisons with other truth commissions, especially regarding the NRC's features.

[5]See Inter-American Court of Human Rights, *Gomes Lund et al. ("Guerrilha Do Araguaia") v Brazil*, Judgment of 24 November 2010, p. 106, where the court held that the said amnesty law is invalid under international human rights law. The court, recognizing the benefits of truth commissions in establishing accurate records of the past, urged the state of Brazil to utilize a truth commission in a credible and unbiased manner as one way of dealing with its past. See also Cavallaro and Delgado 2012, pp. 90–92; and Comparato and Sarti 2012, p. 8.

[6]Indeed, prior to the establishment of the Comissão Nacional da Verdade, other transitional justice measures, such as reparations and institutional reform had been initiated in the country. The major gap in the country's way of dealing with past human rights violations was the absence of 'justice and restoration of equality before the law' (i.e., the duty of the state to investigate and prosecute certain human rights violations). See Abrão and Tirekky 2012, pp. 153–156, 163–164; and Torelly 2018, pp. 199–201.

[7]See Presidência da República Brasil. Lei N° 12.528, De 18 De Novembro De 2011 (Law No. 12.528, of 18 November 2011) (Law No. 12.528), Article 1; and Comissão Nacional da Verdade, Relatório da Comissão Nacional da Verdade (Report of the Comissão Nacional da Verdade), 10 December 2014, vol 1, para 47.

[8]See Kritz 1995b, pp. 453–454.

3.2 Reasons for the Establishment of the National Reconciliation Commission

Four main legal factors made the establishment of a truth commission a plausible choice in the case of Ghana: the existence of amnesty provisions in Ghana's Constitution, the difficulty of amending these provisions, the absence of a transitional policy in the Constitution for dealing with past human rights violations and the failure to prosecute on account of the principle of legality.

3.2.1 The Amnesty Provisions Under the 1992 Constitution

The amnesty laws that barred prosecution of past human rights violations in Ghana are contained in the transitional provisions provided under the first schedule to the country's Constitution. Section 34(1) of the transitional provisions stipulates that none of the followers of the Provisional National Defence Council or officers who were appointed by them can be made accountable either jointly or severally for any acts or inactions of the council.[9] Section 34(2) proscribes the judiciary from hearing any lawsuits (whether civil or criminal) against the Ghanaian government, any past or present governmental official or appointee or individuals who aided and abetted past military coups in Ghana. The judiciary is also barred by Section 34(2) from making any award or pronouncement with respect to any past military coup d'états in Ghana's history. Furthermore, Sections 34(3) and 34(4) forbid the courts from challenging or making 'orders' or awards in relation to acts of the Provisional National Defence Council and the Armed Forces Revolutionary Council as well as their followers and appointees. This includes actions that contravened the law at the time of their occurrence.[10] Under Section 34(5), the judiciary is further prohibited from hearing lawsuits in relation to the 'acts and omissions' of individuals in response to commands of the Armed Forces Revolutionary Council or the Provisional National Defence Council and their affiliates, whether or not their action was proscribed under law at the time of its occurrence.[11]

Section 35(1) of the transitional provision categorically states that the seizure of properties that occurred during the regime of the Provisional National Defence Council (31 December 1981 to 7 January 1993) and the Armed Forces Revolutionary Council (4 June 1979 to 24 September 1979) are irreversible.[12] However, seizures from individuals as a result of their governmental positions can

---

[9]For further information about the Provisional National Defence Council, see Sect. 2.8 in Chap. 2 of this book.

[10]See Republic of Ghana, Constitution of the Republic of Ghana, 1992 (1992 Constitution), First Schedule, ss 34(3), (4).

[11]Ibid., s 34(5).

[12]Ibid., s 35(1).

be reversed by Ghana's Commission on Human Rights and Administrative Justice, if it is able to prove that the individual was in possession of the asset in question prior to assuming office or that the asset was attained legally.[13]

These provisions grant a de jure, blanket amnesty to perpetrators of human rights violations under Ghana's past military regimes, thereby providing immunity from all kinds of legal actions in relation to the human rights violations they perpetrated. The amnesty provisions apply only to court proceedings and judgements (i.e., criminal and civil actions) and not to out-of-court investigations, including those by a commission of enquiry. On that basis, the government considered the establishment of a truth commission to be a feasible option for dealing with perpetrators of past human rights violations in Ghana's history.[14]

3.2.2 *Complexities with Amending the Amnesty Provisions*

The problems posed by the existence of the amnesty provisions under Ghana's Constitution are compounded further by the complexities of amending these provisions. Section 37 of the transitional provisions categorically proscribes Parliament from amending Sections 34, 35 and 37 of the transitional provisions, regardless of the amendment procedures laid down under Chapter 25 of the 1992 Constitution.[15] Nevertheless, assuming this provision could be circumvented, Parliament would have to contend with Chapter 25 of the 1992 Constitution, which lays down the procedure for amending the Constitution.[16]

Under Chapter 25 of the 1992 Constitution, any bill for amendment of the amnesty provisions shall be submitted to the Council of State by the Speaker of Parliament to seek its suggestions on the bill.[17] Upon receiving the bill, the Council of State is required to provide its recommendations within a period of not more than 30 days from the date that the bill was referred to it.[18] Moreover, the bill can be introduced in Parliament only six months after its publication in the national gazette.[19] Following an initial reading of the bill in Parliament, it must be subjected to a national referendum, which requires a voter turnout of not less than 40% of registered eligible voters. The bill can be passed by Parliament only if the referendum

[13]Ibid., s 35(2).

[14]See Ameh 2006a, pp. 99–100.

[15]See 1992 Constitution, above n 10, First Schedule, s 37.

[16]Since the transitional provisions in the Constitution are given effect by Article 299 of the 1992 Constitution, provisions on their amendment must be inferred from the amendment procedure for Article 299, which is found under Article 290 of the 1992 Constitution.

[17]Under the 1992 Constitution of Ghana, the Council of State is a group of Ghanaians with a high level of integrity, who are appointed to serve as an advisory body to the presidency. See 1992 Constitution, above n 10, Article 89.

[18]See 1992 Constitution, above n 10, Article 290(2).

[19]Ibid., Article 290(3).

yields an approval rate of not less than 75%.[20] Subsequent to these processes, the president can assent to the bill to give it the force of law.[21]

In reality, the procedure for amending the amnesty provisions in the Constitution, as outlined above, is only theoretically possible. The process entails an extremely long and cumbersome process, particularly in view of the 75% approval requirement for the referendum to be used to approve the amendment bill. Indeed, it has been asserted that it would take an unusually popular government to attain 75% approval of an amendment to the Constitution, which is highly unlikely.[22] Given these circumstances, there was almost no possibility of amending the Constitution to enable the country to deal with perpetrators of human rights violations, making a truth commission the most favourable alternative for Ghana.

3.2.3 *Absence of a Transitional Justice Policy for the Country*

The non-existence of a transitional justice policy regarding how to deal with past human rights violations is also a factor that influenced Ghana's decision to pursue a truth-telling exercise. Although the 1992 Constitution contains transitional provisions in its first schedule and has made ample provisions for protecting fundamental human rights, it does not contain provisions that address the question of dealing with human rights violations that occurred prior the 1992 Constitution's adoption.[23] Thus, unlike Liberia, where the establishment of the Liberian TRC was part of a well-laid transitional plan,[24] there is no plan in Ghana's transitional provisions and elsewhere about how to handle past human rights violations.

---

[20]Ibid., Articles 290(4) and (5).

[21]Ibid., Article 290(6). See also Ameh 2006a, p. 101.

[22]See Ameh 2006a, pp. 101–102.

[23]This is probably due to the hollow format, which Ghana's transitional process took, and the high level of control that was exerted by the former military government in the transitional process. According to, Attafuah 2004, pp. 126–127, instead of undertaking a thorough reconciliation exercise, the government of Rawlings resorted to piecemeal measures, such as apologizing to Ghanaians in public and returning some seized assets to their owners. As explained in Sect. 2.9 in Chap. 2 of this book, the country's transition to democracy did not initially bring about much transformation, as most of the members of the new government were also members of the former military government and continued to influence key policies in the country. On this subject, see also Gyimah-Boadi 1994, pp. 78–79; Kandeh 2004, p. 92; Lyons 1997, p. 70; Oduro 2005, pp. 340–341; and Whitfield 2009, pp. 622.

[24]The transitional plan for Liberia derives its roots from the Comprehensive Peace Agreement, which was signed in Accra, Ghana on 18 August 2003. The Comprehensive Peace Agreement provided for the establishment of a truth commission to bring about reconciliation in the country. See the Comprehensive Peace Agreement between the Government of Liberia and the Liberians United for Reconciliation and Democracy (LURD) and the Movement for Democracy in Liberia (MODEL) and Political Parties, Accra (Comprehensive Peace Agreement), 18 August 2003,

The Constitution addresses only human rights violations occurring after it came into existence. The body legally mandated to deal with human rights violations is the Commission on Human Rights and Administrative Justice.[25] This body is authorised to conduct enquiries into all allegations of human rights violations and corruption by public officials and governmental bodies. It also works towards providing redress for such violations and educating the public on their rights.[26] Although the commission has powers like those of a truth commission, it has no power to investigate human rights violations that occurred before the 1992 Constitution came into being.

Other provisions of the 1992 Constitution can be used to buttress the establishment of a truth commission. For instance, Article 12(1) of the 1992 Constitution entreats the three arms of government (the executive, the judiciary and the legislative) to defend human rights and fundamental freedoms of persons, as expressly provided under Chapter 3 of the Constitution.[27] The establishment of a truth commission was, therefore, a move towards fulfilling this constitutional principle, in the absence of an alternative.

3.2.4 The Principle of Legality (Nullum Crimen, Nulla Poena Sine Lege)

The principle of legality is another barrier that hinders prosecutions in the Ghanaian context. The amnesty provisions in the 1992 Constitution apply to only past military regimes. This would presuppose that human rights violations that occurred under former *constitutional* regimes can be prosecuted by the judiciary. However, this would contravene the principle of legality.

The principle of *nullum crimen sine lege* requires that a criminal offence must be expressly spelt out in the meaning of the offence in question and that punishment should not be meted out retrospectively. The principle of *nulla poena sine lege* requires sanctions to be based on a pre-existing law.[28] These principles are expressly endorsed under the 1992 Constitution. Article 19(5) of the 1992 Constitution provides that no individual can be accused of or held liable for 'an act or omission' that did not amount to a crime at the time it occurred.[29] Article 19(6)

Article XIII; and Government of Liberia, An Act to Establish the Truth and Reconciliation Commission (TRC) of Liberia (TRC Act of Liberia), 10 June 2005.

[25]See 1992 Constitution, above n 10, Articles 216 and 217.

[26]See 1992 Constitution, above n 10, Article 218; and Republic of Ghana, Commission on Human Rights and Administrative Justice Act (CHRAJ Act), 1993, Act 456, s7.

[27]Chapter 3 of the 1992 Constitution, under which Article 12(1) falls, contains extensive provisions on protection and upholding of fundamental human rights and freedoms.

[28]See Werle and Jessberger 2014, pp. 39–40.

[29]See 1992 Constitution, above n 10, Article 19(5).

also provides that a person shall not be given a punishment which is ‘severer in degree or description’ than what was prescribed for the act or omission at the time of its occurrence.[30] Furthermore, Article 19(11) categorically proscribes convictions that are not defined or whose punishment is not expressly provided under a law.[31]

Based on these provisions, prosecuting human rights violations committed during past constitutional regimes would have contravened the 1992 Constitution, given the fact that many of the human rights violations perpetrated under constitutional regimes were done under the force of law. In other words, most of these violations could be considered ‘legal’ at the time they occurred. For example, the detention of over 1,000 Ghanaians without trial during Ghana’s first republican era would amount to unlawful detention. Yet these actions occurred under a validly enacted law known as the Preventive Detention Act of 1958.[32]

In some jurisdictions, the barriers posed by the principle of legality in the prosecution of human rights violations would have been resolved through different approaches to interpretation, such as the Radbruch formula.[33] According to the Radbruch formula, even when it is unjust and of no benefit, the positive law must prevail when there is inconsistency between positive law and justice. However, if the conflict between positive law and justice reaches an intolerable level, justice must take supremacy over the positive law, which is a ‘false law’.[34] In Germany, the Radbruch formula has been used in a number of cases to prosecute crimes committed in East Germany and during the Nazi regime.[35] Another approach that has been used in Germany to prosecute human rights violations committed under a validly enacted law is to interpret the law in a manner that is human rights-friendly.[36]

In the Ghanaian context, however, neither the Radbruch formula nor the human rights-friendly approach to interpretation has been adopted so far in any court decision. The Supreme Court of Ghana uses the modern purposive approach to interpretation, which allows the court to look at the intention of the framers of the law, in addition to the literal interpretation. This approach was succinctly stated in the case of *Tuffour v Attorney General*:

---

[30]Ibid., Article 19(6).

[31]Ibid., Article 19(11).

[32]On the Preventive Detention Act, see Sect. 2.3 in Chap. 2 of this book.

[33]The Radbruch Formula was propounded by the German legal theorist, Gustav Radbruch. For further discussion of the Radbruch Formula, see Bix 2011, pp. 45–51; and Werle and Vormbaum 2012, pp. 67–70.

[34]Radbruch 1946, pp. 105–108, as cited in Werle and Vormbaum 2012, pp. 316–317.

[35]See, for instance, Berlin State Court, Trial of Border Guards, 20 January 1992, Docket No. (523) 2 Js 48/90 (9/91). For a discussion of how the Radbruch formula was used in the Trial of Border Guards, see Werle and Vormbaum 2012, pp. 316–317.

[36]See Werle and Vormbaum 2012, pp. 315–316, where they discuss the use of this approach in the Trial of Border Guards in Germany.

> A written Constitution such as ours is not an ordinary Act of Parliament. It embodies the will of a people. It also mirrors their history.... Its language, therefore, must be considered as if it were a living organism capable of growth and development. Indeed, it is a living organism capable of growth and development, as the body politic of Ghana itself is capable of growth and development.... And so a construction should be avoided which leads to absurdity. And when a particular interpretation leads to two, shall we say 'inconsistent' results, the spirit of the Constitution would demand that the more reasonable of the two should be adhered to. We must have recourse to the Constitution as a whole.[37]

In light of the purposive approach to interpretation, it is possible that the barriers to prosecution posed by the principle of legality in the 1992 Constitution could, in the future, be overridden if it can be shown that doing otherwise would be inconsistent with the intention of the framers of the Constitution. However, no such decision has yet been given, and it remains to be seen whether such an approach could be used to permit prosecution of human rights violations perpetrated under validly enacted laws. At the moment, however, this is still not an option.

3.2.5 *Other Factors*

Other factors relating to the legal requirements for prosecution would have made prosecution difficult. To begin with, it would be difficult to meet the standard of proof for criminal cases in Ghana (proof beyond all reasonable doubt) because of the long lapse of time between the commission of most human rights violations and Ghana's transition to democracy. Especially for cases that occurred as far back as the 1950s, it would have been difficult to obtain evidence for prosecution. Moreover, some victims and perpetrators might not have been alive to provide testimonies in such cases. Coupled with this is the fact that prosecuting such cases would take a long time in view of the large number of victims involved.[38] Furthermore, it has been asserted that Ghanaians are generally not assertive of their rights.[39] Perhaps, this is due to the general lack of knowledge about their human rights. Thus, even prior to the enactment of the amnesty provisions, there was no evidence that many Ghanaians attempted to seek remedies for the human rights violations they suffered. There is, therefore, a high probability that they would not utilise the avenue of the courts, even if prosecution was a possible option.[40]

In summary, the NRC was a very practical solution to the realities of the time. Although this approach fulfilled the right to truth, it is questionable whether the use of a truth commission as a substitute, rather than a complement, for prosecutions was an appropriate transitional choice. This issue is revisited later in this study.[41]

---

[37]Court of Appeal, Sitting as the Supreme Court of Ghana, *Tuffour v Attorney General*, 23 September 1980, 1980 Ghana Law Reports, pp. 647–648. See also Supreme Court of Ghana, *Asare v Attorney-General*, 2003–2004 Supreme Court of Ghana Law Reports, p. 823.

[38]See Ameh 2006a, pp. 103–104.

[39]Ibid., p. 102.

[40]Ibid.

[41]See Sect. 6.2 in Chap. 6 of this book.

3.3 The Features of the National Reconciliation Commission

The features of a truth commission can usually be ascertained from the legal document under which it is created. The legal document may be a presidential decree, a peace accord, a parliamentary act or a royal decree. In Morocco, for instance, the truth commission was established through a royal decree, whilst those of Argentina, Chile and Ecuador were created by presidential decrees. In Sierra Leone, Guatemala, Liberia and El Salvador, truth commissions were established through peace accords, whilst the truth commission in East Timor was established via a regulation of the United Nations. Generally, none of these options is preferable, as one mode of establishment may be more favourable in one context than another.[42]

In Ghana, the legal document that brought the NRC into existence was an act of Parliament: the National Reconciliation Commission Act, 2002. However, the basis for its establishment and the passage of the act of Parliament was derived from the 1992 Constitution. Therefore, the framework for the establishment of the NRC can, in fact, be placed under two legal documents, the 1992 Constitution and the NRC Act.

Although various provisions in the 1992 Constitution could be interpreted to support the establishment of a truth commission,[43] the provision that expressly deals with the matter is Article 278 of the 1992 Constitution. This article grants the president of Ghana the power to establish a 'commission of enquiry' to conduct investigations in relation to 'matters of public interest' in three instances: the president personally believes that such a commission should be established; the president is counselled by the Council of State that 'it is in the public interest to do so'; or Parliament, through a resolution, asks for the establishment of such a commission for the investigation of an issue of 'public importance'.[44] In effect, the 1992 Constitution contains the broader framework for establishment of the NRC

[42]For instance, it has been asserted that even though truth commissions are easy to establish by an executive act, there is a tendency for the executive decree to leave out the details on the commission's scope and features. However, legislative involvement in the establishment of a truth commission creates room for providing all details related to the work of the truth commission. See Hayner 2011, pp. 210–211. See also Freeman 2006, p. 27.

[43]A good case for the establishment of a body to investigate past human rights violations can also be made under the Directive Principles of State Policy (i.e., Chapter 6 of the 1992 Constitution) which are supposed to be the guiding principles underlying the interpretation of the Constitution. Under Article 35(4) of the 1992 Constitution, the state is required to inculcate in all Ghanaian nationals, the habit of cherishing 'fundamental human rights and freedoms and the dignity of the human person'. See 1992 Constitution, above n 10, Article 35(4).

[44]See 1992 Constitution, above n 10, Article 278(1).

(under Articles 278 to 283), whilst the NRC Act sets out all other details relating to the commission.[45]

The NRC's mode of establishment (i.e., by parliamentary act) is comparable to that of the Comissão Nacional da Verdade of Brazil, which was established through Law No. 12.528 of 18 November 2011.[46] A distinguishing feature of the mode of establishment of the Comissão Nacional da Verdade, however, was that aside from Law No. 12.528, there were by-laws that provided further details on the features of the Comissão Nacional da Verdade.[47]

From a general outlook, the NRC's mode of establishment was appropriate within the Ghanaian context, as it provided all the needed details relating to every aspect of the NRC's work.[48] Indeed, the need for detailed legal provisions regarding the features of a truth commission is evinced by the fact that some truth commissions that are initially established through peace accords and executive decrees are eventually elaborated through parliamentary acts that spell out all the

---

[45]The said Act is divided into four parts and is made up of 27 sections. Part 1 deals with the establishment and functions of the NRC, Part 2 covers investigative and procedural matters, Part 3 deals with completion of the NRC's report, offences and penalties under the Act and the accountability of the NRC and its members of staff. Finally, Part 4 of the Act covers administration, finance and other miscellaneous matters.

[46]In comparison with existing standards in Latin America, the mode of establishing the Comissão Nacional da Verdade was unique, as the usual practice in the region was to establish such bodies through executive decrees. In this regard, the Comissão Nacional da Verdade, by virtue of its mode of establishment was to have more powers, as is usually the case with bodies established through a Parliamentary law within the region. See Report of the Comissão Nacional Da Verdade, above n 7, para 46. See also Law No. 12.528, above n 7, Article 11; and Commissão Nacional da Verdade 'The Comissão Nacional da Verdade'. http://www.cnv.gov.br/institucional-acesso-informacao/a-cnv.html. Accessed 19 October 2019.

[47]These by-laws were passed under a Decree that empowered the Comissão Nacional da Verdade to create by-laws to provide further detailed regulations of its actions. See Presidência da República Brasil, Decreto Nº 7.919, De 14 De Fevereiro De 2013 (Decree No. 7.919 of 14 February 2013) (Decree No. 7.919), Article 4. One such by-law which outlines more details about the Comissão Nacional da Verdade's features is Resolution No. 8 of 4 March 2013. See Comissão Nacional Da Verdade 2013. http://www.cnv.gov.br/institucional-acesso-informacao/a-cnv/59-regimento-interno-da-comissao-nacional-da-verdade.html. Accessed 19 October 2019. Aside the Comissão Nacional da Verdade of Brazil, other examples of truth commissions that have been established through a parliamentary act include: the South African TRC, which was established under the Promotion of National Unity and Reconciliation Act No. 34 of 1995, assented to 19 July 1995 (entered into force 1 December 1995) (South African TRC Act); South Korea's Presidential Truth Commission on Suspicious Deaths, established under the Special Act to Find the Truth on Suspicious Deaths, 15 January 2000; the 2005 South Korean Truth and Reconciliation Commission which was established by the Framework Act on Clearing up Past Incidents for Truth and Reconciliation, Enacted by Law No. 7542, 31 May 2005; the Truth and Justice Commission of Mauritius, established under the Truth and Justice Commission Act No. 28, 1 February 2009; and the Truth and Justice Commission of Paraguay, established under Ley Nº 2225 (Law No. 2225), 15 October 2003. See United States Institute of Peace. http://www.usip.org/category/publications/truth-commission. Accessed 27 October 2019.

[48]During the tenure of the NRC, Attafuah 2004, p. 125, described the NRC Act as 'simple', with no prospects of generating complicated 'legal issues'.

particulars of their operations. In Liberia, for instance, the legal document that brought the Liberian TRC into being was the Accra Peace Agreement, which put in place a transitional programme for Liberia after a 14-year civil war.[49] Subsequently, the Truth and Reconciliation Commission Act of 2005 was passed to provide further details about the commission.[50] This was also the case in Sierra Leone, where the peace accord between the Sierra Leone government and the rebel Revolutionary United Front provided for the establishment of a truth commission. Subsequently, the Truth and Reconciliation Commission Act of 2000 was passed to provide further details about the mandate, features and scope of the Sierra Leone Truth Commission.[51]

In the absence of detailed provisions about the features and scope of a truth commission, several legal questions may eventually arise about the extent of the truth commission's powers. Nigeria's Oputa Panel, established through Statutory Instrument No. 8 of 1999 by the president under his powers under the Tribunals of Inquiry Act of 1990, offers a vivid example.[52] With the exception of the commission's mandate, which was clearly spelt out in Statutory Instrument 8 of 1999, other specific details relating to the truth commission's powers and limitations were to be inferred from the Tribunals of Inquiry Act.[53] In this instance, the legal framework for the Oputa Panel was considered fragile as there was no thorough parliamentary enactment focused on the truth commission. This was particularly evident as regards the tenets of its jurisdiction within the federal state of Nigeria, whose individual states also wield the power to establish similar bodies.[54] Based on this example, it can be established that the manner in which the NRC was created carved out a firm foundation for its future operations. The NRC Act, under which the NRC was established, contained provisions for the NRC's time frame for

---

[49]See the Comprehensive Peace Agreement, above n 24, Article XIII.

[50]About the mode of establishing the Liberian TRC, see Long 2008, p. 1; Wiebelhaus-Brahm 2013, p. 282; and TRC Act of Liberia, above n 24, Article III.

[51]For details of the Sierra Leonean TRC, see the United States Institute of Peace. http://www.usip.org/publications/truth-commission-sierra-leone. Accessed 26 October 2019.

[52]According to Freeman 2006, p. 27, this mode of establishment could be considered a 'hybrid', as the truth commission derived its source from both the executive and the legislature. The said Statutory Instrument No. 8, 1999 was subsequently amended by Statutory Instrument No. 13, 4 October 1999, to make changes in the membership and mandate of the commission. See Human Rights Violations Investigation Commission 2002, vol 1, paras 2.36, 2.37.

[53]Yusuf 2013, p. 337.

[54]As a result of the weak legal foundation of the commission, the tenets of the Oputa panel's powers were challenged in a number of lawsuits, which adversely affected its work. See, for instance, Supreme Court of Nigeria, *Chief Gani Fawehinmi et al. v General Ibrahim Babangida (Retired) et al.* (Case Chief Gani Fawehinmi), 31 January 2003, SC.360/2001, where it was held that Section 19 of the Tribunals of Inquiry Act, 1990, under which the President derived his powers to establish the Oputa Panel provided that some of the powers of tribunals as outlined within the Act could be excluded by the authority that establishes the tribunal. Thus, although the Tribunals of Inquiry Act, 1990 contained some details about how a tribunal should function, not all the powers could actually be exercised by the Oputa Panel. See also Yusuf 2007, pp. 272–273, 277–279, 284–285, for a discussion of the case.

operation, membership, independence, confidentiality of information related to its work, objects and mandate, powers, funds, the commission's reporting requirements and the offences and penalties related to the commission's work.

3.3.1 Time Frame for Operation

The operational time frame is a relevant feature of truth commissions that can make or unmake their work. Whereas a long working time for a truth commission can affect the level of attention it receives from the public, particularly if its report is published late, a short time frame may also affect the work quality of a truth commission.[55] An example of this is the case of Guatemala, where the truth commission was required to complete its work within six months, with a possibility of renewal for a further six months. The initial first six months was supposed to begin the day that the Oslo Agreement (which created the truth commission) was adopted. This time frame eventually became problematic for the truth commission, which was not able to commence its activities on the day the agreement was concluded. Moreover, the small number of commissioners compounded the problem, preventing the commission from meeting its deadline. In the end, it took two years for the truth commission to complete its work.[56]

In the case of Ghana, the NRC was to work for one year commencing the day it heard its first complaint.[57] This period was, however, extendable for up to six months, by the president, if the commission gave it compelling reasons to do so.[58] In practice, it is not unusual to make a truth commission's operational time frame extendable. A look at other truth commissions reveals the common nature of this practice. The Oputa Panel of Nigeria was mandated to complete its work within a year of commencing proceedings, although this time frame was extendable.[59] Likewise, in the case of the Liberian TRC, it was given a time frame of two years to complete its work and an additional three months to conclude all its operations and deliver a report.[60] This statutory time frame was nevertheless extendable for 'three months at a time' if the commission provided a good basis for such an extension.[61] In Brazil, the Comissão Nacional da Verdade was empowered under Law

[55]See Hayner 2011, p. 216.

[56]For details about this, see Tomuschat 2001, pp. 240–241.

[57]The activities of the NRC were to commence not later than 14 days from the nomination of its commissioners. See Republic of Ghana, National Reconciliation Commission Act, 2002, Act 611 (NRC Act), s 5(1).

[58]See the NRC Act, above n 57, s 5(1).

[59]See Human Rights Violations Investigation Commission 2002, vol 1, para 2.36, 2.37.

[60]See TRC Act of Liberia, above n 24, s 5.

[61]Ibid., s 6.

No. 12.528 of 18 November 2011 to operate for two years.[62] Although there was no express provision in the law that made this time extendable, the two-year period that was originally supposed to end in May 2014 was eventually extended to end on 16 December 2014 under Law 12,998 of 2014.[63]

Comparing the NRC's operational time frame with that of other states, the NRC's time frame seemed realistic and feasible. Moreover, the extendibility of its time frame was a positive feature for the outcome of its work, as a lack of flexibility with regard to a truth commission's time frame can have negative consequences, especially in cases where the truth commission cannot finish its work within the stipulated time.

3.3.2 *Membership and Staffing*

The most definitive aspect of a truth commission is its membership. In the end, the members are the main projectors of the commission's image and can heavily impact its credibility. Particularly, the leadership of the commission (i.e., the chairperson), is instrumental in creating a good reputation for the body.[64] In view of that, the mode of selecting members of a truth commission and the calibre of persons that partake in its work are critical factors to consider. Preferably, the competence of a truth commission can be assured by including international human rights law experts in the membership, whilst independence can be ensured by making membership of the commission irremovable, except in cases of gross misconduct or incompetence.[65] Membership of commissions must make room for equal and fair representation of all segments of the community, especially women.[66] In order to achieve this, adoption of the mandate and appointment of the commission's membership must be the result of 'broad consultation' of the general populace, especially from victims and survivors.[67] Also, the members of a truth commission should be well respected in the community and not popularly affiliated to a particular faction in the society. Moreover, they should be selected through a consultative process.[68]

These parameters were, however, not all fulfilled in the case of the NRC. For instance, the requirement for broad consultation in member selection was not met. Prior to the passage of the NRC bill into law, the issue of how NRC members should be appointed became a subject of huge debate in Ghana. In particular, the

---

[62]See Law No. 12.528, above n 7, Articles 1, 11; and Report of the Comissão Nacional Da Verdade, above n 7, para 55.

[63]See Report of the Comissão Nacional Da Verdade, above n 7, para 55.

[64]See Freeman 2006, p. 30; and 2010, p. 211.

[65]See United Nations Commission on Human Rights 2005, para 7.

[66]Ibid., paras 6 and 7.

[67]Ibid., para 6.

[68]See Office of the United Nations High Commissioner for Human Rights 2006, p. 13.

Ghana Civil Society Coalition suggested that the process should be as participatory and objective as possible.[69] Aside from civil society groups, the minority in Parliament voiced their opinion that Parliament should take part in the nomination process by subjecting the nominees to the same screening process required by ministers of state.[70]

In spite of these modest views from civil society bodies and the minority in Parliament, the ruling parliamentary majority argued that based on Article 70(1) of the 1992 Constitution, the president is required to nominate all important office holders in consultation with the Council of State (such as the members of the Commission on Human Rights and Administrative Justice and the Public Services Commission). They, therefore, argued that similarly, nomination of members of the NRC must be done by the president in consultation with members of the Council of State.[71] In the end, the majority's argument carried the day, and the president was granted the power of appointing the commissioners of the NRC, thereby excluding the public from the nomination process.[72] However, the president was mandated under the NRC Act to seek advice from the Council of State, in the appointment process.[73]

In reality, Ghana is not the only country in which the suggestions of civil society regarding appointment of truth commission members has been rejected. In Guatemala, for instance, civil society suggestions regarding the power of the Clarification Commission to name perpetrators as well as its time frame for operation were disregarded. Thus, the commission was established on terms that were very different from those proposed by the civil society bodies.[74]

Although rejection of civil society suggestions is not laudable, in some cases, over-involvement of different actors, such as victims and civil society, in the appointment process, can give rise to inconsistencies and misunderstandings. In

---

[69]According to Nesiah 2001, p. 2, transparency and objectivity in the process is relevant because it will involve all sections of the society in the process and ensure that different classes in the country are properly represented in the commission. She also holds the opinion that the manner of appointing members of the commission can have immense effect on the legitimacy of the commission and the eventual outcome of its work, as it can determine the level of transparency, and the general feeling of participation in the commission's work by the general public. See also Valji 2006, p. 7.

[70]See Ameh 2006b, p. 354; and Boafo-Arthur 2005, pp. 122–123; and Boafo-Arthur 2006, p. 143.

[71]In particular, they relied on Article 70(1e) of the 1992 Constitution of Ghana, which provides that the President should nominate the 'holders of such other offices as may be prescribed by the Constitution or by any other law not inconsistent with the Constitution'. For a discussion of these parliamentary debates, see Boafo-Arthur 2006, pp. 143–144.

[72]This aspect of the NRC Act did not go down well with a section of Ghanaians, particularly the minority in Parliament. See Valji 2006, p. 7; and the NRC Act, above n 57, s 2(2).

[73]The Council of State in Ghana is a constitutional body appointed by the President of Ghana, pursuant to Article 89 of the 1992 Constitution to provide advice to the President in his official duties. See 1992 Constitution, above n 10, Chapter 9. About the appointment process, see also NRC Act, above n 57, s 2(2).

[74]See Hayner 2011, p. 32.

Paraguay, the requirement for members of the Truth and Justice Commission to be appointed by different sectors of the country (i.e., the executive, legislature, civil society and victim groups) resulted in disagreements amongst these groups, which delayed the commencement of the commission's work.[75] There is, therefore, the need for balance regarding the extent of civil society involvement, although it generally has a positive effect of enabling broad consultation in the work of a truth commission.

Other instances show that even when the mode of appointment is devoid of disagreement, the appointment of truth commission members usually gives rise to controversy in several cases. In Nigeria, for instance, a section of Nigerians considered the composition of the Oputa Panel not to be fully representative of the country's population and societies, as there was no Muslim to represent the interests of Muslims, who constitute more than half of the country's population.[76] Similarly in Liberia, the initial selection of members of the Liberian TRC by the president gave rise to intense criticism due to the fact that, at the time of the selection, the law used to establish the Liberian TRC had not yet been adopted. Owing to these developments, the Truth and Reconciliation Commission Act required the establishment of a selection panel of seven individuals, including representatives from the United Nations, the Economic Community of West African States, civil society groups and political bodies in Liberia to take part in vetting the commissioners. However, the president still retained the power to formally appoint the commissioners.[77] In Peru, the composition of the Comisión de la Verdad y Reconciliación was a subject of high criticism, with allegations that there was unequal representation of different political groups and the army in the commission.[78]

Another matter of grave importance regarding membership of the NRC is the number of commissioners. The NRC was made up of nine commissioners, all Ghanaian, including one chairperson, who was authorised to supervise its proceedings.[79] Considering the geographical and population size of Ghana and in view of the fact that the extent of human rights violations in Ghana was not as high as

[75]For details of the truth commission in Paraguay, see Hayner 2011, p. 63.

[76]See Yusuf 2007, p. 281.

[77]Following the massive criticisms of this process, it was decided that the already selected people should be vetted, hence the existence of a requirement for a vetting committee in the Truth and Reconciliation Commission Act. In the end, only two of the final members of the commission were part of the initially selected group. See James-Allen et al. 2010, pp. 5–6; and Ojielo 2010, p. 8. https://sabarometerblog.files.wordpress.com/2010/05/ijr-ap-op-1-general-liberia.pdf. Accessed 4 September 2019.

[78]Although some changes were later made in the membership to add some members from the armed forces, none of other players in the conflict were added as members. See Malca 2015, p. 106.

[79]Members of the NRC were supposed to be people with a high level of honesty and 'a sense of fairness' and the requisite capabilities needed to achieve the aims of the NRC. In situations where the chairman was not present, the commissioners could elect one person to act in place of the chairman. See the NRC Act, above n 57, ss 2(3) and 6(2).

that of its neighbours within the West African subregion, the number of commissioners was adequate. A larger number of commissioners would have been required in a country with a very large population and large numbers of violations, such as Nigeria, where the number of commissioners of the Oputa Panel (i.e., seven) was considered low in view of the large population and the diversity of cultures in the country.[80] This is because the population size and the magnitude of human rights violations invariably correlates with the workload of a truth commission. Hence, it is practicable that these factors be considered when deciding the number of commissioners for a truth commission.

Also, by virtue of all its members being citizens of Ghana, the NRC was obviously a national truth commission in the true sense of the word, a feature that is shared by several other truth commissions.[81] This feature may either serve as an advantage or disadvantage, depending on the peculiar circumstances of each country.[82] In the same vein, truth commissions with international input also have benefits or disadvantages of their own.[83] There are also instances in which a truth commission composed of only nationals of the country will have features that bring about the involvement of some international players. The Liberian TRC was

---

[80]See Yusuf 2007, p. 281. In South Africa for instance, the South African TRC's membership of 17 was very large, in comparison with many truth commissions (for example, Paraguay: nine, Haiti: seven, East Timor: seven, Liberia: nine, Bolivia: eight and Brazil: seven). Nevertheless, a critical look at the peculiarities of South Africa highly resonates with the high number of commissioners. The country has a high population rate. Besides, the commission had to deal with a large number of human rights violations, thereby justifying the need for a bigger commission. On the membership of the South African TRC, see South African TRC Act, above n 47, s 7(1).

[81]See Buergenthal 2006, pp. 105–106, where he classifies truth commissions as national, mixed and international. In Nigeria for instance, all members of the Oputa Panel were Nigerians, appointed by the President through Statutory Instrument No. 8, 1999. The chairman of the Oputa Panel was a retired justice of the Nigerian Supreme Court. Subsequently, four of the commissioners were changed after Statutory Instrument 8 of 1999 was amended by Statutory Instrument No. 13, 4 October 1999. Similarly, in Brazil, the seven members of the Comissão Nacional da Verdade were all Brazillian nationals who were appointed by the President. The Comissão Nacional da Verdade was headed by a chairman who was appointed by the other members for a renewable term of three months. The Comissão Nacional da Verdade was also assisted in its work by an executive secretary, project managers, technical advisors and assistants, coordinators and some assistants. The executive secretariat was responsible for organizing, supervising and coordinating the activities of the other sub bodies within the Comissão Nacional da Verdade. Other truth commissions which were composed of only nationals of the country involved are those of Argentina, Brazil, Chile, South Africa and Morocco. See Law No. 12.528, above n 7, Article 2; Comissão Nacional da Verdade's 2013, Articles 2, 6. http://www.cnv.gov.br/institucional-acesso-informacao/a-cnv/59-regimento-interno-da-comissao-nacional-da-verdade.html. Accessed 19 October 2019; Hayner 2011, p. 249; and Human Rights Violations Investigation Commission 2002, vol 1 paras 2.34, 2.38 and 2.39.

[82]See Buergenthal 2006, p. 107.

[83]For instance, in countries where prolonged conflict has eroded all forms of trust amongst citizens, and everyone has taken sides in the conflict (such as El Salvador), it may be necessary to bring on board some neutral foreigners in the truth telling process. In the case of El Salvador, all the working staff of the commission were foreigners, as a result of the need to keep the commission objective. See Tomuschat 2001, pp. 237–238.

composed of nine members, all citizens of Liberia.[84] Nevertheless, it had the advantage of working alongside an International Technical Advisory Committee, constituted of three individuals.[85] The functions of the International Technical Advisory Committee were mainly to provide recommendations and make suggestions. However, its members were given the same rights and privileges as the commissioners of the Liberian TRC, including attendance of all meetings and full disclosure rights.[86]

Within the context of Ghana, however, there was no need for involvement of foreigners in the NRC. The country had not experienced a protracted period of conflict to derail domestic capacities regarding an objective transitional exercise. Moreover, although Ghana had experienced prolonged political instability, the country had already transitioned to constitutional rule (albeit feeble) at the time of the NRC's establishment and therefore had in place the appropriate means for undertaking a truth-telling exercise on its own. This is, however, not to say that more international involvement in the process would not have been beneficial, especially in relation to enhancing the credibility of the process.[87]

Regarding the need for equal and fair representation in truth commission membership, the membership of the commission made room for equal religious representation and had representation from different professional backgrounds. However, there was unequal gender representation, with only three women amongst the nine members.[88] This gap is also found with the Oputa Panel of Nigeria, where

[84]The Chairperson and vice-Chairperson were supposed to be appointed by the members of the commission. It also had a National Secretariat that was tasked with the duty of providing 'technical, professional, administrative and clerical assistance' to the commission. The head of the National Secretariat (i.e., the Executive Secretary) was responsible for all the commission's secretarial work. See the TRC Act of Liberia, above n 24, ss 7, 13, 33 and 34.

[85]TRC Act of Liberia, above n 24, s 10.

[86]Ibid., s 10. The exception to their privileges was that they did not have the right to vote at meetings of the commission.

[87]Regarding the challenges that the NRC faced with its credibility, see Sects. 4.3.3 and 4.3.4 in Chap. 4 of this book.

[88]The members of the commission and their respective professions were as follows: Mr. Justice Kweku Etrew Amua-Sekyi, a retired Supreme Court Judge (Chairman); Most Reverend Charles Gabriel Palmer-Buckle, Catholic Bishop; Maulvi Abdul Wahab Bin Adam, Ameer, Head and Missionary-in-Charge, Ahmadiyya Muslim Mission of Ghana; Professor Florence Abena Dolphyne, former Pro-Vice-Chancellor of the University of Ghana; Lieutenant General Emmanuel Alexander Erskine, First Force Commander of the United Nations Interim Force in Lebanon; Dr. Sylvia Awo Mansah Boye, former Registrar of the West African Examinations Council; Mr. Christian Appiah Agyei, former Secretary-General, Trades Union Congress of Ghana; Uborr Dalafu Labal II, Paramount Chief of Sanguli Traditional Area of then Northern Region; and Professor Henrietta Joy Abena Nyarko Mensa-Bonsu, Associate Professor, Faculty of Law, University of Ghana. Regardless of the diverse professional representation in the commission, some views consider the professional representation in the commission to have been unbalanced. For instance, Ansah-Koi K, Department of Political Science, University of Ghana, Personal Interview (18 August 2016), has observed that although the commission was dealing with social issues, it had no social scientist in its membership. Rather, more lawyers were appointed. In relation to the controversial nature of the membership, see Gyimah-Boadi 2002, p. 3.

only two out of the seven members were female.[89] Brazil's Comissão Nacional da Verdade has also been criticised for lacking fair professional representation, given that most members were lawyers and did not include any historian.[90] In the case of the Liberian TRC, however, the need for fair and equal representation is partly provided for under the Liberian Truth and Reconciliation Commission Act, which expressly advocated for gender balance amongst the commission's membership by providing that not less than four of the commissioners were to be females.[91] Although this is not a requirement, the existence of such provisions enhance, rather than detract, from the work of truth commissions, which are by nature human rights bodies, and should in that regard, demonstrate protection of all social segments of communities, including minorities, in the course of their work. In the Ghanaian context, a provision on gender balance would have been particularly helpful to the NRC, especially for the purposes of encouraging women to appear before the commission and feel at ease about sharing their experiences on sensitive issues such as rape and sexual assault.[92]

3.3.3 Independence of the National Reconciliation Commission

The independence of a truth commission is a major feature that impacts directly on the level of confidence bestowed on its work by the public or the extent to which it is considered legitimate.[93] A truth commission must be able to work autonomously towards fulfilling its terms of reference and must not experience any form of meddling in its affairs by the government or any other body or individual.[94] In order to attain the requisite level of independence, truth commission members should be appointed through a credible and legitimate process.[95] Moreover, members should be legally insulated against arbitrary dismissals and any threats to their safety.[96] The

[89]See Nigerian Muse 2006. https://www.nigerianmuse.com/nigeriawatch/oputa/?u=commission_timeline.htm Accessed 23 November 2019.

[90]See Torelly 2018, p. 202.

[91]See TRC Act of Liberia, above n 24, s 7.

[92]Indeed, it is believed that the NRC, in practice did not receive as many reports about rape and public assault as was anticipated. This has been attributed to the social stigma that is attached to such experiences in the Ghanaian society. See Hayner 2011, p. 57. Similarly, in Nigeria, such provisions would have been useful to create equal representation amongst Christians and Muslims in the country. On this subject, see also Yusuf 2007, p. 281.

[93]The Office of the United Nations High Commissioner for Human Rights 2006, p. 6.

[94]See González and Varney 2013, p. 16. https://www.ictj.org/sites/default/files/ICTJ-Book-Truth-Seeking-2013-English.pdf. Accessed 2 November 2019.

[95]See United Nations Commission on Human Rights 2005, para 7(a).

[96]Ibid., para 7(a).

truth commission must also have full control over all monetary, supervisory and operational aspects of its work.[97]

These paradigms were partially present in the NRC. There were no restrictions on the venue and timing of the commission's proceedings.[98] Moreover, the commission could exercise decisions only with unanimity or a majority approval through voting.[99] Also, in instances where a commissioner was prone to be biased on account of a personal interest (whether pecuniary or not), the commissioner in question was obligated under the NRC Act to inform the commission of the supposed interest and refrain from participating in the case in question.[100] Aside from these provisions, the NRC Act specifically provides that the NRC was supposed to undertake its work autonomously, without the manipulation or regulation of any person or body. In this regard, the commissioners were tasked to conduct their duties 'impartially and independently and perform the duties of office in good faith and without fear, favour, bias or prejudice'.[101]

The inclusion in the enabling act of express provisions to protect the independence of truth commissions is not limited to the NRC. In Liberia, the independence of the commission and its members was guaranteed under the Truth and Reconciliation Commission Act, which expressly stated that the Liberian TRC was to enjoy the full benefit of the nation's resources in order to protect its independence.[102] Moreover, the commission and its individual commissioners and staff were supposed to operate independently, without any political influence or pecuniary interest on the part of any commissioner or staff member.[103]

The presence of such legal provisions does not, however, provide conclusive indication that the truth commission has absolute independence. The NRC's case offers a clear example. Despite the existence of the above-mentioned provisions, other provisions in the NRC Act show governmental control in its affairs. A key example is the fact that the president was the sole person in charge of appointing the members of the commission, although he could be advised by the Counsel of State. In addition, the NRC's managerial staff was required to be nominated by the president in 'consultation with the Attorney General and the Public Services

[97]See González and Varney 2013, p. 16. https://www.ictj.org/sites/default/files/ICTJ-Book-Truth-Seeking-2013-English.pdf. Accessed 2 November 2019.

[98]See NRC Act, above n 57, s 6(1).

[99]Ibid., s 6(3), 6(4). In this regard, the proceedings of the commission could only be held with a quorum of five (with the chairman included) and the chairman could exercise a 'casting vote' where there was a draw after voting. This was also the case with the Nigerian Oputa Panel, where the Chairman had the power to exercise 'a casting vote' in relation to all decisions of the commission. See Nigeria, Tribunals of Inquiry Act, Laws of the Federation of Nigeria, Chapter 447, 1990, s 4.

[100]Failure to comply with this provision could result in a dismissal of the person from the commission. See NRC Act, above n 57, s 6(5) and 6(6).

[101]Ibid., s 8.

[102]See TRC Act of Liberia, above n 24, s 21–22.

[103]Ibid., s 39.

Commission', although this power could be assigned to another person or body.[104] Also, public officers from other governmental institutions could be reassigned to the NRC, thereby creating the possibility of conflicting interests.[105]

Thus, unlike Brazil's Comissão Nacional da Verdade, which had powers to make its own resolutions to regulate all aspects of its administration, some aspects of the NRC's administrative powers were reserved for the president. The NRC can, therefore, not be said to have enjoyed the utmost level of independence required to enhance the credibility of a truth commission's work.[106]

3.3.4 Confidentiality of Information

Truth commissions need to obtain information from different sections of the public in the course of their work, thus confidentiality rules are critical for their work and must be expressly provided for.[107] Victims' privacy and confidentiality requests must, therefore, be respected.[108] This is particularly relevant because disclosure of information can sometimes be at the expense of peoples' security. In Ghana, this need was adequately provided for under the NRC Act. All NRC commissioners and staff had to abide by strict confidentiality rules in relation to their work. NRC members were, therefore, duty bound under the NRC Act not to divulge any information they obtained in the course of their work about the commission. The only exceptions were when such information was requested by the courts or under another law or was necessary for carrying out the work of the NRC.[109] NRC commissioners were also required to take the oaths of secrecy and the official oaths as provided under the second schedule of Ghana's 1992 Constitution, prior to commencing their work.[110] In the same vein, NRC appointees and staff who may have access to confidential information about the commission in the course of their work were also required to take oaths of confidentiality under the NRC Act.[111]

---

[104]See NRC Act, above n 57, s 23(1) and (3).

[105]Ibid., s 23(2).

[106]See Decree No. 7.919, above n 47, Article 4.

[107]According to Bisset 2012, p. 120, the existence of confidentiality rules could serve as an incentive to certain individuals who would otherwise not be willing to divulge information to provide testimony, thereby enabling the truth commission to have access to more information. The availability of such information could also be useful for courts, where prosecutions are also being conducted. See also Freeman 2006, pp. 182–186, on how truth commissions should treat confidential information during statement taking.

[108]See the United Nations Commission on Human Rights 2005, para 10.

[109]NRC Act, above n 57, s 19(1), 19(4), 19(8), 19(9).

[110]NRC Act, above n 57, s 27; and 1992 Constitution, above n 10, Second Schedule.

[111]NRC Act, above n 57, s 19(2), (3), (4), (8) and (9). Under these provisions, the rules of confidentiality are backed by penal consequences in case of any breach. Thus, the NRC Act provides that commissioners' exposure of information about the NRC's work, utilization of the

The NRC's rules on confidentiality are nearly identical to those of the Liberian TRC. Members, employees and proxies of the Liberian TRC were required to uphold the confidentiality of all information they acquire in the course of their work and were prohibited from using such information for their personal gain or any purposes except to further the objects and work of the commission.[112] Moreover, the members and workers of the commission were required to take oaths prior to assuming their duties.[113]

The confidentiality provisions of the NRC and the Liberian TRC evince a general broadness, which can be related to all aspects of the truth commissions' operations. This is, however, not the case with every truth commission. In Nigeria, although the Tribunals of Inquiry Act of 1990 contained some confidentiality rules, they were not as broad as those of the NRC. The commissioners of the Oputa Panel and the interpreters who worked for the commission were required to take oaths prior to their assumption of office, to carry out their obligations to the commission in a loyal and unbiased manner and not to disclose any confidential information relating to the proceedings, votes or the other issues related to the commission.[114] Nevertheless, there was no provision that barred the use of the commission's information by members and other employees for personal or private gain. Likewise, in Brazil, the confidentiality rules relating to the Comissão Nacional da Verdade were not as broad as those of the NRC and the Liberian TRC. The only related provision prohibits disclosure of the commission's information to third parties.[115] It is therefore difficult to ascertain whether the members of the Comissão Nacional da Verdade are bound to uphold any other strict principles of confidentiality.[116]

These instances amply illustrate that the NRC's confidentiality rules adequately covered all aspects of its work. Given the broad nature of the confidentiality rules, it can safely be stated that NRC Act provided enough protection to the NRC's members as well as victims and other informants to encourage individuals to freely divulge information to the commission.

---

commission's information to make personal gains by commissioners and conducts which brought the image of the commission into disrepute amount to a crime and offenders could face a penalty of either a fine or imprisonment upon conviction.

[112]See TRC Act of Liberia, above n 24, ss 25, 41(a), 41(b), 41(c).

[113]Ibid., ss 25, 41(b), 41(c).

[114]See Tribunals of Inquiry Act, above n 99, ss 3, 7.

[115]See Law No. 12.528, above n 7, Article 4(2).

[116]Ibid. See also Comissão Nacional da Verdade 2013. http://www.cnv.gov.br/institucional-acesso-informacao/a-cnv/59-regimento-interno-da-comissao-nacional-da-verdade.html. Accessed 19 October 2019.

3.3.5 Objects and Mandate of the National Reconciliation Commission

The objects and mandate of truth commissions form the crux of their work, as they define the very essence and aim of their existence. Usually, the objects and mandates of truth commissions vary depending on the context, and it is, therefore, not generally feasible to compare their mandates. Nevertheless, a look at each truth commission's mandate may sometimes reveal unique features.[117] It must be noted, however, that despite the variances in truth commission mandates, their primary components are to establish a true record of past human rights violations by ascertaining their causes and to seek the promotion of reconciliation.[118]

In Ghana, these core paradigms were captured in the mandate of the NRC. Under the NRC Act, the commission was supposed to pursue and enhance national reconciliation by providing a holistic account of human rights violations that were perpetrated by governmental institutions and members of the public service. Moreover, the NRC was empowered to make suggestions to the president in relation to providing appropriate remedy for the human rights violations that occurred in the respective periods it was mandated to investigate.[119] In order to carry out its mandate, the NRC had the following specific duties:

- Conduct an enquiry into the human rights violations that occurred within the stipulated period of its investigations. Specifically, the human rights violations

[117] An example is the Truth and Reconciliation Commission of Liberia, whose mandate, unlike that of most truth commissions, expressly called for the investigation of 'economic crimes, such as the exploitation of natural or public resources to perpetuate armed conflicts' and human rights violations perpetrated on 'women, children and vulnerable groups' as well as 'gender-based' violations. See TRC Act of Liberia, above n 24, s 4(a) and (e).

[118] This feature can be inferred from the mandate of every truth commission and various instances can be cited. In Nigeria for example, the Oputa Panel was mandated to find out the causes and degree of human rights violations between 15 January 1966 and 28 May 1999, identify the perpetrators and victims, ascertain whether the occurrence of the human rights violations was deliberate and suggest measures to redress the human rights violations. In Liberia, the mandate of the Liberian TRC, was 'to promote national peace, security, unity and reconciliation' through investigation of human rights violations that occurred from January 1979 to 14 October 2003, as well as ascertain the causes and perpetrators of these human rights violations, and also to compile a true and historical record of the country's past; and in Brazil, the Comissão Nacional da Verdade was mandated to clarify and provide details of the facts and circumstances surrounding the human rights violations that occurred in the country between the period of 1946 to 1988, identify the individuals and institutions that were responsible for such human rights violations, recommend measures and policies for redressing these violations and enhance national reconciliation. See Human Rights Violations Investigation Commission 2002, vol 1 paras 2.36, 2.40; TRC Act of Liberia, above n 24, s 4(a), (d) and (f); and Law No. 12.528, above n 7, Articles 1, 3.

See Duffy 2010. http://news.bbc.co.uk/2/hi/8451109.stm. Accessed 19 October 2019.

[119] These periods are: 24 February 1966 to 21 August 1969; 13 January 1972 to 23 September 1979; and 31 December 1981 to 6 January 1993. See NRC Act, above n 57, s 3(1).

that the NRC was mandated to investigate were 'killings, abductions, disappearances, detentions, torture, ill-treatment and seizure of properties'.[120]
- Enquire into the basis and reasons for the occurrence of these human rights violations and identify the perpetrators of these human rights violations.[121]
- Provide details of the victims of human rights violations and give the requisite suggestions for compensation.[122]
- Enquire into and ascertain whether the violations in question were intentionally commissioned by the perpetrators.[123]
- Undertake any other enquiry that is significant for the performance of its mandate and the enhancement and realisation of reconciliation in the country including consultation with the police and other bodies, where necessary in order to further its enquiries.[124]
- Provide education to the general populace about its work in order to inspire maximum public participation.[125]

The drafting process of a truth commission's mandate provides the basis for the truth commission's work and must therefore be done vigilantly.[126] Ideally, members of the public must be given the opportunity to be involved in the preparation stage for the truth-telling.[127] In Liberia, the drafting of the Truth and Reconciliation Commission Act was the result of much interaction and involvement amongst individual victims, civil society organisations and the United Nations.[128] Likewise in Ghana, the drafting of the NRC's mandate was perceived as a very interactive one, which involved maximum participation from all segments of the populace.[129] The civil society bodies in the country came together to form the Ghana Civil Society Coalition on National Reconciliation in 2001, led by the Ghana Centre for Democratic Development to help with the truth-telling exercise. The Ghana Civil Society Coalition adopted its own framework for the national reconciliation exercise by conducting a nationwide survey to obtain public views, reviewing the then National Reconciliation Commission Bill and providing suggestions. It also

[120]NRC Act, above n 57, s 4(a).

[121]Ibid., s 4(b).

[122]Ibid., s 4(c).

[123]Ibid., s 4(d).

[124]Ibid., s 4(e), 4(f).

[125]Ibid., s 4(g).

[126]See González 2013, p. 1. https://www.ictj.org/sites/default/files/ICTJ-Report-DraftingMandate-Truth-Commission-2013_0.pdf. Accessed 13 November 2019.

[127]See International Covenant on Civil and Political Rights, opened for signature 16 December 1966 (entered into force 23 March 1976) (Covenant on Civil and Political Rights), Article 25, where it is provided that citizens of a state have the right to be involved in public affairs' of the state; and United Nations Commission on Human Rights 2005, para 6.

[128]See Wiebelhaus-Brahm 2013, p. 283.

[129]See Boafo-Arthur 2005, p. 119.

educated other civil society bodies on the national reconciliation exercise, advised the NRC in some instances and provided some financial support to the NRC.[130]

The parliamentary committee in charge of the drafting process took several steps to ensure as much public involvement as possible. In doing so, the committee harnessed individual views as well as the opinions of political parties, non-governmental organisations and civil society groups. Moreover, it held seminars, conducted public outreaches and publicised the proposed NRC bill in the print media.[131]

Despite the high level of interaction in its drafting, the NRC's mandate gave rise to much controversy prior to enactment of the NRC Act.[132] Under Article 280(1a) of the 1992 Constitution, the NRC was supposed to conduct a complete, truthful and independent enquiry based on its mandate, by virtue of being a commission of enquiry established under the Constitution.[133] Whilst expanding this mandate under the proposed NRC bill, some Ghanaians believed that a wider mandate that enabled the commission to investigate all past human rights violations without regard to the political regime of its occurrence would satisfy the underpinnings of this constitutional provision. It would also create room for greater credibility and effectiveness of the truth-telling process, rather than a mandate that was selective regarding the political regimes it investigated.[134] Nevertheless, views of the parliamentary majority and minority greatly diverged on this issue. The bone of contention amongst the parliamentarians related to the historical time frame that the NRC should be mandated to investigate, although their collective support for establishing a truth commission was not in doubt. The expectations of the minority in Parliament for the impending truth commission were lowered when the proposed bill sought to limit the NRC's investigative mandate to military regimes in Ghana's history, excluding past constitutional regimes. Two factions thus emerged after the bill was introduced in Parliament.

The majority New Patriotic Party wanted to limit the work of the NRC to military regimes. They opined that the long lapse of time since Ghana's first constitutional regime made it very likely that most victims of the human rights violations were dead. They asserted that since reconciliation is for 'the living', there was no longer a need to investigate such abuses.[135] The parliamentary majority also argued that some other commissions of enquiry had been set up in the past to investigate the regimes of the first republican era. Thus, in their view, there was no need for a second investigation into the very matters that had been previously

[130] See Alidu and Ame 2012, pp. 106–107, 124–129; and National Reconciliation Commission 2004, vol 1, 'Acknowledgements', p. ii.

[131] See Boafo-Arthur 2005, p. 119, 2006, p. 138; Gyimah-Boadi 2002, p. 3; and Oduro 2013, p. 212.

[132] Boafo-Arthur 2006, p. 139.

[133] See 1992 Constitution, above n 10, Articles 278 and 280(1a).

[134] On this subject, see for instance, Nesiah 2001, p. 1.

[135] Boafo-Arthur 2005, p. 119, and 2006, p. 140.

investigated. They argued vehemently that the regimes that required urgent redress for human rights violations were the military regimes.[136]

The minority in Parliament, however, sought an investigation into all past political regimes after independence, whether military or constitutional.[137] They argued that although most victims may have died, there was still the need to initiate reconciliation for the benefit of their offspring. Moreover, they argued that several human rights violations had also occurred under civilian rule, which equally demanded redress.[138] Further, they opined that limiting the commission's work to only military regimes would diminish the credibility of the entire reconciliation exercise, as some periods would still be unexamined.[139]

The minority stance was premised on their inclination that the NRC could be used by the ruling party to attack former president Jerry John Rawlings, under whose leadership many human rights violations occurred.[140] Also, the minority felt that the exclusion of civilian regimes was an effort by the majority to avert investigation of human rights violations committed by their political predecessors during Ghana's First and Second Republics.[141] For example, excluding non-military governments from the investigative time frame of the NRC would have excluded all acts of violence committed during the government of Kwame Nkrumah and the harsh governmental policies of the Progress Party during the Second Republic.[142] The disagreement on the NRC's mandate intensified when the minority in Parliament attempted to disrupt the passage of the NRC Act by refusing to vote on the bill.[143]

---

[136]Ibid.

[137]According to Alidu and Ame 2012, pp. 17–18, these political disagreements are grounded in the fact that the manner of recounting the human rights violations in Ghana's history may vary based on the political affiliations of the person giving the narration. In this regard, members of the New Patriotic Party support the basis of the 1966 coup that overthrew the government of Kwame Nkrumah but disapprove of the military coups that were staged by Jerry John Rawlings in 1979 and 1981. Members of the National Democratic Congress however think the contrary.

[138]Examples of human rights violations under civilian rule were the numerous cases of unlawful detention that occurred under the leadership of Kwame Nkrumah. See Sect. 2.3 in Chap. 2 of this book.

[139]For a discussion of the different views of the majority and minority in Parliament, see Ameh 2006b, pp. 351–352; Boafo-Arthur 2005, pp. 119–121, 2006, pp. 139–141; and Seidu 2010, pp. 159–160.

[140]See Ameh 2006b, p. 351; Boafo-Arthur 2005, pp. 122, 2006, p. 142; and Gyimah-Boadi 2002, p. 3.

[141]This is because the then ruling New Patriotic Party traces its roots from the National Liberation Movement and the Progress Party. See Ameh 2006b, 351; Boafo-Arthur 2005, p. 121, and 2006, p. 142.

[142]See Ameh 2006b, p. 353.

[143]According to Valji 2006, p. 5, the high level of disagreement amongst the minority and majority on this subject reduced the high hopes and expectations that people had of the idea of establishing a truth commission, prior to the passage of the NRC Act. About the refusal of the minority to vote on the bill in Parliament, see Ameh 2006a, p. 86, b, p. 351; and Seidu 2010, p. 156.

The great degree of disagreement that accompanied the drafting of the NRC's mandate could be attributed to the continued presence of members of the former military regime in Ghanaian politics, which granted them a stake in the discussions leading to the drafting of the NRC's mandate. This state of affairs could be likened to that of Brazil, where certain prominent members of the Brazilian military considered the establishment of the Comissão Nacional da Verdade as an attempt to subvert the country's amnesty law and thus threatened to vacate their positions in the military.[144]

In the case of Ghana, the majority eventually softened its stance on the issue, after public deliberations and persuasion by civil society groups. The initial provisions in the bill that limited the NRC's mandate to military regimes was changed, and a provision was added to give the NRC additional jurisdiction over all political regimes in Ghana since independence.[145] The NRC's mandate thus covered human rights violations that occurred during Ghana's past military regimes (i.e., 24 February 1966 to 21 August 1969, 13 January 1972 to 23 September 1979, and 31 December 1981 to 6 January 1993).[146] Individuals could also apply to the NRC to hear cases falling outside the listed time frames but occurring between 6 March 1957 and 6 January 1993.[147] In such instances, the NRC had the discretion whether to hear the case.[148] Similar provisions are found in Liberia's Truth and Reconciliation Commission Act, which granted the commission the liberty to investigate cases falling outside the mandated time frame (in instances where an application was made to the commission for such a purpose).[149] The existence of this comparable provision in Liberia's Truth and Reconciliation Commission Act and the fact that this provision did not cause controversy in Liberia show that limitations on truth commission mandates may be feasible in certain contexts. However, where the extent of human rights violations is very high, an absence of limitations on the truth commission's mandate can create an overwhelming workload for the commission and compromise its truth-finding duty.[150]

Within the Ghanaian context, however, it was argued by the minority National Democratic Congress that the provisions provided 'a door of opportunity' for people who suffered human rights violations under military regimes whilst only gesturing to 'a window of hope' for redressing the human rights violations that

[144]See Duffy 2010. http://news.bbc.co.uk/2/hi/8451109.stm. Accessed 19 October 2019.

[145]See Ameh 2006b, p. 351; and Valji 2006, p. 6.

[146]See NRC Act, above n 57, s 3(1).

[147]Ibid., s 3(2).

[148]Ibid., s 3(2).

[149]See TRC Act of Liberia, above n 24, s 4(a).

[150]On this subject, see Zalaquett 1995, p. 8, who argues that although it is very relevant that the truth is exposed and publicised, tradeoffs may be necessary in some instances. For example, where the human rights violations are very extensive, he believes that it may be necessary to focus on the more severe human rights violations, to avoid jeopardising the limited resources of the state and placing little emphasis on the more serious violations.

occurred outside the military regimes.[151] The crux of this argument was that the NRC Act expressly stated that all military regimes in Ghana's history constituted the NRC's mandate but merely gave the NRC the discretion to investigate other regimes. In effect, the nature of the NRC's mandate could work to the disadvantage of victims from Ghana's past constitutional regimes, particularly if the NRC decided to exercise this discretion negatively by disallowing investigation of human rights violations that occurred outside the military regimes expressly mentioned in the NRC Act.[152] Indeed, this explanation by the minority was plausible because the limitation on the commission's investigative time frame could diminish the extent to which it could allay doubts about past human rights violations and create a detailed record in that regard.

However, it should be noted that placing limitations on the historical time frame for a truth commission's investigations could sometimes be necessary to avoid overburdening a commission's work and adversely impacting its effectiveness. In the case of the NRC, however, such a limitation was not necessary because the magnitude of human rights violations during Ghana's past constitutional regimes could not have given rise to such complications.

3.3.6 Powers of the National Reconciliation Commission

The ability of a truth commission to effectively carry out its duties and mandate depends largely on its powers. Such powers can form a basis for classifying them. Some truth commissions possess powers akin to those of courts, such as the power to issue subpoenas (e.g., East Timor, Sierra Leone and South Africa), the power to grant amnesties (e.g., Liberia and South Africa),[153] the power to issue warrants for searches and seizure (e.g., East Timor, Sierra Leone and South Africa), the power to hold hearings in public (e.g., Brazil, Liberia, Nigeria, Peru and South Africa) and the power to name the perpetrators of human rights violations (e.g., Liberia, East Timor, El Salvador, Sierra Leone and South Africa).[154] There are, however, truth

[151]In relation to this argument, see Ameh 2006b, p. 352.

[152]Ibid., p. 352.

[153]The Liberian TRC had the power to suggest the granting of conditional amnesties to perpetrators who applied to the commission to make full disclosures for human rights violations they committed, where such violations did not constitute 'violations of international humanitarian law and crimes against humanity in conformity with international laws and standards'. The commission was also empowered to provide immunity against trial for individuals who provided testimony before it. See TRC Act of Liberia, above n 24, s 26(g) and 30. Similarly in South Africa, the enabling law of the South African TRC empowered it to grant amnesties to 'persons who make full disclosure of acts associated with a political objective'. See South African TRC Act, above n 47, s 3(1)(b).

[154]See Freeman 2006, pp. 34–35, where he asserts that although these added powers of truth commissions could enhance their work, they could also divert the focus of truth commissions from their traditional roles.

commissions that possess little or none of the above-mentioned powers (e.g., Guatemala). In practice, there is no fixed rule on the nature and extent of a truth commission's powers and such powers depend, to a large extent, on the circumstances of each case.

In the case of the NRC, its powers can be generally classified as administrative powers, subpoena powers, powers related to witnesses, the power to hold public proceedings, the power to name perpetrators and search and seizure powers. The nature and extent of these powers are outlined below.

3.3.6.1 Administrative Powers

According to the NRC Act, the right of appointing the commission's administrative staff rested with the president of Ghana.[155] The NRC's only administrative powers related to its working structure. For instance, the NRC was required under the NRC Act to set up an investigation unit to be responsible for carrying out some of the commission's enquiry-related functions by obtaining information from individuals whose rights had been violated.[156] Aside the Investigative Unit, the NRC was authorised to establish any committees it considered useful in carrying out its mandate. Committee membership could include non-members of the NRC. However, such committees could be headed only by an NRC commissioner.[157]

The administrative powers of the NRC could be regarded as narrow, compared with, for instance, the Liberian TRC and Brazil's Comissão Nacional da Verdade. The Liberian TRC had the power to appoint its own chairman and vice-chairman from amongst its members. It could regulate all aspects of its work and proceedings, including the power to come up with instructions and strategies regarding its operations.[158] Moreover, the commission had the power to appoint administrative staff and to determine the terms and conditions of their employment.[159] In Brazil, the extent of the Comissão Nacional da Verdade's administrative powers are evinced by its ability to pass by-laws to regulate its administration.[160] In this regard, 16 resolutions were passed by the commission.[161]

Arguably, the possession of such powers by the Comissão Nacional da Verdade of Brazil and the Liberian TRC was a positive feature, as such powers gave them an avenue to independently create relevant structures to suit their work. In the case of

---

[155]NRC Act, above n 57, s 23(1) and (3).

[156]Ibid., s 9.

[157]Ibid., s 7.

[158]See TRC Act of Liberia, above n 24, s 13 and s 26(i).

[159]Ibid., ss 18 and 35.

[160]See Decree No. 7.919, above n 47 Article 4, which empowered the Comissão Nacional da Verdade to create bye laws to provide further detailed regulations of its actions.

[161]See the Comissão Nacional da Verdade. http://www.cnv.gov.br/institucional-acesso-informacao/a-cnv/59-regimento-interno-da-comissao-nacional-da-verdade.html. Accessed 19 October 2019.

the NRC, however, the lack of extensive administrative powers did not cripple the commission, in light of the commission's ability to decentralise its work and involve non-members in subcommittees. For instance, the power to create subcommittees was utilised to employ the services of experts as necessary for the purposes of investigations.

3.3.6.2 Subpoena Powers and Other Witness-Related Powers

The NRC was equipped with the same powers, rights and privileges as the High Court of Ghana, allowing it to compel witnesses to appear before it and provide testimony under either oath or affirmation, to bring documentary evidence and to demand interrogation of witnesses outside the borders of Ghana.[162] Thus, the commission could interrogate any individual in relation to matters under investigation and compel persons to reveal documents and any other data or evidence they possessed about a case under investigation irrespective of whether the evidence was incriminating.[163] It could also administer oaths to witnesses and other individuals who appeared before it.[164]

In addition, the NRC was empowered to issue subpoenas for the appearance of individuals before the commission and production of documents.[165] In this regard, the NRC could cause individuals who disregarded the commission's orders to be charged with contempt.[166] Nevertheless, the ultimate decision regarding whether official documents could be disclosed in furtherance of public interest and state security was reserved for the Supreme Court of Ghana.[167]

Regarding protection of witnesses, individuals who gave testimony before the NRC were accorded the same rights and protections as witnesses that appeared before the High Court of Ghana.[168] Moreover, persons could not be prosecuted or sued in a civil matter by virtue of their adherence to the NRC's dictates.[169]

[162] 1992 Constitution, above n 10, Article 279(1).

[163] See NRC Act, above n 57, ss 10, 13(a), 13(c), 15(1).

[164] Ibid., s 13(b).

[165] Ibid., s 13(c).

[166] Ibid., s 13(d).

[167] 1992 Constitution, above n 10, Article 135; and NRC Act, above n 57, s 16.

[168] 1992 Constitution, above n 10, Article 283; and NRC Act, above n 57, s 14(1). Under Article 19 of the 1992 Constitution, some of the rights of witnesses before the High Court are provided as: the existence of a presumption of innocence, the right to be adequately informed of one's charges, the right to sufficient time and facilities to set up one's defence, the right to defend oneself in court, the right to question prosecution witnesses and bring other witnesses to testify on one's behalf, the right to the services of an interpreter, and the individual's right to be tried in his presence (except where he refuses to be present or his conduct does not permit his presence at the trial). Other provisions under Article 19 deal with the principle of legality, the double jeopardy rule and compellability of witnesses in criminal trials.

[169] See NRC Act, above n 57, s 14(2).

Witnesses who gave incriminating evidence to the NRC were indemnified against civil and criminal suits with respect to the evidence given to the NRC.[170] Persons who gave testimony before the NRC or who had some connection with any subject under the investigation by the NRC were entitled to the services of a lawyer, and the NRC was required to inform all persons who appeared before it of this right.[171] Aside the services of lawyers, the services of experts could be utilised by such persons in order to safeguard their interests.[172] The NRC could also provide a lawyer for persons who it believed could not afford such services on their own but needed representation to serve 'the interests of justice'.[173]

These powers of the NRC are comparable to those of the Liberian TRC. To begin with, the Liberian TRC could compel the production of any information, just as the NRC.[174] Nevertheless, the TRC's subpoena powers differ significantly, as its subpoena powers were exercised through a special magistrate appointed based on the commission's recommendations.[175] The position of the special magistrate was analogous to that of a circuit judge and worked to facilitate the functioning of the commission by issuing 'arrest warrants for contempt and subpoenas'.[176] In effect, the Liberian TRC's subpoena powers were not direct like that of the NRC. Unlike the NRC, which was able only to charge individuals for contempt, the special magistrate was empowered to conduct its own contempt proceedings to enable it carry out its duties effectively.[177] Like the NRC, the Liberian TRC could also administer oaths and could compel any individual to appear before it.[178] The commission also had some witness protection powers akin to those of the NRC. Persons who appeared before the commission had a right to a lawyer, and the commission was tasked with considering the safety and other needs of victims and witnesses in its proceedings. It was also tasked with accounting for the peculiarities of each case, particularly in relation to women and children.[179]

In the case of Brazil, the Comissão Nacional da Verdade had no express subpoena powers, as was the case with the NRC. However, the commission could seek information and help from public agencies and other bodies through positive partnerships in order to carry out its work.[180] For the purposes of safeguarding the effectiveness of its work, members of the civil service and government agencies

---

[170]Ibid., s 15(1) and (2).

[171]Ibid., s 17; and 1992 Constitution, above n 10, Article 282.

[172]1992 Constitution, above n 10, Article 282.

[173]NRC Act, above n 57, s 17.

[174]See TRC Act of Liberia, above n 24, ss 27(a), 26(i).

[175]Ibid., s 27(b).

[176]Ibid., s 27(b)(i).

[177]Ibid., s 27(b)(ii).

[178]Ibid., ss 27(c) and (d).

[179]Ibid., ss 26(n), 26(o), 31.

[180]See Law No. 12.528, above n 7, Articles 3(V), 4(II), (VII), (VIII).

were required to be co-operative with the Comissão Nacional da Verdade.[181] Although the Comissão Nacional da Verdade had no autonomy to issue subpoenas, it had the power to obtain all manner of information (whether public or private) from the law courts through applications.[182] The Comissão Nacional da Verdade also had the discretion to act in conjunction with the public institution in charge of the country's records and 'the Committee on Amnesty, and the Special Commission on Political Deaths and Disappearances' in order to effectively carry out its obligations.[183] It could enter into partnerships with private, public, domestic and international bodies or individuals to facilitate acquisition of information and evidence.[184] Regarding witnesses, the Comissão Nacional da Verdade was empowered to provide protection for witnesses and victims whose safety could be compromised as a result of providing it with evidence.[185]

In Nigeria, the powers of the Oputa Panel were minimal, in comparison with those of the NRC. Initially, it was perceived that by virtue of being established under the Tribunals of Inquiry Act of 1990, the commission could exercise subpoena and other witness-related powers in that legislation.[186] The purported exercise of these powers was, however, overruled by the Supreme Court of Nigeria as being unconstitutional.[187]

The examples in the above instances illustrate that subpoena and other witness-related powers could vary in form and breadth depending on the context. For instance, the non-possession of wide subpoena and other witness-related powers by the Comissão Nacional da Verdade and the Oputa Panel, show the extent to which the investigative powers of truth commissions can be limited. In the case of the NRC, however, its subpoena and other witness-related powers were very extensive. Considering the fact that few truth commissions are ever given such powers, the possession of such powers by the NRC was a foundation for a strong

---

[181]Ibid., Article 4, s 3.

[182]Ibid., Article 4, s 5.

[183]Ibid., Article 6.

[184]See the Comissão Nacional da Verdade 2013, Article 9. http://www.cnv.gov.br/institucional-acesso-informacao/a-cnv/59-regimento-interno-da-comissao-nacional-da-verdade.html. Accessed 19 October 2019.

[185]See Law No. 12.528, above n 7, Article 4(VI).

[186]Under the Tribunals of Inquiry Act, above n 99, s 5 and s 6, the perceived powers were the powers to: obtain all the needed evidence from individuals as it required under oath, the power to compel the appearance of individuals and the production of documents and other forms of evidence before it, the power to issue warrants for the appearance of persons who had previously refused to appear before the commission and to recover the costs incurred by virtue of the person's failure to appear before the commission, the power to admit all evidence, including evidence which would be inadmissible before a court of law, and the power to hire the services of interpreters. Also, the chairman of the Oputa panel initially had the power to issue all manner of summonses and subpoenas, in order to effectively conduct the work of the commission.

[187]See the case of *Chief Gani Fawehinmi*, above n 54. See also Oshio 2001–2002, pp. 117–118; and Yusuf 2007, p. 278.

investigative competency, to enable it to fulfil its other mandates.[188] Also, the NRC's possession of witness protection powers was a necessary component of its work, as it gave the commission the ability to sustain the cooperation of witnesses in its work. These powers, however, institutionalised the commission from the outset and gave it a legalistic outlook, a feature that had both pros and cons, as demonstrated later in this study.[189]

3.3.6.3 Search and Seizure Powers

Aside its subpoena powers, the NRC was equipped with extensive search and seizure powers. The commission was authorised to enter any premises for the purposes of carrying out its investigations.[190] It was also given a right of access to all archives and data that were necessary to execute its mandate.[191] The NRC's powers of entry, search and seizure were equivalent to the powers of the Ghana Police Service. In instances where it believed that obtaining a search warrant would interfere with a search, the commission could enter any premises, conduct a search and confiscate items on the condition that the appropriate warrant would be acquired no later than a day after the search.[192]

The NRC's search and seizure powers are somewhat similar to those of the Liberian TRC, which had the power to enter any premises to facilitate the acquisition of evidence and could also issue citations to enable the commission to obtain evidence.[193] However, unlike the NRC, which could exercise these powers directly, the Liberian TRC could exercise its search and seizure powers through the special magistrate.[194] In the case of Brazil, the Comissão Nacional da Verdade had no express search and seizure powers. However, the commission could seek information and help from public agencies and other bodies through positive partnerships in order to carry out its work.[195] For the purposes of safeguarding the effectiveness of its work, members of the civil service and government agencies were required to be co-operative with the Comissão Nacional da Verdade.[196] In Nigeria as well, the Oputa Panel did not have any search and seizure powers. These powers were limited by the Supreme Court of Nigeria, which overruled the commission's exercise of such powers under the Tribunals of Inquiry Act of 1990 and

---

[188]For further details on how the NRC actually performed in its investigations, see Sect. 4.3.2 in Chap. 4 of this book.

[189]See Sects. 3.3.6.5 in Chap. 3 and 4.4.2.3 in Chap. 4 of this book.

[190]See NRC Act, above n 57, s 10.

[191]Ibid., s 10(a).

[192]Ibid., s 11.

[193]TRC Act of Liberia, above n 24, s 27(b)(i).

[194]Ibid., s 27(b)(i).

[195]See Law No. 12.528, above n 7, Articles 3(V), 4(II), 4(VII), 4(VIII).

[196]Ibid., Article 4, s 3.

declared that the exercise of such a power by the commission was unconstitutional.[197]

In light of these instances, the NRC's search and seizure powers were extensive. Indeed, given the long lapse of time between the actual commission of human rights violations in Ghana and the establishment of the NRC, these powers were much needed to properly equip the commission to carry out its fact-finding mandate properly.

3.3.6.4 Proceedings of the National Reconciliation Commission

The nature of a truth commission's proceedings can have significant effect on the overall outcome of its work. Preferably, members of the public must be given the opportunity to be involved in the truth-telling process as much as possible.[198] In practice, however, not all truth commissions are empowered to hold their hearings in public.[199] In the case of the NRC, the provisions on the nature of its hearings are found under Article 281(1) of the 1992 Constitution, which requires all hearings of commissions of enquiry to be conducted publicly. However, commissions of enquiry are empowered to hold their sessions in camera if doing so can jeopardise 'public morality, public safety or public order'.[200] Pursuant to this provision, the hearings of the NRC were supposed to be conducted in public, although some proceedings could be held in camera, if the commission considered this necessary or if a request for an in-camera hearing was made to the commission by a person being examined in a hearing.[201] Moreover, the commission had the discretion to withhold information about witnesses and its hearings from the public, for cases heard in camera.[202]

These powers of the NRC are similar to those of the Oputa Panel in Nigeria, the Liberian TRC and the Comissão Nacional da Verdade of Brazil. In Nigeria, the

[197]See the case of *Chief Gani Fawehinmi*, above n 54. See also Oshio 2001–2002, pp. 117–118; and 2007, p. 278. See also Tribunals of Inquiry Act, above n 99, s 5(g), where it is stated that a tribunal could exercise 'the power to enter upon any land or premises personally or by any agent or agents duly authorised in writing by the members, for any purpose which, in their opinion is material to the inquiry, and in particular, for the purpose of obtaining evidence or information or of inspecting or taking copies of any documents required by or which may be of assistance to, the tribunal, and for safeguarding any such document or property which in the opinion of the members ought to be safeguarded for any purpose of the inquiry'.

[198]See Covenant on Civil and Political Rights, above n 127, Article 25, where it is provided that citizens of a state have the right to be involved in public affairs of the state; and United Nations Commission on Human Rights 2005, para 6.

[199]Examples of truth commissions that had no power to hold public hearings are the Comisión Nacional sobre la Desaparición de Personas of Argentina and the Clarification Commission of Guatemala.

[200]1992 Constitution, above n 10, Article 281(1).

[201]See NRC Act, above n 57, s 12(2).

[202]Ibid., s 12.

Oputa Panel was empowered to hold public hearings, although it reserved the power to hold proceedings in camera, when necessary.[203] Likewise in Brazil, the hearings of the Comissão Nacional da Verdade could be held in public, except when the commission considered it necessary to hold its hearings in camera for the purposes of ensuring confidentiality.[204] The proceedings of the Liberian TRC could also be held in public if the commission believed that doing so would not jeopardise justice or the safety of individuals. Nevertheless, it could entertain applications from individuals about whether certain proceedings should be held in camera. In such circumstances, the discretion was left with the commission to decide.[205]

Undoubtedly, the power of these commissions to hold public hearings was a positive feature, as it provided a forum for victims to make their experiences known.[206] In reality, however, the relevance of public hearings depends on the specific context. Public hearings could increase the expenses of a truth commission and put it under financial and infrastructural strain. However, it can be useful in other instances, particularly for victims, by providing them a means for airing their grievances.[207] Even in the absence of such a power, a truth commission may still manage to fulfil their fact-finding mandate. Key examples are the Comisión Nacional sobre la Desaparición de Personas of Argentina and the Clarification Commission of Guatemala. In the Ghanaian context, however, one cannot think of a reason why such a power would be inappropriate. On the contrary, the power to hold public hearings served to promote the publicity of the commission's work.[208]

3.3.6.5 The Power to 'Name Names'

The power of truth commissions to mention the names of perpetrators is one of the most contentious issues on the subject of truth-telling.[209] A key issue that regularly arises is whether it is appropriate to empower truth commissions to assign criminal responsibility to perpetrators.[210] One argument, based on the scope of the right to truth, is that failing to disclose perpetrators' identities to victims amounts to placing

[203] See Human Rights Violations Investigation Commission 2002, vol 1 para 2.45; and Tribunals of Inquiry Act, above n 99, s 1(2d).

[204] See the Comissão Nacional da Verdade 2013, Article 16. http://www.cnv.gov.br/institucional-acesso-informacao/a-cnv/59-regimento-interno-da-comissao-nacional-da-verdade.html. Accessed 19 October 2019.

[205] See TRC Act of Liberia, above n 24, s 26(p)(i) and (ii).

[206] See Freeman 2006, pp. 222–223.

[207] Ibid.

[208] For details of how the commission utilised its public hearings, see Sects. 4.3.2 and 4.3.5 in Chap. 4 of this book.

[209] Regarding the debates on this issue, see Buergenthal 2006, pp. 109–112; and Hayner 2011, pp. 121–122.

[210] On the controversial nature of this issue, see Méndez 1997, p. 265; and United Nations Commission on Human Rights 2006, p. 11.

a limitation on victims' right to know the complete truth.[211] However, it is also argued that naming perpetrators of human rights violations contravenes the principles of due process.[212] Since truth commissions do not follow due process requirements, it is considered inappropriate for them to assign criminal responsibility for an offence.[213] Furthermore, the naming of perpetrators by truth commissions risks false incrimination, since they do not apply the same standards as courts in their investigations.[214] Indeed, the United Nations has stated that it is only criminal courts who have the authority to assign criminal responsibility for crimes, with the aim of imposing sanctions. Thus, if perpetrators are to be named by a truth commission, the evidence against them must be corroborated and the individuals in question should be given a chance to narrate their side of the story or respond to the evidence against them.[215] Also, individuals whose names appear in any state archives should be made aware of this fact and are entitled to challenge the information in relation to which their name appears in the archive.[216] Regardless of its controversial nature, the possession of such a power is one of the most influential aspects of a truth commission's work, as it can serve as a mild form of retribution.[217]

---

[211]See for instance the United Nations Human Rights Committee 1994, paras 12.3 and 14, where it was stated that the obligation of Uruguay to investigate acts of torture committed on its territory included identifying the perpetrators.

[212]This includes informing individuals promptly of any allegations against them, notifying them of the intention to name them in a public report and providing them with an opportunity to respond to the allegations. Also, the rights of individuals who appear before the commission must be upheld. Examples are the right to be presumed innocent until proven guilty, the right to be informed of the charges brought against any person, the right to a defence, the right to a lawyer, freedom from self-incrimination, the right to call witnesses to support one's claim, the right to examine witnesses making claims against a person and the right to an interpreter where necessary. See Covenant on Civil and Political Rights, above n 127, Articles 9(2) and 14; and Rome Statute of the International Criminal Court, opened for signature 17 July 1998, ICC-PIDS-LT-01-002/11_Eng (entered into force 1 July 2002) (Rome Statute), Article 55. See also Freeman and Hayner 2003, p. 136; and Hamber and Kibble 1999. http://www.csvr.org.za/index.php/publications/1714-from-truth-to-transformation-the-truth-and-reconciliation-commission-in-south-africa.html. Accessed 28 September 2019.

[213]The jurisprudence of the Inter-American Court of Human Rights indicates a preference for this argument. See the Inter-American Court of Human Rights, *Gómez-Paquiyauri Brothers v Peru*, 8 July 2004, p. 54 para 146, where the court stated that states should observe principles of due process when conducting investigations to ascertain the perpetrators of human rights violations.

[214]See Freeman and Hayner 2003, p. 136.

[215]See United Nations Commission on Human Rights 2005, para 9. On the naming of perpetrators only when there is overwhelming evidence of their complicity, see also Freeman and Hayner 2003, p. 136; and Hamber and Kibble 1999. http://www.csvr.org.za/index.php/publications/1714-from-truth-to-transformation-the-truth-and-reconciliation-commission-in-south-africa.html. Accessed 28 September 2019; and Méndez 1997, p. 265.

[216]See United Nations Commission on Human Rights 2005, para 17.

[217]See Weiner 2005, p. 130.

In the case of Ghana, the NRC Act granted the commission discretion regarding whether to reveal in its report the names and identities of individuals who appeared before it or submitted a complaint to it.[218] Persons whose names are revealed are also covered by the witness protection laws of the NRC Act. Therefore, individuals who felt that the revelation of any information would threaten their safety could ask the NRC to provide them with the requisite protection.[219]

Similar powers were possessed by the Liberian TRC and the Oputa Panel of Nigeria. The Liberian Truth and Reconciliation Commission Act empowered the commission to point out the perpetrators of human rights violations where feasible and ensure that perpetrators are held accountable.[220] The Oputa Panel was also empowered under its mandate to identify the individuals and bodies to be held liable for the human rights violations under investigation.[221] No such express powers were given to the Comissão Nacional da Verdade, although it was authorised to point out the institutions and bodies that caused human rights violations.[222]

The question of appropriateness regarding the possession or non-possession of this power in the above instances depends largely on the specific circumstances in each context. If trials are being held, it would be unnecessary to burden a truth commission with that responsibility. In such a case, it would be best to leave the task of naming perpetrators to the courts.[223] In contrast, where no trials are being held, then the process of truth-telling should comply with due process requirements and must be fair and be perceived as credible by the society.[224]

In the case of the NRC, its massive legal powers properly equipped it to fulfil due process requirements. For instance, its subpoena and search and seizure powers involved processes similar to those of normal courts. Also, the fact that individuals who appeared before the commission were entitled to the services of a lawyer and swore an oath implies that normal courtroom procedure was to be applied in the commission's proceedings. Nevertheless, whether the exercise of such a power by the commission was appropriate will be addressed later, on the basis of its actual work.[225]

---

[218] NRC Act, above n 57, s 18.

[219] Ibid., s 18(2).

[220] See TRC Act of Liberia, above n 24, s 26(b) and (d).

[221] See Human Rights Violations Investigation Commission 2002, vol 1 para 2.36(b).

[222] See Law No. 12.528, above n 7, Article 3(III).

[223] See Méndez 1997, p. 265.

[224] See Freeman and Hayner 2003, p. 136; and Hamber and Kibble 1999. http://www.csvr.org.za/index.php/publications/1714-from-truth-to-transformation-the-truth-and-reconciliation-commission-in-south-africa.html. Accessed 28 September 2019.

[225] See Sect. 4.4.2.3 in Chap. 4 of this book.

3.3.7 *Funds of the National Reconciliation Commission*

Funding for truth commissions is a very crucial aspect of their work, as truth-telling exercises usually require substantial funds. The state must, therefore, provide the requisite financial support and logistics for truth commissions.[226] Relevant issues to consider in this regard are the source of funds, adequacy of funds, the possibility of financial independence for the truth commission and the observance of good accounting standards by the commission.

In Ghana, the funds for the NRC were to be obtained from Parliament through the Consolidated Fund as well as 'any other public funds', 'donations' and 'grants'.[227] In this regard, the NRC was required to abide by good accounting practices and standards by keeping the requisite records of its accounts, which were supposed to be submitted to the auditor general not later than three months after submitting its report to the president.[228] These books and records of accounts were also supposed to be reviewed by the auditor general, who was required to provide Parliament with a report on the said accounts.[229]

The funding-related provisions of the NRC create a general impression that the NRC had a firm legal foundation regarding adequacy of its funds and observance of good accounting standards. The NRC's degree of financial independence cannot, however, be discerned from the provisions. The funding methods of other truth commissions suggests that funding sources differ, depending on the existing circumstances. In Liberia, for instance, the funding source was not specific, as the TRC was expected to be funded with money from the national coffers as well as international and local 'donations', 'loans' and 'grants'.[230] In Brazil, the country's president was required to provide the finances of the Comissão Nacional da Verdade.[231] In principle, no particular funding method is preferable over another. Considering that societies in transition usually have poor economic conditions,[232] the most relevant factor regarding funding is that the source should be practical enough to ensure that the commission does not face financial difficulties.

[226]See United Nations Commission on Human Rights 2005, para 11; and the United Nations Economic and Social Council 1989, paras 10, 17.

[227]The Consolidated Fund in Ghana is one of three types of public funds mentioned under Article 175 of the 1992 Constitution of Ghana. It comprises funds that are generated, obtained or acquired through a trust 'for the purposes of or on behalf of the government of Ghana', with the exception of funds that are to be allocated under another fund for a particular usage under a legislation. See 1992 Constitution, above n 10, Article 175; and NRC Act, above n 57, s 24.

[228]NRC Act, above n 57, s 26(1) and 26(2).

[229]Ibid., s 26(3).

[230]TRC Act of Liberia, above n 24, s 36.

[231]See Law No. 12.528, above n 7, Article 10.

[232]On the economic status of transitional societies, see de Greiff 2009, p. 29.

3.3.8 Provisions on the Report

Although there are varied mechanisms through which the progress of a truth commission may be monitored, the final means of doing so is to require a report after it concludes work.[233] Also, the state must publicise and distribute the report of a truth commission extensively.[234] In some instances, the reporting requirements of truth commissions may include additional requirements. Nigeria's Oputa Panel was required to submit occasional interim reports to the president, in addition to one final report at the end of its work.[235] In Liberia, aside from the usual duty to recommend reparations and suggest reforms in its report, a unique aspect of the Liberian TRC's reporting duties was the presence of provisions to ensure the effectiveness of the commission's recommendations. Thus, unlike most truth commissions, implementing the recommendations of the Liberian TRC was safeguarded under the Truth and Reconciliation Commission Act, which mandated the Independent National Human Rights Commission of Liberia to ensure that the recommendations are executed.[236] Moreover, the president of Liberia is mandated to provide quarterly updates to the nation's legislature on the implementation of the commission's recommendations.[237] In addition, the records of the Liberian TRC are supposed to remain public even after completion of its work, with the exception of records considered confidential by the commission.[238]

The NRC was also required to complete and submit its report no later than 90 days after ending its proceedings. The report was required to give a detailed account of the human rights violations suffered, provide an account of the cases into which it enquired, offer details of the individuals who suffered the human rights violations, provide suggestions on the requisite ways to meet the needs of victims based on their specific requirements, provide advice on the best means to deter future

[233]For example, in Brazil the Comissão Nacional da Verdade was required to provide a report not later than two years after its establishment; in Nigeria, the Oputa Panel was required to submit a final report within a year after commencement of its proceedings, or such other time as may be extended by the President; and in Liberia, the Liberian TRC had the power to make suggestions to the President as regards reparations, reforms, conduct of further enquiries into specific matters and the holding of prosecutions for some cases. See Law No. 12.528, above n 7, Article 11; the Comissão Nacional da Verdade 2013, Article 1(2). http://www.cnv.gov.br/institucional-acesso-informacao/a-cnv/59-regimento-interno-da-comissao-nacional-da-verdade.html. Accessed 19 October 2019; Human Rights Violations Investigation Commission 2002, vol 1 para 2.37; Tribunals of Inquiry Act, above n 99, s 14; and TRC Act of Liberia, above n 24, s 26(j).

[234]See United Nations Commission on Human Rights 2005, para 13.

[235]See Human Rights Violations Investigation Commission 2002, vol 1 para 2.37; and Tribunals of Inquiry Act, above n 99, s 14.

[236]TRC Act of Liberia, above n 24, s 46.

[237]Ibid., s 48.

[238]Ibid., s 47.

occurrences of similar human rights violations; provide suggestions on the changes needed for the commission to fulfil its mandate, promote 'healing and reconciliation' and provide advice about provision of remedies for victims.[239] NRC commissioners and other people who performed tasks for the commission were indemnified against any liability for the contents of the report, provided the content was not written in bad faith.[240]

The basis for the reporting requirements of the NRC can be found under Article 280(1)(b) and (c) of the 1992 Constitution, which requires all commissions of enquiry to provide the outcome of their enquiries in a report that outlines the basis for their findings. Moreover, Article 280(2) accords the status of a High Court decision to a commission of enquiry's investigation results with respect to 'adverse findings against any person' after the lapse of six months from the time of its publication or when the president declares his intention of not publishing a white paper on the findings of the commission of enquiry.[241] Conclusions of a commission of enquiry are appealable only to Ghana's Court of Appeal. However, this right can be asserted only within a trimester after the commission's finding obtains the status of a High Court decision.[242] Nevertheless, the deadline for appeal can be extended with permission from the High Court or the Court of Appeal.[243] These features of the NRC also portray its court-like structure, as noted earlier.

Under Article 280(4) of the 1992 Constitution, the publication of reports produced by commissions of enquiry and the accompanying white paper must be done by the president within half a year after the report's presentation to the president.[244] Nevertheless, the president reserves the right not to go ahead with such a publication. In such instances, the president is required to provide the basis of non-publication publicly.[245]

The reporting requirements of the NRC contain a major gap: the absence of a provision to ensure its proper publicity and implementation, as was the case with the Liberian TRC, containing rules regarding implementation of the recommendations in the report.[246] Although the existence of such a provision does not guarantee absolute implementation of a truth commission's report, such a requirement would have been particularly useful in the Ghanaian context, given the country's tardiness in implementation of past commission of enquiry reports.

[239] NRC Act, above n 57, s 20.

[240] Ibid., s 21.

[241] 1992 Constitution, above n 10, Article 280(2)(5).

[242] Ibid., Article 280(2)(6).

[243] Ibid., Article 280(6).

[244] Ibid., Article 280(3).

[245] Ibid., Article 280(4).

[246] TRC Act of Liberia, above n 24, s 46.

3.3.9 *Offences and Penalties*

Since truth commissions do not have all the powers of courts of law, it may be necessary to safeguard their work, by meting out penalties for conduct that jeopardises their work. In Nigeria for instance, the Oputa panel was given such safeguards against giving of false testimony before the commission or providing the commission with false interpretation and against individuals who in any manner obstructed people from providing the commission with evidence.[247] Similarly, acts of contempt against the Oputa Panel and failure to honour its invitations to provide testimony were deemed punishable offences.[248] In Liberia, the Truth and Reconciliation Commission Act similarly safeguarded the work of the Liberian TRC. Obstruction of the work of the commission or any of its workers was deemed an offence punishable by either a fine or prison sentence or both.[249]

The work of the NRC was also safeguarded in a similar but broader manner, by criminalising various acts that were likely to interfere with its effectiveness. These acts (offences) were punishable either by a fine or imprisonment or both.[250] Some of the actions that were criminalised were the following:

- Actions that were likely to impact negatively on the possible outcome of any of the NRC's cases and investigations.
- Actions that could affect the commission's processes or discoveries.
- Acts regarded as contemptuous to the work of the courts under the laws of Ghana.
- Interfering with, impeding or resisting the NRC's work without a legal explanation.
- Voluntarily providing the commission with false testimony or deceiving or attempting to deceive the commission, its workers and other persons in relation to carrying out the NRC's mandate.
- Failing to abide by the orders of the NRC without legal cause.
- Failure to comply with a subpoena order and all its requirements without 'sufficient cause'.
- Failure to comply with the requirements of the NRC Act.
- Breaches of the confidentiality rules under the NRC Act.
- Destruction of evidence (whether documentary or not) connected to the work of the NRC.[251]

---

[247]Such conduct was punishable with a prison sentence of not less than two years. See Tribunals of Inquiry Act, above n 99, s 9.

[248]Individuals who failed to honour an invitation by the commission to provide testimony had the same privileges and rights against self-incrimination, as was applicable before the law courts. See Tribunals of Inquiry Act, above n 99, ss 10, 11, 12.

[249]See TRC Act of Liberia, above n 24, s 28.

[250]See NRC Act, above n 57, s 22.

[251]Ibid., s 22(a)–22(k).

Overall, the existence of these penalties under the NRC Act were crucial for solidifying the powers of the commission. Nevertheless, such penalties could also pose a potential threat of discouraging individuals from involvement in the work of the commission. This, however, depended largely on how the court handled its powers, as shall be seen in Chap. 4.

3.4 Chapter Summary

This chapter has illustrated that the NRC was established against the backdrop of four main legal hurdles: amnesty provisions that barred prosecutions, difficulties with amending the amnesty provisions, absence of a transitional justice policy to deal with past human rights violations and failure to prosecute on account of the principle of legality. Given the framework for the establishment of the NRC, it is apparent that the commission was established on a detailed and comprehensive legal footing. The key shortcomings in the features of the commission have also been identified. This includes the lack of equal gender representation in its membership, lack of full independence of the commission and the absence of broad consultation regarding the appointment of the commission's members. Overall, the features of the NRC evince an institution that is almost akin to a court. The key court-like aspects of the commission include the requirement for lawyers in its proceedings, the commission's power to administer oaths and the extensive nature of its subpoena and other witness-related powers. Regardless of this fact, the detailed provisions on the NRC's powers and features created clarity from the very outset regarding how the commission was supposed to function.

References

Abrão P, Tirekky MD (2012) Resistance to change: Brazil's persistent amnesty and its alternatives for truth and justice. In: Lessa F, Payne LA (eds) Amnesty in the age of human rights accountability: Comparative and international perspectives. Cambridge University Press, New York, pp 152–181.

Alidu S, Ame R (2012) Civil society activism and the Ghanaian National Reconciliation Commission: The case of the Civil Society Coalition on National Reconciliation. Transitional Justice Review 1(1):104–136.

Ameh RK (2006a) Doing justice after conflict: The case for Ghana's National Reconciliation Commission. Canadian Journal of Law and Society 21(1):85–109.

Ameh RK (2006b) Uncovering truth: Ghana's National Reconciliation Commission excavation of past human rights abuses. Contemporary Justice Review 9(4):345–368.

Attafuah KA (2004) An overview of Ghana's National Reconciliation Commission and its relationship with the courts. In: Schabas WA, Darcy S (eds) Truth Commissions and courts: The tension between criminal justice and the search for truth. Kluwer Academic Publishers, Dordrecht, pp 125–134.

Bisset A (2012) Truth commissions and criminal courts. Cambridge University Press, Cambridge.

Bix BH (2011) Radbruch's formula and conceptual analysis. American Journal of Jurisprudence 56:45–57.
Boafo-Arthur K (2005) National reconciliation or polarisation? Preliminary reflections on the politics of the Ghana National Reconciliation Commission. In: Fawole WA, Ukeje C (eds.) The crisis of the state and regionalism in West Africa. Codesria, Dakar, pp 105–126.
Boafo-Arthur K (2006) The quest for national reconciliation in Ghana: Challenges and prospects. In: Boafo-Arthur K (ed) Voting for democracy in Ghana: The 2004 elections in perspectives. Freedom House Publishing, Accra, pp 127–155.
Buergenthal T (2006) Truth commissions: Functions and due process. In: Dupuy et al (eds) Fest-schrift für Tomuschat. Engel, Kehl, pp 103–113.
Cavallaro JL, Delgado F (2012) The paradox of accountability in Brazil. In: Popovski V, Serrano M (eds) After oppression: Transitional justice in Latin America and Eastern Europe. United Nations University Press, New York, pp 86–115.
Comissão Nacional da Verdade (2012) Resolução No 1, De 2 De Julho De 2012. http://cnv.memoriasreveladas.gov.br/images/pdf/regimento_interno_cnv_130712.pdf Accessed 19 October 2019.
Comissão Nacional Da Verdade (2013) Regimento Interno da Comissão Nacional da Verdade, Resolução No. 08 De 04 De Março De 2013. http://www.cnv.gov.br/institucional-acesso-informacao/a-cnv/59-regimento-interno-da-comissao-nacional-da-verdade.html. Accessed 19 October 2019.
Comissão Nacional da Verdade (2014) Relatório da Comissão Nacional da Verdade, vol I-III. http://cnv.memoriasreveladas.gov.br/. Accessed 3 November 2019.
Comparato BK, Sarti C (2012) Amnesty, memory and reconciliation in Brazil: Dilemmas of an unfinished political transition. http://files.isanet.org/ConferenceArchive/f2ecc7f25f6147f9ac79067fb7142135.pdf. Accessed 24 October 2019.
De Greiff P (2009) Articulating the links between transitional justice and development: Justice and social integration. In: de Greiff P, Duthie R (eds) Transitional justice and development: Making connections. Social Science Research Council, New York, pp 28–75.
Duffy G (2010) Brazil truth commission arouses military opposition. http://news.bbc.co.uk/2/hi/8451109.stm. Accessed 18 November 2019.
Freeman M (2006) Truth commissions and procedural fairness. Cambridge University Press, New York.
Freeman M, Hayner PB (2003) Truth telling. In: Bloomfield D et al (eds) Reconciliation after violent conflict. A handbook. International Institute for Democracy and Electoral Assistance, Stockholm, pp 122–144.
González E (2013) Truth and memory: Drafting a truth commission mandate – A practical tool. https://www.ictj.org/sites/default/files/ICTJ-Report-DraftingMandate-Truth-Commission-2013_0.pdf. Accessed 13 November 2019.
González E, Varney H (2013) Truth seeking: Elements of creating an effective truth commission. https://www.ictj.org/sites/default/files/ICTJ-Book-Truth-Seeking-2013-English.pdf. Accessed 2 November 2019.
Gyimah-Boadi E (1994) Ghana's uncertain political opening. Journal of Democracy 5(2):75–86.
Gyimah-Boadi E (2002) National reconciliation in Ghana: Prospects and challenges. https://www.files.ethz.ch/isn/100438/2004-05-01_Briefing_Vol4-No1.pdf. Accessed 4 September 2019.
Hamber B, Kibble S (1999) From truth to transformation: The Truth and Reconciliation Commission in South Africa. http://www.csvr.org.za/index.php/publications/1714-from-truth-to-transformation-the-truth-and-reconciliation-commission-in-south-africa.html. Accessed 28 September 2019.
Hayner PB (2011) Unspeakable truths: Transitional justice and the challenge of truth commissions, 2nd edn. Routledge, London.
Human Rights Violations Investigation Commission (2002) Human Rights Violations Investigation Commission Report, vol I-IX. https://dawodu.com/oputa1.htm. Accessed 3 November 2019.

James-Allen P et al (2010) Beyond the Truth and Reconciliation Commission: Transitional justice options in Liberia. International Centre for Transitional Justice, New York.
Kandeh JD (2004) Coups from below: Armed subalterns and state power in West Africa. Palgrave Macmillan, New York.
Kritz NJ (1995a) Brazil: Editor's introduction. In: Kritz N (ed) Transitional justice: How emerging democracies reckon with former regimes, vol. II. United States Institute of Peace Press, Washington DC, pp 431–432.
Kritz NJ (1995b) Chile: Editor's introduction. In: Kritz N (ed) Transitional justice: How emerging democracies reckon with former regimes, vol. II. United States Institute of Peace Press, Washington DC, pp 453–454.
Long WA (2008) Liberia's Truth and Reconciliation Commission: An interim assessment. International Journal of Peace Studies 13(2):1–14.
Lyons T (1997) A major step forward. Journal of Democracy 8(2):65–77.
Malca CG (2015) Peru: Changing contexts for transitional justice. In: Skaar E et al (eds) After violence: Transitional justice, peace, and democracy. Routledge, Abingdon and New York, pp. 94–124.
Méndez JE (1997) Accountability for past abuses. Human Rights Quarterly 19(2):255–282.
Mezarobba G (2013) Brazil. In: Stan L, Nedelsky N (eds) Encyclopedia of transitional justice, vol 1. Cambridge University Press, New York, pp 67–73.
National Reconciliation Commission (2004) Report of the National Reconciliation Commission, vol 1–4.
Nesiah V (2001) Key elements of a sustainable national reconciliation program in Ghana. http://cddgh.org/publications/Briefing-Papers. Accessed 4 September 2019.
Nigerian Muse (2006) Oputa Panel (HRVIC) timeline. https://www.nigerianmuse.com/nigeriawatch/oputa/?u=commission_timeline.htm. Accessed 23 November 2019.
Oduro F (2005) Reconciling a divided nation through a non-retributive justice approach: Ghana's national reconciliation initiative. International Journal of Human Rights 9(3):327–347.
Oduro F (2013) National Reconciliation Commission (Ghana). In: Stan L, Nedelsky N (eds) Encyclopedia of transitional justice. Cambridge University Press, Cambridge, pp 317–322.
Office of the United Nations High Commissioner for Human Rights (2006) Rule-of-law tools for post conflict states: Truth commissions. United Nations, New York and Geneva. https://www.ohchr.org/Documents/Publications/RuleoflawTruthCommissionsen.pdf. Accessed 2 November 2019.
Ojielo O (2010) Critical lessons in post-conflict security in Africa: The case of Liberia's Truth and Reconciliation Commission. https://sabarometerblog.files.wordpress.com/2010/05/ijr-ap-op-1-general-liberia.pdf. Accessed 4 September 2019.
Oshio PE (2001–2002) The constitutionality and powers of The Human Rights Violations Investigation Commission (Oputa Panel). University of Benin Law Journal 7(1):116–135.
Radbruch G (1946) Gesetzliches unrecht und übergesetzliches recht. Süddeutsche Juristenzeitung 1:105–108.
Roht-Arriaza N (2006) The new landscape of transitional justice. In: Roht-Arriaza N, Mariezcurrena J (eds) Transitional justice in the Twenty-First Century. Cambridge University Press, Cambridge and New York, pp 1–16.
Seidu A (2010) The National Reconciliation Commission and reconciliation in Ghana: An assessment. Review of International Affairs LXI (1138–1139):153–177.
Tomuschat C (2001) Clarification Commission in Guatemala. Human Rights Quarterly 23(2): 233–258.
Torelly M (2018) Assessing a late truth commission: Challenges and achievements of the Brazilian National Truth Commission. International Journal of Transitional Justice 12(2):194–215.
United Nations Commission on Human Rights (2005) Promotion and protection of human rights: Impunity, Report of the independent expert to update the set of principles to combat impunity, Diane Orentlicher, Addendum – Updated set of principles for the protection and promotion of human rights through action to combat impunity, E/CN.4/2005/102/Add.1.

United Nations Commission on Human Rights (2006) Promotion and protection of human rights: Study on the right to the truth – Report of the Office of the United Nations High Commissioner for Human Rights, E/CN.4/2006/91.

United Nations Economic and Social Council (1989) Principles on the effective prevention and investigation of extra-legal, arbitrary and summary executions. https://www.ohchr.org/Documents/ProfessionalInterest/executions.pdf. Accessed 2 November 2019.

United Nations Human Rights Committee (1994) Views of the Human Rights Committee under Article 5, paragraph 4 of the Optional Protocol to the International Covenant on Civil and Political Rights, concerning Communication No. 322/1988, CCPR/C/51/D/322/1988.

United States Institute of Peace. Truth commission: Sierra Leone. http://www.usip.org/publications/truth-commission-sierra-leone. Accessed 26 October 2019.

Valji N (2006) Ghana's National Reconciliation Commission: A comparative assessment. https://www.ictj.org/sites/default/files/ICTJ-Ghana-Reconciliation-Commission-2006-English_0.pdf. Accessed 24 October 2019.

Weiner MA (2005) Defeating hatred with truth: An argument in support of a truth commission as part of the solution to the Israeli-Palestinian conflict. Connecticut Law Review 38:123–156.

Werle G, Jessberger F (2014) Principles of international criminal law. Oxford University Press, Oxford.

Werle G, Vormbaum M (2012) After the fall of the Berlin Wall: Transitional justice in Germany. In: Popovski V, Serrano M (eds) After oppression: Transitional justice in Latin America and Eastern Europe. United Nations University Press, New York, pp 298–332.

Whitfield L (2009) Change for a better Ghana: Party competition, institutionalization and alternation in Ghana's 2008 elections. African Affairs 108/433:621–641.

Wiebelhaus-Brahm E (2013) Liberia. In: Stan L, Nedelsky N (eds) Encyclopedia of transitional justice. Cambridge University Press, New York, pp 280–286

Yusuf HO (2007) Travails of truth: Achieving justice for victims of impunity in Nigeria. International Journal of Transitional Justice 1:268–286.

Yusuf HO (2013) Nigeria. In: Stan L, Nedelsky N (eds) Encyclopedia of transitional justice. Cambridge University Press, New York, pp 333–339.

Zalaquett J (1995) Confronting human rights violations committed by former governments: Principles applicable and political constraints. In Kritz N (ed) Transitional justice: How emerging democracies reckon with former regimes, vol. I. United States Institute of Peace Press, Washington DC, pp 3–31.

Chapter 4
The National Reconciliation Commission in Practice

Contents

4.1 Introductory Remarks ... 104
4.2 The Work of the National Reconciliation Commission ... 104
4.2.1 Interpretation and Implementation of the Mandate ... 105
4.2.2 Structures and Offices ... 106
4.2.3 Statement Taking and Processing ... 109
4.2.4 Conduct of Investigations ... 110
4.2.5 Hearings ... 111
4.2.6 Assistance of Witnesses ... 112
4.3 Challenges ... 113
4.3.1 Inadequacy of Funds and Logistics ... 114
4.3.2 Weak Investigative Capacity ... 115
4.3.3 Condemnation of and Resistance to the Commission's Work ... 116
4.3.4 Political Resistance to the Commission's Work ... 119
4.3.5 Difficulty in Engaging Perpetrators ... 121
4.4 Outcome of the Commission's Work ... 124
4.4.1 Overview of the Report ... 124
4.4.2 Interim Analysis of the Commission's Report and Recommendations ... 132
4.4.3 Publicity of the Report ... 137
4.4.4 Implementation of the Report ... 139
4.5 Chapter Summary ... 142
References ... 142

Abstract In transitional societies where the rule of law is in limbo and state institutions are usually fragile, implementation of mechanisms to address gross human rights violations can prove to be an arduous journey, and the establishment of truth commissions in such contexts is filled with several uncertainties. In as much as the work of a truth commission depends on its enabling laws, the extent to which the commission's procedures comply with international human rights law is a defining element in meeting the outsized anticipations that usually accompany such

M. Yankson-Mensah, *Transitional Justice in Ghana*, International Criminal Justice Series 25, https://doi.org/10.1007/978-94-6265-379-5_4

mechanisms. In order to assess how the legal framework of Ghana's National Reconciliation Commission was implemented, this chapter employs normative and comparative approaches to analyse how the commission carried out and fulfilled its mandate. It also reflects on the commission's procedure, identifies the core challenges that hindered its work and assesses the strengths and weaknesses of the commission's report. The accentuation of the commission's structure, hearings and report provide insight into how the features and mandate of the National Reconciliation Commission defined and shaped its outcome.

Keywords National Reconciliation Commission · Challenges of Truth Commissions · Structure of the National Reconciliation Commission · Report of Truth Commissions · Implementation of Truth Commission Reports

4.1 Introductory Remarks

Following the establishment of a truth commission, a society can anticipate a variety of outcomes regarding how the commission's mandate is fulfilled. Bowden, Charlesworth and Farrall allude to Charles Dickens' novel *Great Expectations* to describe the extent to which high hopes accompany mechanisms for dealing with past human rights violations.[1] In reality, however, the path towards dealing with past human rights violations is like a roller-coaster ride, with many ups and downs. Regardless of a truth commission's mandate and features, its actual work could turn out differently from what it was perceived to be. In order to ascertain how the NRC fared in practice, this chapter discusses the commission's actual work, the challenges it faced and the measures it took in response to those challenges. In doing so, the chapter also compares the work of the NRC with that of truth commissions in other countries. In addition, the chapter discusses the final report and recommendations of the NRC, reactions to the work of the commission and the major steps that were taken to implement its recommendations.

4.2 The Work of the National Reconciliation Commission

The NRC Act was passed by Parliament in December 2001 and became effective on 11 January 2002.[2] On 6 May 2002 (two weeks after the appointment of the members of the NRC), the president of Ghana administered the respective oaths of office to the members of the NRC in conformity with the NRC Act and the 1992

[1]See Bowden et al. 2009, p. 3.

[2]See National Reconciliation Commission 2004, vol 1, para 2.1.1.

Constitution.[3] After its inauguration, the NRC was put through an orientation by the International Centre for Transitional Justice and a civil society body known as the Ghana Centre for Democratic Development.[4] Following its orientation, the NRC was able to come up with an interpretation for its mandate as well as a course of action to enable it achieve this mandate.

4.2.1 Interpretation and Implementation of the Mandate

The NRC interpreted its core mandate to entail 'seeking and promoting national reconciliation'.[5] In particular, this interpretation entailed providing a detailed account of human rights violations that occurred within the time frame for its investigations and suggesting measures for reparations and institutional reform.[6] The NRC also utilised doctrines of international human rights law and the common law to give what, in their view, amounted to broad interpretations to the types of human rights violations that it was mandated to investigate (i.e., 'killings, abductions, disappearances, detentions, torture, ill-treatment and seizure of properties').[7] Torture, for instance, was construed to include 'mock executions and forced cannibalism', whilst 'ill-treatment' included 'dehumanising treatment and some forms of administrative injustice'.[8]

From the outset, the commission decided that it could not hear petitions related to cases falling outside the period between 6 March 1957 and 7 January 1993, in light of the provisions of the NRC Act. Moreover, it would not hear cases that could not be categorised under any of the types of human rights violations expressly stated in its mandate.[9] In those instances, the named perpetrators in the petitions in question were not invited to appear before the commission.[10]

As stated in Chap. 3, the historical time frame that the NRC was mandated to investigate was limited to military regimes, although the commission could decide to hear cases that did not occur during military regimes.[11] In reality, however, the NRC resolved that it would not deny hearing cases that occurred in non-military regimes within the mandated period in order to achieve utmost national reconciliation. Thus, the commission received all petitions relating to human rights

[3]Ibid., vol 2, para 1.4.1.
[4]Ibid., vol 2, para 2.0.1.
[5]Ibid., vol 1, para 2.1.1; and vol 2, para 2.1.1.
[6]Ibid., vol 1, para 2.2.1; and vol 2, para 2.2.1.1.
[7]Ibid., vol 1, para 2.3.3.2.1 and s 4(a) of the NRC Act.
[8]Ibid., vol 2, para 2.3.3.2.1.
[9]Ibid., vol 1, para 2.3.3.4.1 at note 1.
[10]Ibid., vol 1, para 2.3.3.4.1 at note 1.
[11]About this aspect of the NRC's mandate, see Sect. 3.3.5 in Chap. 3 of this book.

violations that occurred between 6 March 1957 and 6 January 1993.[12] This move by the NRC was laudable, as doing otherwise would have given rise to issues of selectivity and created doubts about the credibility of the commission. Moreover, denying such victims access to the commission's work would have reduced the level of confidence in the commission's work. In Brazil, the failure of the Comissão Nacional da Verdade to gain support from the military in its investigations can be attributed partly to the skewed nature of the commission's mandate towards only the military regimes. Indeed, this factor was cited by the military in its criticism of the commission, that the mandate of the commission disregarded the opponents of the military regime.[13] In effect, the manner in which the NRC handled its mandate afforded victims from non-military regimes the same opportunities for seeking redress as afforded victims of cases that occurred during military regimes.

4.2.2 Structures and Offices

The main offices of the NRC were located in Accra. Most of the hearings and work of the commission were conducted from this location.[14] The commission also had zonal offices located in five other regions of Ghana.[15] The aim of the zonal offices was to enhance access to the commission's work in all parts of the country.[16] Although each zonal office was led by a manager, its activities were coordinated by the executive secretary, who oversaw the activities of the leaders of the zonal offices.[17] The structure of the NRC is shown in Fig. 4.1.

As indicated in Fig. 4.1, the NRC set up a secretariat, comprised of five sub-committees, and also created five thematic committees. The secretariat was led by an executive secretary who had been appointed by the president.[18] The five sub-committees of the secretariat dealt with the areas of finance and administration, investigations and research, legal issues, public affairs and community liaison and counselling and support services.[19]

[12]See National Reconciliation Commission 2004, vol 1, para 2.3.3.1.2.

[13]See Pensamento Do Clube Militar. http://clubemilitar.com.br/pensamento-do-clube-militar-14/. Accessed 15 October 2019.

[14]Although the NRC initially operated from a short-term location at Ghana's Independence Square Building in Accra, it was eventually based permanently at the Old Parliament House in Accra. See National Reconciliation Commission 2004, vol 1, para 1.11; vol 2, para 1.14.1.

[15]According to the NRC, zonal offices were established rather than regional offices as a result of the lack of funds and logistics to set up offices in all ten regions of Ghana. See National Reconciliation Commission 2004, vol 2, para 1.10.1.

[16]See National Reconciliation Commission 2004, vol 2, para 1.10.1.

[17]Ibid., vol 2, para 1.12.1; and vol 1, para 1.10.3.

[18]Ibid., vol 1 para 1.10.1; and vol 2, para 1.5.1.

[19]Ibid., vol 1, para 1.10.1; and vol 2, para 1.10.1.

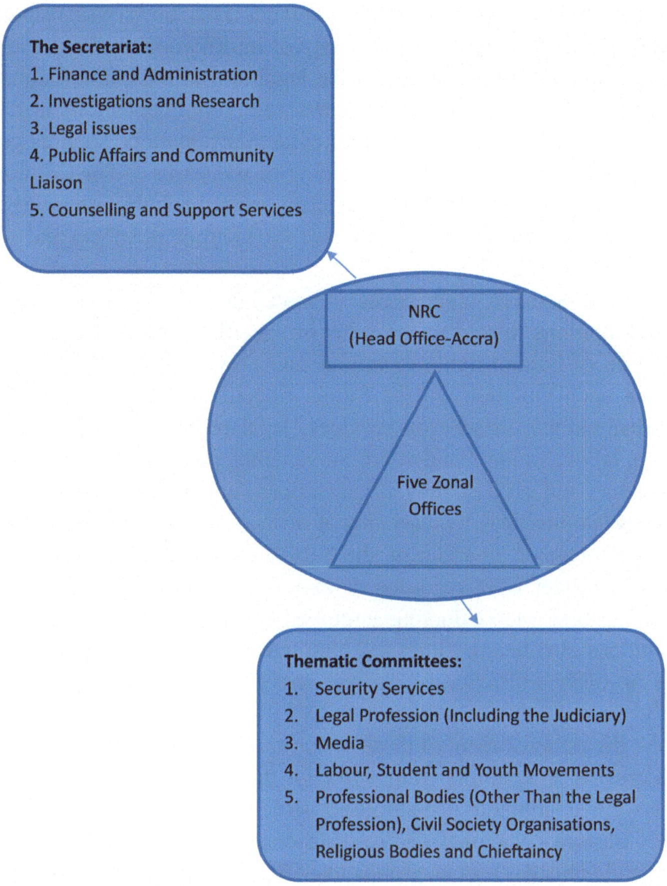

Fig. 4.1 Organisational structure of the NRC (*Source* The author 2018)

Each of these sub-committees was headed by a director and assigned different functions.[20] The major roles of the Finance and Administration Directorate was to manage all financial matters of the commission such as its planned expenses, remuneration of commissioners and staff, acquisition of logistics and maintenance of the required financial records.[21] The Public Affairs and Community Liaison Directorate was in charge of the commission's public relations. Specifically, this directorate publicised the work of the commission and all its activities, educated the public about the NRC and was in charge of transmitting information from the commission to the public.[22] The Investigations and Research Directorate oversaw

[20]Ibid., vol 2, paras 1.11.1, 1.13.0.

[21]Ibid., para 1.13.1(1).

[22]Ibid., para 1.13.1(2).

statements and petitions that the NRC received. This body was responsible for conducting enquiries to ascertain the veracity of information received and reporting its findings.[23] The Legal Directorate, as the legal arm of the commission, provided legal services, such as provision of its views and recommendations in response to investigative findings.[24] It also dealt with evidentiary matters, such as preparation and service of subpoenas as well as examining of witnesses.[25] The Counselling and Support Directorate fulfilled the NRC's victim-centred role by providing advice as well as psychological and emotional support for victims, members and staff of the commission.[26]

The six other thematic committees indicated in Fig. 4.1 were established to conduct investigations related to the roles of specific governmental institutions in the perpetration of human rights violations and how such government institutions could prevent such violations in the future. Specifically, the committees were to conduct investigations on security services, legal profession (including the judiciary), media, labour, student and youth movements, professional bodies (other than legal profession) and civil society organisations, and religious bodies and chieftaincy.[27] These committees, comprising of at least five individuals each, were all led by an NRC member. In addition, the NRC's chairman, executive secretary and senior research officer were regarded as ex-officio members of all these committees.[28] In the course of conducting enquiries on their respective thematic areas, these committees also heard witnesses, although such witnesses were not made to take oaths or make affirmations, as was the case in the commission's regular hearings.[29]

Arguably, the establishment of these structures within the NRC served to prevent delays and created an enabling framework for the commission's work. Other truth commissions have adopted decentralised structures to facilitate their work. In Brazil, the Comissão Nacional da Verdade decentralised its work amongst three committees and created 13 focus groups to enable it carry out its work effectively.[30]

[23]Ibid., para 1.13.1(3).

[24]Ibid., para 1.13.1(4).

[25]Ibid., para 1.13.1(4).

[26]Ibid., para 1.13.1(5).

[27]Ibid., para 2.7.1.

[28]Ibid., para 2.7.2.

[29]Ibid., para 2.7.3.

[30]The said three committees were in the areas of research and systemization of information, liaison with civil society groups and institutions, and external communications. The 13 focus areas as outlined by the commission related to dictatorship and gender; the Araguaia armed group; contextualization, grounds and reasons for the 1964 civil-military coup; dictatorship and the justice system; dictatorship and repression of workers and trade union movement; the repression structure; the dead and disappeared; serious human rights violations against indigenous people; Operation Condor; the role of churches during the dictatorship; military persecution; human rights violations of Brazilians abroad and foreigners in Brazil; and the dictatorial military rule. See Comissão Nacional da Verdade 2015. http://www.cnv.gov.br/institucional-acesso-informacao/grupos-de-trabalho.html. Accessed 19 October 2019. Despite the existence of these divisions, the unfixed

Likewise in South Africa, the TRC was made up of three committees in charge of 'amnesties, reparations and rehabilitation and human rights violations'.[31] In contrast, the Liberian TRC failed to create an organisational and staffing framework prior to commencement of its work, and the commission's initial operations were weighed down significantly, hampering its progress.[32] Based on these instances, the decentralisation of the NRC's work can be seen as a positive step towards successful implementation of its mandate.

4.2.3 Statement Taking and Processing

The NRC commenced taking statements from victims on 3 September 2002, with more than 120 petitions received on the first day.[33] In total, the commission received 4, 240 from inside and outside Ghana.[34]

The commission utilised two main methods to obtain information from the public.[35] One approach was for individuals to report to any of the NRC's offices for their statements to be recorded by trained statement takers. The statement takers recorded the received information onto a standardised form in English. The recorded information was then read by the statement takers to confirm the petitioner's understanding and the accuracy of the recorded information, after which the petitioner was required to sign or thumbprint the form.[36] Alternatively, literate petitioners could complete the statement form on their own or send a prepared statement to the NRC's office. Such prepared statements were thereafter attached to the standardised statement form for completion by the petitioner. This method was

nature of the Comissão Nacional da Verdade's leadership position gave rise to some complaints from the commission's staff, regarding inconsistency caused by regular changes in the commission's leadership. It was alleged that each new leader of the commission came with new demands. See Magalhães and Leitão 2013, http://www1.folha.uol.com.br/poder/2013/04/1262356-apos-quase-um-ano-comissao-da-verdade-e-alvo-de-criticas.shtml. Accessed 15 October 2019.

[31]See South Africa, Promotion of National Unity and Reconciliation Act No. 34 of 1995, assented to 19 July 1995 (entered into force 1 December 1995) (South African TRC Act), s 3(3).

[32]The slow progress of its work was also compounded by misunderstandings between some international workers of the commission and its members. This reduced its credibility both locally and internationally. See James-Allen et al. 2010, pp. 7–8, who write that one member of the commission's International Technical Advisory Committee vacated his position as a result of tensions between him and the commissioners. In reality, the International Technical Advisory Committee had no other members during a greater period of the commission's work because one appointed member never assumed his position, whilst the third member assumed her position for a brief period.

[33]See BBC News 2002. http://news.bbc.co.uk/2/hi/africa/2235853.stm. Accessed 9 October 2019; and National Reconciliation Commission 2004, vol 1, para 2.5.

[34]See National Reconciliation Commission 2004, vol 1, paras 2.3.2.4, 2.5.2.1.

[35]Ibid., vol 1, para 2.3.2.

[36]Ibid., vol 1, para 2.3.2; and vol 2, para 2.3.2.1.

particularly useful for petitioners abroad who could not go to Ghana immediately to provide their statements.[37]

The commission also engaged in what it called 'a mopping-up exercise' to reach individuals in remote areas or individuals unable to report to its offices by virtue of their financial incapability. This exercise was made possible through the financial and technical assistance of the Ghana Center for Democratic Development. As a result, the NRC was able to visit rural communities where it educated the population about its work and took statements from individuals who could otherwise not give their statements.[38]

Statements received by the commission were first evaluated by its senior statement taker, who was supposed to forward the statement to either the commission's legal department, for a legal opinion or the department in charge of investigations.[39] Enquiries were conducted on cases that were sent to the investigations department, after which the discoveries were forwarded to the legal department.[40] The legal department then provided its suggestions to the executive secretary, who made further suggestions to the commission.[41]

The commission could subsequently decide whether the matter would be a subject of public hearing.[42] Various paradigms were used to select the cases to be heard at the commission's public proceedings. The NRC considered factors such as the level of severity of the human rights violations, whether the case required further investigations, whether investigations on the case had been concluded to enable hearing to commence and which cases were referred first to the commission.[43]

4.2.4 Conduct of Investigations

In fulfilment of its investigative function, the NRC requested individuals who had been accused of human rights violations to provide written responses to their accusations. Perpetrators who were to testify to the commission were afforded a chance to appear before the body during its hearings, in order to be cross-examined under oath.[44]

---

[37]Ibid., vol 1, para 2.3.2; and vol 2, para 2.3.2.1.

[38]Ibid., vol 1, para 2.3.2.3; and vol 2 para 2.3.2.3.

[39]Ibid., vol 1, para 2.5.4.1.

[40]Ibid., para 2.5.4.1.

[41]Ibid., para 2.5.4.1.

[42]Ibid., para 2.5.4.1.

[43]Ibid., para 2.5.5.1, and para 2.5.5.1 at note 4, where the commission notes that although it did not underestimate any of the human rights violations reported, it ranked killing as more severe than other violations such as denial of a person's financial entitlements, because of its irreversibility. In the same vein, torture was ranked higher in severity than wrongful dismissal.

[44]National Reconciliation Commission 2004, vol 1, para 2.3.3.6.1.

In ascertaining the veracity of the information that it received, the commission used the civil standard of proof (i.e., on the preponderance of probabilities).[45] Moreover, as mentioned above, the NRC established six thematic committees,[46] aside from the committees within its secretariat, to ascertain the role played by state and civil society bodies in the human rights violations.[47] The commission also undertook exhumation exercises to identify the individuals buried in unmarked graves across the country.[48]

4.2.5 *Hearings*

The NRC commenced its public hearings on 14 January 2003 in Accra. Subsequently, it conducted public hearings in the other regional capitals of the country.[49] The procedure for the commission's public hearings was as follows. The witness was made to either swear an oath or make an affirmation, after which the commission's lawyer led the witness in providing evidence.[50] In its hearings, the commission advertently used the term 'witness' to represent perpetrators and victims alike, for the sole reason that doing otherwise would jeopardise the course of reconciliation.[51] This explains why all individuals were led by the NRC's lawyers in giving their testimony.[52] In practice, however, the commission differentiated between witnesses who had filed petitions with it and those who appeared in response to a filed petition.[53] After being examined, witnesses were questioned again by members of the commission, if necessary, to provide further clarification. Also, any individuals who wished to respond to the already given testimony could cross-examine the witness at this stage, using a lawyer of their choice.[54] Subsequently, alleged perpetrators and other individuals could also provide their testimony, led by a lawyer of their choice.[55] All hearings of the commission were

---

[45] Ibid., para 2.3.3.6.2.

[46] See Sect. 4.2.2.

[47] Ibid., para 2.3.3.6.4.

[48] See Republic of Ghana, National Reconciliation Commission Act, 2002, Act 611 (NRC Act), s 4 (f); and National Reconciliation Commission 2004, vol 1, paras 2.3.3.7.1, 2.3.3.7.2.

[49] See National Reconciliation Commission 2004, vol 1, para 2.6.3.1.

[50] Ibid., paras 2.6.2.1, 2.3.4.1.

[51] Ibid., vol 2, para 2.3.4.1.

[52] Ibid., vol 1, para 2.3.4.1.

[53] See Valji 2006, p. 8 at note 31.

[54] It must be noted however that it was not mandatory for perpetrators to provide such testimony. See National Reconciliation Commission 2004, vol 1, paras 2.6.2.2, 2.6.2.1.

[55] See National Reconciliation Commission 2004, vol 1, para 2.6.2.2.

recorded in English and aired live on television by the Ghana Broadcasting Corporation.[56]

In compliance with the provisions of Article 281(1) of the 1992 Constitution and Section 12 of the NRC Act, the NRC also held hearings in camera. In selecting cases for such hearings, the primary considerations for the commission were the nation's security, the safety of the witness and whether hearing the matter in public would compromise the 'public good, morality or decency'.[57]

The nature of human rights violations heard by the commission were killings, abductions, disappearances, maiming, torture, detentions without trial, ill-treatment, invasion of property rights, interference with the right to work, hostage-taking, abuse of judicial process and violation of the right to die in dignity.[58] The NRC's hearings lasted for one year and six months (between 14 January 2003 and 13 July 2004). During this period, 1,866 witnesses appeared at the public hearings.[59] The commission heard 3,840 petitions, out of the total of 4,240; the unheard petitions fell outside the mandate of the commission.[60]

In comparison with truth commissions in other countries, where even larger numbers of petitions were received, the number of witnesses who appeared at the NRC's public hearings is relatively high. In Nigeria, for instance, the commission received over 10,000 petitions but selected only 40 cases to be heard in public, using the criteria of whether the case represented a 'gross violation of human rights' in accordance with its mandate.[61] Similarly, the South African TRC received over 21,000 petitions, but only 2,000 were heard in the public hearings.[62] The high number of public hearings in the case of the NRC is a positive feature because it provided an avenue for a large number of victims to narrate their experiences and express their emotions.

4.2.6 Assistance of Witnesses

In its report, the NRC identified several steps that were taken to assist victims and other witnesses. For instance, the commission acquired a list of lawyers from the Ghana Bar Association willing to provide free legal aid; these lawyers provided

[56]See Wain 2003, p. 8.

[57]See National Reconciliation Commission 2004, vol 1, para 2.6.4.2.

[58]Ibid., para 5.0.2.

[59]Ibid., para 5.0.1.

[60]The commission considered these petitions to exceed its mandate because they did not fall within the mandated period for the commission's investigations (i.e., the said cases occurred either prior to 6 March 1957 or after 6 January 1993) or were not about a public official or public institution as was required in the NRC's mandate. See National Reconciliation Commission 2004, vol 1, para 5.0.1.

[61]See Human Rights Violations Investigation Commission 2002, vol 4, para 1.12.

[62]See Gready 2011, p. 160.

legal services to individuals who could not afford to pay for these services.[63] According to the commission, this was done to ensure utmost observance of fair hearing principles.

The NRC also conducted extensive public outreach programmes in Ghanaian languages and English in different parts of the country. These outreach programmes served as platforms for educating and providing awareness of the work of the commission as well as for encouraging victims to appear before it.[64] Members of the general public who had knowledge of past human rights violations were invited to report them to the commission, regardless of whether or not they were victims. Such individuals were to help identify victims who would otherwise not be known to the commission.[65]

The form used to take statements from victims was designed to be as user-friendly as possible, to simplify the process by which victims relayed their stories. Moreover, professional assistance and interpretation services were provided for victims to help them complete of the forms.

Victims and petitioners were also given the advantage of having access to free counselling services, medical screening, first aid and other medical responses in instances where they had difficulty in communicating their experiences.[66] The commission provided counselling services to victims whilst taking their statements and during its hearings (whether in public or in camera). Some victims even received counselling services in their homes, when necessary.[67] Witnesses who travelled long distances to reach the offices of the NRC were reimbursed with the cost of their transportation, when they asked for such reimbursements.[68]

4.3 Challenges

Despite setting out a very comprehensive, well-planned structure and procedure, the NRC experienced a number of hurdles in the pursuit of its mandate. These have been analysed below.

[63] See National Reconciliation Commission 2004, vol 1, para 2.3.3.4.3.
[64] Ibid., para 2.3.3.5.2.
[65] Ibid., para 2.3.3.5.2.
[66] Ibid., para 2.3.3.5.2.
[67] Ibid., para 2.5.3.1.
[68] Ibid., para 2.3.3.5.2.

4.3.1 Inadequacy of Funds and Logistics

When the NRC was established, questions were raised about the use of state funds for a reconciliation exercise when more fundamental challenges such as poverty needed to be addressed in the country.[69] In the wake of this criticism, it is not surprising that the commission did not gain all the funds and resources it required.

Funding from the government to the commission was grossly inadequate and inconsistent, thereby hampering the body's investigative abilities.[70] The commission's required budget was initially assessed at five million USD.[71] However, due to constraints, the budget was subsequently cut down to three million USD, two-thirds of which was provided by the government. The remainder of this sum was generated from international donors.[72] For instance, the United States Agency for International Development provided the commission with a grant of 25,000 USD.[73]

Truth commissions in states that have experienced long periods of conflict or political dictatorship often face financial difficulties, due to the poor economic conditions in such countries. Indeed, the financial plights of the NRC are minimal in comparison with those of Liberia and Nigeria. In Liberia, the truth commission's initially proposed budget of 13 million USD had to be reduced to eight million, due to lack of funding. Eventually, the Liberian TRC was forced to halt its work for nearly one year because of financial constraints.[74] Similarly in Nigeria, the Oputa Panel was rendered inactive for nearly one year after its inauguration as a result of unavailability of funds. The commission's budget was never agreed upon, and it was able to commence its work only after it obtained a donation of 400,000 USD from the Ford Foundation.[75]

Although the extent of the NRC's financial difficulties was comparatively limited, there is no doubt that it hampered the commission's processes in significant ways. For instance, the live television broadcast of the proceedings were stopped before the commission completed its work.[76] The state's failure to provide full financial support to the commission thus deviated from the requisite needs of Ghana's truth-telling process.

---

[69]See Valji 2006, p. 4.

[70]Ibid., p. 19.

[71]See Ameh 2006, p. 359.

[72]See Hayner 2011, p. 57.

[73]Aside this grant, other bodies like the Open Society Initiative for West Africa provided some funding and logistics, whilst the International Centre for Transitional Justice provided the commission with technical assistance. See National Reconciliation Commission 2004, vol 1, p. ii.

[74]See Wiebelhaus-Brahm 2013, p. 283, who writes that some expected international donations for the commission's work were delayed, thereby compounding the commission's financial difficulties.

[75]About the lack of agreement on the commission's budget, see Samuel and Green 2017, p. 111 at note 134. See also Yusuf 2013, p. 337.

[76]Ameh 2006, p. 359.

4.3.2 *Weak Investigative Capacity*

Another challenge faced by the NRC was its inadequate capacity to carry out investigations effectively. Owing to funding problems, the commission worked with a lower number of staff and compromised on the expertise it required for its work.[77] For instance, less than halfway into the completion of its work, the commission laid off about 50% of its staff. Also, the commission resorted to the services of former police officers in its work, rather than utilising the services of specifically trained individuals. This hampered the body's investigations, as victims and witnesses felt intimidated by the presence of police and felt unable to freely narrate their experiences.[78] This state of affairs also likely resulted in low turnout of petitions related to human rights violations involving sexual and gender-based violence.[79]

The commission's investigation problems were further compounded by the long lapse of time between its establishment and the occurrence of the human rights violations it was mandated to investigate. Many victims and perpetrators had died long before the commission was established, whilst the whereabouts of individuals in exile could not be traced.[80] In the circumstances, the commission did not have the benefit of all witnesses needed in its truth-finding venture, worsening its already weak investigative capacity.

In an effort to remedy its investigative lapses, the NRC tried to use public hearings to obtain as much information as possible, expanding the purpose of the public hearings beyond serving as a means for victims to air their grievances.[81] Nevertheless, the weak investigative tendencies adversely affected the commission, as many Ghanaians started to question its competence. Also, it has been averred that about 70% of the cases that were presented to the NRC were not investigated, before the petitioners in those cases were publicly heard in the commission's proceedings. The commission focused more on the petitions of people who claimed they had personally suffered human rights violations, disregarding petitions from relatives of victims who did not know what had happened to their relations.[82]

The commission's failure to undertake comprehensive investigations created an avenue for individuals to propagate lies at the hearings, knowing that their

[77]Ibid., p. 360.

[78]It is also believed that the predominantly male staff base of the NRC intimidated witnesses sometimes, owing to traditional and social beliefs in Ghana, which make it difficult for female victims to freely open up to the male statement takers. See Valji 2006, p. 20.

[79]See Valji 2006, p. 20, who iterates a respondent's opinion that although it was common knowledge within Ghanaian society that several rapes and sexual assaults occurred during the era of the Provisional National Defence Council, a minute number of such cases were actually reported to the commission. On this subject, see also Hayner 2011, p. 57.

[80]See Oduro 2013, p. 321.

[81]See Valji 2006, p. 19, where she refers to this assertion made by a respondent she interviewed.

[82]Ansah-Koi K, Department of Political Science, University of Ghana, Personal Interview (18 August 2016).

assertions would never be verified.[83] Critics of the commission cited examples of witnesses giving testimonies that were likely untrue. For instance, the main opposition political party, the National Democratic Congress, in a memorandum written to the NRC on 24 February 2003, cited the testimony of a woman who had stated at the commission's public hearings that members of the military inserted gunpowder and pepper into her genitals. According to the memorandum, there was a high likelihood that this testimony was untrue, given that the Ghanaian military had ceased using gunpowder at the time of the purported incident. The memorandum thus bemoaned the fact that the veracity of this testimony, despite its obvious loopholes, had not been verified by the commission.[84]

4.3.3 Condemnation of and Resistance to the Commission's Work

Numerous criticisms levelled against the NRC in the course of its existence also risked derailing its work. To begin with, the commission's proceedings were criticised for having a legalistic outlook. It was alleged that the venue used for public hearings resembled a courtroom. Also, critics asserted that the proceedings involved too many lawyers.[85] These critics noted that the chairman of the commission, who was a retired Supreme Court judge, and two other members, who were lawyers, treated the proceedings as if they were courtroom proceedings.[86] According to critics, the legalistic nature of the commission's proceedings did not create a conducive forum for witnesses to recount their experiences.[87] In response to this criticism, the commission attempted to make witnesses feel more at ease.[88] Nevertheless, not all legal features of the commission's proceedings were removed. Some, such as the broad involvement of lawyers, remained throughout its work.[89]

---

[83]See Valji 2006, p. 20, where she cites this assertion made by a respondent she interviewed.

[84]For this and further examples of such possibly untrue testimonies, see Ghana Web 2003a. http://www.ghanaweb.com/GhanaHomePage/economy/artikel.php?ID=33294. Accessed 27 October 2019; and Gyimah-Boadi 2003, p. 3, where he discusses this issue.

[85]In his description of the NRC proceedings, Gyimah-Boadi 2003, p. 1, writes that members of the commission sat on an elevated platform that overlooked the witness and an interpreter, with perpetrators and their lawyers seated at one remote side of the witness and the NRC's workers on another side. The witness was led in evidence by the NRC's lawyer and then discharged. See also Valji 2006, p. 12; and Wain 2003, p. 8.

[86]See Valji 2006, p. 11.

[87]Ibid., p. 12.

[88]See Gyimah-Boadi 2003, p. 2.

[89]See Valji 2006, p. 11.

The NRC was also criticised for being biased. In particular, it was alleged that witnesses who appeared before the commission were given different treatment, depending on their political affiliation and whether they were perpetrators.[90] The leadership of the commission also proved to be a source of controversy, as the chairman was considered predisposed to bias because of bitter past encounters with the opposition.[91] It was asserted that the chairman treated some witnesses harshly, especially when such witnesses were affiliated to the political party of former president Jerry John Rawlings.[92] On one occasion, the chairman made a hostile comment about the testimony of a witness from the opposition party, which unknown to him, was captured by his microphone and was heard live on national television.[93]

Other key instances of the allegations of bias against the chairman can be cited. In March 2003, the major opposition party at the time (the National Democratic Congress) wrote a petition to the president of Ghana seeking the dismissal of the NRC's chairman, on the grounds of the chairman's alleged bias.[94] In the petition, the party claimed that the chairman bore grudges against them because of past bitter encounters he had with their party.[95] The petition alleged that on account of those past experiences, the chairman was not neutral and should be dismissed.[96] In support of these claims, the petition described instances when the chairman, during the commission's hearings, acted hostilely towards people affiliated to either the Provisional National Defence Council or the Armed Forces Revolutionary Council, both led by Jerry John Rawlings.[97] The petition was, however, not successful. Following this incident, another opposition party in the country, the Convention People's Party, also criticised the work of the NRC, claiming it was biased and fraught with various irregularities. According to this critique, the commission was

[90]Ibid., pp. 8–9.

[91]See for instance Asamoah 2014, p. 502, who writes that the chairman was one avenue through which members of the opposition were treated in an unfair manner; and Ghana Web 2003b. http://www.ghanaweb.com/GhanaHomePage/NewsArchive/Remove-NRC-Chairman-NDC-34445 Accessed 13 October 2019.

[92]Regarding the biased attitude of the Chairman, see Asamoah 2014, pp. 502–504, where he describes his own appearance before the commission. See Oduro 2013, p. 321; and Valji 2006, pp. 8–9.

[93]See Asamoah 2014, p. 502; and Oduro 2013, p. 321.

[94]See Ghana Web 2003b. http://www.ghanaweb.com/GhanaHomePage/NewsArchive/Remove-NRC-Chairman-NDC-34445. Accessed 13 October 2019; and Gyimah-Boadi 2003, p. 5.

[95]For instance, the petition cited a past incident where the property of the Chairman's father was confiscated by their party during their political regime. Also, the petition stated that the Chairman's father was a victim of the kangaroo courts that were established by the government of the Provisional National Defence Council. See Ghana Web 2003b. http://www.ghanaweb.com/GhanaHomePage/NewsArchive/Remove-NRC-Chairman-NDC-34445. Accessed 13 October 2019.

[96]See Ghana Web 2003b. http://www.ghanaweb.com/GhanaHomePage/NewsArchive/Remove-NRC-Chairman-NDC-34445. Accessed 13 October 2019.

[97]Ibid.

prioritising cases related to specific military regimes, whilst disregarding other military regimes.[98] On another occasion, a former national security chief who was a prominent member of the National Democratic Congress initiated a lawsuit against the chairman of the NRC, alleging that the chairman had treated him with hostility and unfairness. He asked the court to order the chairman to act in a manner that would uphold the commission's independence and continued 'credibility, impartiality or integrity'.[99] The suit was dismissed by the court, which stated that the conduct of the chairman did not constitute bias according to the NRC Act's description of the commission's mandate and how the commission should conduct its activities.[100] Although the numerous allegations against the NRC were never substantiated and could, in fact, have been politically motivated, they undoubtedly reduced the credibility of the commission in the eyes of many Ghanaians.

Indeed, because truth commissions are usually established in highly charged political environments, it is rare that a commission completes its work without becoming the subject of widespread criticism and condemnation. In some instances, a truth commission may face security threats as a result of intense opposition to its work. In Peru, for instance, the Comisión de la Verdad y Reconciliación encountered widespread criticism and antagonism towards its work, including eight lawsuits against the commission's chairman, following release of the body's report.[101] The findings of the commission were challenged fiercely by some political factions and members of the country's military, and death threats were made against the chairman of the commission.[102] In Brazil, the Comissão Nacional da Verdade was criticised for weak investigative tendencies because of its inability to obtain enough testimonies from the armed forces, who many believed to be the major force behind the country's past human rights violations.[103] Less than halfway into the completion of its work, the Comissão Nacional da Verdade was severally criticised for allegedly being unable to reveal any new relevant information about past human rights violations perpetrated by the military.[104] In Liberia, the truth commission's credibility was endangered when three of its members were accused by witnesses of

[98]See the Daily Graphic 2003. http://www.ghanaweb.com/GhanaHomePage/NewsArchive/NRC-Is-Biased-CPP-38400. Accessed 13 February 2018.

[99]Ghana News Agency 2004a. http://www.ghanaweb.com/GhanaHomePage/NewsArchive/Court-dismisses-Tsikata-s-application-against-NRC-Chairman-614. Accessed 13 October 2019.

[100]Ibid.

[101]See Root 2013, pp. 426–427.

[102]Ibid., p. 427. See also Amnesty International 2004, p. 27. https://www.essex.ac.uk/armedcon/themes/international_courts_tribunals/amnestyaugust2004.pdf. Accessed 18 October 2019; and International Centre for Transitional Justice. https://www.ictj.org/news/ten-years-after-peru-truth-commission. Accessed 18 October 2019.

[103]See Deutsche Welle. http://www.dw.com/pt/brasil-encara-responsabilidade-na-ditadura-diz-historiadora/a-18112450. Accessed 20 October 2019.

[104]See Magalhães and Leitão 2013, http://www1.folha.uol.com.br/poder/2013/04/1262356-apos-quase-um-ano-comissao-da-verdade-e-alvo-de-criticas.shtml. Accessed 15 October 2019.

having participated actively in the Liberian civil war.[105] The South African TRC and the Oputa Panel had to battle with lawsuits challenging their powers.[106]

The examples above illustrate the high degree of adversity that can characterise the working environments of truth commissions. In the midst of such criticisms, the credibility of a truth commission can be maintained if such criticisms are handled carefully. Allegations of bias must be investigated and when necessary, neutral commissioners must be appointed to handle cases where commissioners may be biased. In the Ghanaian case, the commission's lack of credibility was worsened by the continued leadership of the chairman despite the allegations of bias. Arguably, the failure of the president to address the opposition's petition for removal of the chairman reaffirmed their view that the NRC was a political witch-hunt. This explains why the commission never gained serious recognition from members of the opposition.

4.3.4 Political Resistance to the Commission's Work

Although the NRC was established nearly a decade after the end of the last military regime, its work was regularly hampered by the continuous influence of prominent political figures from the military era, who felt that the national reconciliation exercise was meant to discredit their reputation.[107] The initial political disagreements that characterised the drafting stage of the NRC bill in Parliament, with respect to the historical time frame of its mandate and the manner of selecting its members, raised doubts about the intentions of political leaders in advocating for the establishment of the commission.[108]

Key incidents during the existence of the commission indicate the continued political resistance to the body's work. On the day of the inaugural ceremony for the first hearing of the NRC, all opposition political party officers invited to the event did not attend, with the exception of representatives from the Convention Peoples Party.[109] Also, on 24 February 2003, the National Democratic Congress forwarded a memorandum to the NRC in which it cited a number of occurrences in

---

[105]See James-Allen et al. 2010, p. 9.

[106]In South Africa, one of the country's ex-Presidents was sued, following his failure to honour a subpoena invitation by the commission. In another lawsuit, an order was obtained against the South African TRC to provide individuals who were to be named as perpetrators in its hearings with due notice. In a third suit, the commission's authority to award amnesties was the subject of one lawsuit, in which it was claimed that this power was unconstitutional. The suit was however unsuccessful. See Hayner 2011, pp. 30–31.

[107]See Gyimah-Boadi 2002, p. 3; and Valji 2006, p. 5.

[108]Regarding the debates that surrounded the establishment of the NRC, see Boafo-Arthur 2006, pp. 138–145; and Boafo-Arthur 2005, pp. 118–124.

[109]Ghana Web 2003c. http://www.ghanaweb.com/GhanaHomePage/NewsArchive/NDC-Other-Parties-Boycott-NRC-Hearings-31573. Accessed 13 February 2019.

the commission's proceedings that indicated to the party that the commission was merely a tool for furthering the New Patriotic Party's political agenda. In the memorandum, the National Democratic Congress cited instances regarding procedural impropriety. It alleged that the members of the National Democratic Congress had not been given equal opportunity to accurately respond to allegations made against them.[110] The memorandum expressed doubts about the accuracy of the commission's investigations, citing already given testimonies at the NRC's hearings, which, in their view, were blatantly untrue.[111] Although the commission attempted to refute some of these allegations, the accusations undoubtedly sowed seeds of doubt regarding the body's competence.[112]

Apart from the above incidents, the NRC had to contend with episodes of verbal abuse from key opposition figures. The commission became an object of name-calling. It was nicknamed the 'Nail Rawlings Commission' and was publicly referred to as an illegal body and a medium for propagating falsehood about the past military regime.[113] Moreover, members of the opposition regularly subjected the commission to negative propaganda and expressed cynicism about its competence through the media.[114] In particular, the continued presence and popularity of former president Rawlings on the political scene hampered the work of the commission.[115] Regardless that such name-calling was a product of politics, it undeniably diminished the NRC's credibility.

The harsh political antagonism experienced by the NRC was also seen in Brazil and Ecuador. In Brazil, the problems of the Comissão Nacional da Verdade did not stem from political mudslinging but was rather posed by the power wielded by the military and the minimal control exercised over the military by the presidency.[116] Early attempts by former president Luiz Inácio Lula da Silva to establish the truth

---

[110] See Ghana Web 2003a. http://www.ghanaweb.com/GhanaHomePage/economy/artikel.php?ID=33294. Accessed 27 October 2019; and Gyimah-Boadi 2003, p. 3. See also Alidu 2010, pp. 163–164.

[111] See Ghana Web 2003a. http://www.ghanaweb.com/GhanaHomePage/economy/artikel.php?ID=33294; and Gyimah-Boadi 2003, p. 3.

[112] See Alidu 2010, pp. 163–164.

[113] For instance, a former National Security Chief from the regime of the Provisional National Defence Council, alleged in a media briefing that the NRC was making attempts to ambush him with untruthful witnesses. See the Ghanaian Chronicle 2004. http://www.ghanaweb.com/GhanaHomePage/NewsArchive/Kojo-T-Raises-Alarm-NRC-Planning-To-Ambush-me-60506. Accessed 13 October 2019. See also Alidu 2010, pp. 156–157.

[114] For instances of such negative propaganda, see Gyimah-Boadi 2002, p. 3.

[115] In one instance, the former President alleged on radio that lies had been concocted by affiliates of the ruling party at the hearings of the NRC. In his view, such lies were part of a grand scheme by the ruling party to divert the minds of Ghanaians from the failures of their government. See the Ghanaian Lens 2004. http://www.ghanaweb.com/GhanaHomePage/NewsArchive/Rawlings-Grants-Interview-On-The-Lies-At-The-NRC-61820. Accessed 13 October 2019; and Valji 2006, p. 5.

[116] See Quinalha 2014. http://ohrh.law.ox.ac.uk/50-years-later-still-in-search-of-truth-challenges-facing-truth-commissions-in-brazil/. Accessed 15 October 2019.

commission were met with stiff resistance from the military, some of whom threatened to vacate their posts.[117] After the establishment of the Brazilian truth commission by the government of Dilma Rousseff, the military persisted in their resistance towards the Comissão Nacional da Verdade. This resistance and the limits that the military placed on the commission's access to military records were major challenges that jeopardised the commission's investigations.[118] In Ecuador, the truth commission created in 2008 faced similar political opposition from ex-president Febres Cordero, who had led the country's most abusive political regime. Other members of the opposition and the army also resisted its work fiercely.[119]

These examples show that the work of truth commissions can hardly be divorced from political factors. Nevertheless, the ability of a truth commission to surpass political interference lies in how it manoeuvres through existing political conditions to undertake its work in an objective and credible manner. In the case of the NRC, an overriding factor that helped the commission to finish its work was its focus on its set task, not allowing its affairs to be dictated by the occurrences on the political landscape.

4.3.5 Difficulty in Engaging Perpetrators

The work of the NRC was also adversely affected by the unwillingness of perpetrators to divulge information to the commission. This situation, which has been partly attributed to the political atmosphere in Ghana at the time, created an impression that the perpetrators were not remorseful for their actions.[120] Most of the perpetrators appearing before the commission were prominent members of either the ruling party or the main opposition party, who felt that any information disclosed to the commission would adversely affect their political credibility. Thus, political figures who appeared as witnesses before the commission used the platform to save face and earn political credibility, instead of honestly recounting their

[117]Duffy 2010. http://news.bbc.co.uk/2/hi/8451109.stm. Accessed 15 October 2019.

[118]The Comissão Nacional da Verdade was unable to effectively trace disappeared and dead individuals owing to the minimal support they obtained from the country's military. In one instance, the commission's attempt to obtain certain evidential records from an ex-military official was put on hold for about six months, due to an injunction that was obtained by the military official's wife. Eventually, the injunction was overturned, thereby enabling the Comissão Nacional da Verdade to have access to the said records. See Arruda 2014. http://politica.estadao.com.br/blogs/roldao-arruda/comissao-tera-acesso-a-informacoes-sobre-militar-apontado-como-chefe-da-casa-da-morte/. Accessed 15 October 2019; Folha de São Paulo 2014. http://www1.folha.uol.com.br/poder/2014/12/1558801-grupo-fracassa-na-tentativa-de-encontrar-mortos-e-desaparecidos.shtml. Accessed 15 October 2019; and see Quinalha 2014. http://ohrh.law.ox.ac.uk/50-years-later-still-in-search-of-truth-challenges-facing-truth-commissions-in-brazil/. Accessed 15 October 2019.

[119]See Hayner 2011, p. 69.

[120]On this subject, see Valji 2006, p. 13.

experiences to the commission.[121] Also, perpetrators who appeared before the commission refuted the allegations made against them or remained unrepentant about their past actions, at times even appearing defensive.[122] These difficulties triggered high drama during the NRC's hearings, with perpetrators rebutting with counter-allegations against victims, rather than apologising.[123] In light of these circumstances, doubts began to emerge about whether the commission intended to reconcile the country.[124]

Although the commission was not at fault for this situation, the way it handled key witnesses exacerbated it further. A notable example was the manner in which the commission handled the appearance of former president Jerry John Rawlings. Pursuant to its subpoena powers under the NRC Act, the commission had sent a request to the former president, in which he was given a deadline to respond to some allegations about certain murder and torture cases.[125] By virtue of their lack of contentment with the responses he provided, the NRC eventually invited him to appear before it in person.[126] Considering the large number of petitions made to the commission involving human rights violations committed during Rawlings' two political regimes, it was not surprising that his invitation aroused interest in Ghanaians, who eagerly waited to see the outcome of his appearance before the commission. The numerous individuals who lined the streets of Accra on that day expected the NRC to question the former president broadly regarding gross human rights violations perpetrated during his two political regimes. To the disappointment of many, however, the former president was questioned only about the whereabouts of recordings relating to the murder of three high court judges in 1982. After admitting that he had once been in possession of these tapes, Rawlings informed the commission that he was not aware of their current whereabouts, and he was thereafter dismissed by the commission.[127] Ghanaians were deeply disappointed, as it was felt that the NRC did not utilise the session properly to obtain relevant information.[128] Indeed, many individuals believed that the commission had wasted

---

[121]Ibid.

[122]Ibid. According to her, only two cases are popularly cited by the public in which the perpetrators openly admitted their wrong and asked for forgiveness from the victims.

[123]See Ghana Web 2004. http://www.ghanaweb.com/GhanaHomePage/NewsArchive/NRC-ends-on-a-low-note-61664. Accessed 13 October 2019.

[124]Ibid.

[125]See Sakyi-Addo 2003. http://news.bbc.co.uk/2/hi/africa/2860489.stm. Accessed 9 October 2019.

[126]See Valji 2006, p. 15.

[127]Ghana News Agency 2004b. http://www.ghanaweb.com/GhanaHomePage/NewsArchive/Rawlings-At-NRC-No-Drama-51645. Accessed 13 October 2019; and Valji 2006, pp. 15–16.

[128]For instance, more than a year after the appearance of Rawlings before the NRC, a son of one of the murder victims (i.e., the murder of three High Court judges in 1982, which was the subject matter of Rawlings' appearance before the commission) expressed on radio his desire for the commission to recall the former President for further questioning. This indicates a general dissatisfaction with the commission's earlier questioning of Rawlings. See Peace FM 2004. http://www.ghanaweb.com/GhanaHomePage/NewsArchive/Prez-Spokesman-Dares-Rawlings-60179.

an opportunity that could have been used to clarify issues relating to Ghana's past. The most probable cause for this failure of the commission was its weak investigative capacity, which disabled it from finding substantive evidence regarding the former president's possible complicity in any past human rights violations. In the absence of such substantive evidence, the commission did not have any precise questions to ask him. It is possible that the commission's invitation of the former president was a mere façade, to create an impression that it was making efforts to ascertain facts regarding human rights violations that occurred during Rawlings' leadership.

However disappointing the manner in which the NRC handled Rawlings' appearance, the mere invitation of the former president gave an indication that no one is above the law and signalled the effective use of the commission's powers. Indeed, not all truth commissions are able to boldly utilise their powers to deal with influential politicians. For instance, the South African TRC was alleged to have scarcely utilised its subpoena and search and seizure powers, because of sensitivity to the reactions of specific institutions and prominent members of the society.[129] Thus, the NRC took a step in the right direction by issuing a subpoena against former president Rawlings.

It is also important to note that the difficulties the NRC faced in obtaining information from perpetrators are typical of truth-telling exercises, particularly in the case of commissions whose investigative capacities have been diminished by low funding. Such commissions often encounter challenges with contradictory stories from perpetrators and victims.[130] In Liberia, for instance, several individuals generally known to have participated in the Liberian civil war openly denied their deeds before the commission.[131] The Oputa Panel experienced a similar challenge. As in the case of the NRC, a large number of perpetrators who appeared before the panel denied allegations against them, despite overwhelming witness testimonies to the contrary.[132] Moreover, the Oputa Panel was faced with a greater challenge when three summoned witnesses failed to appear in court and challenged the powers of the commission to compel their appearance. Pursuant to these lawsuits, the commission's subpoena and search and seizure powers were declared unconstitutional, and the commission was prohibited from dealing with petitions against which

Accessed 23 October 2019. See also Valji 2006, pp. 15–16, who opines that the manner in which the NRC handled Rawlings' appearance gives a vivid picture of the difficulties that truth commissions have in dealing with prominent political figures. She asserts that if such moments are not handled with care, the appearance of such political figures could rather create a platform to display more scorn rather than to foster the reconciliatory agenda of the truth commission.

[129]See Gready 2011, p. 31, where he makes reference to this criticism.

[130]Even in instances where a commission is well-funded to conduct all its investigations, such problems could still arise. In Germany, several ex-government officials refused to give testimony at the hearings of the Commission of Inquiry for the Assessment of History and Consequences of the SED Dictatorship, owing to their fear of being tried in future on account of their testimonies. See Hayner 2011, p. 52.

[131]See Weah 2012, p. 7.

[132]See Yusuf 2007, p. 8.

lawsuits had been filed.[133] This court decision posed significant challenges to the work of the Oputa Panel, and the government later cited it as a reason for its failure to implement the commission's recommendations.[134]

In summary, soliciting information from alleged perpetrators is never an easy task, and should thus be handled cautiously to fulfil a commission's truth-finding mandate. The practice of other truth commissions indicates that there is no apt solution to this problem. Even in South Africa and Liberia, where conditional amnesties were awarded in return for truth, it is still doubtful whether the respective commissions engaged perpetrators effectively. A plausible solution for the NRC would have been to utilise its powers in a more stringent manner. For instance, the offences and penalties provided under the NRC Act could have come in handy in this regard. Yet, this could also be futile since perpetrators know that at the end of the day, a truth commission's decisions and findings are not binding. In the circumstances, whether or not the NRC would have succumbed to this problem depended largely on how well it controlled perpetrators during its proceedings.

4.4 Outcome of the Commission's Work

4.4.1 Overview of the Report

The NRC ended its hearings in July 2004, after sitting for 18 months, and submitted its report to the president on 12 October 2004.[135] For unknown reasons, the report was made accessible to the public only after six months, on 22 April 2005.[136] In the report, the NRC outlined the manner in which the commission had been established and the historical and social factors that led to human rights violations. In addition,

---

[133]See Supreme Court of Nigeria, *Chief Gani Fawehinmi et al. v General Ibrahim Babangida (Retired) et al.* (Case Chief Gani Fawehinmi), 31 January 2003, SC.360/2001, where, the Supreme Court of Nigeria held amongst other things that summons by the Oputa Panel constituted a violation of the rights of the individuals involved. The court also held that the Tribunals of Inquiry Act, under which the Oputa Panel derived authority to issue warrants and compel the appearance of witnesses, was a law that was applicable only to the federal capital of Abuja and not the whole of Nigeria. Moreover, the aspects of the respective provisions of the Tribunals of Inquiry Act that empowered the commission to impose fines and imprisonments was a contravention of the Nigerian Constitution and was thus unconstitutional. For further discussion of this decision, see also Yusuf 2007, pp. 277–279. See also Human Rights Violations Investigation Commission 2002, vol 4, para 1.15.

[134]See Yusuf 2007, p. 16, 2013, p. 337.

[135]See the Daily Graphic 2004. http://www.ghanaweb.com/GhanaHomePage/NewsArchive/NRC-Winds-Up-Business-68901. Accessed 13 October 2019; and Ghana Web 2004. http://www.ghanaweb.com/GhanaHomePage/NewsArchive/NRC-ends-on-a-low-note-61664. Accessed 13 October 2019.

[136]See Amnesty International 2005–2007, p. 2. http://lib.ohchr.org/HRBodies/UPR/Documents/Session2/GH/AI_GHA_UPR_S2_2008anx_annualreportentries.pdf. Accessed 9 October 2019.

it provided an overview of how different state institutions contributed to or prevented the occurrence of human rights violations in the country. The report also summarised the petitions that the commission received as well as their statistical details and patterns. It gave recommendations on how to redress the human rights violations and prevent similar occurrences in future.

4.4.1.1 Summary of Findings

The NRC recorded a total of 8,766 human rights violations that occurred from 1957 to 1992.[137] The specific number of cases recorded under each type of violation are as follows: 37 cases of execution-style killings, 151 cases of killings not classified under executions, 1,323 cases of abductions, 2,304 cases of unlawful detention, 186 cases of forced displacement, 20 cases of disappearance, 1,480 cases of property seizure, 1,362 cases of beatings, 46 cases of sexual abuse, 505 cases of property destruction, 301 cases of specified torture, 406 cases of unspecified torture, 67 cases of head shaving, 59 price control cases (i.e., government limits placed on the prices of essential commodities to the detriment of entrepreneurs and traders), 45 cases of extortion, 103 cases of forced sale, 69 cases of media dismissals, 218 cases of other dismissals and 84 cases of psychological torture.[138] The overall findings of the NRC can be summarised as follows:

- Human rights violations did not occur merely under unconstitutional governments. Both periods of constitutional and unconstitutional rule were tainted with high levels of violations, although the violations that occurred in unconstitutional regimes outnumbered those that occurred in constitutional regimes.[139]
- In total, 84% of the human rights violations that were recorded by the NRC occurred under the political regimes of the Armed Forces Revolutionary Council (4 June 1979 to 24 September 1979) and the Provisional National Defence Council (31 December 1981 to 7 January 1993). The regimes of the Armed Forces Revolutionary Council and Provisional National Defence Council also recorded the highest levels of abductions and detentions in comparison with other political regimes, although similar violations occurred in the other regimes.[140]
- Most of the human rights violations were perpetrated by security forces—namely, the military, the police and prisons services. In total, 66.3% of the cases that were heard by the commission were committed by the military.[141]

[137]See National Reconciliation Commission 2004, vol 3, para 8.

[138]Ibid.

[139]Ibid., vol 1, para 6.1.1(1).

[140]Ibid., vol 1, para 6.1.1(2), (6).

[141]Ibid., vol 1, para 6.1.1(3), (4).

- A majority of the human rights violations that occurred were recorded in three of the then ten regions of Ghana—namely, the Greater Accra, Ashanti and Western (currently divided into Western and Western-North) regions.[142]
- A majority of victims of human rights violations were adults, 81% of which were male adults. Nevertheless, some victims of sexual abuse and 'other killings' as defined by the commission were minors.[143]
- Guns were the main instrument used to perpetrate violations. In some cases, however, boots, sticks and canes and even hands were also used.[144]
- Petitioners to the NRC provided three major bases for coming before the commission—namely, monetary compensations, material compensations and the need to know the facts and circumstances of the human rights violations suffered.[145]
- The major impacts of the human rights violations on victims were financial constraints, inability to gain access to education, family disintegration and health problems.[146]

4.4.1.2 Summary of Recommendations

The NRC observed in its report that a solid constitutional democracy cannot be built on a system that allows perpetrators of past human rights violations to escape being subjected to the full rigours of the law by virtue of the amnesty provisions in the Constitution. It therefore suggested that steps should be taken to amend the transitional provisions in the 1992 Constitution, which have granted blanket amnesties to perpetrators of human rights violations in military regimes.[147] This recommendation of the NRC can be compared with the recommendations of other truth commissions, such as the Brazilian Comissão Nacional da Verdade in relation to the amnesty law in Brazil. The Comissão Nacional da Verdade, referring to some decisions of the Inter-American Court of Human Rights also advocated for punishment of the perpetrators named in its report, although the attitude of some politicians in the country reflect a general lack of political will to reverse the amnesty law.[148]

The NRC also recommended the abolition of specific practices such as the formation of private military bodies, politicisation of the army and the other security bodies in the country and indoctrination of members of security bodies. In

[142] Ibid., vol 1, para 6.1.1(4).

[143] Ibid., vol 1, para 6.1.1(5).

[144] Ibid., vol 1, para 6.1.1(7).

[145] Ibid., vol 1, para 6.1.1(8).

[146] Ibid., vol 1, para 6.1.1(9).

[147] Ibid., vol 3, para 3.2.9.2.

[148] See Ramalho 2014. http://g1.globo.com/politica/noticia/2014/12/ministros-defendem-decisao-do-stf-e-questionam-revisao-da-lei-da-anistia.html. Accessed 15 October 2019.

addition, it recommended the establishment and sustenance of proper institutional memory through good record-keeping practices in public institutions and initiation of steps to foster ethnic unity in the country.[149] It was also recommended that national educational curricula should incorporate human rights education at all educational levels and include the commission's findings in teaching materials to create nationwide awareness.[150] The NRC recognised the role played by student youth bodies in ensuring democratic governance. In this regard, it made recommendations regarding the need for political leaders to respect the needs of students and appropriately involve them in decisions that affect students. It also suggested the need for democratic practices in student bodies.[151] Moreover, it recommended that youth be given civic education.[152]

4.4.1.3 Recommendations for Institutional Reform

The NRC also suggested a number of institutional reform measures. In relation to the Ghana Armed Forces, the NRC recommended the following:

- Joint training should be provided for leaders of the military and high-level political officials on their respective roles.[153]
- A consistent command structure should be maintained within the military and respected by political leaders to ensure continued discipline within the army.[154]
- An effective means of communication between the army, political rulers and other security bodies should be created in the country, through the establishment of a strong system of intelligence. Intelligence information should be proved at all times and handled with utmost care.[155]
- Members of the Ghanaian military should be educated on their duties in ensuring democratic rule and be awakened to the allegiance they owe to the state, through education.[156]
- All leaders within the military should ensure a strict sense of discipline in the army by ensuring that military codes are faithfully adhered to.[157]
- Employment of individuals into the army should be done through a well-structured and credible process that takes the behaviour of recruits into account. Appointment and recruitment of officers into the army should be done

[149] National Reconciliation Commission 2004, vol 3, paras 3.12.1–3.12.3, 3.12.6, 3.12.11.
[150] Ibid., para 7.7.4.
[151] Ibid., paras 3.8.1–3.8.15.
[152] Ibid., para 3.9.3.
[153] Ibid., para 3.3.1.
[154] Ibid., Chap. 1, paras 3.3.2–3.3.3.
[155] Ibid., paras 3.3.5, 3.3.8, 3.3.17.1.
[156] Ibid., para 3.3.6.
[157] Ibid., para 3.3.7.

in a well-balanced manner that ensures equal representation of all ethnic groups in the army.[158]

- Members of the army should be given adequate education, including regular in-service education on human rights and humanitarian law as necessary to fulfil their duties. Moreover, members should be regularly assessed to ensure that standards are maintained.[159]
- Adequate remuneration and accommodation as well as all appropriate monetary settlement for death and injury should be provided for members of the military to enhance their loyalty to the army.[160]
- Counselling and career guidance services should be instituted for members of the army.[161]
- The rules and standards pertaining to promotions of army officers and release of incompetent officers should be followed at all times to ensure that all officers remain satisfied with their work. Moreover, officers who are released' from the army should be properly resettled.[162]
- The secondment of military officers into civil establishments should be discontinued.[163]
- The Ghanaian army should be properly funded and resourced by the government.[164]

The institutional reform recommendations made regarding the Police Service and the Prisons Service largely mirrored those for the army. These included reforming the command system of the respective services to transfer some power to the regional commanders, creating ethnic balance within the services and appointing officers through a credible process. The recommendations also called for providing officers education including on human rights, reviewing the terms of service and providing adequate remuneration and proper accommodation for officers. Moreover, they advocated the provision of adequate compensation for death and injury, creation of schemes for proper resettlement of discharged officers, control of the high level of police corruption by drafting a new code of conduct and strict monitoring and improvement of remuneration of police officers.[165]

Recommendations were also made on reforming the judiciary. The NRC recognised that the actions of lawyers had created a perception of legality to some cases of human rights violations. In this regard, it was recommended that lawyers should be given training in human rights as part of their continuing legal education. Moreover, it was suggested that strict punitive and monitoring procedures should be

[158]Ibid., para 3.3.9.

[159]Ibid., para 3.3.11.

[160]Ibid., paras 3.3.12.1, 3.3.12.2, 3.3.12.5.1.

[161]Ibid., para 3.3.12.3.

[162]Ibid., paras 3.3.12.4 and 3.3.12.6 and 3.3.12.7.

[163]Ibid., para 3.3.13.

[164]Ibid., para 3.3.15.

[165]Ibid., paras 3.3.19–3.3.27, 3.3.28–3.3.35.

established within the judiciary to ensure that members of the judiciary do not act according to the whims and caprices of the government in power.[166] The NRC's recommendations also stated that an objective criterion should be developed and followed in awarding positions to judges and other members of the judiciary.[167] It proposed that steps should be taken to ensure speedy delivery of justice in the courts, as well as proper use of discretion in relation to cases at the attorney general's department, although no specific means of attaining these were mentioned in the report.[168] Also, the commission expressed the need for the 'prerogative of mercy' to be scarcely utilised to avoid creating a culture of impunity. It urged the judiciary to ensure at all times that human rights are upheld with respect to accused persons, so as to avoid torture and unlawful detentions.[169] In addition, the recommendations pointed out the need to take steps to prevent the passage of retroactive laws by lawmakers.[170]

The NRC recognised the important role played by the media in strengthening democracy and therefore made recommendations to safeguard the role of the media. It recommended that the media should be supported as much as possible by the government, by abstaining from unnecessarily interfering in their work and from side-lining privately owned media. It also proposed the incorporation of human rights education in the curricula of institutions where journalists are trained.[171]

As regards labour groups, it was recommended that trade unions should adhere to existing rules when asserting their rights and embarking on strikes.[172] Moreover, the commission expressed the need for leaders of trade unions to be independent from political influence.[173] It suggested that steps should be taken to establish effective labour dispute resolution mechanisms to prevent labour-related violence in

---

[166]Ibid., paras 3.4.7, 3.4.9.

[167]Ibid., paras 3.4.11–3.4.14. This recommendation of the NRC can be explained against the backdrop that under the 1992 Constitution it is provided that justices of the Supreme Court should be appointed by the President with advice from the Judicial Council, in consultation with the Council of State. The Chief Justice is also appointed by the President in consultation with the Council of State and with approval from Parliament. However, Court of Appeal and High Court judges must be appointed by the President in consultation with the Judicial Council. The Constitution does not however provide the detailed steps for appointment, to ensure objectivity. Besides, a majority of the members of the Council of State, who advise the President are also appointed by the President. In the circumstances, the President of Ghana wields a large amount of power regarding the caliber of persons who join the bench. This problem is further exacerbated by the fact that there is no constitutional limit on the number of Supreme Court judges in Ghana. In light of these circumstances, credibility of the appointment process of judges is rather doubtful.

[168]National Reconciliation Commission 2004, vol 3, paras 3.4.18–3.4.19.

[169]Ibid., paras 3.4.21, 3.4.22–3.4.25.

[170]Ibid., para 3.4.26.

[171]Ibid., paras 3.5.1–3.5.9.

[172]Ibid., paras 3.6.2, 3.6.3.

[173]Ibid., para 3.6.3.

the future.[174] It also recommended that employee dismissals should follow properly laid-down procedures.[175]

The NRC also made propositions relating to other non-legal professional groups, including civil society bodies. In this regard, it was suggested that such groups should encourage human rights protection and incorporate human rights education in their activities.[176] The commission also suggested the need for the Commission on Human Rights and Administrative Justice to be well-resourced by the government to enhance its ability to protect human rights.[177] Moreover, the NRC expressed the need for the Commission on Human Rights and Administrative Justice and the National Commission on Civic Education to carry out a consistent human rights educational programme throughout the country.[178]

Regarding traditional rulers (i.e., local chiefs), it was recommended that they should desist from meddling in political affairs and seeking political favours, and should act as custodians of human rights protection.[179] Moreover, the NRC recommended that the Regional House of Chiefs and Traditional Councils should devise proper and effective mechanisms for resolving chieftaincy disputes.[180] It was also suggested that a proper land tenure system should be devised in relation to lands under the authority of traditional leaders so as to curb the situation of numerous land disputes in the country.[181]

Lastly, the NRC recognised the potential role of religious bodies in combatting human rights violations. The commission condemned discrimination on the basis of religion and the use of religion to give legitimacy to dubious political acts. It encouraged the use of religion to propagate and enhance education on human rights protection.[182]

4.4.1.4 Recommendations for Reparations

The NRC acknowledged the need to award reparations to the victims of the human rights violations it had investigated. The commission opined that reparations were necessary to fulfil individuals' right to obtain relief for abuse of their rights as well as to fulfil the state's obligation to respect 'human rights, the rule of law and democratic accountability'.[183] Moreover, the NRC believed that provision of

[174]Ibid., para 3.6.9.

[175]Ibid., paras 3.6.10, 3.6.11.

[176]Ibid., para 3.7.1.

[177]Ibid., para 3.7.7.

[178]Ibid., para 3.7.6.

[179]Ibid., paras 3.10.2–3.10.3, 3.10.8–3.10.9, 3.10.15, 3.10.17.

[180]Ibid., paras 3.10.4, 3.10.5.

[181]Ibid., paras 3.10.11–3.10.14, 3.10.16.

[182]Ibid., paras 3.11.1–3.11.10.

[183]Ibid., para 7.3.1.1.

reparations would fulfil the need to formally acknowledge the abuses suffered by victims, initiate a process of healing for victims and serve as the basis for deterring future occurrences through reformation.[184]

Pursuant to the provisions of Article 20(2)(h) of the NRC Act, the commission made recommendations regarding the creation of a Reparations and Rehabilitation Fund.[185] The commission suggested key funding sources for the award of reparations, such as the government, voluntary awards and grants by perpetrators, private companies and the general public.[186] The reparative measures suggested by the NRC are summarised below:

- Make a one-time payment to victims of human rights violations as compensation for the abuses suffered. Different compensatory sums were proposed by the commission for various categories of human rights violations and in accordance with the commission's definition of the violation in question.[187]
- Return seized fixed assets to the rightful owners.[188]
- Pay a fixed compensatory sum to victims of vehicle confiscation.[189]
- Grant scholarships to one offspring each of the victims of killings, disappearances and unlawful seizure of property as well as victims who acquired disabilities as a result of human rights violations.[190]
- Rendering written apologies by the president, including a special apology to all females in the country and the relatives of the three High Court judges murdered in June 1982.[191]
- Deliver public apologies by the leaders of government bodies implicated in the commission of human rights violations from the findings of the NRC. This was to include an apology from the president himself as commander-in-chief of the Ghana Armed Forces.[192]
- Grant awards to army officers for their defence of the country in times of military takeovers.[193]
- Erect memorials in all regional capitals in memory of the victims of killings, disappearances and other human rights violations.[194]

---

[184]Ibid., paras 7.3.1.2, 7.3.1.3, 7.3.1.4.

[185]See NRC Act, above n 47, s 20(2)(h), which provides that one of the elements of the report is recommendations on the creation of a 'reparations and rehabilitation fund'. See also National Reconciliation Commission 2004, vol 1, para 7.1.1.

[186]See National Reconciliation Commission 2004, vol 1, paras 7.2.1(1)(2)(3) and (7).

[187]Ibid., paras 7.4.3.2, 7.4.3.3 and 7.5.

[188]Ibid., para 7.4.2.1.

[189]Ibid., para 7.4.2.2.

[190]Ibid., para 7.4.1.5.

[191]Ibid., vol 1, para 7.4.1.3; vol 3, paras 3.2.1, 3.2.3.

[192]Ibid., vol 1, para 7.4.1.3; vol 3, para 3.2.1.

[193]These officers were specifically named in the report. See National Reconciliation Commission 2004, vol 3, para 3.2.7.3.

[194]See National Reconciliation Commission 2004, vol 1, para 7.4.1.4.

- Hold a one-time special event on national reconciliation to publicly deliver the recommended apologies and launch the recommended national reparative monuments.[195]
- Create commemorative objects such as coins, badges and stamps in honour of the country's reconciliation.[196]
- Present yearly lectures on reconciliation to ensure future safeguarding of 'human rights, rule of law and democratic principles'.[197]
- Establish units in all regional and district hospitals to deal with trauma and counselling.[198]
- Build a market at Namoo in the Upper East Region of Ghana in memory of traders whose goods were unlawfully confiscated.[199]

4.4.2 Interim Analysis of the Commission's Report and Recommendations

4.4.2.1 Assessment of the Recommendations

Although the recommendations by the NRC largely mirror the recommendations of other truth commissions, they evince a soft approach to addressing past human rights violations, without many recommendations intended to ensure accountability for gross human rights violations or to address specific cases of human rights violations by recommending how to deal with perpetrators. Apart from the commission's call for the repeal of the amnesty provisions and payment of reparations, the NRC did not specifically address how individual perpetrators were to be dealt with to ensure accountability. Also, the commission's recommendations for institutional reform are all soft recommendations, with no legal consequences, much like the institutional reform recommendations of Nigeria's Oputa Panel. The Oputa Panel's recommendations also identified the underlying causes of human rights violations in Nigeria and suggested measures for reforming the country's prisons, police and army but did not deal with specific accountability issues or perpetrators.[200]

Other truth commissions have been able to address very specific issues in their recommendations to ensure accountability. For instance, the Liberian TRC's report listed 124 persons and recommended their trial by an extraordinary tribunal to be

[195]Ibid., para 7.4.1.4.
[196]Ibid., para 7.4.1.4.
[197]Ibid., para 7.4.1.4.
[198]Ibid., para 7.4.1.6.2.
[199]Ibid., para 7.4.1.7.
[200]For details of the findings and recommendations, see Human Rights Violations Investigation Commission 2002, vol 7.

set up for the purpose.[201] In Peru, the Comisión de la Verdad y Reconciliación dispatched 44 cases to the Office of the Public Prosecutor to be investigated and tried, following the release of the commission's report.[202] Similarly, in Timor Leste, the report of the Commission for Reception, Truth and Reconciliation outlined the names of Indonesian army officers who controlled specific areas in Timor Leste where heinous human rights violations had been committed.[203] Similarly to institutional reform measures, some commissions have made recommendations that have a legal effect. The Liberian TRC, for instance, recommended the disqualification of 49 named perpetrators, including the country's then sitting president, from holding offices in public service. Those who had been elected to official positions could finish their term but could not be re-elected, whilst those who held positions by appointment were to resign or have their work contracts terminated.[204]

In principle, although the NRC was not a court of law and was not expected to come out with binding decisions, such specific recommendations would have given its work more force and made its impact more profound in the Ghanaian society. From another dimension however, such recommendations could have been detrimental because the NRC did not have all the powers bestowed to courts for enforcing decisions and judgements. Enforcement could be possible only if the commission made recommendations to ensure proper implementation or if there was an existing law to ensure implementation. This was the case in Sierra Leone, where the truth commission's enabling law contained provisions making it mandatory for the government to implement the commission's report.[205]

In summary, although the NRC would have benefitted from recommendations with legal force, the eventual outcome of the commission's work cannot be entirely said to depend on the absence of such recommendations. The lack of such recommendations served to enhance the commission's prime focus on reconciliation, since such recommendations could also have undermined the commission's reconciliation agenda by creating further misunderstanding in the country.

4.4.2.2 Strengths of the Report

The NRC's report has a number of merits. It shed more light on Ghana's history by providing a detailed account of the historical and social contexts within which human rights violations occurred between 6 March 1957 and 7 January 1993. In the process, the report reveals the respective roles played by the judiciary, the army, the police and prisons services, religious groups, traditional rulers and state institutions

[201]See Truth and Reconciliation Commission of Liberia 2009, vol II, paras 12.2–12.4.

[202]See Root 2013, p. 426.

[203]See Hayner 2011, p. 41.

[204]See Truth and Reconciliation Commission of Liberia 2009, vol II, p. 353 para 12.5, pp. 360–361 paras 14.2–14.3.

[205]See Sierra Leone, Truth and Reconciliation Commission Act 2000, 2 March 2000, s 17.

in committing and preventing human rights violations. Significantly, the historical record given by the report points out the existence of ethnic and political factions when Ghana gained independence. It also highlights unequal levels of economic development between the northern and southern parts of the country and between the colonial territories and the trust territory of the Trans-Volta Togoland.[206]

The report also provides an account of the specific human rights violations experienced from 6 March 1957 to 7 January 1993, thereby demonstrating an acknowledgement by the state of the various abuses that occurred during the period. In this regard, it provides statistical records of the total number and types of human rights violations that occurred from 1957 to 1993. Previously, no such records existed, although some historical events were common knowledge in the country. Thus, the report has given a proper perspective on the magnitude of human rights violations in the period.[207]

The report also set the stage for remedies for victims of human rights violations through its extensive recommendations for reparations. Besides, the detailed facts contained in the report offered a formal acknowledgement by the state of past human rights violations.

4.4.2.3 Weaknesses of the Report

Despite the above-mentioned strengths, the NRC's report has various weaknesses in terms of its content and structure. To begin with, the report is very repetitive. In particular, the first volume, whilst titled the executive summary, is not a summary but rather a full reproduction of the contents of the report's other volumes. Thus, the reader encounters the same information in parts of Volumes Two and Three, thereby interrupting the flow of ideas in the report.

Another weakness is the report's lack of precision, depth and clarity regarding how it conducted its investigations to arrive at the facts and details that it presents. In the report, the commission merely outlines the methodology it used for its work, the structural divisions it created in the commission and how it carried out its work. Although the commission also provides details on how it took statements, interpreted its investigative role and processed petitions, the report fails to clarify the exact manner in which the investigations were carried out.[208] Moreover, in explaining how it carried out its investigative role, the commission states only the standard of proof used and mentions that it carried out a number of exhumations. Thus, regarding the manner of processing petitions, the report states:

[206]See National Reconciliation Commission 2004, vol 2, para 3.1.5.1. For details of the trust territory of the Trans Volta Togoland, see Sect. 2.2.3 in Chap. 2 of this book.

[207]For instance, see Valji 2006, p. 21, where she cites the statement of a Ghanaian professor, who admits that in spite of his academic knowledge and experience, he acquired a large amount of new information from the NRC's report.

[208]See National Reconciliation Commission 2004, vol 2, paras 2.3.0, 2.4.0, 2.5.0, 2.60.

> Where the complaint was referred to the Investigations Department, the necessary investigation was conducted and an investigation report submitted to the Legal Department for a recommendation on the matter to the Executive Secretary, who, in turn, made a recommendation to the Commission.[209]

This quotation from the report merely indicates that the commission undertook investigations. These do not provide enough detail about the method employed in investigations. The lack of specificity in this regard detracts from the value of the report, in view of the concerns that arose in the course of the commission's work about its low investigative capacity. The information contained in the report would have gained further credibility if there were more transparency regarding how the investigations were conducted.[210]

Lastly, although the report offered details of human rights violations, it failed to provide adequate information about specific prominent cases of human rights violations, which had incited much curiosity upon its inception. In particular, despite the commission's broad powers under the NRC Act to identify perpetrators, the report did not extensively name perpetrators, especially with regard to popular cases that had garnered the attention of a large number of Ghanaians. Notable amongst these is the 1982 murder of three High Court judges, which was a matter of prime concern to many Ghanaians throughout the work of the NRC. Prior to the establishment of the NRC, a number of people were insinuated to have committed the murders, and many anticipated that the work of the commission would lay these insinuations to rest. Yet little progress was made by the NRC regarding this case. The report merely gives an account of how the judges were abducted from their homes and murdered and how earlier investigations into the matter had failed. The report then recounts the NRC's own attempts to find the facts behind the murders, without providing a definite conclusion on the real culprits.[211] Ansah-Koi has also recounted the case of a popular traditional ruler from the Eastern Region of Ghana, whose disappearance was reported to the commission but never investigated.[212] Moreover, the whereabouts of 200 abducted and disappeared individuals, whose names were published in 1982 by a former leader of the Ghana Bar Association, Sam Okudzeto, were not traced by the NRC.[213] Due to this gap in the report, people are still in the dark regarding the perpetrators of those murders and enforced disappearances.

---

[209]Ibid., para 2.5.4.1(2).

[210]Regarding the weak investigative capacity of the commission, see Sect. 4.3.2 in the present chapter.

[211]See National Reconciliation Commission 2004, vol 2, paras 8.4.1–8.4.26; and Sarpong 2004. http://www.worldpress.org/Africa/1827.cfm. Accessed 19 October 2019.

[212]According to Ansah-Koi, above n 82, several other cases of disappearances that were reported to the commission were not investigated, and the truth is still unknown.

[213]See Myjoyonline TV, Scars of the revolution (Video File) published by Myjoyonline TV on YouTube, 12 December 2019. https://www.youtube.com/watch?v=p2BC4LNhnIE. Accessed 3 January 2020.

In principle, four key arguments back the NRC's failure to name perpetrators. First, since the commission used the civil standard of proof (i.e., on the preponderance of probabilities) in its investigations, its findings cannot be considered to meet the threshold for assignment of criminal responsibility to perpetrators. Second, key incidents that occurred during the commission's existence cast doubt on its credibility and created the impression that it was not competent to assign criminal responsibility to perpetrators. A key example is the allegations by some witnesses that they were not given equal opportunities to respond to accusations against them. Besides, the numerous allegations of bias levelled against the commission cast a long shadow on its credibility. Third, the proceedings of the commission were broadcast on national television, which deviates from the rules of court in Ghana. Fourth, the weak investigative capacity of the commission evince its high level of judicial incompetence. Indeed, the commission's weak investigative capacity was the key cause of the gaps in its report.

No matter how extensive the work of a truth commission, there may invariably be limitations in the extent of truth revealed in their work. In Liberia, the truth commission failed to uncover the full truth regarding sexual violence against females. Besides, the commission's report was said to have lacked consistency on account of failing to provide sufficient information to substantiate its findings and recommendations.[214] Similarly, in South Africa many victims felt that the TRC did not conduct further investigation into cases for which they had provided testimony and was unable to provide the full truth about all cases.[215]

Due to the large number of cases, spanning over a large period of time, that truth commissions hear, it is inconceivable that they would be able to reveal the detailed facts about every past human rights violation. Also, since truth commissions are usually supposed to complete their work within a short time frame, it is nearly impossible for them to reveal the truth about every case. In the circumstances, what should be expected from a truth commission is a general overview of the violations suffered, rather than the specifics of each case. Moreover, since assignment of criminal responsibility is already in the ambit of the judiciary, which is properly equipped to perform that function, it is unnecessary to saddle a truth commission with that responsibility. The commission's power to name perpetrators and its adherence to due process requirements should be viewed as facilitators of the commission's work and not as imputing an authority that is akin to that of criminal courts. The information disclosed in a truth commission's report about perpetrators of human rights violations should thus be regarded as merely complementary, for the purposes of future prosecutions.

Nonetheless, the NRC should have made an exception for high-profile cases such as the murder of the three High Court judges and utilised its perpetrator-naming powers. This was necessary given the fact that the amnesty provisions in the 1992 Constitution have blocked other avenues for victims to know

[214]See James-Allen et al. 2010, pp. 14–15.

[215]See Campbell 2000, pp. 51–52; and Hamber 2003, pp. 1078, 1084–1085.

the truth. Besides, naming perpetrators in such high-profile cases would not have contravened due process requirements, because of the commission's similarity to a court. Actions of the commission that conform to due process requirements observed in normal courts include: informing individuals of allegations against them in writing, allowing alleged perpetrators to respond to allegations in writing, providing lawyers for witnesses and permitting witnesses to examine other witnesses through their lawyers.[216] The NRC's failure to name perpetrators in its report can, therefore, be considered as a key limitation of its work. Indeed, nearly 15 years after closure of the commission, the mystery surrounding the death of the three judges continues to resurface in public discourses. On 2 October 2018, a documentary published by a popular Ghanaian television network, MyJoyOnline Television,[217] on the issue revived questions about why the state has not followed up on bringing perpetrators of the murders to justice.[218] Perhaps such questions would have been laid to rest if the NRC had named the perpetrators of the murders.

4.4.3 Publicity of the Report

Publicising the work of truth commissions is key to realising most of their goals, since revealing their findings and recommendations is one of the core reasons for their establishment. Indeed, the right to truth involves an obligation on the part of states to preserve the memory of the information revealed to victims and their families, facilitate knowledge of such information and prevent it from being lost.[219] It also includes an obligation to prevent absolute destruction of the state's history or alteration of the facts relating to past human rights violations. The state must foster knowledge of its past through creation and protection of records and erection of memorials in relation to its history.[220]

---

[216]Indeed, the commission states in its report that in exercising its mandate to identify perpetrators, it observed rules of natural justice in its hearings. See National Reconciliation Commission 2004, vol 1, para 2.3.3.4.1.

[217]See MyJoyOnline Television, Who killed the judges-Joy News Special Assignment (2-10-18) (Video File), published by Myjoyonline Television on YouTube, 2 October 2018. https://www.youtube.com/watch?v=JxTZiAXbX3I. Accessed 9 October 2019.

[218]See for example Azumah 2018a. https://www.myjoyonline.com/news/2018/October-6th/who-killed-the-judges-baako-scandalised-by-silent-of-subsequent-govts-on-amedeka-.php. Accessed 9 October 2019; Azumah 2018b. https://www.myjoyonline.com/news/2018/October-6th/who-killed-the-judges-baako-reveals-missing-links-of-damning-history.php. Accessed 9 October 2019; and Mordy 2018. https://www.myjoyonline.com/politics/2018/October-5th/who-killed-the-judges-amedeka-was-brought-into-prison-as-mad-man.php. Accessed 9 October 2019.

[219]See United Nations Commission on Human Rights 2005, paras 3, 5, 14 and 15.

[220]Ibid., para 3. See also United Nations Office of the High Commissioner for Human Rights 2015, pp. 3, 4; United Nations General Assembly 2014, para 10; United Nations Human Rights Council 2012, para 10; and United Nations General Assembly 2006, para 24.

Arguably, publication of a truth commission's report is one key avenue for fostering knowledge of and preserving records of information revealed to victims and their families.

In this regard, the reports of truth commissions are usually published extensively on the internet, in newspapers and in hard copies.[221] In Argentina, for instance, the final report of the National Commission on the Disappeared was translated into five languages and published in 25 different versions.[222] This has, however, not been the case with the NRC. The report was released on 22 April 2005, six months after being submitted to the president.[223] Although an executive summary of the report was initially posted on the government's website, it was subsequently removed, and it is no longer available on the internet. Despite the commission's recommendation that copies of its report should be sold as a way of raising funds for payment of monetary compensations, this has not been done. The only part of the report that is easily accessible is a summary compiled by the Ghana Centre for Democratic Development in 2005.[224] In the course of conducting this study, the author found no hard copy of the full report in libraries or bookshops or on the internet. A digital copy of the report was eventually obtained on a compact disc from the Balme Library of the University of Ghana, after a rigorous search, although this was not openly displayed in the library. Rather, the copy was obtained after making a formal request to the library and explaining the reason for requesting the copy.

A number of factors has exacerbated the low-level publicity for the NRC's report. It has been fuelled by the change in Ghana's government, which occurred following the country's presidential elections in 2008. The main opposition party (the National Democratic Congress), which proved to be the major opposing force to the work of the commission, resumed power from January 2009 to January 2017.[225] It is, therefore, not surprising that during their rule, the NRC's report was not publicised. Also, the limited publicity of the report has been aggravated by the commission's failure to create a website during its existence. Thus, no reliable records of its work are available online to date, with the exception of media publications about the commission. The failure of the NRC to create a website during its existence is a big detraction from its work, considering the fact that even earlier truth commissions, such as the South African TRC, created websites that are still easily accessible online. Moreover, Odartey-Wellington and Alhassan believe that the NRC's failure to recommend a clear distribution plan for the report as part of its recommendations has also contributed to its limited publicity.[226] This view is,

[221]Daly 2013, p. 264.

[222]See Cuevas et al. 2002. https://www.apt.ch/content/files_res/Truth%20Comm_Executive%20Summary.pdf. Accessed 4 September 2019.

[223]See Amnesty International 2005–2007, p. 2. http://lib.ohchr.org/HRBodies/UPR/Documents/Session2/GH/AI_GHA_UPR_S2_2008anx_annualreportentries.pdf. Accessed 9 October 2019.

[224]See Ghana Centre for Democratic Development 2005. https://books.google.de/books/about/Never_again.html?id=ZfwUAQAAIAAJ&redir_esc=y. Accessed 29 October 2019.

[225]On this subject, see Odartey-Wellington and Alhassan 2016, p. 41.

[226]Ibid., p. 40.

however, questionable, in light of the commission's recommendation that copies of the report should be sold as a way of raising funds for payment of monetary compensations. The main factor in the limited publicity for the NRC's report is, therefore, likely the lack of political will to do so.

The experience of Ghana regarding the limited publicity for the NRC's report could be likened to that of Nigeria and Timor Leste. In Nigeria, the report of the Oputa Panel was never published officially by the state following completion of the commission's work in 2002. Eventually, the report was published by a civil society body and a nongovernmental organisation in 2005, and the recommendations of the commission were never implemented.[227] Likewise, in Timor Leste the government initially refused to release the report of the Comissão de Acolhimento, Verdade e Reconciliação to the public, until former rebels caused uprisings in the country, which prompted the government to eventually release the report.[228]

The failure to publish a truth commission's report can, indeed, limit its impact, and this is apparent from the persistence used in the above instances to ensure publication of the reports of the Oputa Panel in Nigeria and the Comissão de Acolhimento, Verdade e Reconciliação in Timor Leste. In view of the key role that publication plays in the outcome of truth commissions, even a late publication is still useful for publicising a truth commission's work. Hence, publication of the NRC's report can be reinitiated, although it has been nearly 15 years since the report was initially released.

4.4.4 Implementation of the Report

Following the publication of a truth commission's report, reactions from the public and the government can be critical and may affect the extent to which the commission's recommendations are implemented. For instance, the Liberian TRC's report caused controversy in the country, on account of a recommendation that over 150 individuals, including the country's sitting president, should be prosecuted and banned from public office for 30 years.[229] To date, this recommendation has not been implemented, and a number of the individuals banned from holding public office have been given political appointments despite the TRC's recommendations.[230] In Chile, the release of the report of the Rettig Commission ignited

[227]See the United States Institute of Peace. http://www.usip.org/publications/truth-commission-nigeria. Accessed 16 October 2019; Yusuf Yusuf 2007, pp. 16–17, 2013, p. 337.

[228]González and Varney 2013, p. 66. https://www.ictj.org/sites/default/files/ICTJ-Book-Truth-Seeking-2013-English.pdf. Accessed 2 November 2019.

[229]To compound matters further, some ex-warlords who had been named in the commission's report, threatened to resume violence in the country. See Aning and Jaye 2011, pp. 13–15; James-Allen et al. 2010, pp. 10–11; and Weah 2012, pp. 5–6.

[230]See West African Journal Magazine 2018. https://westafricanjournalmagazine.com/2018/03/23/un-pressures-liberia-to-implement-trc-report/. Accessed 16 October 2019.

criticisms from the country's army and navy, which eventually caused physical assaults on some political factions.[231] Amidst these attacks, three assassinations occurred in a span of 21 days, including of one senator who was a known affiliate of former president Pinochet.[232] Ghana's experience cannot, however, be likened to the above instances.

Following submission of the NRC's report to the government on 12 October 2004, the government issued a white paper on the report in April 2005. In the paper, the government expressed its acceptance of the commission's recommendations regarding the armed forces, the police and the prisons services and stated that it had given orders to the leaders of the respective sectors to commence necessary steps to implement the recommendations. The government also stated in the white paper that steps were being taken to set up the NRC's recommended reparation and rehabilitation fund, which would commence operation by the end of 2005.[233]

The immediate steps taken by the government towards implementation of the NRC's recommendations were minimal. However, the government eventually made significant strides to uphold the recommendations on reparations, after criticisms began to emerge from civil society organisations.[234] In 2006, the government made a budgetary allocation to be paid to victims as reparations.[235] Subsequently in 2007, about 2,000 victims were earmarked to receive reparations totalling approximately 15 billion Ghana cedis (equivalent to about 1.5 million USD at the time of releasing the commission's recommendations). The individual sums allocated for victims ranged from 217 USD to 3,300 USD, based on the extent of human rights violations suffered.[236] Although a majority of the reparations were paid, some victims never received their monetary compensation due to a number of irregularities in the payment process.[237] Names of some victims who had initially been validly earmarked to receive compensation subsequently disappeared from the list, whilst some victims were impersonated by fraudsters.[238] A former deputy

---

[231]See Ferrara 2015, pp. 50–52; Fuentes and Collins 2013, pp. 297–298; Fuentes 2012, pp. 123–124; and Kaye 1997, p. 697.

[232]Ibid.

[233]See Information Services Department of Ghana 2005. http://www.ghanaweb.com/GhanaHomePage/NewsArchive/Govt-Issues-White-Paper-On-NRC-Report-79926. Accessed 13 October 2019.

[234]See the Ghanaian Times 2005 http://www.ghanaweb.com/GhanaHomePage/NewsArchive/CDD-Boss-wants-NRC-report-implemented-83673. Accessed 24 October 2019.

[235]See the Daily Graphic 2007. http://www.ghanaweb.com/GhanaHomePage/NewsArchive/8bn-Paid-To-Human-Rights-Victims-125571. Accessed 13 October 2019; and the Ghana News Agency 2006. http://www.ghanaweb.com/GhanaHomePage/NewsArchive/13-5bn-to-implement-NRC-recommendations-103210. Accessed 13 October 2019.

[236]See Asare 2008, p. 35.

[237]See Myjoyonline TV, Scars of the revolution (Video File) published by Myjoyonline TV on YouTube, 12 December 2019. https://www.youtube.com/watch?v=p2BC4LNhnIE. Accessed 3 January 2020.

[238]Ibid.

attorney general, who led the implementation committee for the NRC's recommendations has also admitted that not all compensations were paid due to different governmental challenges.[239] Even today, some victims continue to pursue payment of their compensation.[240]

Regarding the return of confiscated lands to their rightful owners, in June 2007, the attorney general at the time stated that no funds had yet been allocated for the purpose, although the government had no objection to the recommendation. He admitted that return of assets presented various challenges, owing particularly to the fact that some assets had been legally transferred to third parties after being confiscated. There was thus the need to handle the issue carefully in order to avoid creating new problems.[241] This pronouncement by the government showed its general willingness to implement at least some of the NRC's recommendations, although it did not appear to be a high or urgent priority. Indeed, a display of political will towards implementation of a truth commission's report does not ensure implementation in all instances. In Brazil, for instance, the recommendations of the Comissão Nacional da Verdade in the commission's 2014 report have not yet been implemented even though the country's minister in charge of human rights announced after two months of the submission of the report that steps were being taken to implement 12 of the 29 recommendations.[242]

In the case of Ghana, despite the payment of some reparations to victims and the modest indications by the Ghanaian government that it would implement the NRC's recommendations on institutional reform, the suggested reforms had not been implemented at the time of undertaking this study. Like the limited publicity of the commission's report, the most probable reason for non-implementation of the recommendations is the change in government four years after the release of the report.[243] In 2017, the New Patriotic Party, under whose leadership the NRC was established, regained power, and yet there is no indication at the time of undertaking this study that the government has any plans of implementing the commission's recommendations.

---

[239]Ibid.

[240]Ibid.

[241]See the Daily Graphic 2007. http://www.ghanaweb.com/GhanaHomePage/NewsArchive/8bn-Paid-To-Human-Rights-Victims-125571. Accessed 13 October 2019.

[242]See Arruda 2015. http://politica.estadao.com.br/blogs/roldao-arruda/governo-ja-segue-recomendacoes-da-comissao-da-verdade-afirma-ministra/. Accessed 15 October 2019; and Charner 2015. http://www.americasquarterly.org/content/brazils-truth-commission-many-recommendations-little-action. Accessed 15 October 2019.

[243]See Oduro 2013, p. 214, who notes that judging from the past attitude of Ghanaian governments in the implementation of reports, it is possible that the report of the NRC would at best remain a collection in Ghana's archives.

4.5 Chapter Summary

The NRC's experiences demonstrate the complex nature of truth-telling exercises and the varied responses that they can elicit from different factions of society. The chapter has highlighted some of the commission's weaknesses. For instance, the NRC was unable to carry out thorough investigations due to its weak investigative capacity. Another weakness of the commission relates to its failure to utilise its powers fully, such as the omission to name perpetrators in its report and its failure to utilise its powers to adequately engage perpetrators. This chapter has also shown that the NRC carried out its mandate in a highly categorical manner, as indicated by its interpretation of its mandate, its detailed organisational structure and the way it conducted its hearings. Other laudable aspects of the NRC's work include the payment of reparations as a result of the commission's recommendations as well as the provision of a historical and statistical record for past human rights violations. Moreover, the commission was highly effective in respecting the privacy and confidentiality requests of victims and involving members of the public in the truth-telling. The NRC can thus be seen to have executed its mandate fully, despite its weaknesses and the challenges it faced.

References

Alidu S (2010) The National Reconciliation Commission and reconciliation in Ghana: An assessment. Review of International Affairs LX (1138–1139):153–177.

Ameh RK (2006) Uncovering truth: Ghana's National Reconciliation Commission excavation of past human rights abuses. Contemporary Justice Review 9(4):345–368.

Amnesty International (2004) Peru: The Truth and Reconciliation Commission – A first step towards a country without injustice. https://www.essex.ac.uk/armedcon/themes/international_courts_tribunals/amnestyaugust2004.pdf Accessed 18 October 2019.

Amnesty International (2005–2007) Annual report entries 2005–2007: Ghana. https://lib.ohchr.org/HRBodies/UPR/Documents/Session2/GH/AI_GHA_UPR_S2_2008anx_annualreportentries.pdf. Accessed 9 October 2019.

Aning K, Jaye T (2011) Liberia: A briefing paper on the TRC Report. https://www.africaportal.org/publications/liberia-a-briefing-paper-on-the-trc-report/. Accessed 3 September 2019.

Asamoah OY (2014) The political history of Ghana. The experience of a non-conformist (1950–2013). Authorhouse, Bloomington.

Asare AA (2008) The Ghanaian National Reconciliation Commission: Reparation in a global age. The Global South 2(2):31–53.

Boafo-Arthur K (2005) National reconciliation or polarisation? Preliminary reflections on the politics of the Ghana National Reconciliation Commission. In: Fawole WA, Ukeje C (eds) The crisis of the state and regionalism in West Africa. Codesria, Dakar, pp 105–126.

Boafo-Arthur K (2006) The quest for national reconciliation in Ghana: Challenges and prospects. In: Boafo-Arthur K (ed) Voting for democracy in Ghana: The 2004 elections in perspective. Freedom House Publishing, Accra, pp 127–155.

Bowden B et al (2009) Introduction. In: Bowden B et al (eds) The role of international law in rebuilding societies after conflict: Great expectations. Cambridge University Press, Cambridge, pp 1–14.

Campbell PJ (2000) The truth and reconciliation commission (TRC): Human rights and state transitions-The South Africa model. African Studies Quarterly 4(3):41–63.

Comissão Nacional da Verdade (2015) Grupos de trabalho (Working Groups). http://www.cnv.gov.br/institucional-acesso-informacao/grupos-de-trabalho.html. Accessed 19 October 2019.

Cuevas VE et al (2002) Truth commissions: An uncertain path? Comparative study of truth commissions in Argentina, Chile, El Salvador, Guatemala and South Africa from the perspectives of victims, their relatives, human rights organisations and experts. https://www.apt.ch/content/files_res/Truth%20Comm_Executive%20Summary.pdf. Accessed 4 September 2019.

Daly E (2013) Truth (truth seeking and truth telling). In: Stan L, Nedelsky N (eds) Encyclopedia of transitional justice. Cambridge University Press, Cambridge, pp 259–266.

Ferrara A (2015) Assessing the long-term impact of truth commissions: The Chilean Truth and Reconciliation Commission in historical perspective. Routledge, New York.

Fuentes C (2012) The unlikely outcome: Transitional justice in Chile. In: Popovski V, Serrano M (eds) After oppression: Transitional justice in Latin America and Eastern Europe. United Nations University Press, New York, pp 116–143.

Fuentes C, Collins C (2013) National Commission on Truth and Reconciliation, the Rettig Commission/Comisión Nacional de Verdad y Reconciliación, Comisión Rettig (Chile). In: Stan L, Nedelsky N (eds) Encyclopedia of transitional justice. Cambridge University Press, New York, pp 295–300.

Ghana Centre for Democratic Development (2005) Never again: Summary and synthesis of the National Reconciliation Commission's final report. Ghana Centre for Democratic Development, Accra.

González E, Varney H (2013) Truth seeking: Elements of creating an effective truth commission. https://www.ictj.org/sites/default/files/ICTJ-Book-Truth-Seeking-2013-English.pdf. Accessed 2 November 2019.

Gready P (2011) The era of transitional justice. The aftermath of the Truth and Reconciliation Commission in South Africa and beyond. Routledge, Abingdon.

Gyimah-Boadi E (2002) National reconciliation in Ghana: Prospects and challenges. https://www.files.ethz.ch/isn/100438/2004-05-01_Briefing_Vol4-No1.pdf. Accessed 4 September 2019.

Gyimah-Boadi E (2003) NRC: Matters arising. Democracy Watch 4(1):1–5.

Hamber B (2003) Rights and reasons: Challenges for truth recovery in South Africa and Northern Ireland. Fordham International Law Journal 26(4):1074–1094.

Hayner PB (2011) Unspeakable truths: Transitional justice and the challenge of truth commissions, 2nd edn. Routledge, London.

Human Rights Violations Investigation Commission (2002) Human Rights Violations Investigation Commission Report, vol I-IX. https://dawodu.com/oputa1.htm. Accessed 3 November 2019.

International Centre for Transitional Justice (2013) Ten years after Peru's truth commission. https://www.ictj.org/news/ten-years-after-peru-truth-commission. Accessed 18 October 2019.

James-Allen P et al (2010) Beyond the Truth and Reconciliation Commission: Transitional justice options in Liberia. International Centre for Transitional Justice, New York.

Kaye M (1997) The role of truth commissions in the search for justice, reconciliation and democratisation: The Salvadorean and Honduran cases. Journal of Latin American Studies 29 (3):693–716.

National Reconciliation Commission (2004) Report of the National Reconciliation Commission, vol 1–4.

Odartey-Wellington F, Alhassan A (2016) Disseminating the National Reconciliation Commission report: A critical step in Ghana's democratic consolidation. African Journal of Political Science and International Relations 10(4):34–46.

Oduro F (2013) National Reconciliation Commission (Ghana). In: Stan L, Nedelsky N (eds) Encyclopedia of transitional justice. Cambridge University Press, Cambridge, pp 317–322.

Quinalha RH (2014) 50 years later, still in search of truth: Challenges facing truth commission in Brazil. http://ohrh.law.ox.ac.uk/50-years-later-still-in-search-of-truth-challenges-facing-truth-commissions-in-brazil/. Accessed 15 October 2019.

Root RK (2013) Truth and Reconciliation Commission/Comisión de la Verdad y Reconciliación (Peru). In: Stan L, Nedelsky N (eds) Encyclopedia of transitional justice. Cambridge University Press, Cambridge, pp 423–427.

Samuel S, Green JA (2017) Domestic commissions of inquiry and international law: The importance of normative authority. In: Henderson C (ed) Commissions of enquiry: Problems and prospects. Hart Publishing, Oxford and Portland.

Truth and Reconciliation Commission of Liberia (2009) Final Report, vol I–III. https://web.archive.org/web/20170515044651/http://trcofliberia.org/reports/final-report. Accessed 2 November 2019.

United Nations Commission on Human Rights (2005) Promotion and protection of human rights: Impunity, Report of the independent expert to update the set of principles to combat impunity, Diane Orentlicher, Addendum – Updated Set of principles for the protection and promotion of human rights through action to combat impunity, E/CN.4/2005/102/Add.1.

United Nations General Assembly (2006) Resolution adopted by the General Assembly on 16 December 2005, Basic Principles and Guidelines on the Right to a Remedy and Reparation for Victims of Gross Violations of International Human Rights Law and Serious Violations of International Humanitarian Law, A/RES/60/147. https://documents-dds-ny.un.org/doc/UNDOC/GEN/N05/496/42/PDF/N0549642.pdf?OpenElement. Accessed 2 November 2019.

United Nations General Assembly (2014) Resolution adopted by the General Assembly on 18 December 2013, Right to Truth, A/RES/68/165.

United Nations Human Rights Council (2012) Resolution 21/7 adopted by the Human Rights Council, Right to the truth, A/HRC/RES/21/7.

United Nations Office of the High Commissioner for Human Rights (2015) Rule-of-law tools for post-conflict states: Archives. https://www.ohchr.org/Documents/Publications/HR_PUB_14_4_Archives_en.pdf. Accessed 4 September 2019.

United States Institute of Peace, Truth Commission: Nigeria. http://www.usip.org/publications/truth-commission-nigeria. Accessed 16 October 2019.

Valji N (2006) Ghana's National Reconciliation Commission: A comparative assessment. https://www.ictj.org/sites/default/files/ICTJ-Ghana-Reconciliation-Commission-2006-English_0.pdf. Accessed 24 October 2019.

Wain M (2003) Ghana's National Reconciliation Commission. http://peacemagazine.org/archive/v19n2p18.htm. Accessed 30 November 2019.

Weah A (2012) Hopes and uncertainties: Liberia's journey to end impunity. International Journal of Transitional Justice 6(2):331–343.

West African Journal Magazine (2018) UN pressures Liberia to implement TRC report. https://westafricanjournalmagazine.com/2018/03/23/un-pressures-liberia-to-implement-trc-report/. Accessed 16 October 2019.

Wiebelhaus-Brahm E (2013) Liberia. In: Stan L, Nedelsky N (eds) Encyclopedia of transitional justice. Cambridge University Press, New York, pp 280–286.

Yusuf HO (2007) Travails of truth: Achieving justice for victims of impunity in Nigeria. International Journal of Transitional Justice 1:268–286.

Yusuf HO (2013) Nigeria. In: Stan L, Nedelsky N (eds) Encyclopedia of transitional justice. Cambridge University Press, New York, pp 333–339.

Chapter 5
The National Reconciliation Commission in Hindsight: An Evaluation of Impact

Contents

5.1 Introductory Remarks 146
5.2 The Concepts of 'Impact' and 'Success' 147
5.3 The Assessment Criteria 148
5.4 The Impact of the National Reconciliation Commission on Truth 152
5.4.1 Overview of the Goal of Truth 152
5.4.2 Perceptions of the National Reconciliation Commission's Impact on the Establishment of Truth 153
5.4.3 Discussion 157
5.5 The Impact of the National Reconciliation Commission on Justice 160
5.5.1 The National Reconciliation Commission and the Pursuit of Victims' Rights to Remedies 161
5.5.2 Preventing the Recurrence of Human Rights Violations 167
5.5.3 Summary 173
5.6 The Impact of the Commission on National Reconciliation 173
5.6.1 Perceptions of the Commission's Impact on National Reconciliation 175
5.6.2 Discussion 178
5.7 The Impact of the National Reconciliation Commission on Peace 180
5.7.1 Perceptions of the National Reconciliation Commission's Impact on Peace 181
5.7.2 Discussion 183
5.8 Chapter Summary 185
References 186

Abstract Few studies in transitional justice rely on empirical data to interpret the outcome of truth commissions and to analyse the extent to which truth commissions impact transitional societies. In order to elucidate this aspect of transitional justice, this chapter examines the concepts of 'impact' and 'success' within transitional justice. It also designates criteria for assessing Ghana's National Reconciliation Commission, which can be used for other truth commissions with minor contextual modifications. The established criteria form the basis for discussing the impact of the commission, using quantitative and qualitative data from a survey conducted by

M. Yankson-Mensah, *Transitional Justice in Ghana*, International Criminal Justice Series 25, https://doi.org/10.1007/978-94-6265-379-5_5

the author. The examination of the National Reconciliation Commission's impact not only sheds light on the current perceptions held about the work of the commission in Ghana but also demonstrates how the use of empirical data helps to clarify the uncertainties about the impact of truth commissions.

Keywords Truth Commissions · Impact of Truth Commissions · Assessment Criteria · Success · National Reconciliation Commission · Empirical Assessment of Truth Commissions

5.1 Introductory Remarks

Although there is ample literature on the desired outcomes of truth commissions,[1] great uncertainties abound regarding their effectiveness and success.[2] It has thus been alleged that states have utilised truth commissions in the past based solely on their faith in the process.[3] It has also been purported that truth commissions do not always achieve their acclaimed goals.[4] A study by Wilson, for instance, has found that despite the South African TRC's work, there is still a desire for vengeance amongst South Africans.[5] These claims bring to light the need for empirical assessment of truth commissions' impact and success.

However, this aspect of transitional justice has not yet been developed, and there is still a dearth of scholarship regarding how empirical data can be utilised to determine the impact of a truth commission. There are also diverse views on the criteria for determining the impact of a truth commission and what constitutes its

[1]On some of the expected goals of truth commissions, see for instance Ambos 2015, p. 469; Kritz 2009, p. 13; Mazzei 2011, pp. 434–435; Popkin and Roht-Arriaza 1995, p. 80; and Zalaquett 1995, p. 5.

[2]For further discussions on the need for literature on the impact of transitional justice, see Kritz 2009, p. 17; Van Der Merwe et al. 2009b, p. 4; and Wiebelhaus-Brahm 2010, p. 22. See also Hirsch et al. 2012, pp. 387, 391–392; Lundy 2010, p. 105; and Thoms et al. 2010, p. 330.

[3]See Mendeloff 2004, p. 375. According to Wiebelhaus-Brahm 2010, p. 7, existing studies on truth commissions' effectiveness fail to analyse their impact beyond the immediate completion of their work. Olsen et al. 2010c, p. 981 also assert that even if transitional justice mechanisms attain their perceived objectives, no scholarship has indicated how, when and why they occur. See also Bonacker and Buckley-Zistel 2013, p. 6.

[4]For instance, Hamber 2009, p. 168, argues that the expected outcomes of truth commissions that are excessively highlighted by truth commission advocates are not fully true. Nichols 2019, p. 3 also asserts that the ability of truth commissions to make an impact depends on their institutional features, such as their level of independence from the past regime and transparency in their work. See also Frederking 2015, pp. 15–16; Nwogu 2010, p. 276; Waldorf 2009, p. 111; and Wilson 2001, 161.

[5]See Wilson 2001, p. 161.

success.[6] This chapter seeks to address some of these uncertainties by considering the appropriate criteria for assessing the impact of the NRC. The chapter then assesses the NRC's impact from an empirical perspective, on the basis of the criteria. It relies on both quantitative and qualitative data obtained in the course of this study as well as on quantitative data from independent sources.

Details of the collection of data were explained and discussed in Chap. 1.[7] As stated there, the findings must be understood in light of possible limitations posed by the sample size used for the survey. The findings are not meant to be generalised as the overall impact of the NRC in Ghana or of truth commissions more broadly. Rather, the key aim of the chapter is to highlight different perspectives on the commission's impact. In particular, the chapter's reliance on empirical data enables more inclusive views on the NRC's work by bringing to fore the views of ordinary Ghanaians.

5.2 The Concepts of 'Impact' and 'Success'

The question of what constitutes the 'impact' and 'success' of a truth commission can yield different responses.[8] According to Brahm, impact with regards to truth commissions refers to 'whether the experience resulted in substantive change'.[9] Backiner has also explained impact as the effect it has on government policy and judicial processes, as separate from the impacts of other mechanisms of transitional justice and conflict resolution mechanisms.[10]

Success is, however, defined by Brahm as 'the degree to which a commission fulfilled the duties assigned to it'.[11] Other authors have defined success by limiting it to paradigms that can be used to measure it. For instance, Cassel names three indicators of a commission's success: its receipt of external backing, positive reception of its work by all opposing factions of the society and the ruling class and its resources.[12] Kemp also proposes that the success of a truth commission may be best ascertained by examining the extent to which it has established a record of past human rights violations, enhanced the chances of victims for obtaining redress for the abuses suffered and given rise to 'political' deliberations about the country.[13]

[6]See Office of the United Nations High Commissioner for Human Rights 2006a, p. 32. https://www.ohchr.org/Documents/Publications/RuleoflawTruthCommissionsen.pdf. Accessed 2 November 2019.

[7]See Sect. 1.2.4 in Chap. 1 of this book.

[8]On the difficulties posed by how to define impact and success, see Wiebelhaus-Brahm 2010, p. 22; Brahm 2005, pp. 21–22, 24–25; Hirsch et al. 2012, p. 396; and Thoms et al. 2008, p. 28.

[9]Brahm 2007, p. 18.

[10]See Bakiner 2014, pp. 6–7.

[11]Brahm 2007, p. 17.

[12]See Cassel 1995, pp. 332–333.

[13]Kemp 2004, p. 68.

Posner, however, is of the view that the success of a transition can be judged by the worth of political and economic reforms occasioned in the society as a result of the transition.[14]

In light of these definitions, it is apparent that the two concepts are closely linked, as they both relate to the consequences of a truth commission's work. Nevertheless, 'success' has a purely positive connotation, relating to the positive consequences. 'Impact' however has a broader scope as it extends to both positive and negative results. This study therefore construes the concept of impact to include success. This is because the ascertainment of a commission's impact invariably depends on all the consequences of its work, including positive and negative. Impact is defined here as the implications, repercussions and results generated as a result of the NRC's work as well as the extent to which the NRC attained its goals.

5.3 The Assessment Criteria

The impact of a truth commission can be manifested in diverse ways and over a long period of time.[15] Different factors can be considered when assessing impact. Van Der Merwe, for instance, asserts that impact can be demonstrated by the manner in which the transitional justice mechanism strengthens bodies, laws and societal trends as it creates a new political order.[16] Wiebelhaus-Brahm, in contrast, prefers assessments based on the implications of truth commissions for human rights and democracy, since these two paradigms are regularly mentioned as key goals of truth-telling and lend themselves easily to comparative analysis.[17] Skaar, Malca and Eide have also proposed a framework for impact assessment through empirical analysis based on 'a stepwise approach'.[18] In their four-stage approach, they assess impact by first examining the specific factors (national, regional and global) of the transition in question. This is followed by an assessment of the transitional justice mechanism itself, by examining its objectives, scope, requirement and timing. The third step involves examining the execution of the recommendations of the transitional justice mechanism. Lastly, they assess the impact of the transitional justice mechanism on the basis of two variables: peace and democracy. In doing this, they examine whether the mechanism in question has

[14]See Posner and Vermeule 2003, p. 768.

[15]See Office of the United Nations High Commissioner for Human Rights 2006a, p. 32. https://www.ohchr.org/Documents/Publications/RuleoflawTruthCommissionsen.pdf. Accessed 2 November 2019.

[16]See Van Der Merwe et al. 2009b, p. 5.

[17]See Wiebelhaus-Brahm 2010, p. 17. See also Olsen et al. 2010b, pp. 457–476.

[18]Skaar et al. 2015, pp. 46–47.

attained its goals, after which they link the attainment of the transitional justice mechanism to peace and democracy.[19]

Other criteria used to assess impact include comparing states that have utilised transitional justice mechanisms with those that have not,[20] assessing whether the truth-seeking mandate of the truth commission was fulfilled,[21] examining experiences and reactions of victims and whether they attained psychological healing,[22] exposing the connections between the truth commission and other transitional justice measures that have been employed in the country,[23] ascertaining whether the truth commission brought about reconciliation,[24] examining the implications of the truth commission on national laws and programmes as well as practices of the judiciary,[25] assessing whether the mechanism in question has resulted in positive societal and political transformation,[26] assessing whether the process demonstrates the desire of the general populace and does not contravene international human rights law[27] and investigating whether transitional justice attained the goals of improving human rights and democracy.[28]

The common thread to these assessment approaches is the assessment of impact based on the accomplishment of the perceived goals of transitional justice.[29] This is appropriate in view of the fact that every transitional justice mechanism is invariably tailored towards meeting the goals expected of it. It is, therefore, pertinent to

---

[19]Ibid., pp. 46–55.

[20]According to Sikkink 2012, pp. 30–31, this will constitute 'counterfactual reasoning'. See also Moler 2010, pp. 21–39.

[21]See Long 2008, pp. 1–14.

[22]See Allan and Allan 2000, pp. 459–477; Hamber 2001, pp. 131–148; Millar 2010, pp. 477–496; Silove et al. 2006, pp. 1222–1224; and Van Der Merwe et al. 2009b, p. 5.

[23]See Ferrara 2015.

[24]See for instance Bachmann 2010, pp. 71–100; Gibson 2004, pp. 201–217.

[25]See Bakiner 2014, pp. 6–7.

[26]See Backer 2009, p. 28.

[27]Zalaquett 1995, p. 9.

[28]See Olsen et al. 2010a, pp. 29–42.

[29]See for instance Van Der Merwe et al. 2009b, p. 5; and Wiebelhaus-Brahm 2010, p. 17. See also Olsen et al. 2010b, pp. 457–476. Assessments based on the goals of transitional justice fall into the category of 'comparison with the ideal', according to the classification by Sikkink 2012, pp. 29–30. According to Werle and Vormbaum 2018, p. 34, the goals of transitional justice are the core values that underlie the new democracy. The goals of transitional justice can be broadly categorised as establishment of the truth, enhancement of democracy and rule of law, prevention of the recurrence of human rights violations, attainment of lasting peace, national unity and reconciliation, remedying the harm caused as a result of the human rights violations suffered, and establishing accountability and justice for human rights violations. For a cross-sectional overview of these goals of transitional justice, see African Union Panel of the Wise 2013, p. 13. https://reliefweb.int/sites/reliefweb.int/files/resources/ipi_e_pub_peacejusticeafrica.pdf. Accessed 4 September 2019; Ambos 2015, p. 469; Chapman 2009b, p. 94; Crocker 1999, pp. 53–60, 61–62; De Greiff 2012, pp. 52–58; Kritz 2009, p. 13; Kritz 1995, pp. xx, xxi; Popkin and Roht-Arriaza 1995, p. 80; Posner and Vermeule 2003, p. 768; Sooka 2006, pp. 320–321; the United States Institute of Peace 2008, pp. 1–2; Van Der Merwe et al. 2009b, p. 3; and Zalaquett 1995, pp. 5, 6, 8.

conduct an assessment of the mechanism's impact against the backdrop of attainment of the goals that informed its initiation and guided its work and existence. It should be noted in this regard that methodologically, it is difficult to establish a causal link between a transitional justice mechanism and a particular goal in attempting to ascertain impact.[30] This, according to Ferrara, is because transitional justice mechanisms are 'non-linear processes' and the goals of transitional justice are based on the 'interaction' of different factors.[31] In light of this methodological constraint, this study interprets the attainment of a specific goal as impact only if it can be directly traced to implementation of the NRC's recommendations or if it is largely perceived by a majority of the respondents in this study as an impact of the NRC. Perception of impact was determined based on the percentage of positive and negative responses from the surveys conducted in this study as well as the explanations offered by respondents for their answers. In instances where the responses from the survey do not reflect a majority view on the attainment of a specific goal, the predominant reasons provided by respondents for their answers are discussed to ascertain whether the goal has been achieved in the Ghanaian context.

The discussion of the impact of the NRC is done in relation to the goals of truth, justice, reconciliation and peace. Not only are these goals undisputed and at the core of debates on the goals of transitional justice,[32] they are also relevant in the Ghanaian context.

Truth is considered a relevant goal because prior to establishment of the NRC, Ghanaians were generally in the dark regarding the fate of victims of past human rights violations. Indeed, the basis of truth as a goal of transitional justice is grounded in the individual's 'moral right' to know what happened, coupled with the fact that none of the other goals of transitional justice can be attained in the absence of truth.[33] The absence of truth can give rise to controversies regarding the country's history, and failure to address such uncertainties can cause further harm to victims and downplay the new regime. In view of this, there is the need for truth to conduct an enquiry into the past and in order to usher in the new regime smoothly.[34] From the perspective of victims, revelation of the truth plays a crucial role in their healing process.[35] Besides, public exposure of the truth helps to 'individualise guilt' and is the sole efficient means by which a country can perfectly

[30]On the difficulty of establishing a causal link between a particular paradigm and the work of a transitional justice mechanism, see Wiebelhaus-Brahm 2010, p. 22, who asserts that 'correlation' is often considered as 'causation'. He also proposes in Brahm 2005, pp. 21–22, 24–25, that taking a look at the factors which led to the establishment of a truth commission could be a first step in resolving this difficulty. See also Ferrara 2015, pp. 17–18; and Hirsch et al. 2012, p. 396.

[31]Ferrara 2015, pp. 17–18.

[32]On the goals of truth, justice, reconciliation and peace, see Werle and Vormbaum 2018, pp. 34–38.

[33]Crocker 1999, p. 50.

[34]Ibid., pp. 49–53. See also Kritz 1995, p. xxvi.

[35]See Aldana 2006, pp. 109–114.

document its past.[36] From a legal perspective, the relevance of truth stems from the obligation of states under international human rights law to investigate serious human rights violations, which is a component of the right to truth, as explained in Chap. 1.

The goal of justice is also crucial, given that prior to the establishment of the NRC, a majority of Ghanaians supported a process to address the country's past human rights violations, although there was no consensus regarding the manner in which it was to be done.[37] This is consistent with the general rationale underlying the need for justice in transitional societies. For victims, attainment of justice serves their desire for retribution against perpetrators as well as their need for restitution.[38] Moreover, the acknowledgement of past human rights violations that comes with attainment of justice is essential for the healing of victims.[39] Also, the need for justice can be understood in light of the negative implications of failing to address past human rights violations. These include impunity, continuing human rights violations, disrespect for the rule of law as well as lack of protection and safety of the general populace.[40]

Reconciliation is also important in the Ghanaian context on account of the large degree of polarisation that existed prior to the establishment of the NRC.[41] In fact, the NRC stated expressly in its report that it considered the pursuit of reconciliation in Ghana as its main mandate.[42] In a general sense, the need for reconciliation in a post-conflict or post-dictatorship society is based on the need for individuals from opposing factions and political parties to co-exist following transition.[43]

Finally, the goal of peace is a crucial paradigm for discussing the NRC in light of the long period of political instability that gave rise to the commission's establishment. Although Ghana did not experience war, regular military interventions in constitutional government occasionally caused pockets of violence, which affected rule of law and democracy. Peace is, therefore, a key factor for assessing the NRC's impact, since democracy and rule of law cannot be maintained without peace.[44]

Indeed, the relevance of justice, peace and reconciliation in the Ghanaian context have been indicated in a survey conducted by the Ghana Centre for Democratic

---

[36] Crocker 1999, pp. 49–53. See also Goldstone 1996, pp. 488, 489; and Kritz 1995, p. xxvi.

[37] About the existence of a consensus for undertaking a national reconciliation exercise in Ghana, see Boafo-Arthur 2006, pp. 132, 138, 145.

[38] See Aldana 2006, p. 117.

[39] See Goldstone 1996, p. 489.

[40] See Aldana 2006, p. 118. See also Goldstone 1996, p. 490, on the deterrent effect of justice.

[41] On the need for national reconciliation in Ghana, see Boafo-Arthur 2005, pp. 110–111.

[42] See National Reconciliation Commission 2004, vol 1, para 2.1.1.

[43] See Brounéus 2008, p. 292.

[44] In this regard, see Beetham et al. 2008, pp. 23, 24; and Mihr 2012, pp. 11–12, 19, who writes that solidarity is a key factor for assessing democracy. Solidarity in this sense entails peaceful co-existence amongst the different segments of the society, without regard to differences in beliefs and opinions, as well as the existence of support for democratic ideals by the government.

Development, which asked victims to list three goals that they believed the NRC was established to achieve. 64% of responses related to the goals of justice, helping victims to recover from their experiences, peace and reconciliation.[45]

5.4 The Impact of the National Reconciliation Commission on Truth

5.4.1 Overview of the Goal of Truth

From the perspective of transitional justice, the question of what constitutes truth is still debated. The South African TRC, for example, identified four versions of truth in its report: factual or forensic truth (based on the objective information obtained), personal or narrative truth (as told by the victim or individual in question), social or dialogical truth (as established through social interactions and dialogues) and healing or restorative truth (as acknowledged or admitted by the society).[46] This classification shows that different versions of truth can exist in relation to one event. In the case of the NRC, the commission's truth-finding mandate was to provide an 'accurate, complete and historical record' of past human rights violations.[47] Although the use of 'accurate' and 'complete' creates the impression that the NRC was supposed to provide an absolute truth, the version of truth that is actually relevant for a truth commission's work is a general narrative to serve as the society's formal acknowledgement of the past.[48] This correlates with the concept of healing or restorative truth in the South African TRC's definition. In explaining healing and restorative truth, the South African TRC expressly stated in its report that healing and restorative truth was central to its work[49] and explained:

> It is not merely the actual knowledge about past human rights violations that counts; often the basic facts about what happened are already known, at least by those who were affected. What is critical is that these facts be fully and publicly acknowledged. Acknowledgement is an affirmation that a person's pain is real and worthy of attention. It is thus central to the restoration of the dignity of victims.[50]

Based on this explanation, this study interprets the term 'truth' to entail healing and restorative truth, for two main reasons. To begin with, it is not conceivable that a truth commission can establish all versions of truth and identify the minutest

---

[45]See the Ghana Centre for Democratic Development 2006, p. 10.

[46]See the Truth and Reconciliation Commission of South Africa 1998, vol 1, paras 29–45. See also Borraine 2006, p. 21.

[47]See Republic of Ghana, National Reconciliation Commission Act, 2002, Act 611 (NRC Act), s 3(1).

[48]See Chapman 2009b, p. 109; and Hayner 2011, p. 84.

[49]Truth and Reconciliation Commission of South Africa 1998, vol 1, para 43.

[50]Ibid., para 45.

details of all facts that it encounters in the course of its work.[51] This is especially true due to the large number of cases that a truth commission typically handles over a relatively short period. Besides, in the case of the NRC, providing all versions of truth would have been impossible due to the limitations placed on its mandate under the NRC Act, to investigate mainly human rights violations that occurred only in the course of Ghana's past military regimes.[52] On that basis, the term truth as used in this study refers to society's formal acknowledgement of the facts relating to the causes and conditions of human rights violations.

During the NRC's existence, the key efforts that it made towards fulfilling its truth-finding mandate were the taking of statements from victims and the general public on their experiences and accounts of past human rights violations, the conduct of investigations to ascertain the veracity of the claims of victims (such as exhumations by the commission to find the disappeared), the holding of public and private hearings to further elucidate facts on past human rights violations in Ghana and the release of its report, which gave a detailed account of human rights violations that occurred in Ghana from March 1957 to January 1993. In order to assess how the commission fared in establishing truth, the ensuing discussion focuses on the perceptions of respondents interviewed for this study as well as on data from prior surveys.

5.4.2 Perceptions of the National Reconciliation Commission's Impact on the Establishment of Truth

5.4.2.1 Quantitative Findings

In March 2006, the Ghana Centre for Democratic Development conducted a survey on 102 victims from the northern, middle and southern areas of Ghana, to determine how victims assessed and perceived the NRC.[53] The victims interviewed were either victims who submitted petitions to the NRC and subsequently appeared before it or victims who submitted petitions but did not appear before the commission. When asked whether the NRC had produced an accurate historical record, 80% of the respondents either agreed or strongly agreed that the commission had

---

[51]On this argument, see Hayner 2011, p. 84; and Zalaquett 1995, p. 6.

[52]Aside the expressly mentioned time frames, individuals could apply to the NRC for cases falling outside the specified periods, but which occurred from 6 March 1957 and 6 January 1993, to be heard. See the NRC Act, above n 47, ss 3(1), 3(2). For details on the mandate of the NRC, see Sect. 3.3.5 in Chap. 3 of this book.

[53]See the Ghana Centre for Democratic Development 2006, pp. 3–4. In total, 41% of the respondents were from the then Northern Region (currently Northern, Savannah and North-East Regions), 20% from the Ashanti Region, 19% from the Greater Accra Region, 16% from the then Western Region (currently Western and Western-North Regions) and 4% from the Central Region of Ghana.

Table 5.1 Perceptions of the Commission's Impact on Establishing Truth: What are your opinions regarding the following statements?

Responses	Agree/ Strongly agree	Disagree/ Strongly disagree	Neutral	Unanswered
The NRC produced an accurate and complete record of past human rights violations in Ghana	59	32	38	1
The NRC's work has established the truth about past human rights violations in Ghana	77	14	38	1
Sample size = 130				

(*Source* The author 2018)

produced an accurate record of Ghana's past.[54] In another survey conducted for an independent study by a political science scholar in the University of Ghana, 100 highly educated respondents, that is, persons deemed knowledgeable in national issues, were questioned about their perceptions of the NRC.[55] This survey also yielded results similar to that of the Ghana Centre for Democratic Development, with 86% of the respondents expressing an opinion that the commission had fulfilled its mandate of creating awareness for past human rights violations, which is a key component of truth revelation.[56]

These responses give an indication that there was generally a positive perception about the NRC's truth-finding efforts shortly after conclusion of its work. In order to assess whether similar perceptions were still held almost 15 years after the commission's closure, a survey was conducted in the course of this study on 130 respondents, 67.7% of whom had tertiary education. Respondents in this study were also asked whether they considered the NRC to have produced an accurate and complete record of past human rights violations. As indicated in Table 5.1, 59 out of 130 respondents (45.4%) believed that the NRC produced an accurate record of past human rights violations. However, 23.8% of the respondents disagreed with this assertion. In comparison with the two surveys that were held shortly after completion of the NRC's work, this shows a lower percentage of people who consider the commission as having produced an accurate and complete record of past human rights violations. Nevertheless, the fact that 77 respondents (59.2%) agreed to the assertion that the NRC's work established truth about past human rights violations in Ghana implies that there is still a generally positive perception of the commission's impact on establishing truth. Indeed, this is further backed by the fact that only 14 respondents (10.8%) disagreed with this assertion. These responses have been summarised in Table 5.1.

[54] See the Ghana Centre for Democratic Development 2006, p. 22.

[55] Boafo-Arthur 2006, p. 149.

[56] Ibid.

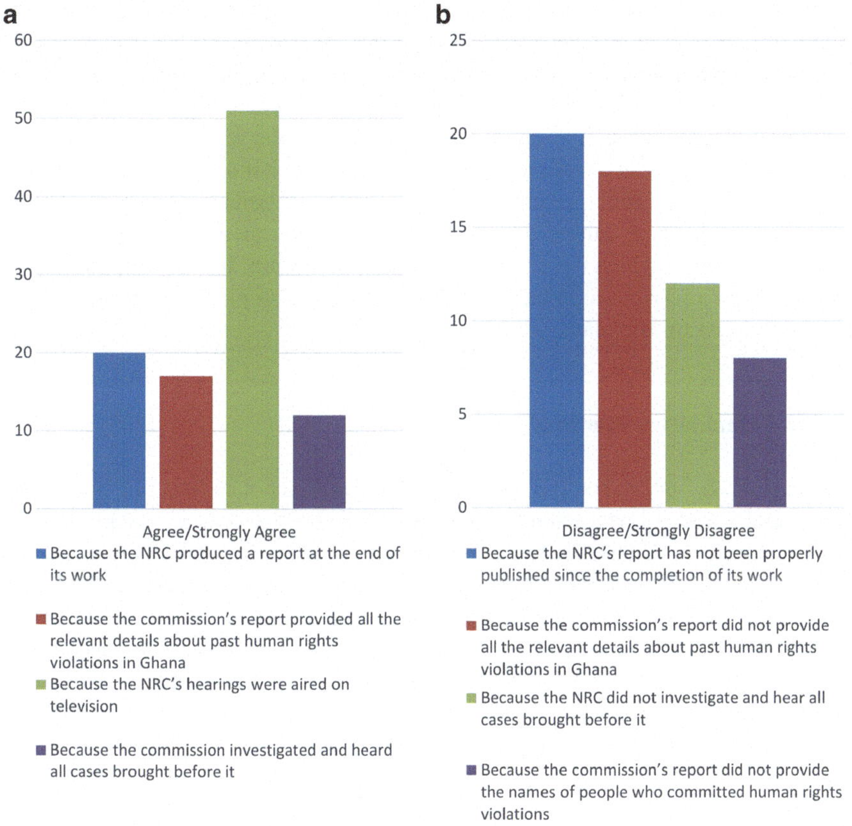

Fig. 5.1 Perceptions of the Commission's Impact on Establishing Truth: What reasons explain your points of view in statements **a** and **b** above? (Please select all that apply) (*Source* The author 2018)

Given the limited publicity for the NRC's report, it is necessary to question how respondents formed an opinion regarding the commission's impact on establishing truth. The most plausible explanation for respondents' perceptions relates to the high level of media publicity that was given to the hearings of the NRC. Even though the commission's report has never been widely disseminated, the experiences narrated during hearings attracted intense media attention, apart from the official broadcasts on national television. Hence, even individuals who did not see the commission's report were informed about victims' experiences through the media. This explains why 51 respondents (39.2%) in Fig. 5.1 based their response on the fact that the hearings of the commission had been aired on television. The public broadcasts were especially important as the basis of information for perceptions about the commission's work amongst individuals who were mere observers of its work. Indeed, this explains why 77 respondents (59.2%) considered themselves either passive or active observers of the NRC's work (i.e., neither victims nor petitioners).

In principle, however, information provided through the media cannot be regarded as truth with respect to the work of the commission. What counts as truth are the records provided by the commission. This may explain why a majority of the reasons provided by respondents to explain their views in Fig. 5.1 related to the content of the commission's report, the production of the report or its publicity.

In comparison with the surveys that were conducted shortly after the commission's closure, the lower percentage of positive perceptions regarding the NRC's impact on establishing truth establishment indicates that there are currently doubts about the extent to which the commission established truth. Indeed, responses from the structured interviews conducted during this study also give an indication of the extent of doubt on the matter.

5.4.2.2 Qualitative Findings

The qualitative survey for this study involved four scholars and practitioners in human rights and political science: Kumi Ansah-Koi, a political science professor at the University of Ghana; Kwame Boafo-Arthur, a lawyer and political science professor at the University of Ghana; Franklin Oduro, deputy director of the Ghana Centre for Democratic Development; and Isaac L. Annan, director and chief investigator at the Commission on Human Rights and Administrative Justice.

Although all respondents who were interviewed in the course of this study agreed that the commission, indeed, provided a record of past human rights violations, they did not regard it as having performed exceedingly well in that regard. The answers given by respondents indicated three main reasons for this assertion. Two respondents were of the view that the NRC compromised its pursuit of the goal of truth by focusing excessively on the goal of reconciliation.[57] In this regard, Boafo-Arthur and Ansah-Koi were of the opinion that the goals of truth and reconciliation cannot be pursued through the same channel. That is, undue emphasis on one would inevitably lead to a compromise of the other.[58] According to Boafo-Arthur and Ansah-Koi, a lesser focus on truth occurred in the Ghanaian case due to the NRC's perception that exposure of negative details about perpetrators might ignite more hatred amongst opponents and therefore hamper reconciliation.[59] In explaining this, Ansah-Koi stated that the commission had a higher tendency to assuage victims who reported the full facts of a case, rather than to investigate cases with many unknowns.[60] Also, Ansah-Koi asserted that the NRC's truth-finding goal was impeded by its screening-out exercise, which was used to dismiss petitions at

[57]Ansah-Koi K, Department of Political Science, University of Ghana, Personal Interview (18 August 2016); and Boafo-Arthur K, Department of Political Science, University of Ghana, Personal Interview (18 August 2016).

[58]Ansah-Koi, above n 57; and Boafo-Arthur, above n 57.

[59]Ansah-Koi, above n 57; and Boafo-Arthur, above n 57.

[60]Ansah-Koi, above n 57; and Boafo-Arthur, above n 57.

the commission's discretion. In his view, this affected the extent of truth that the commission delivered. However, Annan is of the view that the commission was unable to fulfil its truth-finding mandate adequately because of the dominant belief amongst a significant portion of Ghanaians that it was a political witch-hunt. In his opinion, this belief affected the extent to which the commission received nationwide acceptance to enable it carry out its truth-finding mandate effectively.[61]

5.4.3 Discussion

The views of respondents, as outlined above, show a general perception that the NRC established truth, although the responses also indicate the existence of some lapses in the extent of truth establishment. In this regard, the reasons offered by respondents to explain their responses evinced key issues related to the extent to which the commission established truth: whether the lapses in the NRC's truth-finding mandate was caused by an extensive focus on reconciliation, whether placing limits on the petitions heard by the NRC constituted a limitation on truth-finding and whether the perception of the commission as a political witch-hunt affected its truth-finding mandate.

To argue that the lapses in the NRC's truth-finding mandate were caused by an extensive focus on reconciliation would imply that it is impossible to achieve both truth and reconciliation through the same process, as opined by Ansah-Koi and Boafo-Arthur. However, there is no proof that a direct causal relationship exists between truth and reconciliation.[62] Besides, although some studies suggest that there is a relationship between truth and reconciliation, such studies have yielded different results and are context based.[63] They can, therefore, not be applied to the context of the NRC. It should, however, be noted that the commission indeed focused extensively on reconciliation, as evinced by its interpretation of its mandate to comprise national reconciliation in its report.[64] Regardless of this, this interpretation did not necessarily imply that the goal of truth was given a secondary focus. The commission's interpretation was actually based on the wording of the

---

[61] Annan IL, Director and Chief Investigator, Commission on Human Rights and Administrative Justice, Personal Interview (25 August 2016).

[62] On this issue, see for instance Gibson 2004, pp. 215–216, where after analysing empirical data, he does not come to a definite conclusion regarding whether or not there is a causal relationship between truth and reconciliation.

[63] See for instance Gibson 2004, pp. 212, 215–216, where he uses empirical data to establish a positive relationship between truth and reconciliation amongst different groups in South Africa. In contrast, a study conducted by Kaminer 2001, pp. 373–377, revealed that some victims who had appeared before the South African TRC had not been either emotionally healed or forgiven perpetrators. See also Lundy 2010, p. 104, where she writes that 'establishing the 'truth' is no guarantee that beliefs and attitudes change', and that truth can in some instances cause divisions in society.

[64] See Sect. 4.2.1 in Chap. 4 of this book.

NRC Act, which states that the sole object of the NRC was to 'seek and promote national reconciliation amongst the people' of Ghana, 'by establishing an accurate, complete and historical record' of past human rights violations.[65] The use of the word 'by' is an indication that the requirement of truth was a means towards achieving the goal of reconciliation. This does not, however, imply that truth-finding was to be relegated in the pursuit of reconciliation. Rather, one can perceive from this wording that the NRC Act considered truth as a requirement or necessity for achieving reconciliation. It is, therefore, doubtful that the NRC would have neglected the very means prescribed under the NRC Act for attaining its primary goal of reconciliation. In addition, as indicated in Chap. 4, the primary factors that led to the commission's weak investigative capacity were lack of funding, lack of cooperation from key perpetrators and staffing problems. Subsequently, the lack of political will to publish the commission's report was the key cause of the limited publicity for the NRC's report. It is, therefore, not easily discernible from the work of the NRC that the lapses in its pursuit of truth were based on its extensive reliance on the goal of reconciliation. If the commission indeed tried to mollify individuals who wanted to report cases with full facts as a way of promoting reconciliation, that would have been contrary to its mandate, since it would place a limitation on its establishment of truth.[66] Yet the lapses in the NRC's pursuit of truth cannot be imputed to this reason as it is not evident from the commission's work, described in Chap. 4.

Regarding respondents' assertion that the commission's screening-out exercise affected fulfilment of its truth-finding mandate, two key reasons can explain why the commission conducted a screening-out exercise. To begin with, the screening-out exercise was within the discretion that the NRC Act gave to the commission regarding whether or not to receive petitions on human rights violations that occurred in non-military regimes.[67] Besides, the commission screened out cases because they either fell outside the period stated in its mandate or involved acts that could not be categorised under any of the types of human rights violations in its mandate.[68] These reasons imply that the screening-out exercise did not contradict the commission's legal mandate. Moreover, they did not limit the commission's establishment of truth because such limitations cannot be considered as a dent on the commission's truth-finding mandate. Indeed, some trade-offs are acceptable in the truth-finding goal of truth commissions, owing to the numerous challenges in investigating past human rights violations.[69] For instance, it is

[65]NRC Act, above n 47, s 3(1).

[66]On this subject, see Zalaquett 1995, p. 8, who writes that it is not acceptable for a truth commission to compensate victims in order not to disclose the truth. See also Borraine 2006, p. 22; and Mihr 2012, p. 32.

[67]This is because although the commission, in reality, decided to receive all petitions relating to human rights violations that occurred between 6 March 1957 and 6 January 1993, the existence of the discretion, created room for possible selectivity.

[68]See National Reconciliation Commission 2004, vol 1, para 2.3.3.4.1 at note 1.

[69]Zalaquett 1995, pp. 6–8.

acceptable to place a limit on the nature of violations that are investigated.[70] Hence, although the NRC was required under the NRC Act to provide an 'accurate, complete and historical record' of past human rights violations,[71] it is not conceivable that it could have heard all petitions brought before it.

The dominant perception of the commission as a witch-hunt, as opined by Annan, is reflected in the high degree of political resistance that the commission faced in the course of its work. Although no direct link can be established in this regard, there is no doubt that the political resistance faced by the commission affected key aspects of its work, such as the manner in which it handled political witnesses (like former president Jerry John Rawlings). Besides, the resistance to the commission's work was a likely reason for its failure to name perpetrators in its report. Hence, the commission's pursuit of truth can be said to have been affected by the general perception that it was a witch-hunt exercise.

Two other facts can be identified regarding the extent to which the NRC impacted the establishment of truth. First, the basic components of the right to truth, such as preservation of memory and revelation of information to victims, promotion of knowledge of such information and prevention of information loss, have not been pursued in Ghana since the closure of the commission.[72] This may explain why 107 of the respondents (82.3%) in the Fig. 5.1 explained their views with reasons related to either the content of the commission's report, the production of the report or its publicity. In the Ghanaian case, these requirements would have been met through proper publicity of the NRC's report. Second, despite the existence of the NRC's report, there are still divergent views regarding key occurrences in Ghana's history, which suggests that the records that were provided by the NRC regarding Ghana's history is either not known or has not been accepted by the general citizenry. A key case that still forms the basis of divergent views relates to the circumstances surrounding the 1982 murder of three judges. In this regard, accusations are still made occasionally against different political and public figures as perpetrators of those murders.[73]

In light of these facts, one can say that the NRC's truth-finding goal was partially fulfilled. The majority view of respondents in Table 5.1, that the NRC established truth about past human rights violations, can therefore be said to relate to what the commission achieved during its existence—namely, obtaining statements from

[70]Ibid., p. 8.

[71]Ibid., p. 6.

[72]Regarding these aspects of the right to truth, see United Nations Commission on Human Rights 2005, paras 3, 5, 14, 15.

[73]For instance, some news items create the impression that some Ghanaians still consider former President Jerry John Rawlings and his former security adviser as being complicit in the murder, although this is not stated in the NRC's report. See for instance: Quansah 2013. http://thechronicle.com.gh/rawlings-tsikata-cannot-escape-blame-for-murders-so-foul/. Accessed 22 October 2019; The Daily Guide 2007. http://www.ghanaweb.com/GhanaHomePage/NewsArchive/artikel.php?ID=126507. Accessed 22 October 2019; and Johnson 2014. http://www.dailyguideghana.com/3-murdered-judges-remembered/. Accessed 22 October 2019.

victims and the general public, conducting investigations in cases (such as exhumations), conduct of public and private hearings and the release of its report. Since its closure, however, the commission has not sufficiently impacted truth revelation. The commission's work will have a more profound impact in terms of establishing truth if extensive publicising of its report is reinitiated and details of the records in the report are incorporated into school curricula to create more awareness amongst Ghanaians. Also, key human rights violations that were not addressed by the NRC on account of the limitations in its mandate can be revisited by establishing another truth commission to deal specifically with such issues.

5.5 The Impact of the National Reconciliation Commission on Justice

Defining the concept of justice is a difficult task, owing to the fact that its scope has been debated for centuries. This study is concerned with justice only from the perspective of transitional justice. It thus recognises that justice goes beyond the bounds of criminal justice and includes the necessity to address the needs of victims, heal the society from the past and usher in a process for reconciliation.[74] The United Nations has captured the broad nature of justice in the context of transitional justice in its definition:

> an ideal of accountability and fairness in the protection and vindication of rights and the prevention and punishment of wrongs. Justice implies regard for the rights of the accused, for the interests of victims and for the well-being of society at large.[75]

Based on the wording of this definition, justice within the ambit of transitional justice includes prosecutions (i.e., 'accountability and fairness', 'punishment' of wrongs, rights of accused), pursuit of victims' rights to remedies (i.e., 'protection and vindication of rights' and 'regard for the rights of victims') and the prevention of the recurrence of human rights violations (i.e., 'prevention of wrongs' and 'regard for the well-being of society at large').[76] In the Ghanaian context, since prosecutions and punishment of perpetrators have never taken place, they do not form part of this assessment but are rather discussed in Chap. 6 as part of the neglected aspects of transitional justice in Ghana.[77] This section focuses on the pursuit of victims' rights and prevention of the recurrence of human rights violations.

---

[74]See Aldana 2006, p. 117; Ambos 2009, pp. 22–23; and Borraine 2006, pp. 18, 20.

[75]United Nations Security Council 2004, para 7.

[76]For further explanations of the different forms of justice under transitional justice, see Porter 2015, pp. 11, 13–14; and Van Der Merwe 2009a, pp. 115, 119. See also Borraine 2006, p. 18, who identifies the forms of justice as economic, restorative, retributive and distributive.

[77]See Sect. 6.2 in Chap. 6 of this book.

5.5.1 The National Reconciliation Commission and the Pursuit of Victims' Rights to Remedies

As part of the pursuit of justice, provision of remedies to victims is critical because of the deep-seated wounds that conflicts can leave in societies.[78] There is thus the need for subsequent regimes to restore the society by healing those wounds. According to the United Nations, victims' remedies comprise 'equal and effective access to justice; adequate, effective and prompt reparation for harm suffered; and access to relevant information concerning violations and reparation mechanisms'.[79]

Within the Ghanaian framework, fulfilment of the right to a remedy was a key goal, in view of the NRC's duty to identify victims of human rights violations in the country and make recommendations for redress.[80] The commission's efforts to achieve this goal are evidenced by its recommendation for the repeal of the Constitution's amnesty provisions to enable victims of human rights violations to seek redress. Another key effort of the commission was its recommendations for reparations to victims and an apology to the whole nation by the president. Moreover, the commission's remedial efforts and its dedication to facilitating the healing process are evidenced in the many public hearings, which provided an avenue for a large number of victims to air their grievances. Other aspects of the commission's remedial efforts are its provision of counselling services and medical and financial support to victims.

5.5.1.1 Perceptions of the Commission's Impact on the Right of Victims to Remedies: Quantitative Findings

Shortly after the closure of the NRC, there were differing views on its impact in providing remedies to victims. In two surveys of victims conducted by the Ghana Centre for Democratic Development, respondents displayed a positive response to the commission's remedial efforts. The first survey was conducted in April 2005 with 98 victims from the Western (now the Western-North and Western Regions), Volta (now the Volta and Oti Regions) and Greater Accra Regions of Ghana. The second survey, described in Sect. 5.4.2.1, was conducted in March 2006 with 102 victims. In these two surveys, 75% (2005) and 88% (2006) of respondents agreed that the NRC provided an avenue for them to ease their pain.[81] These views do not imply that victims considered the commission to have provided them with the

---

[78]See Hamber 1995. http://www.csvr.org.za/publications/1713-do-sleeping-dogs-lie-the-psychological-implications-of-the-truth-and-reconciliation-commission-in-south-africa. Accessed 15 October 2019; and Hayner 2011, p. 145.

[79]For further details on victims' rights to remedies, see United Nations General Assembly 2006, para 11.

[80]See the NRC Act, above n 47, ss 4(c), 20(2)(h), 20(2)(d).

[81]See the Ghana Centre for Democratic Development 2006, pp. 17–18.

Table 5.2 Perceptions of the Commission's Impact on the Right of Victims to Remedies: What are your opinions regarding the following statements?

Responses	Agree/ Strongly agree	Disagree/ Strongly disagree	Neutral	Unanswered
The NRC's work helped to address the needs of victims of past human rights violations in Ghana	53	32	45	0
The NRC's work has brought healing and restoration to victims of past human rights violations in Ghana	57	27	46	0
Sample size = 130				

(*Source* The author 2018)

healing they wanted. This is evinced by the fact that 80% of the respondents in the second survey considered the commission's work as having made them 'relive' their horrible experiences.[82] Regarding the commission's compensation package, 48% of respondents in the second survey considered it to be adequate, whilst 43% did not agree that it was adequate.[83] These responses indicate that there was no real consensus amongst victims regarding the commission's provision of remedies.

The survey conducted for this study, as outlined in Table 5.2, indicates that there is still a lack of consensus on the issue, although the respondents in this study (130 respondents, including only six victims) represent different demographics from those in the earlier surveys.[84] Despite the fact that 53 respondents (40.8%) agreed that the NRC's work helped to address the needs of victims of past human rights violations, 45 respondents (34.6%) remained neutral, indicating their refusal to take a stance on the issue. However, 32 respondents (24.6%) disagreed with this proposition. Similar views were expressed regarding whether or not the NRC's work has brought healing and restoration to victims of past human rights violations: 57 (43.8%) respondents agreed with the assertion, whilst 27 (20.8%) disagreed. Once again, a notable percentage of respondents (35.4%) remained neutral. The views of respondents are summarised in Table 5.2.

The high rate of neutral responses outlined in Table 5.2 is most likely related to the fact that most respondents were merely observers of the NRC's work, who could not concretely attest to the extent to which the commission provided remedies to victims. In Fig. 5.2, the key factor that informed respondents' views was whether or not the NRC afforded victims an opportunity to recount their experiences. This can be explained in light of the fact that the hearings of the NRC were the main source of knowledge about the commission's work. Indeed, as outlined in Chap. 4, the NRC conducted hearings for a large proportion of the petitions it received. It is, therefore, not surprising that observers of the commission's work would consider

[82]Ibid., pp. 17–18.

[83]Ibid., p. 23.

[84]For the demographic details of all respondents, see Appendix C of this book.

the opportunity for victims to recount their experiences as the most remedial aspect for victims.

Although respondents were not directly questioned about the adequacy of the monetary compensation awarded, the fact that 45 respondents named monetary compensation as a reason that the commission was able to address victims' suffering shows that respondents considered it as a relevant factor. Nevertheless, it is questionable why only 19 out of the 57 respondents, see Fig. 5.2, who held positive

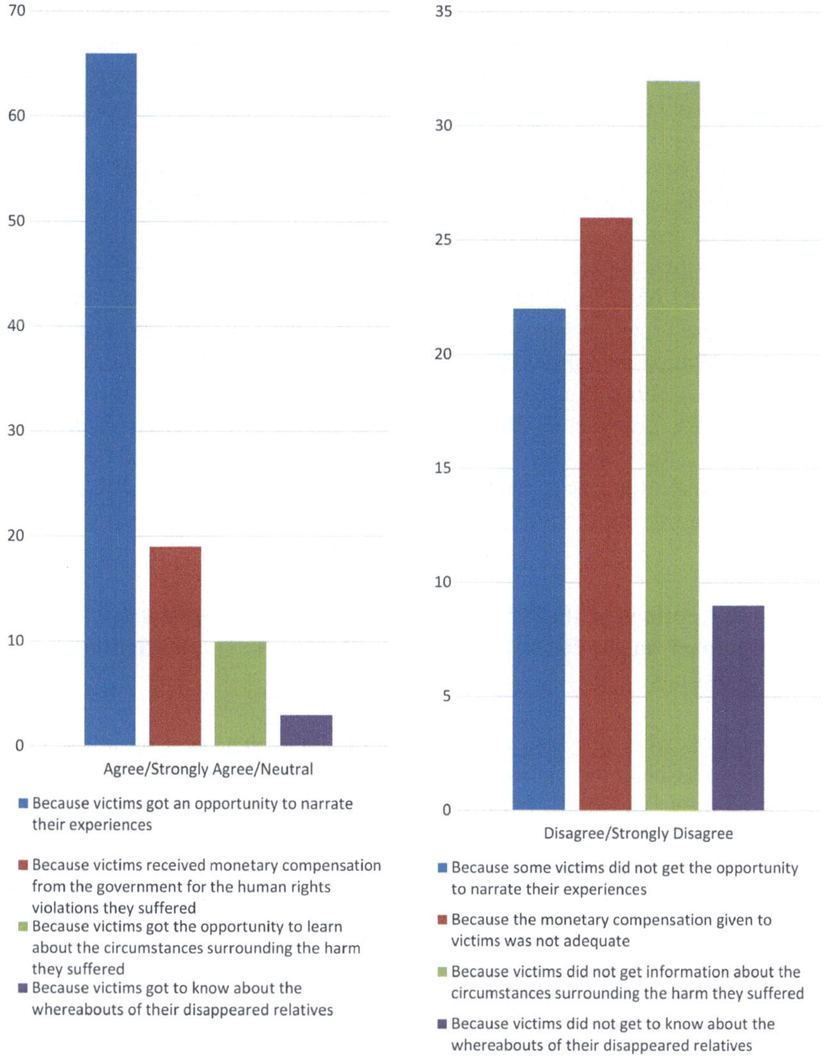

Fig. 5.2 Perceptions of the Commission's Impact on the Right of Victims to Remedies: What reasons explain your points of view in the statement above? (Please select all that apply) (*Source* The author 2018)

perceptions about the NRC's impact on providing remedies to victims, selected the payment of monetary compensation as a reason. It is most likely that the remaining 38 respondents did not consider the monetary compensation to be adequate and therefore did not perceive it as the reason for their view that the NRC had brought healing and restoration to victims of past human rights violations. Indeed, this explains why 26 of the respondents who had negative perceptions in Fig. 5.2 selected the reason related to inadequacy of the compensation paid.

Another key trend shown in Fig. 5.2 is that a majority of the respondents who held a negative perception about the NRC's impact on providing remedies explained their view in terms of the fact that victims were not informed about the circumstances surrounding the harm they suffered. A likely explanation for this is the weak investigative capacity of the NRC, as discussed in Chap. 4 and the limited dissemination of the NRC's report. It also appears that respondents did not regard the availability of opportunities for victims to know the whereabouts of disappeared relatives as a primary factor related to providing remedies to victims, in light of the low number of responses that were based on that reason. A plausible explanation is that few cases of enforced disappearances actually occurred in Ghana. Indeed, in the report of the NRC, only 186 cases of forced disappearances were recorded.[85] Hence, it is not surprising that few respondents considered it a relevant aspect of the commission's impact on providing remedies for victims.

In Table 5.2, although a greater number of responses reflect a positive perception of the NRC's impact regarding providing remedies to victims, it cannot be considered as a majority view, since it represents less than 50% of respondents. This trend in the responses is partly mirrored in the answers generated from experts interviewed during this study.

5.5.1.2 Perceptions of the National Reconciliation Commission's Impact on the Right of Victims to Remedies: Qualitative Findings

All respondents who were interviewed shared the view that the main impact of the commission has been the payment of monetary compensation to some victims of past human rights violations. However, three respondents considered the monetary compensations to have been insufficient, whilst one respondent considered it to have been a practical amount, given the nation's economy at the time.

Despite admitting that the NRC's impact on providing remedies had been positive as a result of the monetary compensation, three respondents agreed that the extent of the commission's impact on providing remedies for victims was adversely affected by the amnesty provisions in the 1992 Constitution. Boafo-Arthur, for instance, was of the view that the wholesale immunity that has been granted to prominent politicians was the key reason for the commission's failure to engage

[85] See National Reconciliation Commission 2004, vol 1, Chap. 6.

them extensively in its investigations and an impediment to the commission's ability to name perpetrators.[86] Oduro also opined that the existence of the amnesty provisions is a permanent hindrance to providing remedies to victims.[87]

5.5.1.3 Discussion

The quantitative and qualitative findings indicate that respondents' perceptions of the NRC's impact on providing remedies for victims related to several factors: victims' knowledge of circumstances surrounding the harm suffered, their ability to recount their experiences, the payment of monetary compensation to victims and the ability to seek redress in court (i.e., due to the amnesty provisions that are believed to hinder the commission's impact on providing remedies for victims). Indeed, these views are actually reflected in the components of remedies for victims as outlined above.[88] Although a greater percentage of respondents indicated positive views about the NRC's impact on provision of remedies, their explanations for their views point to two main issues that might have affected the extent of the commission's remedial impact. These issues relate to whether the monetary compensation that was recommended by the NRC was low and whether the amnesty provisions in the 1992 Constitution have been a hindrance to adequate remedies for victims.

In light of the commission's practical experiences outlined in Chap. 4, the payment of monetary compensation to some victims can be regarded as the main remedial impact that the NRC had on victims. However, its adequacy remains debatable, since it is a highly subjective issue that depends on the type of expectations that victims had for the commission. It should be noted in this regard that in most cases, compensation awarded by a state in the context of transitional justice is merely a symbolic measure, meant to acknowledge the state's wrongs, and to rebuild 'relations of trust' in a divided society.[89] Indeed, the possibility of awarding compensation that is commensurate with the harm suffered poses a number of challenges. Within the context of a transitional society, there are usually a large number of victims from different generations. It is therefore practically impossible to quantify the extent of harm suffered by each victim in exact monetary terms. Moreover, a state that is undergoing transition is most likely to be faced with enormous economic challenges, which makes it financially difficult to compensate

[86]Boafo-Arthur, above n 57.

[87]Oduro F, Deputy Director, Ghana Centre for Democratic Development, Personal Interview (16 August 2016).

[88]See United Nations General Assembly 2006, para 11.

[89]Satz 2012, pp. 140–141.

victims for all the harm caused in tangible terms.[90] Hence, the amount of compensation paid usually depends on the number of victims.[91] Besides, even if it were possible to make atonement for the harm suffered in exact monetary terms, it is doubtful that such claims could be sustained by individuals against a state. This is because although victims of human rights violations have a right to obtain remedies, it is questionable whether the state owes an obligation under customary international law to award compensation to individuals for historical injustices.[92] In light of these factors, the amount of compensation that was allocated for victims cannot be considered insufficient and was therefore not a detraction from the commission's impact on providing remedies. Even if such an argument was tenable, the amount of monetary compensation recommended by the NRC can still be considered a practical amount in light of the state of Ghana's economy at the time.[93] The country's daily minimum wage at the time was 1.90 Ghanaian cedis, whilst the rate of poverty was 31.9%.[94] Nevertheless, the key detraction regarding the payment of compensation is the failure of the state to ensure the compensation that was earmarked by the NRC to be given to victims was actually paid.

Also, respondents' assertion that the amnesty provisions in the 1992 Constitution has been a hindrance to provision of remedies to victims is only partially true. This is because the only remedies that have been barred by the amnesty provisions are judicial remedies. Remedies that are accessible through non-judicial means, such as the reparations recommended by the NRC, are not barred and are still available to victims. Hence, the amnesty provisions have hindered the provision of only judicial remedies.

In summary, the outcome of the survey indicated that the NRC indeed impacted the provision of remedies to victims, by providing them an avenue for narrating their experiences. Another main impact of the commission on victims' rights to remedies is the payment of monetary compensation pursuant to its recommendations, to some of the victims. Other aspects of victims' remedies have not materialised, however, mainly due to the government's failure to implement the remaining reparative measures that were recommended by the commission, and its failure to pay the compensation of some victims who were earmarked by the NRC to receive compensations. Also, the continued existence of amnesty provisions in Ghana's Constitution has hampered the commission's impact on judicial remedies, which is discussed further in Chap. 6.

---

[90]On the economic status of transitional societies, see De Greiff 2009, p. 29.

[91]See Satz 2012, p. 145.

[92]On this issue, see Tomuschat 2005, pp. 582–587, where he argues that individual compensation claims are not a right under customary international law.

[93]The individual sums that were received by victims ranged from 217 USD and 3,300 USD, based on the extent and nature of human right violations suffered. See Asare 2008, p. 35. See also National Reconciliation Commission, vol 1, para 7.4.3.

[94]See the Ghana Statistical Service 2018, p. 12; and The Ghana Statistical Service 2008, p. 27. http://www.statsghana.gov.gh/docfiles/gh_figures_2008.pdf. Accessed 11 November 2019.

5.5.2 *Preventing the Recurrence of Human Rights Violations*

In the pursuit of justice, prevention of further human rights violations is crucial because the basis for a transition to democracy, is to end protracted human rights violations during the previous regime.[95] Besides, the duty of states to provide remedies for human rights violations under international human rights law also entails the need for states to prevent recurrence of violations.[96] A key component of prevention of human rights violations is institutional reform, by which a society can fulfil its obligation to provide guarantees of non-repetition.[97] In this sense, there is the need to create institutions that support the rule of law and respect for human rights, in order to ensure non-recurrence of human rights violations in the society.[98]

In the Ghanaian context, prevention of human rights violations was a key aspect of the NRC's work, since one of the commission's duties was to make suggestions 'to prevent and avoid the repetition of such violations and abuses'.[99] The major work of the commission in this regard are its recommendations for inclusion of human rights education in the curricula at all educational levels; provision of human rights education to members of the military, police, prison officers and members of the judiciary; and the respective recommendations for reforming Ghanaian state institutions, as outlined earlier.[100]

5.5.2.1 Perceptions of the National Reconciliation Commission's Impact on Preventing the Recurrence of Human Rights Violations: Quantitative Findings

Unlike the other paradigms used in this study to assess the NRC's impact, no prior surveys were found that are directly related to the prevention of the recurrence of human rights violations. The only indirectly related survey was conducted by

---

[95]See United Nations General Assembly, Human Rights Council 2013, para 91.

[96]See the United Nations Human Rights Committee 2004, para 19.

[97]On the linkage of institutional reforms to guarantees of non-repetition, see Andreu-Guzmán 2013, p. 4. https://www.files.ethz.ch/isn/164673/80ed6b7fa08ff1e0620fe297f85f63f0.pdf. Accessed 1 November 2019; and Ferstman 2010, p. 23. See also United Nations General Assembly 2006, para 23; and Inter-American Court of Human Rights, *Velásquez-Rodríguez v Honduras*, Judgment of 29 July 1988, Ser. C. No. 4 (Velásquez-Rodríguez 1988), para 174. Regarding the role of institutional reform in prevention of human rights violations, see Ferstman 2010, p. 26.

[98]See Office of the United Nations High Commissioner for Human Rights 2006b, p. 3.

[99]See NRC Act, above n 47, s 20(2)(e).

[100]See National Reconciliation Commission 2004, vol 3, paras 7.7.4, 3.3.11, 3.3.22.2, 3.3.28.1, 3.4.1. Regarding the recommendations for institutional reform, see Sect. 4.4.1.3 in Chap. 4 of this book.

Table 5.3 Perceptions of the Commission's Impact on Preventing the Recurrence of Human Rights Violations: What is your opinion regarding the following statement?

Responses	Agree/ Strongly agree	Disagree/ Strongly disagree	Neutral	Unanswered
The work of the NRC has helped to prevent human rights violations from recurring in Ghana	41	53	35	1
Sample size = 130				

(*Source* The author 2018)

Boafo-Arthur shortly after the completion of the commission's work.[101] In Boafo-Arthur's survey, 86% of the 100 respondents believed that the commission had achieved its goal of creating awareness of human rights violations,[102] which is a requisite basis for preventing a recurrence of human rights violations. In the course of this study, respondents were expressly asked, as indicated in Table 5.3, whether the NRC's work had prevented the recurrence of human rights violations: 53 respondents (40.7%) disagreed with this assertion, whilst 41 respondents (31.5%) agreed.

As Fig. 5.3 shows, the dominant reason given by the 41 respondents who considered the NRC as having prevented recurrence of human rights violations related to the fact that the commission promoted awareness of human rights violations. In general, this implies that there is a higher rate of positive perceptions regarding the extent to which the commission created awareness on human rights. This explains why only 16 respondents held a contrary view. Since the NRC held a large number of public hearings, a likely explanation for this dominant reason relates to the fact that respondents imputed the commission's hearings as creation of awareness of human rights violations. In Fig. 5.3, the other main explanation selected by respondents related to the fact that there is an improved culture of respect for human rights and Ghanaians are more aware of their rights. However, the fact that 38 other respondents disagreed with this assertion implies that there is a divided opinion on the issue. This is because the number of respondents (29) who hold this opinion cannot be considered a majority. The responses also show divided opinion regarding the issues of whether or not the human rights violations that occurred before Ghana's transition to democracy are still rampant and whether or not there is more human rights education in schools since completion of the NRC's work. This explains why the numbers of respondents who selected these reasons in both positive and negative terms are almost equal.

Comparing the views of respondents, there is no majority perception regarding the NRC's impact on preventing the recurrence of human rights violations. In particular, this is evinced by the fact that in Table 5.3, less than 50% of the total respondents either agreed or disagreed with the assertion. Nevertheless, the fact that

[101] Boafo-Arthur 2006, p. 149.

[102] Ibid.

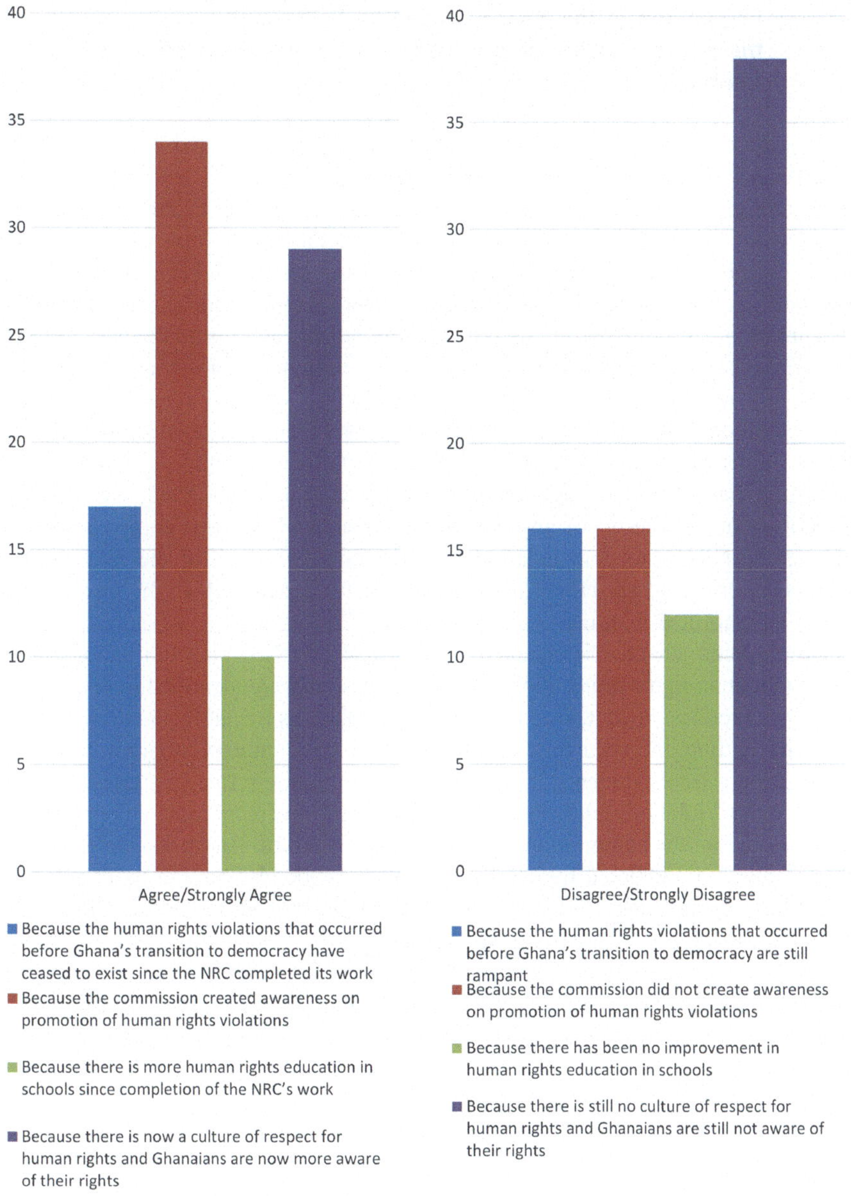

Fig. 5.3 Perceptions of the Commission's Impact on Preventing the Recurrence of Human Rights Violations: What reasons explain your points of view in the statement above? (Please select all that apply) (*Source* The author 2018)

a greater number of respondents (40.3%) did not regard the NRC as having prevented the recurrence of human rights violations means that there is a higher percentage of negative views on the matter.

5.5.2.2 Perceptions of the NRC's Impact on Preventing the Recurrence of Human Rights Violations: Qualitative Findings

The results of the quantitative survey above are partly supported by the views of experts on the subject. All respondents agreed that the NRC had not prevented recurrence of human rights violations. A key example cited in this regard relates to the fact that the NRC's recommendations for institutional reform, which is a key aspect of prevention of human rights violations, have not been implemented. Respondents also reiterated their belief that other factors could be accountable for the current extent of human rights protection in Ghana, apart from the NRC. In this regard, the key factors that were cited were the existence of a vibrant media, civil society, the regulation of the security agencies in the Constitution and the adoption of constitutional rule in Ghana, which laid a comprehensive legal framework for human rights protection.[103] In their view, although few reforms in human rights protection that reflect recommendations of the NRC can be observed, such reforms did not occur as a result of any express governmental effort to comprehensively address the NRC's recommendations. On the contrary, most of the reforms that have occurred over time reflect international best practices, which the government would have to deal with one way or the other.[104]

Despite their stance, respondents admitted that the NRC played a minor role in securing human rights protection. Three main reasons were identified in this regard. First, the commission addressed human rights violations by putting a closure on the past and ending the recurring discourse about past military regimes prior the commission's establishment.[105] Second, the commission's role in addressing past human rights violations related to the fact that victims were afforded an opportunity to appear before the commission and were heard.[106] Third, Ansah-Koi believes that the commission addressed human rights violations merely through its demonstrative effect, by sending a message to perpetrators that similar acts will not be condoned in future.[107] According to Ansah-Koi, one cannot say the commission has prevented human rights from recurring, in so far as the amnesty provisions in Ghana's Constitution are still in existence. In his view, the amnesty provisions hindered the commission's efforts to adequately address past human rights violations.[108]

[103]Annan, above n 61; and Oduro, above n 87.

[104]Oduro, above n 87.

[105]Ibid.

[106]Annan, above n 61.

[107]Ansah-Koi, above n 57.

[108]Ibid. According to him, the commission could have dealt better with human rights if its recommendations had been taken more seriously and the amnesty provisions in Ghana had been repealed.

All respondents were also of the view that although the NRC has not played a role in that regard, Ghana currently has a better human rights regime than it did prior to the establishment of the NRC. The respondents asserted that it is irrelevant to discuss a recurrence of human rights violations in Ghana since there have been no gross human rights violations at the behest of the state. Besides, the state has put in place adequate frameworks to address violations that are committed, such as the courts and the Commission on Human Rights and Administrative Justice; it has also ratified core international human rights treaties.[109]

Whilst admitting the above improvements, three of the respondents also believe that there are still lapses in the system. One respondent was quick to state that the existing human rights framework in Ghana is not very effective in practice. For instance, he stated that there are still struggles for human rights protection regarding inclusion of marginalised groups, such as persons with disabilities or with different sexual orientations. Besides, segments of the society, such as mentally disabled people and prisoners, are not properly cared for and thus face threats of torture.[110] Another respondent also cited instances of abuse of freedom of speech in the country and abuse of judicial freedom.[111]

5.5.2.3 Discussion

Given the above responses from the survey conducted in the course of this study, a greater percentage of respondents (40.8%) held the opinion that the NRC's work has failed to prevent a recurrence of human rights violations. Although the views expressed by respondents in both the qualitative and quantitative surveys show that the commission took significant steps during its existence to promote human rights protection, the higher rate of negative perceptions about the commission's impact on preventing the recurrence of human rights violations are based on the fact that

---

[109] Annan, above n 61; and Oduro, above n 87.

[110] Oduro, above n 87.

[111] In support of his answer, he cited the case of *Montie three*, in which three radio discussion panelists were sentenced to four months imprisonment for publicly threatening to rape the Chief Justice of Ghana and kill some other judges. The said threats were made against the judges for presiding on a case that had been brought against the Ghanaian Electoral Commission to challenge the credibility of the voters register. See Supreme Court of Ghana, *Abu Ramadan and Evans Nimako v The Electoral Commission of Ghana and the Attorney General; In Re the Owner of the Station-Montie FM and three Others*, 27 July 2016, Civil Motion No: J8/108/2016. He also cited the case of the 2012 election petition, in which following the holding of the presidential elections, the then opposition New Patriotic Party, petitioned the Supreme Court of Ghana, to challenge the validity of the election results. Although the decision of the court indicated that there were indeed some electoral irregularities, the petition was dismissed, and the leader of the opposition who had petitioned the court, accepted the court's decision in good faith. See Supreme Court of Ghana, *In the Matter of a Petition Challenging the Validity of the Election of John Dramani Mahama as President of the Republic of Ghana Pursuant to the Presidential Election Held on 7th and 8th December, 2012, Between Nana Addo Dankwa Akufo-Addo and Two Others; and John Dramani Mahama and Two Others*, 2013, Writ No. J1/6/2013.

Ghana has not experienced a better human rights regime since the closure of the NRC.

In this regard, the lapses in human rights protection that were identified by respondents are also indicated by other sources. In a 2016 report submitted by Ghana to the United Nations, it was disclosed that Ghana's Commission on Human Rights and Administrative Justice, which is the country's main body in charge of investigating breaches of human rights violations, is poorly resourced and lacks key powers required to enable it carry out its functions effectively.[112] Besides a report by Amnesty International shows that human rights violations, such as discrimination against the mentally ill and disabled, discrimination on the basis of sexual orientation and gender, domestic violence, police brutality, female genital mutilation, torture of prisoners, child labour and forms of slavery pursuant to traditional practices, are still rife in the country.[113]

The existence of these lapses does not, however, imply that there has been a recurrence of human rights violations. To begin with, these lapses are not reflective of the human rights violations that formed the subject matter of the NRC's work. For instance, no cases of enforced disappearances, extrajudicial killings, unlawful detentions and arbitrary killings have been recorded in the country since the establishment of the NRC. Besides, Ghana's legal framework for protection of fundamental human rights continues to be elaborate, as indicated by the provisions in the 1992 Constitution and the creation of a Human Rights Division at the High Court of Ghana.[114] Indeed, the extent of human rights protection in Ghana is quite laudable, when compared to that of other West African states. Under the 2019 rankings of Freedom House, for instance, Ghana was ranked as 'free' and obtained a high score of 83 out of 100 for observance and respect for political rights and civil liberties.[115]

Regardless of these facts, the outcome of this study's survey suggests that the NRC cannot be considered to have prevented the recurrence of human rights violations. This is also the case because the non-recurrence of human rights violations cannot be attributed to the NRC's work or any of its recommendations. At best, the NRC can be said to have served as an avenue for putting a closure on the past, as reiterated in the responses obtained in the qualitative survey. Yet this cannot be

[112]See Office of the United Nations High Commissioner for Human Rights. http://www.ohchr.org/EN/NewsEvents/Pages/DisplayNews.aspx?NewsID=20180&LangID=E. Accessed 2 October 2019.

[113]See Amnesty International 2013. http://www.amnestyusa.org/research/reports/annual-report-ghana-2013?page=show. Accessed 2 October 2019; and Office of the United Nations High Commissioner for Human Rights 2016. http://www.ohchr.org/EN/NewsEvents/Pages/DisplayNews.aspx?NewsID=20180&LangID=E. Accessed 2 October 2019.

[114]Office of the United Nations High Commissioner for Human Rights. http://www.ohchr.org/EN/NewsEvents/Pages/DisplayNews.aspx?NewsID=20180&LangID=E. Accessed 2 October 2019.

[115]Freedom House is a private watchdog institution that demonstrates its commitment to democracy and world freedom by evaluating determinants of world freedom and conducting advocacy for the promotion of political and civil rights. See Freedom House 2019. https://freedomhouse.org/report/freedom-world/2019/ghana. Accessed 2 October 2019.

considered an impact on preventing the recurrence of human rights violations, since it does not reflect a majority view of respondents.

5.5.3 *Summary*

Given the outcome of the above surveys on the provision of remedies to victims and the prevention of the recurrence of human rights violations, the NRC's key impact on justice relates to providing an avenue for victims to recount their experiences and the payment of monetary compensations to some of the victims of human rights violations. Regarding prevention of the recurrence of human rights violations, the greater percentage of negative perceptions as regards the commission's impact suggest that the commission has not prevented the recurrence of human rights violations. There are, however, more positive views concerning the NRC's impact on providing remedies for victims, which indicates that the commission has resulted in the provision of some remedies for victims. In principle, the extent to which the commission impacted justice has been limited by the non-implementation of the commission's victim-related recommendations, failure to pay the compensation of some victims who were named by the commission to receive reparations and the existence of amnesty provisions in the 1992 Constitution, which is discussed further in Chap. 6.

5.6 The Impact of the Commission on National Reconciliation

Like most concepts in the field of transitional justice, there is no universally accepted definition for reconciliation.[116] The meaning of the concept depends largely on the societal 'context and the nature of transition'.[117] The concept has religious undertones and may be advantageous or even harmful depending on how it is understood. For instance, if reconciliation is part of a process where society forcefully reconciles and merely overlooks and hides the deeds of past regimes, it may be disapproved of by victims. In contrast, where reconciliation comes with 'commitment and sacrifice', it can yield positive results.[118] Reconciliation also has political connotations when used in reference to the political means by which formerly opposed groups in the society are brought back together.[119] The term has thus been given divergent explanations, such as 'putting relationships and societies

[116]See Borraine 2006, p. 22; Chapman 2009a, p. 145; and Mihr 2012, p. 32.

[117]Sánchez and Rognvik 2012, p. 6.

[118]See Borraine 2006, p. 22; and Mihr 2012, p. 32.

[119]Ibid.

back together again',[120] 'the long-term setting aside of disputes between factions that have divided a nation',[121] 'healing the wounds of the past and repairing the broken relationships within a society aiming to achieve a state of lasting sustainable peace'[122] and 'the process of moving from a divided past to a shared future'.[123] Other definitions include 'creating conditions for the removal of violence in various forms, including structural and cultural violence from post-conflict societies',[124] and 'a societal process that involves mutual acknowledgement of past suffering and the changing of destructive attitudes and behavior into constructive relationships towards sustainable peace'.[125] It has also been asserted that reconciliation should not be mistakenly equated with forgiveness, as the latter is a one-sided affair, involving only one party, whereas reconciliation must involve all parties.[126]

Some common inferences can be drawn from these definitions, despite their different nuances. The definitions all consider the resolution of past differences as part of reconciliation. Also, they all evince a goal of bringing together opposed sides. In addition, they recognise the creation of peace and unity as an end goal of reconciliation. Finally, they consider reconciliation as a process, and they entail reconciliation at the societal level.[127] Based on these inferences, reconciliation is defined here as the process of resolving past societal differences and bringing together opposed factions as a means of creating lasting societal peace and unity.

Reconciliation was a key goal of the NRC, as evidenced by the commission's name, as well as its object of 'seeking and promoting national reconciliation amongst the people' of Ghana.[128] In its bid to attain this goal, the NRC relied on the provisions of its enabling law to interpret this goal as entailing 'educating the public on its purpose, mandate, functions, powers and activities', taking statements from petitioners, ascertaining the claims of petitioners through investigations, conducting

---

[120]Chapman 2009a, p. 144.

[121]Mendéz 2001, p. 28.

[122]See Riesenfeld 2008, p. 4.

[123]See Bloomfield 2003, p. 12.

[124]See du Toit 2011, p. 3.

[125]See Brounéus 2003, p. 20.

[126]Brounéus 2009, p. 205; and Larson 2009, p. 125.

[127]Regarding reconciliation at the societal level, Hayner explains that when dealing with reconciliation in post dictatorships and conflicted regimes, one must make a distinction between national (or political) and individual reconciliation. In her view, the kind of reconciliation that is of concern here is national reconciliation. Individual reconciliation is very uncertain regarding the work of truth commissions. See Hayner 2011, p. 183. It has also been asserted that the notion of reconciliation in the private context, which is seen to be a result of forgiveness, is not applicable in transitional justice, where attainment of forgiveness is more complicated. Hence, although forgiveness is not always conceivable in transitional societies, reconciliation can still be plausible. Moreover, forgiveness within the context of transitional justice is not very simple on account of the high number of people involved in the wrongs in question, and the existence of varied views about the possibility of public forgiveness, as opposed to private forgiveness. See Doorn 2008, pp. 382–389.

[128]See NRC Act, above n 47, s 3(1).

hearings to enable petitioners narrate their stories, 'providing healing to victims through counselling and other support services' and making recommendations for remedying the human rights violations that occurred at the instance of the state.[129] These elements of the commission's interpretation constituted the main efforts that the NRC made to enhance national reconciliation. To a great extent, the commission carried out all these components of its reconciliatory agenda. Yet would that be a conclusive basis to say that the commission adequately fulfilled its goal of reconciliation? To do so would be problematic because it would imply that reconciliation was attained right after the closure of the commission, which is practically impossible. It is, therefore, necessary to first ascertain current views on the issue.

5.6.1 Perceptions of the Commission's Impact on National Reconciliation

5.6.1.1 Quantitative Findings

To date, the extent to which the NRC impacted national reconciliation remains a very debatable subject. Hence, existing quantitative surveys that have been conducted about the NRC's reconciliatory attainments have yielded different results. At the tail end of the NRC's existence, the results of a poll conducted by a radio station in Accra revealed that 80% of the respondents did not consider the NRC to have reconciled Ghanaians.[130] However, a survey by the Ghana Centre for Democratic Development yielded a different outcome, with more than 75% of the respondents holding the opinion that the NRC had brought about reconciliation.[131]

The lack of consensus on the issue was revealed once again in the course of this study, as summarised in Table 5.4. Although the highest number of respondents agreed that the NRC had resulted in national reconciliation, the actual percentage of

Table 5.4 Perceptions of the Commission's Impact on Reconciliation: What is your opinion regarding the following statement?

Responses	Agree/ Strongly agree	Disagree/ Strongly disagree	Neutral	Unanswered
The NRC's work has resulted in national reconciliation in Ghana	51	38	38	3
Sample size = 130				

(*Source* The author 2018)

[129]See National Reconciliation Commission 2004, vol 1, para 2.1.2.1.

[130]The number of respondents polled in this survey is however not mentioned in the report. See Ghana Web 2004. http://www.ghanaweb.com/GhanaHomePage/NewsArchive/artikel.php?ID=61664. Accessed 11 September 2019.

[131]See the Ghana Centre for Democratic Development 2006, p. 22.

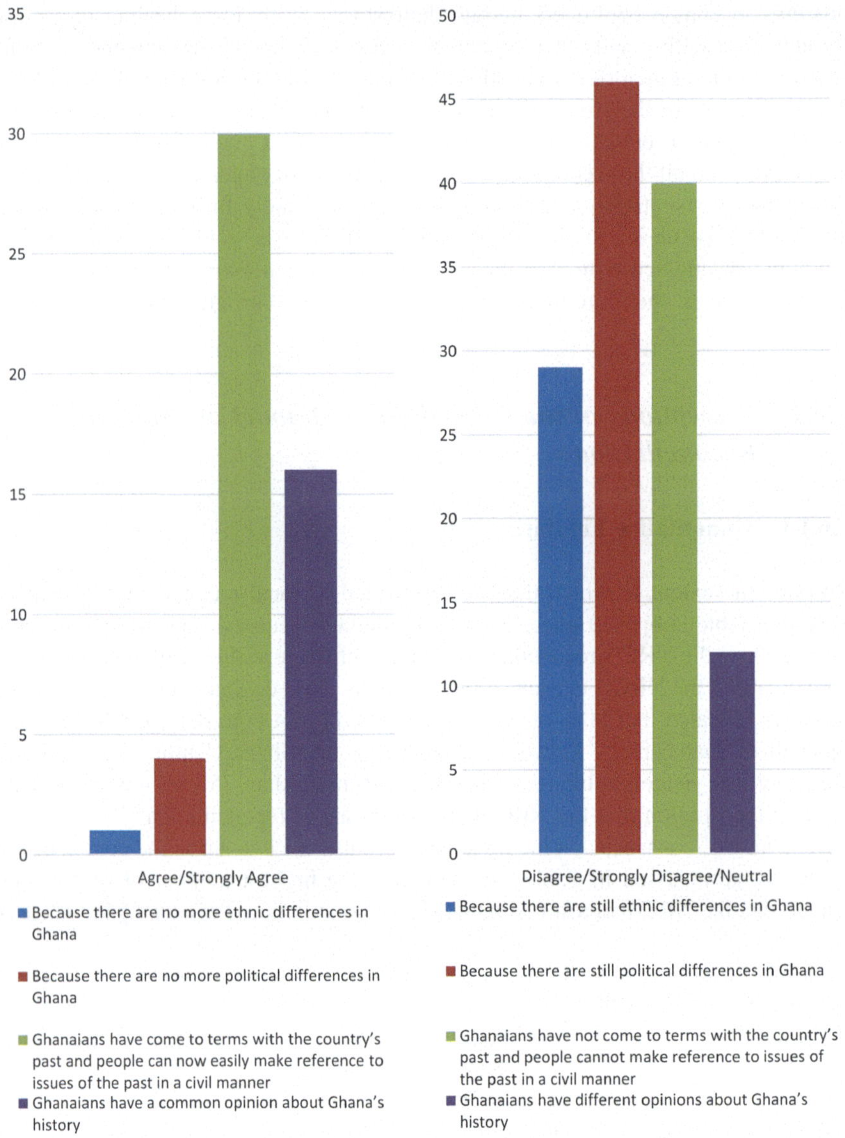

Fig. 5.4 Perceptions of the Commission's Impact on Reconciliation: What reasons explain your points of view in the statement above? (Please select all that apply) (*Source* The author 2018)

respondents who held this view (39.2%) cannot be regarded as a majority in comparison with the percentage who disagreed with the assertion (29.2%). In addition, the fact that 29.2% of respondents remained neutral shows that a significant number of people lack a firm stance on the issue.

A plausible reason for the lack of a majority opinion on the NRC's impact on reconciliation relates to the divergent views on the meaning of reconciliation. Indeed, when questioned about their understanding of reconciliation, 66 respondents selected the response related to apologies or forgiveness, whilst 52 respondents regarded it as the resolution of past societal differences and bringing together opposed factions. In addition, 45 respondents considered reconciliation to entail healing for victims and compensation for harm suffered. A number of respondents also selected more than one of these explanations. Given the different understandings of the concept, it is not surprising that respondents had very diverse views regarding the NRC's impact on reconciliation.

As Fig. 5.4 shows, respondents gave different reasons for their views. Amongst the 51 respondents who agreed that the NRC's work had resulted in national reconciliation, 30 ascribed their view to the fact that Ghanaians have come to terms with the country's past and can now easily make reference to issues of the past in a civil manner. However, 16 respondents selected the reason that Ghanaians have a common opinion of the country's history. Among respondents who did not agree that the NRC had brought about reconciliation, a majority of the reasons selected related to the fact that there are still political differences and the fact that Ghanaians have different opinions about the country's past. Interestingly, a number of the respondents who held a neutral view also selected these reasons. This suggests that their neutrality is tilted more to a negative perception, as opposed to a positive one. The nature of the reasons selected shows that although the NRC may have made efforts in that regard, respondents still see a number of significant challenges to national reconciliation in Ghana. Indeed, the views of respondents from the qualitative data obtained in this study reflect a similar opinion.

5.6.1.2 Qualitative Findings

All respondents who were interviewed indicated that the existence of reconciliation is still questionable. The reasons cited in this regard related to the existence of ethnic and political differences as well as the occasional occurrence of violence in the country. Ansah-Koi, for instance, believes that Ghanaian society has become highly polarised along political and ethnic lines, as evidenced by the recent surge in the use of insulting and abusive language amongst different political groups.[132] Boafo-Arthur also believes that the persistence of opposing factions in the country is evidenced by the recurrent pockets of violence in parts of Ghana. As an example he stated that the country regularly faces problems of disputes between traditional rulers, which in some instances results in violence.[133] Oduro also cited the fact that there are still ethnic undertones in Ghanaian politics, as indicated by the outcomes

[132]See Asamoah et al. 2014, p. 46.

[133]Boafo-Arthur, above n 57.

of presidential elections.[134] Another respondent, Annan, also believes that the commission created more polarisation and political factionism than reconciliation. In explaining his assertion, he stated that the polarisation resulted from the then opposition political party's perception that the national reconciliation exercise was a political witch-hunt. That perception further divided the opposition and ruling parties at the time. He also believes that the information and allegations made during the commission's hearings incited more hatred and division, as people's dirty linen was washed in public. In his view, the extent of the commission's polarisation included even people who were not members of the opposition. This is because such people thought that the commission was established to hold perpetrators accountable, and when nothing was done in this regard, they lost hope in the ruling party.[135]

These responses create an impression that the NRC's impact on national reconciliation was minimal. Yet one respondent asserted that the persistence of factions cannot be used as grounds to minimise the commission's impact on the attainment of reconciliation. This, in his opinion, is because reconciliation is a lengthy process.[136] In particular, he asserted that a key indication of the NRC's impact on reconciliation is the significant reduction in the calls to address past human rights violations, which had formerly dominated public discourse.[137] Hence, he opines that although reconciliation has not been fully achieved, the commission has at least initiated the process.

5.6.2 *Discussion*

Given the findings above, the main factors that informed respondents' views are whether or not there are political and ethnic divisions, whether or not there are divided opinions about the country's past and whether or not Ghanaians have come to terms with the country's past and can easily make reference to issues of the past in a civil manner. These reasons reflect two of the indicators of reconciliation proposed by Hayner: the nature of relationships between former enemies, how the society's history is handled in public and whether or not there are still many narratives of the society's past.[138]

The degree to which these indicators can be observed in Ghana can be judged by a number of factors. For instance, one indication that relationships have not been repaired is the existence of political and ethnic differences, as per the responses above. The high degree of political intolerance in Ghana is evinced by the regular

[134] Oduro, above n 87.

[135] Annan, above n 61.

[136] Oduro, above n 87. About reconciliation being a process, see also Mihr 2012, p. 37.

[137] Oduro, above n 87.

[138] See Hayner 2011, p. 189.

proliferation of insults and abusive language in the media.[139] In addition, the fact that election periods in the country are usually characterised by a high level of tension, on account of persistent fears of political unrest, shows the existence of strong opposing factions in Ghanaian politics. This is further evinced by the fact that electoral periods are usually preceded by calls from civil society groups, religious bodies and, in some instances, international delegations for peace. Indeed, since Ghana's transition to democracy, no presidential election has been held without the occurrence of minor violence, in the form of clashes between political opponents.[140] Ethnic intolerance is also indicated by the fact that Ghanaians usually vote along ethnic lines rather than based on political beliefs.[141] In addition, the absence of a consensus about the country's past has been brought to light in recent times, as a result of an ongoing discourse in the country at the time of this writing, regarding who is the real founder of Ghana.[142]

The above facts may explain why the reasons selected by respondents in Fig. 5.4 were not very reflective of the number of respondents who agreed that the NRC had resulted in national reconciliation.

Another key observation, which could have formed the basis of respondents' perceptions, relates to the fact that people appear to have come to terms with the past. In the interviews for this study, the issue of addressing past human rights violations did not generate a high level of interest amongst respondents. Indeed, most of the people who declined to be interviewed and even those who were interviewed were of the view that the commission's work was completed long ago and there was no need to revisit it. This gives an indication that the work of the NRC sent a message to Ghanaians to put closure on the past, which explains why there is no longer a high demand for the state to address past human rights violations.

In summary, the perceptions of respondents point to the fact that the NRC actually initiated the process of reconciliation in Ghana. This explains why a greater number of respondents agreed that the NRC had resulted in national reconciliation. In particular, the NRC's impact on reconciliation lies in the fact that it indirectly sent a message to all Ghanaians to gain closure on the past. This is further

[139]See National Democratic Institute 2016, p. 2. https://www.ndi.org/sites/default/files/Ghana%20IOM%20Statement%20Final.pdf. Accessed 14 October 2019; and Jimah 2016. https://www.modernghana.com/news/668562/media-independence-key-to-national-development.html. Accessed 19 October 2019.

[140]The Center for African Democratic Affairs 2012. http://www.modernghana.com/news/403939/1/election-violence-in-ghana.html. Accessed 22 October 2019; Ansah-Koi, above n 57.

[141]For instance, whereas the Ashantis in Ghana are known to be predominantly members of the New Patriotic Party, the Ewes are predominantly National Democratic Congress supporters. See Arthur 2009, pp. 53–63; Fridy 2007, pp. 302–303; and Yayoh 2006–2007, pp. 144–145.

[142]For details of these debates, see Ghana Web. https://www.ghanaweb.com/GhanaHomePage/features/dossier.php?ID=725. Accessed 28 September 2019.

evidenced by the fact that the commission was actually able to carry out all its reconciliatory tasks (as per the commission's definition). Moreover, the regular calls for the state to address past human rights violations, which had once dominated public discourses, have lessened since the closure of the NRC. Nevertheless, the lack of a real majority opinion on the issue means that there is no certainty regarding the true extent to which the commission gave rise to reconciliation. Yet the continued existence of ethnic and political divisions in Ghana means that the goal of reconciliation has yet to be achieved, despite its initiation by the NRC.

5.7 The Impact of the National Reconciliation Commission on Peace

The concept of peace has many dimensions. Boulding has defined peace as 'the absence of war'.[143] However, a narrower perspective on peace involves the existence of 'social harmony'.[144] For the purposes of this study, the broader definition is preferred for the sole reason that the major issues in the Ghanaian context that brought forth concerns about peace were the periods of political instability, occasionally leading to violence, between 1957 and 1993. Hence, although Ghana did not experience an internal armed conflict, the question of the NRC's impact on peace still centres on maintaining political stability. Indeed, the NRC acknowledged peace as a key goal in its report:

> Building a future for Ghana that is united, secure, peaceful and humane also demands providing redress, including healing, for those who were hurt in the past by serious human rights violations…. The Commission was seen by the Ghana Parliament as a vehicle to facilitate the attainment of these goals.[145]

The key efforts of the commission to achieve this goal were its recommendations for the abolition of possible violence-causing practices, such as formation of private military bodies, politicisation of the army and the other security bodies in the country and indoctrination of members of security bodies.[146] In order to assess the extent of the NRC's impact on peace, the views of respondents that were interviewed in this study have been outlined below.

---

143 Boulding 1978, p. 6.

144 See Bleiker and Krupanski 2012, p. 12.

145 National Reconciliation Commission 2004, vol 1, para 1.1.5.

146 Ibid., vol 3, paras 3.12.1, 3.12.2, 3.12.3.

Table 5.5 Perceptions of the Commission's Impact on Peace: What is your opinion regarding the following statement?

Responses	Agree/ Strongly agree	Disagree/ Strongly disagree	Neutral	Unanswered
Ghana has been more peaceful since completion of the NRC's work	41	50	37	2
Sample size = 130				

(*Source* The author 2018)

5.7.1 Perceptions of the National Reconciliation Commission's Impact on Peace

5.7.1.1 Quantitative Findings

According to the above-mentioned Ghana Centre for Democratic Development survey,[147] 80% of the respondents either agreed or strongly agreed that the NRC had enhanced peace in Ghana.[148] It appears, however, that this view was based on the commission's immediate completion of its work. Hence, the perceptions of respondents in this study, outlined in Table 5.5, were very different: 38.5% of respondents disagreed with the assertion that Ghana has been more peaceful since completion of the NRC's work, whilst 31.5% of respondents agreed with this assertion.

The outcome of this survey, as summarised in Fig. 5.5, evinces a generally negative perception regarding the NRC's impact on peace. A plausible explanation regarding why a greater number of respondents disagreed with the NRC's impact on peace is their understanding of the term 'peace' to connote an absence of factors that can cause violence. Indeed, 93 respondents considered peace to imply the prevention of situations that are likely to bring about conflicts, rather than the actual absence of conflict. Hence, they perceived the occasional pockets of violence that occur in Ghana to imply a lack of improvement in peace. This explains why 52 respondents in Fig. 5.5 explained their answer by pointing to the occasional occurrence of violence in some parts of Ghana, whilst 37 respondents' explanations related to the pockets of ethnic and political disputes that exist in different parts of the country. Another possible reason for the negative perceptions relates to the fact that Ghana was relatively peaceful between 1992 and the establishment of the NRC. Therefore, respondents only stated an improvement in peace if they could identify concrete improvements in the factors that can enhance peace, without interpreting the absence of a conflict in the Ghanaian context as peace.

[147]See Sect. 5.4.2.1 in the present chapter.

[148]See the Ghana Centre for Democratic Development 2006, p. 22.

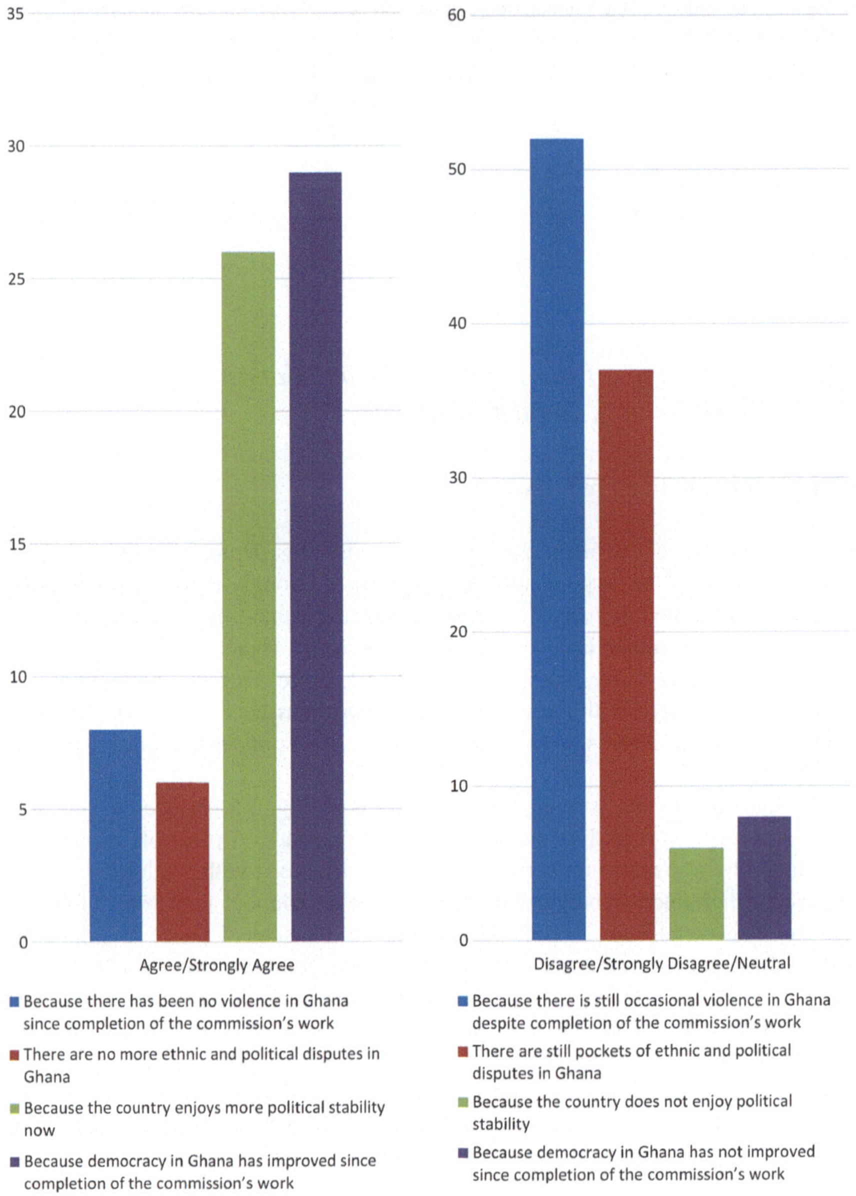

Fig. 5.5 Perceptions of the Commission's Impact on Peace: What reasons explain your points of view in the statement above? (Please select all that apply) (*Source* The author 2018)

Regarding respondents who agreed that Ghana has been more peaceful since completion of the NRC's work, the majority of explanations given related to the country's political stability and democracy. In this regard, the response rate shows that a greater number of respondents consider Ghana to be more democratic and politically stable. In summary, the main factors that were considered by respondents in assessing the NRC's impact on peace were the presence or absence of violence in some parts of Ghana, the occasional ethnic and political disputes and the country's political stability and democracy. These perceptions are backed by the outcome of this study's qualitative study, as outlined below.

5.7.1.2 Qualitative Findings

All respondents interviewed in the course of this study held the opinion that Ghana is peaceful only to the extent that there is no war. However, they pointed to indications in the country that make the existence of peace questionable. These include the current high crime rate, occasional eruptions of violence as a result of chieftaincy disputes and electoral misunderstandings, the occasional discovery of arms in the possession of private individuals and entities as well as the land disputes and traditional boundary disputes in different parts of the country. In their view, although these are not national indicators, they occasionally pose a threat to stability in the country.

In response to the question of whether or not the extent of peace in Ghana could be attributed to the work of the NRC, three respondents believed that the NRC did not play any role, whilst Oduro held the opinion that there were a multiplicity of factors, of which the NRC was one. According to him, the NRC's role in peace-building was to create a forum for initiating reconciliation, which is a key factor for sustaining peace. In his view, another factor that has enhanced peace, apart from the NRC, is the multiparty democracy enjoyed in the country. He believes that due to successful changes in government, the political elite do not need to resort to violence as the sole means of assuming power. If there was, however, no other avenue for the general citizenry to be part of governance, violence could have taken place.[149]

5.7.2 *Discussion*

It is evident from the above data that, unlike the quantitative survey, respondents in the qualitative survey considered peace to imply the absence of war. Nevertheless, the indicators that pose a threat to political stability, as identified in the qualitative findings, are largely identical to the factors that were pointed out by respondents in the quantitative study. Overall, the key factors that affected respondents' views are democracy, political stability, occasional violence, political and ethnic disputes as well as the crime rate.

[149]Oduro, above n 87.

Currently, the existence of these factors can be assessed by different indicators. The existence of pockets of violence and ethnic differences is evinced by the high number of chieftaincy disputes in the country. As of June 2017, for instance, Ghana's Minister for Chieftaincy and Religious Affairs noted that there were 352 unresolved chieftaincy disputes in the country.[150] The high crime rate in the country is also evinced by the recent increase in crime, disclosed by the Ghana Police Service.[151]

Regardless of these facts, Ghana can still be considered a peaceful country, as the problem of political instability, which formerly derailed peace and gave rise to the establishment of the NRC, has not recurred since the closure of the commission. Currently, the existence of political stability in Ghana is indicated by the fact that the country continues to enjoy a vibrant multiparty democracy, which has aided the holding of four successful presidential elections after the closure of the NRC, three of which resulted in a change of government.[152] As of December 2016, there were 24 registered political parties in the country, although not all of them participated in the presidential elections.[153] The country has also seen a massive improvement in freedom of speech and expression. This is evidenced by the important role that the media and civil society continue to play in Ghanaian politics and matters of public interest.[154] Indeed, Ghana was ranked 41st most peaceful out of 163 countries in the 2018 Global Peace Index Report.[155]

---

[150]See Ghana News Agency 2017. https://www.ghanabusinessnews.com/2017/06/01/352-chieftaincy-disputes-remain-unresolved-in-ghana/. Accessed 12 October 2019.

[151]See Ghana Web 2018. https://www.ghanaweb.com/GhanaHomePage/NewsArchive/Crime-rate-shot-up-slightly-in-Ghana-for-2018-first-quarter-Police-CID-654893. Accessed 28 October 2019.

[152]This includes the 2016 presidential elections in which, for the first time in the country's history, a sitting President contested and lost the election to an opposition party.

[153]Only six of these political parties participated in the 2016 presidential elections. See the Electoral Commission of Ghana. http://www.ec.gov.gh/political-parties.html. Accessed 3 October 2019.

[154]For instance, the Coalition of Domestic Election Observers, a group made up of 34 civil society bodies was very instrumental in the peacefulness and transparency of the 2016 presidential elections. This was done by stationing observers at different polling stations during the registration of voters and during the voting as well as making public statements on the process. The group also conducted a Parallel Vote Tabulation' which it used to ascertain the accuracy of the outcome of the elections. See CODEO Ghana. http://www.codeoghana.org/lib-projects.php#domestic. Accessed 14 October 2019; Ghana Web 2016. http://www.ghanaweb.com/GhanaHomePage/NewsArchive/2016-election-results-is-true-reflection-of-people-s-choice-CODEO-493617. Accessed 14 October 2019. Regarding the media, their critical role is illustrated by their contribution to peacefulness and transparency of presidential elections. For instance, during the 2016 presidential elections, media coverage was very extensive to the extent that some media groups accurately predicted the outcome of the elections even before the Electoral Commission announced the results. See also Jockers et al. 2010, pp. 99–100, on the role of the media during the 2008 presidential elections.

[155]See Institute for Economics and Peace 2018. https://reliefweb.int/sites/reliefweb.int/files/resources/Global-Peace-Index-2018-2.pdf. Accessed 20 October 2019.

Nevertheless, the NRC cannot be said to have led to the peace that is enjoyed in Ghana in the absence of any tangible results flowing directly from its work and recommendations. This is further evinced by the fact that no concrete efforts can be identified at the time of this study, regarding implementation of the NRC's peace-related recommendations. This largely explains why a greater number of respondents do not consider the NRC as having resulted in peace. The commission's impact on peace, therefore, relates to the recommendations it made to promote peace during its existence. In the future, the NRC's impact on peace can be made more profound if its peace-related recommendations are implemented by the government.

5.8 Chapter Summary

Although there is no consensus on how to assess the impact of a truth commission, this chapter has shown that the desired outcomes of truth commissions are a plausible way of understanding their impact. The discussions above have also given the scope for assessing the NRC's impact—namely, the goals of truth, justice, reconciliation and peace. Regarding the goal of truth, there is an overall positive perception of the commission's impact. Nevertheless, given key lapses in the dissemination of the NRC's report as well as its inability to properly investigate key human rights violations, the goal of truth can only be considered as partially achieved. Justice has also been achieved through the payment of monetary compensation to some victims as well as through the commission's hearings, which enabled victims to recount their experiences and created awareness for past human rights violations. Yet the continued existence of the amnesty provisions in the 1992 Constitution poses a real challenge to further attainment of justice. This explains why there is no true majority view regarding the extent of the commission's impact on justice. Overall, a greater number of respondents have a positive impression regarding the commission's impact on victims' remedies, whilst a greater number have a negative perception about the commission's impact on preventing the recurrence of human rights violations. In the case of reconciliation, although opinions show a positive view of the commission's impact, the persistence of political and ethnic polarisation shows that the goal of reconciliation is yet to be achieved. The responses also show a negative attitude towards the commission's impact on peace. Despite Ghana's relatively peaceful nature, it is difficult to impute peace to the NRC's work, since there has been no implementation of its peace-related recommendations. In summary, one can say that, in most cases, the commission's impact stems from actions taken when it was still in existence rather than after its closure.

References

African Union Panel of the Wise (2013) Peace, justice, and reconciliation in Africa: Opportunities and challenges in the fight against impunity. https://reliefweb.int/sites/reliefweb.int/files/resources/ipi_e_pub_peacejusticeafrica.pdf. Accessed 4 September 2019.

Aldana R (2006) A victim-centered reflection on truth commissions and prosecutions as a response to mass atrocities. Journal of Human Rights 5:107–126.

Allan A, Allan MM (2000) The South African Truth and Reconciliation Commission as a therapeutic tool. Behavioral Sciences and the Law 18:459–477.

Ambos K (2009) The legal framework of transitional justice: A systematic study with a special focus on the role of the ICC. In: Ambos K et al (eds) Building a future on peace and justice: Studies on transitional justice, peace and development – The Nuremberg Declaration on Peace and Justice. Springer, Berlin, pp 19–103.

Ambos K (2015) Evaluando la eficiencia de la justicia transicional unos comentarios preliminares (Evaluating the efficiency of transitional justice: Some preliminary comments). Zeitschrift für Internationale Strafrechtsdogmatik 9:468–472.

Amnesty International (2013) Annual report: Ghana 2013. http://www.amnestyusa.org/research/reports/annual-report-ghana-2013?page=show. Accessed 2 October 2019.

Andreu-Guzmán F (2013) Peace processes and international law. https://www.files.ethz.ch/isn/164673/80ed6b7fa08ff1e0620fe297f85f63f0.pdf. Accessed 1 November 2019.

Arthur P (2009) Ethnicity and electoral politics in Ghana's Fourth Republic. Africa Today 56 (2):44–73.

Asamoah K et al (2014) Demons of transitional democracies: Politics of insults and acrimony in Ghana. Journal of Social Science Studies 1(1):44–56.

Asare AA (2008) The Ghanaian National Reconciliation Commission: Reparation in a global age. The Global South 2(2):31–53.

Bachmann K (2010) Do truth commissions make a difference? When and how truth commissions contribute to reconciliation. Review of International Affairs LXI (1138–1139):71–100.

Backer D (2009) Cross-national comparative analysis. In: Van Der Merwe et al (eds) Assessing the impact of transitional justice: Challenges for empirical research. United States Institute of Peace, Washington DC, pp. 23–90.

Bakiner O (2014) Truth commission impact: An assessment of how commissions influence politics and society. The International Journal of Transitional Justice 8:6–30.

Beetham D et al (2008) Assessing the quality of democracy: A practical guide. International Institute for Democracy and Electoral Assistance, Stockholm.

Bleiker C, Krupanski M (2012) The Rule of law and security sector reform: Conceptualising a complex relationship. https://dcaf.ch/sites/default/files/publications/documents/SSR%20and%20ROL3%20ONLINE%20VERSION.pdf. Accessed 3 November 2019.

Bloomfield D (2003) Reconciliation: An introduction. In: Bloomfield D et al (eds) Reconciliation after violent conflict: A handbook. International Institute for Democracy and Electoral Assistance, Stockholm, pp 10–18.

Boafo-Arthur K (2005) National reconciliation or polarisation? Preliminary reflections on the politics of the Ghana National Reconciliation Commission. In: Fawole WA, Ukeje C (eds) The crisis of the state and regionalism in West Africa. Codesria, Dakar, pp 105–126.

Boafo-Arthur K (2006) The quest for national reconciliation in Ghana: Challenges and prospects. In: Boafo-Arthur K (ed) Voting for democracy in Ghana: The 2004 elections in perspective. Freedom House Publishing, Accra, pp 127–155.

Bonacker T, Buckley-Zistel S (2013) Introduction: Transitions from violence – Analyzing the effects of transitional justice. International Journal of Conflict and Violence 7(1):4–9.

Borraine AL (2006) Transitional justice: A holistic interpretation. Journal of International Affairs 60(1):17–27.

Boulding KE (1978) Stable Peace. University of Texas Press, Austin.

Brahm E (2005) Getting to the bottom of truth: Examining truth commission success and impact. http://center.theparentscircle.org/images/25239151e8cf4a29a2f3046308307f4a.pdf. Accessed 3 November 2019.

Brahm E (2007) Uncovering the truth: Examining truth commission success and impact. International Studies Perspectives 8(1):16–35.

Brounéus K (2003) Reconciliation: Theory and practice for development cooperation. https://www.urosario.edu.co/Mesas-de-Deliberacion/Documentos/BIBLIOGRAFIA/Reconciliacion/Brouneus,-Karen-Reconciliation-Theory-and-practice/. Accessed 3 November 2019.

Brounéus K (2008) Analyzing reconciliation: A structured method for measuring national reconciliation initiatives. Journal of Peace Psychology 14(3):291–313.

Brounéus K (2009) Reconciliation and development. In: Ambos K et al (eds) Building a future on peace and justice: Studies on transitional justice, peace and development – The Nuremberg Declaration on Peace and Justice. Springer, Berlin, pp 203–216.

Cassel DW (1995) International truth commissions and justice. In: Kritz N (ed) Transitional justice: How emerging democracies reckon with former regimes, vol. I. United States Institute of Peace Press, Washington DC, pp 326–333.

Center for African Democratic Affairs (2012) Election violence in Ghana. https://www.modernghana.com/news/403939/1/election-violence-in-ghana.html. Accessed 4 November 2019.

Chapman AR (2009a) Approaches to studying reconciliation. In: Van Der Merwe H et al (eds) Assessing the impact of transitional justice: Challenges for empirical research. United States Institute of Peace Press, Washington DC, pp 143–172.

Chapman AR (2009b) Truth finding in the transitional justice process. In: Van Der Merwe H et al (eds) Assessing the impact of transitional justice: Challenges for empirical research. United States Institute of Peace Press, Washington DC, pp 91–114.

Crocker DA (1999) Reckoning with past wrongs: A normative framework. Ethics and International Affairs 13:43–66.

De Greiff P (2009) Articulating the links between transitional justice and development: Justice and social integration. In: De Greiff P, Duthie R (eds) Transitional justice and development: Making connections. Social Science Research Council, New York, pp 28–75.

De Greiff P (2012) Theorising transitional justice. In: Williams MS et al (eds) Transitional justice. New York University Press, New York and London, pp 31–77.

Doorn N (2008) Forgiveness and reconciliation in transitional justice practices. Ethical Perspective 15(3):381–398.

Du Toit F (2011) Reconciliation and transitional justice: The case of Rwanda's Gacaca Courts. https://www.africaportal.org/documents/9599/IJR_OP_2_proof_2.pdf. Accessed 4 November 2019.

Electoral Commission of Ghana. Registered political parties. https://ec.gov.gh/political-parties.html. Accessed 3 October 2019.

Ferrara A (2015) Assessing the long-term impact of truth commissions: The Chilean Truth and Reconciliation Commission in historical perspective. Routledge, New York.

Ferstman C (2010) Reparation as prevention: Considering the law and practice of orders for cessation and guarantees of non-repetition in torture cases. Essex Human Rights Review 6 (2):7–27.

Frederking BK (2015) Putting transitional justice on trial: Democracy and human rights in post-civil war societies. International Social Science Review 91(1):1–19.

Freedom House (2019) Freedom of the World 2019: Ghana. https://freedomhouse.org/report/freedom-world/2019/ghana. Accessed 2 November 2019.

Fridy KS (2007) The elephant, umbrella, and quarrelling cocks: Disaggregating partisanship in Ghana's Fourth Republic. African Affairs 106(423):281–305.

Ghana Centre for Democratic Development (2006) Opinions of victims of past human rights abuse in Ghana after the National Reconciliation Commission public hearings. Ghana Centre for Democratic Development, Accra.

Ghana Statistical Service (2008) Ghana in figures http://www.statsghana.gov.gh/gssmain/fileUpload/pressrelease/gh_figures_2008.pdf. Accessed 11 November 2019.

Ghana Statistical Service (2018) Poverty trends in Ghana (2005–2017). http://www2.statsghana.gov.gh/docfiles/publications/GLSS7/Poverty%20Profile%20Report_2005%20-%202017.pdf. Accessed 4 November 2019.

Gibson JL (2004) Does truth lead to reconciliation? Testing the causal assumptions of the South African truth and reconciliation process. American Journal of Political Science 48(2):201–217.

Goldstone RJ (1996) Justice as a tool for peace-making: Truth commissions and international criminal tribunals. New York University Journal of International Law and Politics 28:485–503.

Hamber B (1995) Do sleeping dogs lie? The psychological implications of the Truth and Reconciliation Commission in South Africa. http://www.csvr.org.za/publications/1713-do-sleeping-dogs-lie-the-psychological-implications-of-the-truth-and-reconciliation-commission-in-south-africa. Accessed 15 October 2019.

Hamber B (2001) Does the truth heal? A psychological perspective on political strategies for dealing with the legacy of political violence. In: Nigel B (ed) Burying the past: Making peace and doing justice after civil conflict. Georgetown University Press, Washington DC, pp 155–174.

Hamber B (2009) Transforming societies after political violence: Truth, reconciliation, and mental health. Springer, New York.

Hayner PB (2011) Unspeakable truths: Transitional justice and the challenge of truth commissions, 2nd edn. Routledge, London.

Hirsch MBJ et al (2012) Measuring the impacts of truth and reconciliation commissions: Placing the global 'success' of TRCs in local perspective. Cooperation and Conflict 47(3):386–403.

Institute for Economics and Peace (2018) Global Peace Index 2018 https://reliefweb.int/sites/reliefweb.int/files/resources/Global-Peace-Index-2018-2.pdf. Accessed 20 October 2019.

Jimah M (2016) Media independence: Key to national development. https://www.modernghana.com/news/668562/media-independence-key-to-national-development.html. Accessed 19 October 2019.

Jockers H et al (2010) The successful Ghana election of 2008: A convenient myth? The Journal of Modern African Studies 48(1):95–115.

Kaminer D et al (2001) The truth and reconciliation commission in South Africa: Relation to psychiatric status and forgiveness amongst survivors of human rights abuses. British Journal of Psychiatry:373–377.

Kemp S (2004) The inter-relationship between the Guatemalan Commission for Historical Clarification and the search for justice in national courts. In: Schabas WA, Darcy S (eds) Truth commissions and courts. The tension between criminal justice and the search for truth. Kluwer Academic Publishers, Dordrecht, pp 67–103.

Kritz NJ (1995) The dilemmas of transitional justice. In: Kritz N (ed) Transitional justice: How emerging democracies reckon with former regimes, vol. I. United States Institute of Peace, Washington DC, pp xix-xxx.

Kritz NJ (2009) Policy implications of empirical research on transitional justice. In: Van Der Merwe et al (eds) Assessing the impact of transitional justice: Challenges for empirical research. United States Institute of Peace, Washington DC, pp 13–22.

Larson CC (2009) As we forgive: Stories of reconciliation from Rwanda. Zondervan, Michigan.

Long WJ (2008) Liberia's Truth and Reconciliation Commission: An interim assessment. International Journal of Peace Studies 13(2) 1–14.

Lundy P (2010) Commissioning the past in Northern Ireland. The Review of International Affairs LX (1138–1139):101–133.

Mazzei JM (2011) Finding shame in truth: The importance of public engagement in truth commissions. Human Rights Quarterly 33(2):431–452.

Mendeloff D (2004) Truth-seeking, truth-telling, and post conflict peacebuilding: Curb the enthusiasm? International Studies Review 6:355–380.

Méndez JE (2001) National reconciliation, transnational justice, and the International Criminal Court. Ethics & International Affairs 15(1):25–44.

Mihr A (2012) Transitional justice and the quality of democracy – from democratic institution building to reconciliation. In: Mihr A (ed) Transitional justice: Between criminal justice, atonement and democracy. Netherlands Institute of Human Rights, Utrecht, pp 11–50.
Millar G (2010) Assessing local experiences of truth-telling in Sierra Leone: Getting to 'why' through a qualitative case study analysis. International Journal of Transitional Justice 4:477–496.
Moler J (2010) Justice in transition: The effectiveness of truth commissions in Africa and recommendations for the Kenyan Truth, Justice, and Reconciliation Commission. Minnesota Journal of International Law 19:21–39.
National Democratic Institute (2016) Preliminary statement of the National Democratic Institute's international observer mission to Ghana's December 7 presidential and legislative elections. https://www.ndi.org/sites/default/files/Ghana%20IOM%20Statement%20Final.pdf. Accessed 14 October 2019.
National Reconciliation Commission (2004) Report of the National Reconciliation Commission, vol 1–4.
Nichols AD (2019) Impact, legitimacy, and limitations of truth commissions. Palgrave Macmillan, Cham.
Nwogu NV (2010) When and why it started: Deconstructing victim-centered truth commissions in the context of ethnicity-based conflict. International Journal of Transitional Justice 4:275–289.
Office of the United Nations High Commissioner for Human Rights (2006a) Rule-of-law tools for post conflict states: Truth commissions. https://www.ohchr.org/Documents/Publications/RuleoflawTruthCommissionsen.pdf. Accessed 2 November 2019.
Office of the United Nations High Commissioner for Human Rights (2006b) Rule-of-law tools for post-conflict states. Vetting: an operational framework. https://www.ohchr.org/Documents/Publications/RuleoflawVettingen.pdf. Accessed 4 September 2019.
Office of the United Nations High Commissioner for Human Rights (2016) Human Rights Committee considers the report of Ghana. http://www.ohchr.org/EN/NewsEvents/Pages/DisplayNews.aspx?NewsID=20180&LangID=E. Accessed 2 November 2019.
Olsen TD et al (2010a) The justice balance: When transitional justice improves human rights. Human Rights Quarterly 32(4):980–1007.
Olsen TD et al (2010b) Transitional justice in balance: Comparing processes, weighing efficacy. United States Institute of Peace, Washington DC.
Olsen TD et al (2010c) When truth commissions improve human rights. The International Journal of Transitional Justice 4:457–476.
Popkin M, Roht-Arriaza N (1995) Truth as justice: Investigatory commissions in Latin America. Law and Social Inquiry 20(1):79–116.
Porter E (2015) Connecting peace, justice and reconciliation. Lynne Rienner Publishers, Boulder.
Posner EA, Vermeule A (2003) Transitional justice as ordinary justice. Harvard Law Review 117:762–825.
Riesenfeld G (2008) Instruments of reconciliation? Potentials and risks of reparation measures in post-conflict Guatemala. https://www.pcr.uu.se/digitalAssets/654/c_654492-l_1-k_mfs_riesenfeld.pdf. Accessed 2 November 2019.
Sánchez E, Rognvik S (2012) Building just societies: Reconciliation in transitional settings. https://professorbellreadings.files.wordpress.com/2017/10/building-justice-societies.pdf. Accessed 4 September 2019.
Satz D (2012) Countering the wrongs of the past: The role of compensation. Transitional Justice 51:129–150.
Sikkink K (2012) Models of accountability and the effectiveness of transitional justice. In: Popovski V, Serrano M (eds) After oppression: Transitional justice in Latin America and Eastern Europe. United Nations University Press, New York, pp 19–38.
Silove D et al (2006) Do truth commissions heal? The East Timor experience. The Lancet 367 (9518):1222–1224.

Skaar E et al (2015) Towards a framework for impact assessment. In: Skaar E et al (eds) After violence: Transitional justice, peace, and democracy. Routledge, Abingdon and New York, pp 29–66.
Sooka Y (2006) Dealing with the past and transitional justice: Building peace through accountability. International Review of the Red Cross 88(862):311–325.
Thoms ONT et al (2008) The effects of transitional justice mechanisms. A summary of empirical research findings and implications for analysts and practitioners. http://aix1.uottawa.ca/~rparis/CIPS_Transitional_Justice_April2008.pdf. Accessed 23 October 2019.
Thoms ONT et al (2010) State-level effects of transitional justice: What do we know? International Journal of Transitional Justice 4:329–354.
Tomuschat C (2005) Darfur - Compensation for the victims. Journal of International Criminal Justice 3:579–589.
Truth and Reconciliation Commission of South Africa (1998) The Truth and Reconciliation Commission of South Africa Report, vol I. http://www.justice.gov.za/trc/report/. Accessed 3 November 2019.
United Nations Commission on Human Rights (2005) Promotion and protection of human rights: Impunity, Report of the independent expert to update the set of principles to combat impunity, Diane Orentlicher, Addendum – Updated Set of principles for the protection and promotion of human rights through action to combat impunity, E/CN.4/2005/102/Add.1.
United Nations General Assembly (2006) Resolution adopted by the General Assembly on 16 December 2005, Basic Principles and Guidelines on the Right to a Remedy and Reparation for Victims of Gross Violations of International Human Rights Law and Serious Violations of International Humanitarian Law, A/RES/60/147. https://documents-dds-ny.un.org/doc/UNDOC/GEN/N05/496/42/PDF/N0549642.pdf?OpenElement. Accessed 2 November 2019.
United Nations General Assembly, Human Rights Council (2013) Report of the Special Rapporteur on the promotion of truth, justice, reparation and guarantees of non-recurrence, Pablo De Greiff, A/HRC/24/42.
United Nations Human Rights Committee (2004) General Comment No. 31, The nature of the general legal obligation imposed on states parties to the Covenant, CCPR/C/21/Rev.1/Add. 13.
United Nations Security Council (2004) The rule of law and transitional justice in conflict and post-conflict societies, Report of the Secretary-General, S/2004/616.
United States Institute of Peace (2008) Transitional justice: Information handbook. https://www.usip.org/sites/default/files/ROL/Transitional_justice_final.pdf. Accessed 4 September 2019.
Van Der Merwe H (2009a) Delivering justice during transition: Research challenges. In: Van Der Merwe H et al (eds) Assessing the impact of transitional justice: Challenges for empirical research. United States Institute of Peace, Washington DC.
Van Der Merwe H et al (2009b) Introduction. In: Van Der Merwe H et al (eds) Assessing the impact of transitional justice: Challenges for empirical research. United States Institute of Peace, Washington DC, pp 1–12.
Waldorf L (2009) Ex-combatants and truth commissions. In: Patel AC et al (eds) Disarming the past. Transitional justice and ex-combatants. Social Science Research Council, New York, pp 108–131.
Werle G, Vormbaum M (2018) Transitional justice. Springer, Berlin.
Wiebelhaus-Brahm E (2010) Truth commissions and transitional societies. The impact on human rights and democracy. Routledge, London and New York.
Wilson RA (2001) The politics of truth and reconciliation in South Africa: Legitimizing the post-apartheid state. Cambridge University Press, Cambridge.
Yayoh KW (2006–2007) Resurgence of multiparty rule in Ghana, 1990–2004: A historical review. Transactions of the Historical Society of Ghana 10:125–147.
Zalaquett J (1995) Confronting human rights violations committed by former governments: Principles applicable and political constraints. In: Kritz N (ed) Transitional justice: How emerging democracies reckon with former regimes, vol. I. United States Institute of Peace Press, Washington DC, pp 3–31.

Chapter 6
After the National Reconciliation Commission: The Way Ahead

Contents

6.1 Introductory Remarks 192
6.2 Issues Related to the Duty to Prosecute 193
  6.2.1 The Scope of the Duty to Prosecute 193
  6.2.2 Discussion 197
6.3 Issues Related to the Amnesty Provisions in the 1992 Constitution 202
  6.3.1 The Legality of Amnesties under International Law 202
  6.3.2 Ghana's Amnesty Law Under International Law 206
6.4 Issues Related to the Right to Reparations 209
  6.4.1 The Scope of the Right to Reparations 209
  6.4.2 Has Ghana Fulfilled Victims' Rights to Reparations? 210
6.5 Institutional Reforms 213
  6.5.1 The Basis and Scope of Institutional Reform 213
  6.5.2 Gaps in Institutional Reform 215
6.6 Chapter Summary 216
References 217

Abstract Despite the full implementation of a particular transitional justice mechanism, some needs of a transitional society may remain unfulfilled. Tying the loose ends after a specific mechanism has executed its function would thus require resorting to other transitional justice mechanisms to complement and make amends for the limitations of the mechanisms that have already been implemented. In an effort to ascertain the transitional needs that remain unaddressed in Ghana after the work of the National Reconciliation Commission, this chapter utilises a normative approach to assess the commission's work in relation to other transitional justice mechanisms—namely, prosecutions, amnesties, reparations and institutional reforms. Drawing on emerging and established principles of international human rights law, it identifies key loopholes and outstanding issues in Ghana's transitional

M. Yankson-Mensah, *Transitional Justice in Ghana*, International Criminal Justice Series 25, https://doi.org/10.1007/978-94-6265-379-5_6

process. The chapter provides an insight into the legality of the amnesty provisions under Ghana's 1992 Constitution, the country's duty to prosecute gross human rights violations that were perpetrated from 1957 to 1993 and the extent of the fulfilment of victims' rights to reparations.

Keywords Duty to Prosecute · Amnesties · 1992 Constitution of Ghana · Recurrence of Human Rights Violations · Institutional Reforms · Right to Reparations

6.1 Introductory Remarks

After the use of a particular transitional justice mechanism, it is still possible that some needs of a transitional society may not be fully addressed. Hence, even though states have discretion regarding how to address serious human rights violations,[1] some studies suggest that transitional justice mechanisms work best when they are utilised as complements to each other rather than alternatives.[2] Indeed, as De Greiff has noted, the limitations of each transitional justice mechanism can only be remedied by drawing on the strengths of other mechanisms.[3] In the case of Ghana, however, the NRC remains the major transitional justice mechanism that was pursued, in the absence of a comprehensive transitional justice policy. This chapter thus seeks to identify the loopholes in Ghana's transitional justice process. The chapter reflects on other transitional justice mechanisms (i.e., prosecutions, amnesties, reparations and institutional reforms) in light of the NRC's work to ascertain what remains to be done in Ghana's transitional process. The discussion focuses on four main themes: the duty to prosecute under international law, the

[1]About the arguments that there is no fixed approach for addressing human rights violations, see for instance Ambos 2015, pp. 469, 470; and Kritz 2009, pp. 13–14.

[2]See Olsen et al. 2010, pp. 458, 464–465, who assert that the ability of truth commissions to enhance protection of human rights in a society depends on the presence of other transitional justice mechanisms. See also De Greiff 2012, pp. 35–36; and International Centre for Transitional Justice https://www.ictj.org/about/transitional-justice. Accessed 5 November 2019. Indeed, the Inter-American Court of Human Rights has held that a state's engagement in a truth telling exercise does not obviate from its duty to utilise judicial measures in dealing with past human rights violations. See Inter-American Court of Human Rights, *Garay Hermosilla et al. v Chile*, 15 October 1996, Case 10.843, Report No. 36/96 (Garay Hermosilla 1996), paras 74, 75, 77, where the court held that although the state of Chile had established a truth commission to investigate past human rights violations and awarded reparations to victims, the truth commission could not be considered as a judicial institution. Moreover, the court held that since the commission's terms of reference did not empower it to name perpetrators and punish them, the truth telling exercise could not be regarded as a substitute for a judicial trial. See also Mallinder 2007, p. 216; and Méndez 1997, pp. 255, 263, 269.

[3]De Greiff 2012, pp. 35–36.

validity of amnesties under international law, the right of victims to reparations and institutional reforms.

6.2 Issues Related to the Duty to Prosecute

6.2.1 The Scope of the Duty to Prosecute

The duty to prosecute entails the duty of a state, under international law, to conduct 'effective, prompt, thorough and impartial' investigation of human rights violations that occur on its territory and 'take action against those allegedly responsible in accordance with domestic and international law'.[4] The duty to prosecute arises from three main grounds. First, there are specific crimes that give rise to the duty to prosecute under customary international law and treaty law. For instance, it is established under customary international law that the state in which the crimes of genocide, crimes against humanity and war crimes occur owes a duty to prosecute those crimes.[5] Aside provisions under customary international law, the duty to prosecute by the state in which a crime under international law is committed is also treaty-based for the crime of genocide and war crimes committed in the course of international armed conflict.[6] A duty to prosecute crimes against humanity has its basis in treaty law only in circumstances where there is an express treaty requirement to prosecute the individual act that amounts to the crime against humanity. For instance, torture, enforced disappearances and the crime of apartheid can amount to crimes against humanity, and the respective treaties that deal with these crimes

[4]See United Nations General Assembly 2006, para 3(b).

[5]See Tomuschat 2002, p. 325; and Werle and Jessberger 2014, pp. 79–83.

[6]See Convention on the Prevention and Punishment of the Crime of Genocide, opened for signature 9 December 1948, No. 1021 (entered into force 12 January 1951) (Genocide Convention), Article IV; Geneva Convention (IV).

Relative to the Protection of Civilian Persons in Time of War, opened for signature 12 August 1949, 75 UNTS 287 (entered into force 21 October 1950) (Fourth Geneva Convention), Article 146; Geneva Convention (I) for the Amelioration of the Condition of the Wounded and Sick in Armed Forces in the Field, opened for signature 12 August 1949, 75 UNTS 31 (entered into force 21 October 1950) (First Geneva Convention), Article 49; Geneva Convention (II) for the Amelioration of the Condition of Wounded, Sick and Shipwrecked Members of Armed Forces at Sea, opened for signature 12 August 1949, 75 UNTS 85 (entered into force 21 October 1950) (Second Geneva Convention) Article 50; Geneva Convention (III) Relative to the Treatment of Prisoners of War, opened for signature 12 August 1949, 75 UNTS 135 (entered into force 21 October 1950) (Third Geneva Convention), Article 129; and in relation to torture, the Convention against Torture and Other Cruel, Inhuman or Degrading Treatment or Punishment, opened for signature 10 December 1984 (entered into force 26 June 1987) (Torture Convention), Articles 5 and 7. The duty to prosecute also applies to third party states in respect of war crimes that occur in international armed conflicts. The position of international law is however not settled, regarding whether or not third-party states have a duty to prosecute crimes against humanity and genocide. See also Jones 2015, pp. 99–102; and Werle and Jessberger 2014, pp. 79–82.

expressly require the state of commission to prosecute.[7] In addition to crimes under international law, there are other crimes that may not necessarily amount to any of the four core crimes under international law but can nevertheless give rise to a duty to prosecute under treaty law for the state of commission. For instance, a duty to prosecute exists for the crimes of hijacking, aircraft sabotage, terrorism and hostage-taking, provided that the state in question has ratified the respective treaties that deal with these acts.[8]

Second, the duty to prosecute can be inferred from the duty to protect human rights, as provided in treaties that require states to 'ensure and respect' specific human rights.[9] An example is Common Article 1 to the Geneva Conventions of 1949, where it is stated that 'the High Contracting Parties undertake to respect and to ensure respect for the present Convention in all circumstances'.[10] The terms 'ensure' and 'respect' can also be found in the International Covenant on Civil and Political Rights, the African Charter on Human and Peoples' Rights, the European Convention for the Protection of Human Rights and Fundamental Freedoms, the Charter of Fundamental Rights of the European Union and the American Convention on Human Rights.[11] These terms have been interpreted to give rise to an obligation to investigate and prosecute violations of the human rights addressed in the respective treaties. For instance, the United Nations Human Rights Committee has acknowledged that states in which human rights violations are

[7]See the Torture Convention, above n 6, Articles 5, 7; International Convention for the Protection of All Persons from Enforced Disappearance, opened for signature 20 December 2006 (entered into force 23 December 2010) (Enforced Disappearances Convention), Articles 6, 7, 11; and International Convention on the Suppression and Punishment of the Crime of Apartheid, opened for signature 30 November 1973, A/RES/3068(XXVIII) (entered into force 18 July 1976) (Apartheid Convention), Articles IV and V.

[8]See Convention for the Suppression of Unlawful Seizure of Aircraft, opened for signature 16 December 1970, UNTS 1973 (entered into force 14 October 1971) (Aircraft Seizure Convention), Articles 7 and 22; Convention for the Suppression of Unlawful Acts against the Safety of Civil Aviation, opened for signature 23 September 1971, 974 UNTS 177 (entered into force 26 January 1973) (Safety of Civil Aviation Convention), Articles 7 and 24; and International Convention against the Taking of Hostages, opened for signature 17 November 1979, No. 21931 (entered into force 3 June 1983) (Convention against Hostage Taking), Article 8.

[9]On the duty to prosecute arising from the duty to protect human rights, see Tomuschat 2002, p. 325; and Werle and Jessberger 2014, pp. 317–326.

[10]See the First Geneva Convention, above n 6, Article 1.

[11]See International Covenant on Civil and Political Rights, opened for signature 16 December 1966 (entered into force 23 March 1976) (Covenant on Civil and Political Rights), Article 2(1); African Charter on Human and Peoples' Rights, opened for signature 27 June 1981, CAB/LEG/67/3 rev. 5, 21 I.L.M. 58 (1982) (entered into force 21 October 1986) (Banjul Charter), Article 25; European Convention for the Protection of Human Rights and Fundamental Freedoms, as amended by Protocols Nos. 11 and 14, opened for signature 4 November 1950, ETS 5 (entered into force 3 September 1953) (European Convention on Human Rights), Article 1; Charter of Fundamental Rights of the European Union, opened for signature 26 October 2012, 2012/C 326/02 (entered into force 1 Dec. 2009) (European Charter), Article 51; and American Convention on Human Rights, opened for signature 22 November 1969 (entered into force 18 July 1978) (Pact of San Jose), Article 1(1).

committed have a duty to prosecute by virtue of their duty to ensure protection of human rights under the International Covenant on Civil and Political Rights.[12] In the case of *Velásquez-Rodríguez v Honduras*, the Inter-American Court of Human Rights held that the 'ensure and respect' phrase in Article 1(1) of the American Convention on Human Rights creates an obligation for the state to prevent, investigate and prosecute human rights violations.[13] The African Commission on Human and Peoples' Rights has also stated in the case of *Zimbabwe Human Rights NGO Forum v Zimbabwe* that a state complies with the obligation to respect the rights recognised in the African Charter on Human and Peoples' Rights by not violating them.[14] In this regard, the court stated that 'to ensure' the rights in the African Charter on Human and Peoples' Rights is to take the requisite steps, in accordance with its constitutional process and the provisions of the relevant treaty (in this case, the African Charter), to adopt such legislative or other measures that are necessary to give effect to these rights.[15]

Third, the duty of the state of commission to prosecute can arise from the obligation of states to provide effective remedies to victims of gross human rights violations.[16] The right to a remedy is to the effect that victims of gross human rights violations receive the requisite remedy for the violations suffered.[17] In this regard, the state in question must put in place appropriate judicial or other efficient

[12]See the United Nations Human Rights Committee 2004, para 18. See also Werle and Jessberger 2014, p. 80.

[13]See Inter-American Court of Human Rights, *Velásquez-Rodríguez v Honduras*, Judgment of 29 July 1988, Ser. C. No. 4 (Velásquez-Rodríguez 1988), paras 165–170. Regarding this decision, Tomuschat 2002, pp. 321, 323 and 325–326, comments that the decision of the court was rather rigorous and cannot possibly be applicable to all cases of human rights violations at the instance of the state. In his view, although other bodies have given similar decisions, this position of the law has some limitations in so far as it does not have a binding effect on every country. He however in the end acknowledges that the duty to prosecute has gained enough acceptance to be regarded as 'positive law'.

[14]See the African Commission on Human and Peoples' rights, *Zimbabwe Human Rights NGO Forum v Zimbabwe*, 15 May 2006, Communication No. 245/2002 (Zimbabwe Human Rights NGO case), para 171.

[15]See *Zimbabwe Human Rights NGO case*, above n 14, para 171.

[16]On this subject, see Roht-Arriaza 1990, pp. 474–475.

[17]See Universal Declaration of Human Rights, adopted 10 December 1948, 217 A (III) (Universal Declaration), Article 8; and Covenant on Civil and Political Rights, above n 11, Article 2(3). The basic components of this right have been espoused in the United Nations Basic Principles and Guidelines on the Right to a Remedy and Reparation for Victims of Gross Violations of International Human Rights Law and Serious Violations of International Humanitarian Law, 2005, which sets out the means for complying with the existing rules of international law regarding the rights of victims of human rights violations to remedies. See also United Nations General Assembly 2006, paras 2(c), 8, 9.

non-judicial means for the purposes of fulfilling the remedy.[18] It also comprises a duty to ensure compliance with judgements obtained in the course of seeking redress for human rights violations.[19] Pursuant to the right to an effective remedy, the Universal Declaration of Human Rights, for instance, states that the requisite remedies shall be administered by a 'competent national authority' (whether 'judicial, administrative or legislative') and be 'enforced' when granted.[20] The International Covenant on Civil and Political Rights also creates an obligation for states parties 'to ensure that any person claiming such a remedy shall have his right thereto determined by competent judicial, administrative or legislative authorities, or by any other competent authority provided for by the legal system of the state, and to develop the possibilities of judicial remedy'.[21] In interpreting this obligation, the United Nations Human Rights Committee states that it entails the conduct of investigations by the state in question through the requisite judicial and non-judicial means.[22] Although the Human Rights Committee does not expressly state that the provision amounts to a duty to prosecute, it acknowledges that a failure by the state in question to investigate allegations of gross human rights violations constitutes a breach and that where investigations reveal the commission of human rights violations, the perpetrators must be 'brought to justice'.[23] A duty to prosecute can

---

[18]See African Union 2003, para c(c); Covenant on Civil and Political Rights, above n 11, Article 2 (3); Universal Declaration, above n 17, Article 8; International Convention on the Elimination of All Forms of Racial Discrimination, opened for signature 21 December 1965, UNTS vol 660, p. 195 (entered into force 4 January 1969), Article 6; Torture Convention, above n 6, Article 14; Protocol Additional to the Geneva Conventions of 12 August 1949, and relating to the Protection of Victims of International Armed Conflicts, opened for signature 12 December 1977, 1125 UNTS 3 (entered into force 7 December 1978) (Additional Protocol 1), Article 91; and Rome Statute of the International Criminal Court (last amended 2010), opened for signature 17 July 1998 (entered into force 1 July 2002) (Rome Statute), Articles 75, 79. See also Convention on the Rights of the Child, opened for signature 20 November 1989, UNTS, vol 1577, p. 3 (entered into force 2 September 1990) (Convention on the Rights of a Child), Article 39, where it requires enhancement of physical and psychological recovery and social reintegration of child victims.

[19]See African Union 2003, para c(c); and the United Nations General Assembly 2006, para 17. Regional courts have also elucidated the need for remedies. For instance, the African Commission on Human and Peoples' Rights in the *Zimbabwe Human Rights NGO case*, above n 14, held that states owe an obligation to, where possible, 'restore the right violated and provide appropriate compensation for resulting damage'. See also European Court of Human Rights, *Aksoy v Turkey*, 18 December 1996, 100/1995/606/694, para 95; and European Court of Human Rights, *Kaya et al. v Turkey*, 24 October 2006, Application no. 4451/02, para 50, where the court held that remedies must be effective in both law and fact, in the sense of not being unreasonably withheld by the conduct of the authorities in the state in question. See also *Velásquez-Rodríguez 1988*, above n 13, paras 25, 64, 66; and Inter-American Court of Human Rights, *Osorio Rivera and Family Members v Peru*, 26 November 2013, para 235, where the court stated that customary international law reflects that every violation of an international duty that results in harm gives rise to a duty to provide adequate redress.

[20]Universal Declaration, above n 17, Article 8.

[21]See Covenant on Civil and Political Rights, above n 11, Article 2(3).

[22]United Nations Human Rights Committee 2004, paras 15 and 18.

[23]Ibid.

therefore be inferred from this interpretation, as the Human Rights Committee also expressly states that a failure by a state party to bring perpetrators to justice could constitute a breach of the state's obligation under the International Covenant on Civil and Political Rights.[24] Besides, the Human Rights Committee recognises the relevant role of the judiciary in fulfilling the right of victims to effective remedies.[25] The African Charter on Human and Peoples' Rights also recognises the right to an effective remedy in Article 7(1)(a).[26] The African Commission on Human and Peoples' Rights has stated in the case of *Zimbabwe Human Rights NGO Forum v Zimbabwe* that 'to fulfil the rights' in the African Charter on Human and Peoples' Rights means that any person whose rights are violated would have an effective remedy as rights without remedies have no worth.[27] In summary, the responsibility of states to provide remedies for gross violations of human rights can give rise to a duty to prosecute, since prosecution constitutes one of the avenues through which the right to a remedy can be fulfilled.

6.2.2 Discussion

6.2.2.1 Does Ghana Have a Duty to Prosecute Past Human Rights Violations?

Although Ghana's choice of a truth commission, as opposed to criminal prosecutions, fulfilled the right to truth, there are two reasons that indicate that this response to Ghana's past human rights violations was inadequate.[28] To begin with, the existence of a duty on the part of states to prosecute the above-mentioned crimes as well as the obligation of states to uphold and protect fundamental human rights presupposes that where sufficient evidence is obtained to that effect, perpetrators must be prosecuted, regardless of whether or not a truth commission has been established.[29] A truth commission on its own cannot convict and sentence

[24]Ibid., para 18.

[25]Ibid., paras 15, 17 and 18.

[26]See Banjul Charter, above n 11, Article 7(1)(a), which provides that 'Every individual shall have the right to have his cause heard. This comprises: The right to appeal to competent national organs against acts of violating his fundamental rights as recognized and guaranteed by conventions, laws, regulations and customs in force'. This provision is further expanded in the African Union's Principles and Guidelines on the Right to a Fair Trial and Legal Assistance in Africa, 2003, para c (b). See African Union 2003, para c(b). See also Office of the United Nations High Commissioner for Human Rights 2009, p. 23. https://www.ohchr.org/Documents/Publications/Amnesties_en.pdf. Accessed 4 September 2019.

[27]See *Zimbabwe Human Rights NGO* case, above n 14, para 171.

[28]For the reasons why the NRC was established as opposed to criminal prosecutions being instated, see Sect. 3.2 in Chap. 3 of this book.

[29]See United Nations General Assembly 2006, para 4.

perpetrators of human rights violations. It was, therefore, erroneous to consider the NRC a substitute for actual criminal prosecution rather than a mere complement.[30]

The question then is whether Ghana still has a duty to prosecute. It should be observed in that regard that none of the three international crimes that can occasion a duty to prosecute (i.e., war crimes, genocide and crimes against humanity) occurred in Ghana.

A war crime occurs when there is a breach of international humanitarian law in the course of an international or non-international armed conflict, with a linkage between the breach and the armed conflict, which results in direct criminal responsibility on the part of the perpetrator.[31] The existence of an armed conflict is therefore a prerequisite for the commission of a war crime.[32] In the case of Ghana, however, no armed conflict occurred in the country.

Genocide occurs when the conduct in question is committed with 'an intent to destroy in whole or in part a national, ethnic, racial or religious group'.[33] The human rights violations that occurred in Ghana (as outlined earlier in this study) were, however, power struggles with no relation to the destruction of a national, ethnic, racial or religious group in whole or in part.

Crimes against humanity occur if the respective conduct is 'part of a widespread and systematic attack on a civilian population'.[34] An 'attack' has been defined as 'a course of conduct involving the multiple commission of the act' in question.[35] The 'widespread' element connotes how extensive the act is, including its geographical

---

[30]On the fact that the NRC was established as an alternative to prosecutions, see Ameh 2006, pp. 99–100, where he refers to the argument of a former Attorney General in Parliament during the consideration of the National Reconciliation Bill in Parliament. On the subject of not considering transitional justice mechanisms as alternatives, see United Nations Commission on Human Rights 2005, para 8; and Ambos 2009, pp. 40, 51.

[31]See the Rome Statute, above n 18, Article 8; and Werle and Jessberger 2014, pp. 392, 406–420.

[32]In this regard, it should be noted that there is no internationally accepted definition of an armed conflict. However, one popular definition of the terminology is that of the International Criminal Tribunal for the Former Yugoslavia, which states that an armed conflict occurs 'whenever there is a resort to armed force between states or protracted armed violence between government authorities and organized armed groups or between such groups within a state. See International Criminal Tribunal for the Former Yugoslavia, *Prosecutor v Dusko Tadic A/K/A "Dule"*, Decision on the Defence Motion for Interlocutory Appeal on Jurisdiction, 2 October 1995, para 70. Although this decision is not binding on Ghana, it is useful in this context, as it has been utilized by the International Criminal Court. See International Criminal Court, *the Prosecutor v Thomas Lubanga Dyilo*, Judgment pursuant to Article 74 of the Statute, 14 March 2012, Case No. ICC-01/04-01/06-2843 (Lubanga), para 533; and International Criminal Court, *Prosecutor v Kantanga and Ngudjolo Chui*, Decision on the confirmation of charges, 30 September 2008, Case No. ICC-01/04-01/07-717 (Katanga), para 238, where the court defined international armed conflict.

[33]See the Genocide Convention, above n 6, Article II; and Rome Statute, above n 18, Article 6. For details of the structure of the crime of genocide, see also Werle and Jessberger 2014, pp. 293–294.

[34]See, for example, Rome Statute, above n 18, Article 7.

[35]Ibid., Article 7(2)(a).

reach and the number of people affected.[36] The 'systematic' requirement means that the act must not be unplanned. Rather, it must occur through preparation and 'organisation'.[37] None of the human rights violations in the Ghanaian context, however, can be regarded as an attack, since they occurred through isolated incidents by different perpetrators over a long period of time. Even if one could speak of an attack, the human rights violations in the Ghanaian context cannot be regarded as widespread, considering the small magnitude of violations that occurred with respect to each of the conducts that were highlighted in Chap. 2. It should be noted that although the NRC recorded a total of 8,766 cases of human rights violations,[38] the commission of such human rights violations cannot be considered widespread, in so far as they resulted from isolated acts spanning more than three decades, from 1957 to 1992. Besides, none of the individual acts that brought about human rights violations affected a large number of victims nor extended over a large geographical area. In absence of the elements of 'attack' and 'widespread', it is immaterial whether any of the occurrences in Ghana were systematic. In summary, no duty to prosecute arises in the Ghanaian context based on commission of war crimes, genocide or crime against humanity.

Regardless of the absence of crimes under international law, other bases for Ghana's duty to prosecute would be the United Nations Convention Against Torture and Other Cruel, Inhuman or Degrading Treatment or Punishment (Torture Convention), the International Convention for the Protection of All Persons from Enforced Disappearance and the International Covenant on Civil and Political Rights (as a result of the 'ensure and respect' phrases). However, since the Torture Convention and the International Covenant on Civil and Political Rights were ratified by Ghana only in September 2007, a duty to prosecute would apply only to cases that occurred after ratification and not to the human rights violations that occurred before Ghana's transition to democracy in 1993.[39] Also, a duty to prosecute will not apply to the cases of enforced disappearances that were investigated by the NRC. This is because the International Convention for the Protection of All Persons from Enforced Disappearance has not yet been ratified although signed in 2007.

Another basis for a duty to prosecute past human rights violations in Ghana is the African Charter on Human and Peoples' Rights, on the basis of the decision in

[36]See, for example, *Katanga Case*, above n 32, para 395; and Werle and Jessberger 2014, pp. 339–340.

[37]Werle and Jessberger 2014, p. 340. See also International Criminal Court, the *Prosecutor v Jean-Pierre Bemba Gombo*, Decision on the Prosecutor's Application for a Warrant of Arrest against Jean-Pierre Bemba Gombo, 10 June 2008, Case No. ICC-01/05-01/08-14-tENG (Bemba), para 33.

[38]See National Reconciliation Commission 2004, vol 1, para 6.2.6.5.

[39]Regarding the non-applicability of statutory limitations to certain human rights violations, see United Nations General Assembly 2006, paras 6, 7.

Zimbabwe Human Rights NGO Forum v Zimbabwe.[40] Yet such a duty would apply only to cases that occurred after Ghana ratified the African Charter on Human and Peoples' Rights on 24 January 1989. In reality, the number of cases which occurred after this date are few, since a majority of human rights violations in Ghana occurred before 1989.

Due to the right of victims of human rights violations to obtain remedies, another international human rights document that could give rise to a duty to prosecute is the Universal Declaration of Human Rights. In this regard, it may be argued that the existence of such a duty is questionable, since the Universal Declaration of Human Rights is not a treaty and there is no consensus regarding whether it has attained the status of customary international law.[41] In principle, although there is no consensus on the customary international law status of the Universal Declaration of Human Rights, one could, where applicable, still argue for a customary international law status for the individual rights enshrined in the declaration. For instance, in the *Legal Consequences for States of the Continued Presence of South Africa in Namibia (South West Africa) notwithstanding Security Council Resolution 276 (1970),* Judge Fouad Ammoun argued for the customary status of the right to equality under the declaration, when he stated in his separate advisory opinion that

> the Declaration can bind states on the basis of custom… whether because they constituted a codification of customary law as was said in respect of Article 6 of the Vienna Convention on the Law of Treaties, or because they have acquired the force of custom through a general practice accepted as law . … One right which must certainly be considered a pre-existing binding customary norm which the Universal Declaration of Human Rights codified is the right to equality, which by common consent has ever since the remotest times been deemed inherent in human nature.[42]

This statement implies that specific rights under the Universal Declaration of Human Rights that are recognised as part of customary international law can form the basis of a duty to prosecute human rights violations that occurred in Ghana between 1957 and 1993. To cite an example, the right of freedom from torture, which is enshrined in the Universal Declaration of Human Rights, can form the

---

[40]See Banjul Charter, above n 11, Article 25; and *Zimbabwe Human Rights NGO case*, above n 14, para 171.

[41]On the question of whether the Universal Declaration of Human Rights has attained the status of customary international law, see Charlesworth 2008, para 15. http://opil.ouplaw.com/view/10.1093/law:epil/9780199231690/law-9780199231690-e887#. Accessed 11 October 2019; and Hannum Hannum 1995–1996, pp. 318–352. See International Court of Justice, *South West Africa Cases (Liberia v South Africa)*, Dissenting Opinion of Judge Tanaka, 18 July 1966, p. 288, where he stated that the Universal Declaration of Human Rights 'is no more than a declaration adopted by the General Assembly and not a treaty binding on the member States'.

[42]International Court of Justice, *Legal Consequences for States of the Continued Presence of South Africa in Namibia (South West Africa) notwithstanding Security Council Resolution 276 (1970)*, Advisory Opinion of 21 June 1971, Separate Opinion of Vice-President Ammoun, 21 June 1971, p. 76.

basis of a duty to prosecute since it is considered a part of customary international law.[43]

In summary, Ghana has no duty to prosecute human rights violations that occurred between 1957 and 1993 under the Torture Convention, the International Convention for the Protection of All Persons from Enforced Disappearance and the International Covenant on Civil and Political Rights. Regarding the African Charter on Human and Peoples' Rights, a duty to prosecute exists for human rights violations that occurred after 24 January 1989, when the Charter was ratified. A duty to prosecute also exists with regards to rights in the Universal Declaration of Human Rights, which are recognised as part of customary international law, such as the right of freedom from torture. In this regard, the length of time elapsed since the commission of the human rights violations in Ghana would not be material in the initiation of prosecutions, since criminal cases cannot be time-barred under Ghanaian law.[44]

Even if the small magnitude of human rights violations might be considered an argument against Ghana's duty to prosecute,[45] none of the treaties that create the obligation to prosecute have expressly created a threshold with regards to the number of victims that gives rise to the duty to prosecute. For instance, the Universal Declaration of Human Rights uses the word 'everyone' in relation to the

---

[43]See United Kingdom House of Lords, R*egina v Bartle and the Commissioner of Police for the Metropolis et al. Ex Parte Pinochet, Regina v Evans and Another and the Commissioner of Police for the Metropolis et al. Ex Parte Pinochet* (On Appeal from a Divisional Court of the Queen's Bench Division), 24 March 1999 (Pinochet). https://publications.parliament.uk/pa/ld199899/ldjudgmt/jd990324/pino1.htm. Accessed 30 October 2019, where it was held that the prohibition of torture under international law has gained the status of jus cogens, and therefore entitles states to the exercise of universal jurisdiction with regards to the crime of torture. See also International Criminal Tribunal for the Former Yugoslavia, *Prosecutor v Anto Furundzija*, 10 December 1998, Case No. IT-95-17/1-T (Furundzija), pp. 59–60, where the court held that in view of the jus cogens nature of torture, every state has an obligation to investigate, prosecute and punish or extradite perpetrators of torture who are found on their territories. The Supreme Court of Israel has also held in the case of *Attorney-General of the Government of Israel v Eichmann* that the power of states to prosecute these crimes is owed essentially to the fact that the implications of international crimes go beyond the bounds of domestic law, thereby affecting the wellbeing of the whole international community. See Supreme Court of Israel, *Attorney-General of the Government of Israel v Eichmann*, 29 May 1962, Criminal Appeal No. 336/61, as cited in Amnesty International 2012, p. 6. https://www.amnesty.org/download/Documents/24000/ior530132012en.pdf. Accessed 20 October 2019.

[44]However, civil cases have different periods of limitations, as provided under the Limitations Decree of 1972. See Republic of Ghana, Limitation Decree, 1972, National Redemption Council Decree 54. Hence, claims for reparations for instance would be subject to limitations. See also Supreme Court of Ghana, *Ghana Commercial Bank v Commission on Human Rights and Administrative Justice*, 2003, African Human Rights Law Report, paras 31–43, where the courts stated that Ghana's laws on statutory limitations are applicable to human rights claims, although the limitations do not apply to non-judicial investigations.

[45]On the issue of the low magnitude of human rights violations in Ghana, see Wain 2003, pp. 8–9; and Valji 2006, pp. 2–3.

right to a remedy.[46] Similarly, the International Covenant on Civil and Political Rights, the Convention against Torture and the International Convention for the Protection of All Persons from Enforced Disappearance do not provide any indication of a required number of victims.[47] This implies that even a violation against one individual can trigger the duty to prosecute.[48]

6.3 Issues Related to the Amnesty Provisions in the 1992 Constitution

6.3.1 The Legality of Amnesties under International Law

There is no international treaty that expressly prohibits the use of amnesties by states.[49] Nevertheless, the validity of an amnesty under international law depends on whether it is a blanket amnesty (i.e., an amnesty that 'exempts broad categories of serious human rights offenders from prosecution and/or civil liability without the beneficiaries having to satisfy preconditions')[50] or conditional amnesty (i.e., an amnesty that requires the beneficiary to fulfil specific conditions before being granted the amnesty).[51]

Conditional amnesties may be permissible if they are created as part of a country's efforts to establish the truth and award reparations but not to prevent prosecution.[52] In such instances, amnesties do not amount to contravention of a

[46]See the Universal Declaration, above n 17, Article 8.

[47]See Covenant on Civil and Political Rights, above n 11, Article 2(3); Torture Convention, above n 6, Articles 5, 7; and Enforced Disappearances Convention, above n 7, Article 6. Regarding the crime of enforced disappearances, although Article 5 of the Convention for the Protection of All Persons from Enforced Disappearance, 2006, states that a systematic conduct of the crime constitute crimes against humanity, it does not preclude single cases of the offence from prosecution. This is evident from the use of the crime (i.e., 'enforced disappearance') in its singular form in most parts of the Convention and in particular in Article 6.

[48]Regarding this issue, Roht-Arriaza observes that in the decision of the *Velásquez-Rodríguez case*, which first interpreted the 'ensure and respect' phrase to connote the existence of a duty to prosecute, it was not stated anywhere that the principle is applicable to only instances where there was a systematic pattern of human rights violations. See Roht-Arriaza 1990, p. 472.

[49]See Freeman and Pensky 2012, p. 44; and Freeman 2009, pp. 32–33.

[50]Office of the United Nations High Commissioner for Human Rights 2009, p. 8. See also Werle and Vormbaum 2018, p. 68.

[51]See Werle and Vormbaum 2018, p. 69.

[52]See Constitutional Court of South Africa, *Azanian Peoples Organization et al. v The President of the Republic of South Africa et al.*, 25 July 1996, Case No. CCT 17/96, pp. 33–36, 44–45, where the court stated that an amnesty was essential in order to encourage perpetrators to tell the truth, as well as to enhance the process of reconciliation in the country. See also Ambos 2009, p. 66; and Mallinder 2007, pp. 211–212, 228–229.

state's duty to fulfil the right to a remedy.[53] The United Nations has, however, stated that even where amnesties are used to promote peace and reconciliation, their usage should not be a means for shielding perpetrators of crimes under international law from punishment[54] and must not hamper victims' rights to reparations and truth.[55]

Blanket amnesties, which shield perpetrators of crimes under international law and gross human rights violations from prosecution, are not acceptable under international law. Freeman, for instance, has identified five main justifications for the general disapproval of blanket amnesties, based on the treaty obligation of states:[56] the existence of a duty to prosecute perpetrators of human rights violations;[57] the existence of a right to remedy under Article 8 of the Universal Declaration of Human Rights and Article 2(3) of the International Covenant on Civil and Political Rights;[58] the existence of an obligation for states to investigate human rights violations under the Torture Convention[59] and the International Covenant on Civil and Political Rights;[60] the existence of treaty provisions that forbid the applicability of statutory limitations on war crimes, crimes against humanity, genocide and aggression;[61] and the existence of treaty provisions on 'non-derogability' of the duties of states in respect of specific human rights, such as

[53]See Ambos 2009, p. 66; and Mallinder 2007, pp. 211–212, 228–229.

[54]See United Nations Commission on Human Rights 2005, paras 19 and 24.

[55]Ibid., para 24.

[56]Freeman and Pensky 2012, pp. 45–51. For further details of the five arguments against amnesties, see also Ambos 2009, pp. 31–32, 54–55; and Mallinder 2007, pp. 211–212, 228–229, where she proposes some conditions under which amnesties should or should not be 'intervened' by courts.

[57]See Sect. 6.2.1 in the present chapter of this book. For details of this argument, see Freeman 2009, pp. 36–39.

[58]See Freeman 2009, pp. 39–40.

[59]See Torture Convention, above n 6, Article 12. See also Freeman 2009, pp. 40–41.

[60]See Covenant on Civil and Political Rights, above n 11, Articles 2(1), 2(2) which requires state parties to respect and ensure' realisation of the rights in the convention and to utilise any needed legislation or mechanisms to give effect to' the rights in the treaty. The duty to prosecute arises from the respect and ensure' phrase, which has been interpreted to give rise to such a duty. Also, the duty of states to provide remedies to victims under Article 2(3) of the International Covenant on Civil and Political Rights, 1966 has been interpreted to give rise to a duty to investigate human rights violations. See Roht-Arriaza 1990, p. 483; and United Nations Human Rights Committee 2004, para 15. See also Freeman 2009, pp. 40–41.

[61]For details of this argument, see Freeman 2009, pp. 41–42. See also Rome Statute, above n 18, Article 29; and Convention on the Non-Applicability of Statutory Limitations to War Crimes and Crimes Against Humanity, opened for signature 26 November 1968, A/RES/2391(XXIII) (entered into force 11 November 1970), Article 1.

the right to life, freedom from torture, slavery and false imprisonment.[62] Since a state cannot rely on its domestic law as a reason for its failure to fulfil its treaty obligations,[63] these treaty obligations form a possible argument against blanket amnesties.

The United Nations has also expressed its disapproval for blanket amnesties through soft law documents. For example, Article 18(1) of the 1993 United Nations Declaration on the Protection of All Persons from Enforced Disappearances proscribes the granting of blanket amnesties for perpetrators of enforced disappearances.[64] The Secretary-General, in his 2004 *Report on The Rule of Law and Transitional Justice in Conflict and Post-Conflict Societies*, has also reiterated the commitment of the United Nations to accountability and explicitly recommends a rejection of the use of blanket amnesties for crimes under international law and gross human rights violations. It also recommends that previously granted amnesties should not bar prosecution of such violations.[65]

Regional courts and quasi-judicial bodies, such as the Inter-American Court of Human Rights and the African Commission on Human and Peoples' Rights have also maintained that blanket amnesties that are granted with respect to gross human rights violations contradict state obligations to prosecute and investigate and to provide remedies for human rights violations. In the case of *Barrios Altos v Peru*, the Inter-American Court of Human Rights held that states parties owe a duty to ensure that victims of human rights violations are not deprived of redress, judicial

---

[62]See Covenant on Civil and Political Rights, above n 11, Article 4(2). Also, there are treaties which do not permit derogation of all their provisions. See International Covenant on Economic, Social and Cultural Rights, opened for signature 16 December 1966, UNTS, vol 993, p. 3 (entered into force 3 January 1976); and Convention on the Rights of a Child, above n 18. See also Freeman 2009, pp. 42–43.

[63]See Vienna Convention on the Law of Treaties, opened for signature 23 May 1969, UNTS, vol 1155, p. 331 (entered into force 27 January 1980) (Vienna Convention), Article 27. Under the Covenant on Civil and Political Rights, above n 11, Article 7, however, a state can abrogate its duties under the treaty, where there is a 'public emergency which threatens the life of the nation and the existence of which is officially proclaimed'. Nevertheless, whatever actions which are taken by a state in such a situation should not result in a breach of its other treaty obligations or cause discrimination solely on the ground of race, colour, sex, language, religion or social origin'.

[64]United Nations General Assembly 1992, Article 18(1). See also United Nations Economic and Social Council 1989, para 19, which prohibits the grant of blanket amnesties to protect persons who have committed acts of 'extra-legal, arbitrary or summary executions'; and United Nations Commission on Human Rights 2005, para 24. Moreover, the Human Rights Commission has observed that by virtue of being connected to the duty of the state to investigate gross violations of human rights, the existence of blanket amnesties can contravene the right to truth. See United Nations Commission on Human Rights 2006, para 45.

[65]See the United Nations Security Council 2004, paras 10 and 64. States parties of the UN are therefore urged to investigate, prosecute and punish perpetrators of human rights violations. Also, staff and peace negotiators of the United Nations are not allowed to tolerate amnesties that seek to oust prosecution of international crimes and gross human rights violations, such as torture, forced disappearances, and extrajudicial or arbitrary killings. See United Nations Commission on Human Rights 2005, paras 19 and 24; and Office of the United Nations High Commissioner for Human Rights 2009, p. 27.

protection or full disclosure of the truth regarding the violations in question. Therefore, the amnesty laws adopted in Peru were held to be inadmissible before the court since they prevented investigation and prosecution of international human rights violations, such as torture and extrajudicial killing. It was also stated that such amnesty laws are inconsistent with the right to justice.[66]

The *Barrios Altos* decision has had an impact on some decisions of the African Commission on Human and Peoples' Rights.[67] In the case of *Malawi African Association et al. v Mauritania*, the African Commission on Human and Peoples' Rights held that 'an amnesty law adopted with the aim of nullifying suits or other actions seeking redress that may be filed by the victims or their beneficiaries, whilst having force within Mauritanian national territory, cannot shield that country from fulfilling its international obligations under the Charter'.[68] The African Commission on Human and Peoples' Rights has also stated in the case of *Zimbabwe Human Rights NGO Forum v Zimbabwe* that a clemency law that prevented victims of human rights violations from seeking redress and shielded perpetrators from punishment constitutes a breach of the individual's right to an effective remedy and violated the individual's right to judicial protection under Article 7(1) of the African Charter on Human and Peoples' Rights.[69] Also, the

---

[66]See Inter-American Court of Human Rights, *Barrios Altos v Peru*, 14 March 2001, Series C No. 75 (Barrios Altos), pp. 14–15, 17; and Inter-American Court of Human Rights, *Barrios Altos v Peru*, Concurring Opinion of Judge A.A. Cançado Trindade, 14 March 2001, Series C No. 75, pp. 2, 4. See also Inter-American Court of Human Rights, *Almonacid Arellano et al. v Chile*, 26 September 2006, Series C No 154 (Almonacid Arellano), pp. 51–52, 53, where the court, referring to its prior decision in *Barrios Altos v Peru* stated that states parties owe a duty to prosecute and punish perpetrators of crimes against humanity thereby invalidating any laws which bar such prosecution. The court also stated that amnesty laws are incompatible with the dictates of international human rights law. These decisions of the court have been reiterated in other subsequent decisions of the court. See Inter-American Court of Human Rights, *La Cantuta v Peru*, 29 November 2006, pp. 83, 89–91; Inter-American Court of Human Rights, *Gomes Lund et al. ("Guerrilha Do Araguaia") v Brazil*, 24 November 2010, pp. 55, 64; and Inter-American Court of Human Rights, *Gelman v Uruguay*, 24 February 2011, pp. 69, 80–81.

[67]See, for instance, the *Zimbabwe Human Rights NGO case*, above n 14, paras 203, 204, 206, 144, where the commission referred to various cases of the Inter-American Court of Human Rights.

[68]See African Commission on Human and Peoples' Rights, *Malawi African Association et al. v Mauritania*, 11 May 2000, Communication Nos. 54/91, 61/91, 98/93, 164/97 à 196/97 and 210/98 (Malawi African Association), paras 82–83.

[69]See the case of *Zimbabwe Human Rights NGO*, above n 14, paras 204–216. Similarly, the European Court of Human Rights has stated in some decisions that in order to protect the right to effective remedy, amnesties are not permissible in cases of torture or ill treatment by an agent of state. See European Court of Human Rights, *Abdülsamet Yaman v Turkey*, 2 November 2004, Application no. 32446/96, para 55; and European Court of Human Rights, *Yeter v Turkey*, 13 January 2009, Application no. 33750/03, para 70. Aside from the regional courts, the issue of validity of amnesties has also been dealt with by some ad hoc tribunals. In the *Furundzija case*, above, n 43, pp. 59–60, it was held that the prohibition of torture under international law makes any national measures that either tolerate torture or shield perpetrators of torture from punishment illegitimate under international law. Moreover, the court held that in view of the jus cogens nature of torture, every state has an obligation to investigate, prosecute and punish or extradite

African Union's Principles and Guidelines on the Right to a Fair Trial and Legal Assistance in Africa state that 'the granting of amnesty to absolve perpetrators of human rights violations from accountability violates the right of victims to an effective remedy'.[70]

An explicit exception to these principles arises with regards to internal armed conflicts, in which case Article 6(5) of Additional Protocol II to the Geneva Conventions makes the granting of blanket amnesties permissible under international law. In such instances, blanket amnesties are applicable only to acts that contravene national law and not international law.[71] Besides, blanket amnesties in such cases must not hamper the application of human rights principles but rather to further the protection of human rights in the state.[72]

6.3.2 Ghana's Amnesty Law Under International Law

Given the above principles, the validity of Ghana's amnesty law under international law depends largely on the nature of the amnesty (i.e., whether it is a conditional or blanket amnesty).

The amnesty provisions that have hampered prosecutions in Ghana stipulate that none of the followers or appointed officers of the Provisional National Defence Council can be made accountable either jointly or severally for any of their official acts or inactions.[73] The provisions also proscribe the judiciary from hearing any lawsuits against the government, any past or present governmental official or appointee, or individuals who aided and abetted past military coups in Ghana. Furthermore, the courts are forbidden from challenging or making any orders or awards in relation to acts of the Provisional National Defence Council and the Armed Forces Revolutionary Council as well as their followers and appointees. This includes actions that contravened the law at the time of their occurrence.[74]

---

perpetrators of torture who are found on their territories. The Special Court for Sierra Leone has also ruled that an amnesty that is granted under domestic law cannot bar another state from the prosecution of international crimes that are subject to universal jurisdiction. See Special Court for Sierra Leone, *Prosecutor v Morris Kallon and Brima Bazzy Kamara*, 13 March 2004, Case Nos. SCSL-2004-15-AR72(E)/ SCSL-2004-16-AR72 (E), pp. 30–31.

[70]See African Union 2003, para c(d). Aside international jurisprudence on amnesties, domestic courts have also ruled on the invalidity of amnesties. See, for instance, Corte Suprema de Justicia de la Nación (Supreme Court), Argentina, *Julio Simón et al. v Public Prosecutor*, 14 June 2005, Case No. 17.768, S. 1767. XXXVIII (Julio Simón et al.), in which the Supreme Court of Argentina ruled that Amnesty Laws, 23.492 and 23.521 were invalid.

[71]See Slye 2002, p. 178. See also Méndez 2006, p. 16.

[72]See Slye 2002, pp. 178, who refers to such amnesties as corrective amnesties.

[73]For further information about the Provisional National Defence Council, see Sect. 2.8 in Chap. 2 of this book.

[74]See Republic of Ghana, Constitution of the Republic of Ghana, 1992 (1992 Constitution), First Schedule, ss 34.

In essence, these provisions constitute a blanket amnesty, since they leave no exceptions or avenues for victims of human rights violations to obtain redress. Given their blanket nature, the amnesty provisions are not permissible under international law.[75] The illegality of the amnesty provisions is inferable from the country's duty to prosecute, as outlined above, on the basis of rights stated in the Universal Declaration of Human Rights and the African Charter on Human and Peoples' Rights. Besides, it should be noted that the amnesty provisions in Ghana cannot be classified under the conditions that create an exception for blanket amnesties under Article 6(5) of Additional Protocol II to the Geneva Conventions because these provisions relate to armed conflicts, which did not occur in Ghana.[76]

Moreover, an examination of the means of adopting the amnesty provisions in Ghana seems to reveal that they were not meant to promote peace and reconciliation, since they were not created through a 'democratic and transparent' process. Although the Ghanaian Constitution and the amnesty law were approved through a national referendum, it is questionable whether the amnesty provisions were adopted in a democratic manner.[77] To begin with, most of the members of the consultative assembly that handled the drafting process of the Constitution were members of the Provisional National Defence Council.[78] Also, the amnesty provisions were not subjected to debate on the floor of the consultative assembly that drafted Ghana's Constitution, before being included in the Constitution.[79] In the circumstances, it is doubtful that the need for the amnesty provisions was publicly acknowledged before being adopted. Although the holding of a referendum might indicate that it was adopted democratically, this does not legitimise the amnesty laws under international law. In the Inter-American Court of Human Rights case of *Gelman v Uruguay*, it was held that 'the democratic legitimacy of specific facts in a society is limited by the norms of protection of human rights recognised in international treaties'.[80] Hence, the use of a referendum to adopt the 1992 Constitution and the amnesty laws does not change the fact that they were not adopted in a manner that belied an intention to foster peace and reconciliation.

Given these reasons, the validity of the amnesty laws under Ghana's Constitution is not sustainable under international human rights law. Nevertheless,

---

[75]For details of the amnesty provisions, see Sect. 3.2.1 in Chap. 3 of this book.

[76]See Protocol Additional to the Geneva Conventions of 12 August 1949, and relating to the Protection of Victims of Non-International Armed Conflicts, opened for signature 8 June 1977, 1125 UNTS 609 (entered into force 7 December 1978) (Protocol II), Article 6(5), which states that 'At the end of hostilities, the authorities in power shall endeavour to grant the broadest possible amnesty to persons who have participated in the armed conflict, or those deprived of their liberty for reasons related to the armed conflict, whether they are interned or detained.'

[77]On the need for legitimacy of the process of creating the amnesty, see Ambos 2009, p. 62; and Teitel 2000, pp. 58–59.

[78]See Sect. 2.9 in Chap. 2 of this book.

[79]See Boafo-Arthur 2005, p. 118; and Gyimah-Boadi 1994, pp. 78–79.

[80]See Inter-American Court of Human Rights, *Gelman v Uruguay*, 24 February 2011, paras 238, 239.

the amnesty provisions have not been repealed to date. One probable reason for the failure to repeal the provisions is the lack of consensus amongst Ghanaians on the issue. Also, a section of Ghanaians consider the amnesty provisions as necessary for maintaining peace in the country and protecting the interest of the public, since repealing it will imply questioning the legality of the military coup d'états that occurred in Ghana.[81]

Indeed, from a historical point of view, the amnesty law was a necessary price that had to be paid for democracy, given the fact that one of the political regimes believed to have perpetrated most of the human rights violations in Ghana was the very regime that restored the country to democracy. In the case of *New Patriotic Party v Attorney General*, for example, it was stated that although the 1992 Constitution does not support coup d'états, it is in the spirit of the Constitution to forgive the plotters of the military coups.[82] In essence, the amnesty laws were a critical aspect of the reconciliation process in Ghana.

Regardless of the historical significance of the amnesty provisions, there is still the need to repeal them since blanket amnesties hinder accountability for serious violations of human rights and are not permitted under international law. Indeed, precedents of repealing similar amnesty laws can be found in Argentina, El Salvador and Uruguay. In the Argentinian case of *Simón, Julio Héctor y otros s/ privación ilegítima de la libertad*, for example, the Argentinian Supreme Court pronounced two amnesty laws in Argentina as void and unconstitutional and acknowledged the validity of a law adopted by the Argentinian Congress to repeal the amnesty law.[83] In El Salvador, a similar course was taken by the country's Supreme Court in July 2016, in a landmark decision that nullified an amnesty law enacted in 1993 following the publication of the final report of the United Nations Truth Commission in El Salvador.[84] According to the court, the amnesty law impeded access to justice and promotion of fundamental human rights.[85] In

[81]Annan IL, Director and Chief Investigator, Commission on Human Rights and Administrative Justice, Ghana, Personal Interview (25 August 2016). Oduro F, Deputy Director, Ghana Centre for Democratic Development, Personal Interview (16 August 2016). Also, Ansah-Koi K, Department of Political Science, University of Ghana, Personal Interview (18 August 2016); and Boafo-Arthur K, Department of Political Science, University of Ghana, Personal Interview (18 August 2016), believe that the failure to repeal the said provisions, has largely been a result of protecting the interests of the political elite in the country, who are afraid of facing the consequences of any such attempts.

[82]See Supreme Court of Ghana, *New Patriotic Party v Attorney-General*, 8 March 1994, 1993–1994 Ghana law Reports 2, p. 14.

[83]The said amnesty laws had been enacted to protect perpetrators of human rights violations committed in Argentina between 1976 and 1983. See the case of *Julio Simón et al.*, above n 70.

[84]See Cerqueira and Arteaga 2016, pp. 6–7. http://www.dplf.org/sites/default/files/amnesty_law-final-24june.pdf. Accessed 30 October 2019; and Amnesty International 2016. https://www.amnesty.org/en/latest/news/2016/07/el-salvador-rejects-amnesty-law-in-historic-ruling/. Accessed 30 October 2019.

[85]See Yi 2016, pp. 1, 2, 4. http://www.coha.org/wp-content/uploads/2016/07/PRsalvador_final.pdf. Accessed 30 October 2019.

Uruguay, the Expiry Law of 1986, which granted amnesty to police and military men for gross human rights violations committed between 1973 and 1985, was declared unconstitutional by the Inter-American Court of Human Rights in February 2011 and was subsequently repealed by the country's Congress in October 2011.[86]

These instances show that it is possible to repeal the amnesty law in the 1992 Constitution, although it could be a difficult process.[87] Regardless of this fact, the Ghanaian judiciary, Parliament and nongovernmental organisations can play key roles to make this a reality.

6.4 Issues Related to the Right to Reparations

6.4.1 The Scope of the Right to Reparations

The right to reparations is a component of the right to effective remedies, as outlined in the in the United Nations Basic Principles and Guidelines on the Right to a Remedy and Reparation for Victims of Gross Violations of International Human Rights Law and Serious Violations of International Humanitarian Law.[88] This right entails restitution (i.e., restoring victims to their condition prior to suffering from the human rights violations in question),[89] compensation (i.e., making the requisite amends economically or financially for the harm suffered), rehabilitation (i.e., restoring the physical and mental state of the individual through medical, psychological or social care), satisfaction (i.e., efforts to come to terms with the past as well as to ensure non-recurrence of similar violations in future)[90] and guarantees of non-repetition (i.e., measures for preventing the recurrence of human rights violations).[91] Reparations must also be adequate, effective and prompt.[92]

---

[86]See Amnesty International 2011. https://www.amnesty.org/en/latest/news/2011/10/uruguay-congress-adopts-landmark-law-tackle-impunity/. Accessed 12 October 2019; and Werle and Vormbaum 2018, pp. 293–294.

[87]On the difficult nature of repealing the amnesty provisions, see Sect. 3.2.2 in Chap. 3 of this book.

[88]United Nations General Assembly 2006, para 11. See also the African Union 2003, para c(b)

[89]This could for instance include restoring one's employment or properties lost as a result of human rights violations. See United Nations General Assembly 2006, para 19.

[90]Such efforts could include for example memorialisation, apologies, acknowledgment of past violations by the state and finding the whereabouts of the disappeared. See United Nations General Assembly 2006, para 22.

[91]See United Nations General Assembly 2006, paras 18, 24; United Nations Commission on Human Rights 2005, para 34; and United Nations General Assembly 1985, paras 8–13.

[92]See the United Nations General Assembly 2006, para 15.

6.4.2 Has Ghana Fulfilled Victims' Rights to Reparations?

In the Ghanaian context, restitution and satisfaction were initiated shortly after Ghana's transition, even before the establishment of the NRC. During the first presidential term after the transition to democracy, the then president Jerry John Rawlings rendered two public apologies for the 'excesses' committed during his military rule.[93] Rawlings' government also returned confiscated assets to key members of the opposition.[94] The de-confiscation efforts were partial, however, since they were not based on a well-designed policy and were, for unknown reasons, for the benefit of key opposition politicians.[95]

Following this, Ghana's fulfilment of the four components of reparations were continued through the NRC's work. Restitution was initiated through the NRC's recommendations for the government to return confiscated properties to their owners,[96] whilst compensation was initiated through the recommendations for payment of monetary compensation to victims.[97] Satisfaction was reflected in the NRC's recommendations for the government to apologise to victims[98] and for erection of memorials in all regional capitals.[99] Also, the commission's efforts towards rehabilitation are indicated by its recommendations for the establishment of trauma and counselling centres in regional and district hospitals and the provision of counselling and medical services to victims during the NRC's work.[100] Lastly, the commission's recommendations for reforming the military, police, prisons services and the judiciary can be regarded as its efforts to guarantee non-repetition.[101] Despite the initiation of these reparative measures through the NRC, none of the above-mentioned recommendations have been implemented by the state, with the exception of the payment of some of the monetary compensations recommended for victims.

In effect, the only concrete reparative measures undertaken by the state have been the return of confiscated assets to specific politicians and the payment of monetary compensations to some of the victims. Could these efforts be considered as fulfilment of the right of victims to reparations? As noted above, reparations are supposed to be 'adequate, effective and prompt'.[102] Adequacy means that

[93]Attafuah 2004, pp. 126–127.

[94]Ibid., p. 127.

[95]Ibid.

[96]See National Reconciliation Commission 2004, vol 1, para 7.4.2.1.

[97]Ibid., para 7.4.2.2.

[98]Ibid., vol 1, para 7.4.1.3; vol 3, paras 3.2.1, 3.2.3.

[99]Ibid., vol 1, para 7.4.1.4.

[100]Ibid., para 7.4.1.6.2.

[101]Ibid., vol 3, Chapter 1. For further discussion of institutional reform, see Sect. 6.5 in the present chapter of this book.

[102]See the United Nations General Assembly 2006, paras 15, 2(c), 3(d), 11(b); and United Nations Commission on Human Rights 2005, paras 31, 32, 34.

reparations must be commensurate with the degree of harm or violations suffered,[103] must be capable of redressing the wrong[104] and must erase the effects of the harm suffered, to the extent of restoring the status quo.[105] Adequate reparations must also cater for both the 'material and moral' aspects of the harm suffered.[106]

In the Ghanaian context, it is not possible to measure whether reparations have been commensurate with the harm suffered, given the fact that the human rights violations occurred over a long period of time and many victims died long before the initiation of reparative processes. Indeed, the NRC stressed in its report that 'no reparation, monetary or otherwise can restore victims (direct or indirect) to the *status quo ante*'.[107] Nevertheless, the failure of the state to implement all the reparations proposed by the NRC constitutes non-fulfilment of the adequacy element. For instance, the NRC proposed the erection of a monument in Accra in memory of the killed and disappeared, whose names were to be engraved on the monument. However, no such monument has been erected to date. Also, not all confiscated properties have been restored to victims.[108] In addition, some of the victims who were earmarked to receive reparations in the NRC's recommendations have not received their allocated sums.[109] Thus, the state has failed to address both the 'material and moral' aspects of the harm suffered by victims. Even if some of the recommended monetary compensation was paid to victims,[110] the absence of the above-mentioned measures leaves a gap regarding the adequacy of the reparations.[111]

Concerning the element of effectiveness, the African Commission on Human and Peoples' Rights has stated that a remedy is effective if it 'offers prospects of being successful'.[112] In view of the state's inability to ensure full implementation of

---

[103]See the United Nations General Assembly 2006, para 15.

[104]See the African Commission on Human and Peoples' Rights, *Sir Dawda K. Jawara v The Gambia*, 11 May 2000, Communication No. 147/95 (Sir Dawda), para 32.

[105]See Permanent Court of International Justice, *The Factory at Chorzow (Claim for Indemnity) (The Merits) (Germany v Poland)*, Judgment No. 13, 13 September 1928, 1928 P.C.I.J. (ser. A) No. 17, p. 47; and *Case Concerning The Factory at Chorzów (Claim For Indemnity) (Jurisdiction) (Germany v Poland)*, Judgment No. 8, 26 July 1927, 1927 P.C.I.J. (ser. A) No. 9, p. 21.

[106]Kerbrat 2010, p. 579.

[107]See National Reconciliation Commission 2004, vol 1, para 7.4.1.1.

[108]See Sect. 4.4.4 in Chap. 4 of this book.

[109]See Myjoyonline TV, Scars of the revolution (Video File) published by Myjoyonline TV on YouTube, 12 December 2019. https://www.youtube.com/watch?v=p2BC4LNhnIE. Accessed 3 January 2020.

[110]The question of adequacy of the sums awarded as compensation is still controversial, in light of different views on the subject. For details of this, see Sect. 5.5.1 in Chap. 5 of this book.

[111]See National Reconciliation Commission 2004, vol 1, para 7.4.

[112]See *Sir Dawda Case*, above n 104, para 32. See also REDRESS 2014, p. 19, para 76. http://www.redress.org/downloads/publications/submission-to-special-rapporteur-on-reparations-programmes-public.pdf. Accessed 19 October 2019, where effectiveness of reparations is explained in terms of being beneficial to the victim.

the NRC's reparative measures, the reparations in Ghana cannot be considered effective. For instance, the NRC's recommendation for the return of seized properties to their owners was ineffective due to its low prospects of success from the onset. This recommendation was not practicable in view of the complicated nature of the Ghanaian land tenure system, which made it nearly impossible to return confiscated lands.[113] Moreover, the irregularities in the process of paying monetary compensation and the failure of the state to pay some of the validly allocated sums to victims is an indication of the inefficiency of the reparations.

The promptness of reparations means that they should not be unduly prolonged but must be awarded in a timely manner.[114] The promptness of the reparative efforts in Ghana is doubtful, on account of the delays in initiating a comprehensive process to fulfil the right to reparations. The absence of promptness is also evinced by the delay in implementation of the NRC's recommendations. For instance, the payment of compensations was started nearly after three years of the closure of the commission.[115]

Given the explanations above, the reparations offered in Ghana cannot be said to be adequate, effective and prompt. Although all the four elements of reparations have been tackled in diverse ways, they were done in a piecemeal manner, as indicated by the failure of the state to implement most of the NRC's reparative recommendations. Ghana has therefore not fulfilled all aspects of the right to reparations, and there is the need to address existing gaps. Since the NRC's recommendations reflected all four components of reparations, a comprehensive implementation of the recommendations can meet the need for adequacy, effectiveness and promptness. This can be done by putting in place follow-up measures, such as enactment of a law to implement the NRC's recommendations.

[113] In Ghana, lands are owned by traditional authorities (i.e., local chiefs), clans and the government. The title that is held by traditional authorities is allodial, meaning that they possess the land forever. Hence, although leases and assignments are possible, the land title reverts to the allodial title holders once the lease period has expired. In light of this form of land tenure, it would have been practically impossible to return certain leased properties that were confiscated to their owners, since in some instances the term of the lease would have expired, and title would have reverted back to the traditional authority.

[114] See REDRESS 2014, p. 19, para 76. http://www.redress.org/downloads/publications/submission-to-special-rapporteur-on-reparations-programmes-public.pdf. Accessed 19 October 2019. See also the Banjul Charter, above n 11, Article 50, where it is stated that in instances where exhaustion of local remedies has been 'unduly prolonged', one can refer a matter to the African Commission on Human and Peoples' Rights. This provision can be used to explain the requirement of promptness, in the sense that remedies must not be unduly prolonged.

[115] See Sect. 4.4.4 in Chap. 4 of this book.

6.5 Institutional Reforms

6.5.1 The Basis and Scope of Institutional Reform

Institutional reforms are usually considered a mechanism of transitional justice and have their basis in the obligation of states to provide guarantees of non-repetition, as part of preventing the recurrence of human rights violations.[116] Thus, state institutions that had supported the past dictatorial or conflicted regime must be altered to reflect the change in political orientation and to create institutions that support the rule of law.[117] Also, when institutions such as the military, police and judiciary are properly reformed, it enhances efforts to bring perpetrators to book and also ensures proper exposure of truth and lasting reconciliation.[118]

Currently, there are emerging principles under international law that require states to reform public institutions, following massive human rights violations.[119] For instance, the African Commission on Human and Peoples' Rights has indirectly reiterated the relevance of institutional reform in the case of *Malawi African Association et al. v Mauritania*, in which it recognised the existence of discrimination against specific social groups in Mauritania and held that the state should employ measures to eliminate such discriminatory practices from the society.[120] The Inter-American Court of Human Rights ruled in the case of *Velásquez Rodríguez v Honduras* that the right of prisoners to attain respect for their rights

---

[116]See for instance the United Nations 2010, p. 2, where institutional reforms are mentioned as one of the mechanisms of transitional justice. On the linkage of institutional reforms to guarantees of non-repetition, see Andreu-Guzmán 2013, p. 4. https://www.files.ethz.ch/isn/164673/80ed6b7fa08ff1e0620fe297f85f63f0.pdf. Accessed 1 November 2019; and Ferstman 2010, p. 23. See also the United Nations General Assembly 2006, para 23; and the case of *Velásquez-Rodríguez 1988*, above n 13 para 174.

[117]See Office of the United Nations High Commissioner for Human Rights 2006, p. 3. https://www.ohchr.org/Documents/Publications/RuleoflawVettingen.pdf. Accessed 4 September 2019.

[118]See Borraine 2006, p. 23; and see Office of the United Nations High Commissioner for Human Rights 2006b, pp. 3, 23–24. https://www.ohchr.org/Documents/Publications/RuleoflawVettingen.pdf. Accessed 4 September 2019, where it is written that due to the relevance of institutional reform, truth commissions should conduct institutional hearings, apart from individual hearings, to enable them to uncover institutional failures that led to serious human rights violation. For instance, the South African TRC undertook some form of institutional hearing, by calling representatives from state institutions like the police and military during its work.

[119]See United Nations Commission on Human Rights 2005, para 36. See also Méndez 1997, p. 261, where he writes that such an obligation is emerging, with regards to crimes against humanity, in the sense of the state preventing known perpetrators from assuming authoritative positions in law enforcement and other institutions of influence in the society.

[120]See *Malawi African Association* case, above n 68, para 142.

involves an obligation on the part of the state to put in place 'reasonable' measures that will guarantee protection of those rights.[121]

The need for institutional reform flows from the obligation of states to prevent the recurrence of human rights violations. This includes all means of a legal, political, administrative and cultural nature that promote the protection of human rights and ensure that any violations are treated as illegal acts.[122] Thus, institutional reforms can be achieved by using requisite means to promote the rule of law and ensure protection and respect for human rights and by reforming governmental institutions to re-establish their credibility.[123] Measures that can be used in this regard include vetting ('assessing integrity to determine suitability for public employment'),[124] lustration (using parliamentary legislation to 'restrict members and collaborators of former repressive regimes from holding a range of public offices, state management positions or other jobs with strong public influences')[125] and purges ('removal of individuals from employment positions through dismissal, job transfer, or forced retirement, bans of individuals from future employment, or restrictions on civil and political rights', without using parliamentary legislation).[126] The state must also follow due process to ensure that individuals who took part in perpetration of human rights violations do not continue holding governmental positions, and the judicial sector must be reformed to make it independent, unbiased and efficient.[127] There should also be civilian oversight over security agencies and the military, and the state must disintegrate unofficial armed bodies.[128] Reforms could also entail revising or creating public sector workers' code of conduct, eliminating festivities and symbols associated with the old regime, improving working conditions of public sector workers and merging, closing down or

---

[121]See *Velásquez-Rodríguez 1988*, above n 13, paras 187 and 188. See also Inter-American Court of Human Rights, *Myrna Mack Chang Guatemala*, Judgment of 25 November 2003 (Merits, Reparations and Costs), 25 November 2003, para 284, where the court held that the state of Guatemala should ensure that monitoring of intelligence activities by the military and police is done thoroughly so as to prevent these bodies from violating peoples' human rights and freedoms.

[122]See United Nations General Assembly 2006, paras 1 and 2; and the case of *Velásquez-Rodríguez 1988*, above n 13, para 174.

[123]See United Nations Commission on Human Rights 2005, para 35.

[124]Office of the United Nations High Commissioner for Human Rights 2006b, p. 4. https://www.ohchr.org/Documents/Publications/RuleoflawVettingen.pdf. Accessed 4 September 2019. See also United Nations Security Council, para 52, where it is written that vetting usually involves 'a formal process for the identification and removal of individuals responsible for abuses, especially from police, prison services, the Army and the judiciary'.

[125]Nalepa 2013, pp. 46–47.

[126]Lynch 2013, pp. 61, 62.

[127]See United Nations Commission on Human Rights 2005, paras 35, 36, 38; and the United Nations General Assembly 2006, paras 23(c) and 23(h).

[128]See United Nations Commission on Human Rights 2005, paras 35, 36, 37; and the United Nations General Assembly 2006, paras 23(a).

restructuring certain governmental bodies.[129] Institutional reforms can also entail repeal of laws that foster human rights violations as well as protection of democratic practices and institutions.

6.5.2 Gaps in Institutional Reform

Within the Ghanaian context, no explicit policies were adopted to reform state institutions as part of the transition to democracy. Nevertheless, a number of ad hoc reforms could be identified. Prior to the adoption of the 1992 Constitution, the government of the Provisional National Defence Council employed different measures to prevent the recurrence of military coups d'états. These reforms included disconnecting the army from political movements, improving the command system within the army and increasing the level of governmental control over the activities of the army.[130] The 1992 Constitution also brought additional reforms by proscribing the establishment of any 'armed force' without authorisation by an Act of Parliament.[131] The Constitution also provides different institutionalised means for overseeing the work of the military, the police, the prisons and the judiciary through oversight bodies like the National Security Council, the Prisons Service Council, the Police Council, the Armed Forces Council and the Judicial Council.[132] Following the establishment of the NRC, another indication of the state's institutional reform measures has been the NRC's recommendations regarding the reformation of the Ghana army, police, prisons and the judiciary.[133] These include the commission's recommendations regarding measures on abolishing the practice of forming private armies, providing human rights education to public workers, improving working conditions of workers in respective government sectors, amending workers' codes of ethics and applying strict disciplinary measures at workplaces.[134]

Nevertheless, these recommendations have not been implemented and the key sectors of the NRC's institutional reform recommendations (i.e., the judiciary, the police, the prisons service and the military) are still facing administrative lapses that the NRC recommended be reformed. For instance, the remuneration and working

[129]See United Nations Office of the High Commissioner for Human Rights 2006b, p. 4. https://www.ohchr.org/Documents/Publications/RuleoflawVettingen.pdf. Accessed 4 September 2019.

[130]For details of the different measures used, see Hutchful 1997, pp. 252–264.

[131]See 1992 Constitution, above n 74, Article 210(2).

[132]See 1992 Constitution, above n 74, Articles 84, 153, 154, 201, 203, 206, 208, 211, 214

[133]For a summary of the commission's recommendations on institutional reform, see Sect. 4.4.1.3 in Chap. 4 of this book.

[134]See United Nations Commission on Human Rights 2005, paras 35, 36 and 37; and United Nations General Assembly 2006, para 23(a).

conditions of the police and prisons services are still very poor.[135] But does Ghana, in principle, hold an obligation to implement these reforms? Whilst the state has an obligation to guarantee non-recurrence of human rights violations, the non-reform of state institutions does not in itself imply a failure to take preventive measures.[136] Also, the persistence of some human rights violations does not amount to a violation of an international obligation.

In the Ghanaian context, these lapses are, however, an indication that more efforts are needed to promote human rights protection. In addition, there is the need to reinitiate institutional reform measures as a way of strengthening the rule of law and democracy. A possible way of doing this is implementation of the NRC's recommendations, such as improving the command structure within the army, police and prisons services, creating ethnic balance within the public sector, providing human rights education for public officials, improving the conditions of service of public workers, drafting a codes of conduct and improving disciplinary measures within the public sector.[137] However, other measures, such as vetting, purging and lustrating, may give rise to practical difficulties in the Ghanaian context, given the fact that more than two decades have lapsed since Ghana's transition to democracy. It will therefore be difficult to identify the specific public officials to be dismissed from the public sector.

An additional approach is to introduce human rights education into the curricula of Ghanaian schools and incorporate the relevant findings of the NRC in school curricula. Also, there is the need to equip human rights bodies such as the Commission on Human Rights and Administrative Justice properly to make them more effective in fighting human rights violations.

6.6 Chapter Summary

This chapter has highlighted the gaps in Ghana's transitional justice efforts and has shown that not all relevant aspects regarding addressing past human rights violations have been tackled. Ghana has a duty to prosecute violations of the rights in the Universal Declaration of Human Rights that are recognised as part of customary international law. Moreover, the amnesty provisions that have barred prosecutions are not tenable under international law and need to be repealed. Ghana has taken significant steps towards institutional reform and the right of victims to remedies. However, there is still the need to implement all recommendations made by the NRC. Finally, there is the need to enhance human rights protection in the country to strengthen the foundation laid by the NRC.

---

[135]Regarding the low resourcing of the prisons, see Benjamin 2009. https://briarpatchmagazine.com/articles/view/prison-reform-in-ghana. Accessed 3 October 2019.

[136]See Velásquez-Rodríguez 1988, above n 13, para 175.

[137]National Reconciliation Commission 2004, vol 3, paras 3.3.19–3.3.27, 3.3.28–3.3.35.

References

African Union (2003) Principles and Guidelines on the Right to A Fair Trial and Legal Assistance in Africa, DOC/OS(XXX)247. http://hrlibrary.umn.edu/research/ZIM%20Principles_And_G.pdf. Accessed 4 November 2019.

Ambos K (2009) The legal framework of transitional justice: A systematic study with a special focus on the role of the ICC. In: Ambos K et al (eds) Building a future on peace and justice: Studies on transitional justice, peace and development. The Nuremberg Declaration on Peace and Justice. Springer, Berlin, pp 19–103.

Ambos K (2015) Evaluando la eficiencia de la Justicia Transicional: Unos comentarios preliminares (Evaluating the efficiency of transitional justice: Some preliminary comments). Zeitschrift für Internationale Strafrechtsdogmatik 9:468–472.

Ameh RK (2006) Doing justice after conflict: The case for Ghana's National Reconciliation Commission. Canadian Journal of Law and Society 21(1):85–109.

Amnesty International (2011) Uruguay: Congress adopts landmark law to tackle impunity. https://www.amnesty.org/en/latest/news/2011/10/uruguay-congress-adopts-landmark-law-tackle-impunity/. Accessed 12 October 2019.

Amnesty International (2012) Eichmann Supreme Court judgment 50 years on: Its significance today. https://www.amnesty.org/download/Documents/24000/ior530132012en.pdf. Accessed 20 October 2019.

Amnesty International (2016) El Salvador rejects Amnesty Law in historic ruling. https://www.amnesty.org/en/latest/news/2016/07/el-salvador-rejects-amnesty-law-in-historic-ruling/. Accessed November 2019.

Andreu-Guzmán F (2013) Peace Processes and International Law. https://www.files.ethz.ch/isn/164673/80ed6b7fa08ff1e0620fe297f85f63f0.pdf. Accessed 1 November 2019.

Attafuah KA (2004) An overview of Ghana's National Reconciliation Commission and its relationship with the courts. In: Schabas WA, Darcy S (eds) Truth Commissions and courts. The tension between criminal justice and the search for truth. Kluwer Academic Publishers, Dordrecht, pp 125–134.

Benjamin C (2009) The detestable solution: Prison reform in Ghana. https://briarpatchmagazine.com/articles/view/prison-reform-in-ghana. Accessed 3 November 2019.

Boafo-Arthur K (2005) National reconciliation or polarisation? Preliminary reflections on the politics of the Ghana National Reconciliation Commission. In: Fawole WA, Ukeje C (eds) The crisis of the state and regionalism in West Africa. Codesria, Dakar, pp 105–126.

Borraine AL (2006) Transitional justice: A holistic interpretation. Journal of International Affairs 60(1):17–27.

Cerqueira D, Arteaga L (2016) Challenging the amnesty law in El Salvador: Domestic and international alternatives to bring an end to impunity http://www.dplf.org/sites/default/files/amnesty_law-final-24june.pdf. Accessed November 2019.

Charlesworth H (2008) Universal Declaration of Human Rights (1948). In: Max Planck Encyclopedia of Public International Law. http://opil.ouplaw.com/view/10.1093/law:epil/9780199231690/law-9780199231690-e887#. Accessed 11 October 2019.

De Greiff P (2012) Theorising transitional justice. In Williams MS et al (eds) Transitional Justice. New York University Press, New York and London, pp 31–77.

Ferstman C (2010) Reparation as prevention: Considering the law and practice of orders for cessation and guarantees of non-repetition in torture cases. Essex Human Rights Review 6(2):7–27.

Freeman M (2009) Necessary Evils: Amnesties and the search for justice. Cambridge University Press, New York.

Freeman M, Pensky M (2012) The amnesty controversy in international law. In: Lessa F, Payne LA (eds) Amnesty in the age of human rights accountability: Comparative and international perspectives. Cambridge University Press, Cambridge, pp 42–46.

Gyimah-Boadi E (1994) Ghana's uncertain political opening. Journal of Democracy 5(2):75–86.

Hannum H (1995–1996) The status of the Universal Declaration of Human Rights in national and international law. Georgia Journal of International and Comparative Law 25:287–397.
Hutchful E (1997) Military Policy and Reform in Ghana. Journal of Modern African Studies 35(2):251–278.
Jones A (2015) Tailoring justice for mass atrocities: The constraints of international law and the ICC's complementarity regime. In: Saul M, Sweeney JA (eds) International law and post-conflict reconstruction policy. Routledge, London and New York, pp 95–116.
Kerbrat Y (2010) Interactions between the forms of reparation. In: Crawford J et al (eds) The law of international responsibility. Oxford University Press, Oxford, pp 573–588.
Kritz N (2009) Policy implications of empirical research on transitional justice. In: Van Der Merwe H et al (eds) Assessing the impact of transitional justice: Challenges for empirical research. United States Institute of Peace, Washington DC, pp 13–22.
Lynch M (2013) Purges. In Stan L, Nedelsky N (eds) Encyclopedia of transitional justice. Cambridge University Press, New York, pp 61–65.
Mallinder L (2007) Can amnesties and international justice be reconciled? (2007) International Journal of Transitional Justice 1(2):208–230.
Méndez JE (1997) Accountability for past abuses. Human Rights Quarterly 19(2):255–282.
Méndez JE (2006) Peace, justice and prevention: Dilemmas and false dilemmas. In: Bleeker M (ed) Dealing with the Past and Transitional Justice: Creating Conditions for Peace, Human Rights and the Rule of Law. Federal Department of Foreign Affairs, pp 15–20. https://www.swisspeace.ch/fileadmin/user_upload/Media/Publications/Journals_Articles/Publications_by_staff/Sisson__Jonathan__Dealing_with_the_Past_and_Transitional_Justice.pdf. Accessed 4 November 2019.
Nalepa M (2013) Lustration. In: Stan L, Nedelsky N (eds) Encyclopedia of Transitional Justice. Cambridge University Press, New York, pp 46–51.
National Reconciliation Commission (2004) Report of the National Reconciliation Commission, vol 1–4.
Office of the United Nations High Commissioner for Human Rights (2006) Rule-of-law tools for post-conflict states. Vetting: an operational framework. https://www.ohchr.org/Documents/Publications/RuleoflawVettingen.pdf. Accessed 4 September 2019.
Office of the United Nations High Commissioner for Human Rights (2009) Rule-of-law tools for post-conflict states: Amnesties. https://www.ohchr.org/Documents/Publications/Amnesties_en.pdf. Accessed 4 September 2019.
Olsen TD et al (2010) When truth commissions improve human rights. The International Journal of Transitional Justice 4: 457–476.
REDRESS (2014) Articulating minimum standards on reparations programmes in response to mass violations. https://redress.org/wp-content/uploads/2017/12/submission-to-special-rapporteur-on-reparations-programmes-public.pdf. Accessed 19 October 2019.
Roht-Arriaza N (1990) State responsibility to investigate and prosecute grave human rights violations in international law. California Law Review 78(2): 449–513.
Slye R (2002) The legitimacy of amnesties under international law and general principles of Anglo-American law. Virginia Journal of International Law 43(173):173–247.
Teitel RG (2000) Transitional Justice. Oxford University Press, New York.
Tomuschat C (2002) The duty to prosecute international crimes committed by individuals. In: Cremer H-J et al (eds) Tradition und Weltoffenheit des Rechts: Festschrift für Helmut Steinberger. Springer, Berlin, pp 315–349.
United Nations (2010) Guidance Note of The Secretary-General, United Nations Approach to Transitional Justice. https://www.un.org/ruleoflaw/files/TJ_Guidance_Note_March_2010FINAL.pdf. Accessed 4 November 2019.
United Nations Commission on Human Rights (2005) Promotion and protection of human rights: Impunity, Report of the independent expert to update the set of principles to combat impunity, Diane Orentlicher, Addendum – Updated Set of principles for the protection and promotion of human rights through action to combat impunity, E/CN.4/2005/102/Add.1.

United Nations Commission on Human Rights (2006) Promotion and protection of human rights, Study on the right to the truth, Report of the Office of the United Nations High Commissioner for Human Rights, E/CN.4/2006/91.

United Nations Economic and Social Council (1989) Principles on the Effective Prevention and Investigation of Extra-legal, Arbitrary and Summary Executions, Recommended by Economic and Social Council resolution 1989/65 of 24 May 1989 1. https://www.ohchr.org/Documents/ProfessionalInterest/executions.pdf. Accessed 15 October 2019.

United Nations General Assembly (1985) Declaration of Basic Principles of Justice for Victims of Crime and Abuse of Power, Adopted by General Assembly resolution 40/34 of 29 November 1985, A/RES/40/34. https://www.ohchr.org/EN/ProfessionalInterest/Pages/VictimsOfCrimeAndAbuseOfPower.aspx. Accessed 4 November 2019.

United Nations General Assembly (1992) Declaration on the Protection of all Persons from Enforced Disappearance, Adopted by General Assembly resolution 47/133 of 18 December 1992. https://www.ohchr.org/en/professionalinterest/pages/enforceddisappearance.aspx. Accessed 4 November 2019.

United Nations General Assembly (2006) Resolution adopted by the General Assembly on 16 December 2005, Basic Principles and Guidelines on the Right to a Remedy and Reparation for Victims of Gross Violations of International Human Rights Law and Serious Violations of International Humanitarian Law, A/RES/60/147. https://documents-dds-ny.un.org/doc/UNDOC/GEN/N05/496/42/PDF/N0549642.pdf?OpenElement. Accessed 2 November 2019.

United Nations Human Rights Committee (2004) General Comment No. 31, The nature of the general legal obligation imposed on states parties to the Covenant, CCPR/C/21/Rev.1/Add. 13.

United Nations Security Council (2004) The rule of law and transitional justice in conflict and post-conflict societies, Report of the Secretary-General, S/2004/616.

Valji N (2006) Ghana's National Reconciliation Commission: A comparative assessment. https://www.ictj.org/sites/default/files/ICTJ-Ghana-Reconciliation-Commission-2006-English_0.pdf. Accessed 24 October 2019.

Wain M (2003) Ghana's National Reconciliation Commission. http://peacemagazine.org/archive/v19n2p18.htm. Accessed 30 November 2019.

Werle G, Jessberger F (2014) Principles of international criminal law. Oxford University Press, Oxford.

Werle G, Vormbaum M (2018) Transitional Justice. Springer, Berlin.

Yi J (2016) El Salvador's Amnesty laws overturned: Implications for Colombia. http://www.coha.org/wp-content/uploads/2016/07/PRsalvador_final.pdf. Accessed 2 October 2019.

Chapter 7
Conclusion

Contents

7.1 Research Summary and Findings 221
7.2 Recommendations 224
7.3 Final Thoughts 226
References 227

7.1 Research Summary and Findings

This book has examined Ghana's NRC through an assessment of its features, competencies and effectiveness. It has also developed general assessment criteria for the impact of truth commissions, addressing gaps in the existing literature. Six main objectives inspired the author's research.

One objective of this book related to why Ghana opted for the NRC as a mechanism of transitional justice. In this regard, the book has examined the historical context as well as the legal framework that formed the basis for the establishment of the commission. Following Ghana's attainment of democracy in 1993, not much transformation was initially witnessed, owing to the continued rule of Jerry John Rawlings, the leader of the country's military regime from 1981 to 1993. With the election of a new leader in 2000, the new government of the New Patriotic Party was faced with the challenge of addressing past human rights violations. The establishment of a truth commission in Ghana was a way of circumventing existing barriers to utilising other transitional justice mechanisms. The blanket amnesty in Ghana's Constitution proved to be nearly impossible to repeal. This derailed all chances of prosecution, and Ghana's Constitution did not contain any provisions to regulate how to deal with past human rights violations. The principle of legality, from the viewpoint of Ghanaian law, also closed doors to prosecution of the remaining human rights violations not covered by the amnesty laws.

M. Yankson-Mensah, *Transitional Justice in Ghana*, International Criminal Justice Series 25, https://doi.org/10.1007/978-94-6265-379-5_7

The duty to prosecute specific crimes under international law was effectively relegated to the background through establishment of the NRC, whilst an amnesty law untenable under international law continues to exist. In the absence of a transitional justice policy and plan, Ghana's transitional justice approach proved fragmentary. Indeed, the establishment of the NRC outside a pre-existing transitional plan or policy limited how much it could achieve, beyond undertaking its mandate successfully, since, there were no prior measures in place to ensure that its efforts outlived the commission's existence.

The features, mandate and competencies of the NRC have also been analysed by conducting a comparative analysis in light of its enabling law as well as the commission's actual work and practical experiences. A unique feature of the NRC was its extremely legalese outlook, as borne out by its key features that were akin to those of a court of law. Despite its possession of extensive legal features and powers, the commission was unable to fulfil its investigative mandate fully. This indicates that although the possession of extensive powers is significant for the work of a truth commission, the extent to which such powers are beneficial depends on how the truth commission utilises such powers. The main reason the NRC encountered lapses in its investigative function was because it did not take full advantage of the powers granted to it. Besides, although the court-like nature of the commission fulfilled international due process requirements, it had an adverse effect on the extent to which victims felt at ease during its proceedings, which undermines an essential goal of truth commissions.

Another objective of the book, regarding how the NRC turned out in practice, was addressed by examining how the features and mandate of the NRC defined its work. In this regard, the key factors that defined the effectiveness of the NRC's work were finances and resources, its powers, mandate, perceptions of credibility within the eyes of the general populace, the extent of its autonomy as derived from its mandate and powers and the existence of an amnesty at the time of the commission's operations and of its establishment. The NRC experienced excessive political resistance, and the above-mentioned factors were all influenced by politics. The extreme politicisation of the commission's work was because the government failed to make the opposition see the truth-telling exercise as a national issue. The absence of broad consultations in creating the mandate and appointing the members of the commission partly accounted for this situation. This made the opposition apprehensive towards the truth-telling exercise, and they considered it a witch-hunt rather than a process of which they were also a part. The result was the high-level political drama that accompanied the commission's work.

In relation to the criteria for assessing the impact of the NRC, a number of transitional justice assessment methods were examined, and their commonalities used as the basis for criteria to assess the NRC. The study indicated that on account of the interplay of a wide array of factors that affect the work and outcome of truth commissions, definitional paradigms for measuring their impact should be broad enough to accommodate all the possible factors that affect their work. Such criteria can be utilised in assessing other truth commissions, with contextual modifications. An appropriate means of arriving at such criteria is to find out what truth commissions are set up to do. It is on such a basis that this study considered the goals of transitional justice as variables appropriate for assessing the work of the NRC. For the purpose of this study, the NRC's effectiveness was discussed in terms of the goals of truth, justice, reconciliation and peace. Based on these criteria, this study has established that the impact of a truth commission should not be perceived as being limited to mere completion of its work or fulfilment of its mandate. On the contrary, the goals that inform the establishment of truth commissions must be attained even beyond the existence of the truth commission.

In addressing the extent of the NRC's effectiveness, the book discussed the variables of the defined assessment criteria in light of the NRC's features, mandate, work experiences and outcome. In particular, the discussion relied on empirical data from two surveys conducted as part of this study in addition to data from existing surveys. A key observation regarding the responses from the surveys conducted in this study is the high rate of neutral responses for questions on the goals of truth, justice, peace and reconciliation. This indicates the low level of knowledge on issues related to the NRC. The most logical explanation for this relates to the poor dissemination of the commission's report, which has limited the extent of the public's knowledge about the commission's work. Indeed, in the course of the survey, most individuals who declined to be interviewed or to respond to the questionnaire mentioned the fact that they were likely to have forgotten some facts and might not be able to make any meaningful assessments. This means that although the NRC partially fulfilled some of its goals, there is still a large gap to be filled regarding increasing awareness of the commission's work as part of Ghana's history.

Although the work of the NRC reflected its active pursuit of the goals of truth, justice, reconciliation and peace, there has been limited action towards the fulfilment of these goals since the closure of the NRC. Hence, the commission's impact did not outlive its closure. Overall, the empirical findings of this study show that there is no extremely positive or negative perception regarding the NRC's impact, although there are divergent views regarding the four goals. Even where there is a greater percentage of positive views, respondents identified key lapses that have hindered the depth of the commission's impact. The case of the NRC is a clear example of the fact that truth commissions are temporary bodies that can only do as much as they are authorised within a short period of time. In practice, it is difficult for their goals to be achieved after they complete their work unless they receive the requisite political backing. This does not imply that truth commissions are entirely ineffective. On the contrary, a positive aspect of the NRC's work is that it managed to document Ghana's past, albeit with some limitations. Unreasonably high expectations should not be imposed on the work of truth commissions. Rather, they should be seen for their real value: their ability to document a society's past in a considerably short period. Besides, truth commissions should be considered as measures for breaking away from the society's past, laying the groundwork for a reformed society and devising an avenue for healing of victims.

The loopholes in Ghana's transitional justice process were assessed by examining how other mechanisms of transitional justice were fulfilled through the NRC's work. This assessment has made it evident that although transitional justice mechanisms strive to attain the same goals, they do not work well when they are utilised as substitutes rather than as complements. This is because each mechanism of transitional justice has a basis in the norms of international law, which give rise to duties to be fulfilled by a state in rebuilding a society after protracted conflict or authoritarian rule. Besides, each mechanism has limitations, which may hinder its ability to attain all the goals of transitional justice. Transitional justice mechanisms thus work well when they are used on a complementary basis, to ensure that they make up for their respective weaknesses. In the case of the NRC, no comprehensive steps were taken to adhere to relevant international standards whilst addressing past human rights violations. A key factor that resulted in this was the absence of a transitional plan. Also, the amnesty provisions in Ghana's Constitution are one of the key obstacles to fully addressing past human rights violations. Eliminating existing gaps in how Ghana addressed past human rights violations requires enhancing the country's human rights protection regime and properly reforming state institutions in response to the recommendations of the NRC.

7.2 Recommendations

To ensure more effective ways of dealing with past human rights violations, various measures can be taken into account for future practice in Ghana. As this book has shown, the transitional justice goals of truth, justice, reconciliation and peace are long-term goals, whose realisation can take several years to accomplish. By contrast, truth commissions are temporary bodies whose efforts usually do not outlive their existence. Their effectiveness can thus be ensured through continual follow-up efforts after their closure. One way of doing this is to establish successive truth commissions to fill in the gaps from the work of earlier truth commissions and undertake activities to ensure implementation of the earlier commission's work. An example is the case of Chile, where the Valech Commission was established more than a decade after the closure of the Rettig Commission to deal with non-fatal human rights violations, which were not dealt with by the Rettig Commission.[1] South Korea has also had a number of truth commissions. These include the Jeju Commission, which was established in 2000 to investigate the massacre on the island of Jeju; the Presidential Truth Commission on Suspicious Deaths in the Republic of Korea, which operated from 2000 to 2004 and had the mandate to investigate killings of civilians that occurred between 1975 and 1987; and the TRC,

[1]For details of this commission, see The United States Institute of Peace. https://www.usip.org/publications/2003/09/commission-inquiry-chile-03. Accessed 25 October 2019.

established in 2005 to investigate human rights violations that had occurred between 1910 and 1993.[2]

Responses to human rights violations should be proactive and not reactive. States can consider setting up permanent autonomous bodies whose sole function is to follow up on the work of truth commissions after their closure. Such transitional commissions should not be subsidiary to the national ombudsman but should focus solely on undertaking activities to promote human rights, democracy, national unity and reconciliation. The work of these bodies can be made effective if they are made to publish annual reports to detail their findings for the year and their recommendations. A good model of such a commission is Rwanda's National Unity and Reconciliation Commission. Although this body was not set up as a follow-up to a truth commission's work, it undertakes activities to promote peace, national reconciliation and respect for human rights. Despite not having any investigative powers, it can condemn acts that are discriminatory, xenophobic and intolerant.[3]

Given their numerous limitations, the effectiveness of truth commissions can be ensured if they are established as part of a broader transitional plan that entails other mechanisms to deal with aspects of past human rights violations that the truth commission is unable to address. An example is the transitional justice policy of Uganda, which l is the first of its kind in the world.[4]

It must be borne in mind, however, that regardless of how many follow-up efforts are made and which policies are drafted, the work of truth commissions will continue to be ineffective if there is no political will to enforce their ideals. One way of instilling political will is through involvement of the international community in efforts to address past human rights violations. It is, therefore, laudable that the African Union has adopted a transitional justice policy to serve as a guideline for members states of the African Union.[5]

Finally, truth commissions can be made effective by instilling credibility in their work. This can be done by dissociating their work from politics. Although truth commissions emerge from politics, their work can be detached from politics if there is more involvement from the international community. The political nature of truth commissions can also be reduced if there is equal representation from all segments of the society in their membership. This can be ensured by, for instance, allowing each region in the country to nominate one commissioner through voting or vetting.

[2]See Werle and Vormbaum 2018, pp. 222–223, where they give an overview of truth commissions established in South Korea.

[3]See the United States Institute of Peace. https://www.usip.org/publications/1999/03/truth-commission-rwanda-99. Accessed 29 October 2019.

[4]See African Centre for Media Excellence. https://ugandajournalistsresourcecentre.com/overview-of-ugandas-national-transitional-justice-policy/. Accessed 22 December 2019.

[5]African Union 2019. https://au.int/sites/default/files/documents/36541-doc-au_tj_policy_eng_web.pdf. Accessed 15 October 2019.

7.3 Final Thoughts

Is truth-telling an end? The case of Ghana has illustrated the strengths and potential flaws that accompany the work of truth commissions. Although they undoubtedly contribute to post-conflict and post-dictatorship state reconstruction, they cannot be considered an end, considering their potential limitations. Rather, truth commissions should be considered a part of a long-term process of effecting change in a society. The discussion of the NRC's impact shows the lack of a definitive answer to the question of whether a truth commission is effective. Indeed, the continuous discourse on the efficacy of truth commissions, although not flawed, cannot generate a specific answer. This is mainly because the level of effectiveness depends heavily on context. Hence, the question should not be whether truth commissions work, but rather what factors make them work. There is, therefore, the need for future research to address questions regarding why truth commissions fail in certain contexts and what factors influence their outcomes. Moreover, future research must examine how societies can tie all loose ends after undergoing a truth-telling exercise.

Given the hurdles faced by the NRC as a result of political conditions in the country, should the quest to address past human rights violations always be carried out in line with the classical mechanisms of transitional justice, or must the question of how to deal with past human rights violations be context-based? Within the African context, where leaders show little political will to implement truth commission recommendations, is the recurrent establishment of truth commissions worthwhile? Indeed, research should be addressed towards whether truth commissions are a suitable means for addressing past human rights violations in all contexts. Beyond these recurring questions, however, it must be known that truth commissions can leave long-term legacies in transitional societies only if more emphasis is placed on building strong institutions as opposed to reconciliation.

In the case of Ghana, there are significant gaps regarding how past human rights violations were addressed, due to absence of prosecutions, the existence of amnesty provisions in the Constitution, and the failure to implement the recommendations of the NRC fully. Yet it is questionable whether additional steps will ever be taken to address the country's past, in light of other pressing economic challenges that the country is currently facing. Indeed, even at the time that the NRC was established, some Ghanaians argued that a truth commission was not needed. Nevertheless, the work of the NRC, once it was established, proved otherwise. Perhaps Ghana's current democratic dispensation can be strengthened further by addressing the gaps in the manner in which it has addressed its past. Sweeping the work of the NRC under the carpet has not helped in this regard. In order to properly forge ahead as a country, Ghana must embrace its past and tie all loose ends.

References

African Centre for Media Excellence (2019) Overview of Uganda's national transitional justice policy. https://ugandajournalistsresourcecentre.com/overview-of-ugandas-national-transitional-justice-policy/. Accessed 22 December 2019.

African Union (2019) Transitional justice policy. https://au.int/sites/default/files/documents/36541-doc-au_tj_policy_eng_web.pdf. Accessed 15 October 2019.

United States Institute of Peace (1999) Truth commission: Rwanda 99. https://www.usip.org/publications/1999/03/truth-commission-rwanda-99. Accessed 25 October 2019.

United States Institute of Peace (2003) Commission of inquiry: Chile 03. https://www.usip.org/publications/2003/09/commission-inquiry-chile-03. Accessed 25 October 2019.

Werle G, Vormbaum M (2018) Transitional justice. Springer, Berlin.

Appendix A
Qualitative Survey Questions

Questions

1. Has Ghana sufficiently dealt with human rights violations in its history or there are more measures needed to address past human rights violations? Please give reasons for your answer.
2. Do you think that there is currently respect for human rights in Ghana? Why?
3. Did the NRC play a role in the current state of human rights in Ghana? Please explain your answer.
4. Apart from the NRC, what other factors have enhanced or hindered respect for human rights in Ghana?
5. How did the NRC impact the following in Ghana?

   a. Democracy
   b. Rule of Law

6. Apart from the NRC, what other factors have enhanced or hindered rule of law and democracy in Ghana?
7. Has the NRC impacted justice in Ghana negatively or positively? Please explain and give examples.
8. How has the work of the NRC enhanced or hindered the exposure of the truth about Ghana's past? Please explain and give examples.
9. How have the transitional provisions in the 1992 Constitution affected the work of the NRC?
10. What factors have hindered the amendment of the transitional provisions in Ghana?

M. Yankson-Mensah, *Transitional Justice in Ghana*, International Criminal Justice Series 25, https://doi.org/10.1007/978-94-6265-379-5

11. How has the work of the NRC resulted in institutional reform in Ghana? Please give examples.
12. Apart from the NRC, what other factors have enhanced or hindered institutional reform in Ghana? Please explain your answer.
13. In your opinion, is Ghana currently a peaceful country? If yes, why? If no, why not?
14. Did the NRC play a role in the extent of peace in Ghana now? Why?
15. Would you say that Ghanaians are currently reconciled? And did the NRC play a role in this or not? Please explain.

Appendix B
Quantitative Survey Questions

Introduction

Section A: Demographic and Background Information

1. How best would you describe your occupational category? (Please select all that apply)

- ☐ Academia
- ☐ Public sector
- ☐ Private sector
- ☐ Informal sector
- ☐ Non-profit sector
- ☐ Human rights/civil society
- ☐ Trade/labour union
- ☐ Student
- ☐ Retired/pensioner
- ☐ Unemployed
- ☐ Other (please specify)

2. What is your gender?

- ☐ Male
- ☐ Female

M. Yankson-Mensah, *Transitional Justice in Ghana*, International Criminal Justice Series 25, https://doi.org/10.1007/978-94-6265-379-5

3. Please specify your age category.

- ☐ Less than 30 years
- ☐ 30-39 years
- ☐ 40-49 years
- ☐ 50-59 years
- ☐ 60-69 years
- ☐ 70-79 years
- ☐ 80+ years

4. What is your highest level of education?

- ☐ Primary or junior high school
- ☐ *Senior high/middle/elementary* school
- ☐ Ordinary/advanced level
- ☐ Diploma/certificate (e.g., higher national diploma, teacher training certificate etc.)
- ☐ Bachelor's or undergraduate degree
- ☐ Postgraduate qualification (e.g., master's degree, PhD etc.)
- ☐ No education
- ☐ Other (please specify)

5. Are you a citizen of Ghana?

- ☐ Yes
- ☐ No

6. If you answered yes to question 5 above, which region(s) in Ghana do you come from? (Please select all that apply)

- ☐ Greater Accra Region
- ☐ Central Region
- ☐ Western Region
- ☐ Volta Region
- ☐ Eastern Region
- ☐ Ashanti Region
- ☐ Brong-Ahafo Region
- ☐ Northern Region
- ☐ Upper West Region
- ☐ Upper East Region

7. If you answered no to question 5 above, which country are you a citizen of?

8. How familiar are you with the work of Ghana's NRC?

- ☐ Very Familiar
- ☐ Familiar
- ☐ Neutral
- ☐ Unfamiliar
- ☐ Totally Unfamiliar

9. If you are very familiar or familiar with the NRC, where did you obtain information regarding the commission's work? (Please select all that apply)

- ☐ The media (e.g., newspapers, radio, television etc.)
- ☐ Family
- ☐ Friends
- ☐ School
- ☐ Work
- ☐ Other (please specify)

10. With respect to the work of the NRC, how best would you describe yourself? (Please select all that apply)

- ☐ Victim of past human rights abuses
- ☐ Relative/friend of victim of past human rights abuses
- ☐ Active observer of NRC proceedings
- ☐ Passive observer of NRC proceedings
- ☐ Citizen or resident who was unaware of the proceedings o f the NRC
- ☐ Other (please specify)

Section B: Effects of the NRC on Truth, Justice, Peace and Reconciliation in Ghana

11. With respect to the NRC's work, what is your understanding of human rights? (Please select all that apply)

- ☐ Freedom from torture or abuse
- ☐ Freedom of speech or expression
- ☐ Enforcement of the rule of law
- ☐ Ability to carry out one's daily activities without fear or intimidation
- ☐ Other (please specify)

12. What are your opinions regarding the following statements?

(a) The NRC produced an accurate and complete record of past human rights violations in Ghana.

- ☐ Strongly Agree
- ☐ Agree
- ☐ Neutral
- ☐ Disagree
- ☐ Strongly Disagree

(b) The NRC's work has established the truth about past human rights violations in Ghana.

- ☐ Strongly Agree
- ☐ Agree
- ☐ Neutral
- ☐ Disagree
- ☐ Strongly Disagree

13. What reasons explain your points of view in statements 12(a) and (b) above? (Please select all that apply)

- ☐ Because the NRC produced a report at the end of its work
- ☐ Because the commission's report provided all the relevant details about past human rights violations in Ghana
- ☐ Because the NRC's hearings were aired on television
- ☐ Because the commission investigated and heard all cases brought before it
- ☐ Because the NRC report has not been properly published since the completion of its work
- ☐ Because the commission report did not provide all the relevant details about past human rights violations in Ghana
- ☐ Because the NRC did not investigate and hear all cases brought before it
- ☐ Because the commission's report did not provide the names of people who committed human rights violations
- ☐ Other (please specify)

14. What are your opinions regarding the following statements?

(a) The NRC's work helped to address the needs of victims of past human rights violations in Ghana.

- ☐ Strongly Agree
- ☐ Agree
- ☐ Neutral
- ☐ Disagree
- ☐ Strongly Disagree

(b) The NRC's work has brought healing and restoration to victims of past human rights violations in Ghana.

- ☐ Strongly Agree
- ☐ Agree
- ☐ Neutral
- ☐ Disagree
- ☐ Strongly Disagree

15. What reasons explain your points of view in statements 14(a) and (b) above? (Please select all that apply)

- ☐ Because victims got an opportunity to narrate their experiences
- ☐ Because victims received monetary compensations from the government for the human rights violations they suffered
- ☐ Because victims got the opportunity to learn about the circumstances surrounding the harm they suffered
- ☐ Because victims got to know about the whereabouts of their disappeared relatives
- ☐ Because some victims did not get the opportunity to narrate their experiences
- ☐ Because the monetary compensations given to victims was not adequate
- ☐ Because victims did not get information about the circumstances surrounding the harm they suffered
- ☐ Because victims did not get to know about the whereabouts of their disappeared relatives
- ☐ Other (please specify)

16. What is your opinion regarding the following statement?

The work of the NRC has helped to prevent human rights violations from recurring in Ghana.

- ☐ Strongly Agree
- ☐ Agree
- ☐ Neutral
- ☐ Disagree
- ☐ Strongly Disagree

17. What reasons explain your position in 16 above? (Please select all that apply)

- ☐ Because the human rights violations that occurred before Ghana's transition to democracy have ceased to exist since the NRC completed its work
- ☐ Because the commission created awareness on promotion of human rights violations
- ☐ Because there is more human rights education in schools since completion of the NRC's work
- ☐ Because there is now a culture of respect for human rights and Ghanaians are now more aware of their rights
- ☐ Because the human rights violations that occurred before Ghana's transition to democracy are still rampant
- ☐ Because the commission did not create awareness on promotion of human rights violations
- ☐ Because there has been no improvement in human rights education in schools
- ☐ Because there is still no culture of respect for human rights and Ghanaians are still not aware of their rights
- ☐ Other (please specify)

18. With respect to the NRC's work, what is your understanding of national reconciliation? (Please select all that apply)

☐ Apologies or forgiveness for past abuses suffered

☐ Resolution of past societal differences and bringing together opposed factions to create lasting societal peace and unity

☐ Restoration of rights or privileges of victims of human rights violations

☐ Healing for victims and compensation for losses suffered under past governments

☐ Other (please specify)

19. What is your opinion regarding the following statement?

The NRC's work has resulted in national reconciliation in Ghana.

☐ Strongly Agree

☐ Agree

☐ Neutral

☐ Disagree

☐ Strongly Disagree

20. What reasons explain your point of view in statement 19 above? (Please select all that apply)

☐ Because there are no more ethnic differences in Ghana

☐ Because there are no more political differences in Ghana

☐ Ghanaians have come to terms with the country's past and people can now easily make reference to issues of the past in a 'civil' manner

☐ Ghanaians have a common opinion about Ghana's history

☐ Because there are still ethnic differences in Ghana

☐ Because there are still political differences in Ghana

☐ Ghanaians have not come to terms with the country's past and people cannot make reference to issues of the past in a 'civil' manner

☐ Ghanaians have different opinions about Ghana's history

☐ Other (please specify)

21. With respect to the NRC's work, what is your understanding of peace? (Please select all that apply)

☐ Absence of war or conflict

☐ Prevention of situations which have the potential to create conflicts

☐ Non-violent incidents during elections and other political events

☐ Use of non-violent approaches during political debates and discussions

☐ Other (please specify)

22. *What is your opinion regarding the following statement?*

Ghana has been more peaceful since completion of the NRC's work.

- ☐ Strongly Agree
- ☐ Agree
- ☐ Neutral
- ☐ Disagree
- ☐ Strongly Disagree

23. What reasons explain your point of view in statement 22 above? (Please select all that apply)

- ☐ Because there has been no violence in Ghana since completion of the commission's work
- ☐ There are no more ethnic and political disputes in Ghana
- ☐ Because the country enjoys more political stability now
- ☐ Because democracy in Ghana has improved since completion of the commission's work
- ☐ Because there is still occasional violence in Ghana despite completion of the commission's work
- ☐ There are still pockets of ethnic and political disputes in Ghana
- ☐ Because the country does not enjoy political stability
- ☐ Because democracy in Ghana has not improved since completion of the commission's work
- ☐ Other (please specify)

24. In your opinion, what other key effects did the NRC have on Ghana?

____

____

____

25. Particulars of Respondent (Optional): Please fill in the following details only if you wish to receive copies of the findings of this research

Name:

____

Contact Details (e.g., e-mail address, postal address etc.):

____

Appendix C
Demographic Details of Respondents

1. Gender

Gender	Frequency
Male	77
Female	53
Other	0

NB Sample Size = 130

2. Age

Age group	Frequency
Below 30	12
30–39	49
40–49	33
50–59	22
60–69	10
70–79	3
Above 80	1

NB Sample Size = 130

3. Level of education

Level of education	Frequency
Tertiary level	88
High school	26
Primary	13
No education	3

NB Sample Size = 130

M. Yankson-Mensah, *Transitional Justice in Ghana*, International Criminal Justice Series 25, https://doi.org/10.1007/978-94-6265-379-5

4. Regional representation of respondents

Region	Frequency
Greater Accra	21
Central	26
Western (currently Western-North and Western Regions)	5
Eastern	25
Ashanti	26
Brong-Ahafo (currently Bono, Bono-East and Ahafo Regions)	2
Northern (currently Northern,Savannah and North-East Regions)	5
Volta (currently Volta and Oti Regions)	17
Upper East	2
Upper West	3

NB Sample Size = 130

5. With respect to the work of the NRC, how best would you describe yourself?

Category	Frequency
Victim of past human rights abuses	6
Relative/friend of victim of past human rights abuses	25
Active observer of NRC proceedings	36
Passive observer of NRC proceedings	41
Citizen or resident who was unaware of the proceedings of the NRC	15
Unanswered	7

NB Sample Size =130

Index

A
Accountability, 130, 132
Accra Peace Agreement, 68
Act of Parliament, 65, 66
Actual performance, 17
Administrative powers, 77, 85, 86
Advocacy, 7, 8, 17
African Charter on Human and Peoples Rights, 194, 195, 197, 199–201, 205, 207
Aftermaths of the First World War, 4
Aliens Compliance Order, 37
Amnesty, 58–63, 65, 83, 84, 88, 98
Amnesty International, 172
Amnesty law, 17
Amnesty provisions, 161, 164–166, 170, 173, 185
Argentina, 9
Armed Forces Revolutionary Council, 117, 125
  executions, 42
  holy war on corruption, 42
  house cleaning exercise, 42, 43, 45
  Jerry John Rawlings, 41, 44, 45
  Junior Jesus, 41
  Peoples' Revolutionary Courts, 42, 43
  Special courts, 42, 44, 45
Army, 34–36, 39, 41, 42, 44
Ashanti, 30, 32, 35
Assassination, 32, 33, 35
Assessment criteria, 148
Assistance of Witnesses, 112
Avoidance of Discrimination Act, 1957, 32

B
Balkan Wars of 1912, 7
Benefits, 1, 12, 16
Bias, 117–119, 136
Blanket amnesty, 57, 58, 61
Brazil, 58, 59, 67, 69, 73, 75, 77–79, 83–85, 87, 89–91, 94, 95, 106, 108, 118, 120, 126, 141
Bureau of National Investigations, 48
Byelaws, 85

C
Chile, 59, 66, 73, 224
Citizens Vetting Committees, 47
Cold War, 4, 8
Colonel Ignatius Kutu Acheampong, 38, 39
Colonel Kotoka, 36
Comisión Nacional sobre la Desaparición de Personas (CONADEP), 9
Comissão Nacional da Verdade, 16, 17, 59, 67, 69, 70, 73, 75, 77–79, 83, 85, 87–91, 93–95
Commission of enquiry, 61, 66, 81, 96
Commission on Human Rights and Administrative Justice, 61, 63, 71
Comparative analysis, 16, 18
Comparisons, 6, 15–17
1960 Constitution, 32, 33
1969 Constitution, 37
1992 Constitution, 57, 60–66, 71, 77, 81, 86, 87, 90, 94, 96
Convention Peoples' Party, 27, 29–36, 38

M. Yankson-Mensah, *Transitional Justice in Ghana*, International Criminal Justice Series 25, https://doi.org/10.1007/978-94-6265-379-5

Corruption scandal, 37, 45
Coup attempt, 36, 41, 48
Credibility, 106, 118–121, 135, 136
Crimes against humanity
  attack, 198
Criminal responsibility to perpetrators, 91
Criticisms, 106, 114, 116, 118, 119, 140

D

Dealing with past human rights violations, 224
Death sentence, 43, 46
Democracy, 2, 4, 5, 8, 9, 12, 17, 20
Deportation, 34
Deterrence, 12
Disappearances, 47
Disappeared individuals, 10
Dismissal, 38
Drafting process
  public involvement, 81
Duty to prosecute
  duty to protect human rights, 194
  effective remedies, 195, 197, 209
  ensure and respect, 194, 195, 199, 202
  grounds, 193, 204
  Velasquez-Rodriguez v Honduras, 195, 213

E

Economic hardships, 28, 41
Economic recovery program, 49
Ecuador, 120, 121
Effectiveness, 146, 189
El Salvador, 9
Empirical analysis, 14, 17, 19, 20
Empirical data impact assessment, 145–147
Enforced disappearances, 10, 11
Engaging perpetrators, 121
Expectations, 104
Expected outcomes of truth commissions, 17

F

Far Eastern and Pacific Commission, 7
Features, 57–59, 66–70, 73, 75, 79, 85, 89, 91, 96, 98
Features of a truth commission
  broad consultation, 70, 72, 98
  civil society suggestions, 71
  commissioners of the NRC, 71
  confidentiality rules, 77, 78, 97
  equal and fair representation, 70, 74
  independence, 58, 75–77
  involvement of foreigners, 74
  mandate, 58, 59, 68–70, 79–81, 83, 84
  membership, 58, 70, 73–75
  mode of establishment, 66–68
  number of commissioners, 69, 73
  objects, 69, 79
  operational timeframe, 58, 69, 70
  parliament, 81
  powers, 57, 58, 63, 66, 68, 69, 84, 85, 88, 92, 93, 97
  selection of members, 72
  staffing, 70
Financial independence, 94
Findings, 108, 118, 124, 125, 127, 131, 136, 137
Firing squad, 46
Funding for truth commissions, 94

G

Genocide, 193, 198, 199, 203
Ghana, 1, 2, 13–16, 19–21
  first republican regime, 31
Ghana's duty to prosecute, 199, 201
Ghana's independence, 28, 30, 31, 35
Ghana's transitional justice process
  loopholes, 191, 192
Goals of transitional justice
  justice, 149, 150
  peace, 151
  reconciliation, 149–151, 156, 158, 174, 175, 180, 185
  truth, 149, 150
Gold Coast, 28–31, 37
Guatemala, 9

H

Healing and restoration, 162, 164
Healing of victims, 151
Hearings
  procedure, 111
  public hearings, 110–112, 115, 116
Hearings in camera, 112, 113
Historical context, 28
Human rights violations, 103–106, 108–111, 113, 115, 118, 122–126, 128, 130–137, 140, 142
Human Rights Violations Investigation Commission, 16

I

Identity of perpetrators, 91
Immunity, 41
Implementation of the mandate, 105
Inadequacy of funds and logistics, 114
In comparison with courts, 6
Independence, 28–32, 34, 35
Independence from British colonial rule, 2
Institutional reforms

human rights education, 215, 216
lapses, 215, 216
International Covenant on Civil and Political Rights
respect and ensure, 10
Investigation problems, 115
Investigations, 105, 106, 108, 110, 115, 120, 121, 134–136, 142
Investigations of past human rights violations, 10

J
J.B. Danquah, 33, 51
Jerry John Rawlings, 117, 122
Judicial and non-judicial mechanisms, 10
June 4 Movement, 44
Justice, 145–152, 156, 157, 160, 161, 165, 167, 171–174, 185

K
Killings, 28, 32, 42
Kofi Abrefa Busia, 33, 37
Kwame Nkrumah, 29, 34–36

L
Legalistic outlook, 116
Legality of amnesties
Argentina, 206, 208
Barrios Altos, 204, 205
conditional amnesties, 202
disapproval of blanket amnesties, 203
El Salvador, 208
means of adopting the amnesty provisions, 207
New Patriotic Party v Attorney General, 208
Peru, 205
regional courts, 204
repeal, 208, 209, 215
United Nations, 203
Uruguay, 205, 207–209
Legal nature of its proceedings, 116
Liberia, 58, 62, 66, 68, 69, 72–76, 78–80, 83–85, 87, 89, 91, 93–97, 114, 118, 123, 124, 136
Limann government, 44

M
Magnitude of human rights violations, 201
Major General Ankrah, 36
Malawi African Association et al. v. Mauritania, 205, 213
Methodology, 1, 13, 20
Military, 105, 106, 116, 118–121, 125–128, 131
Modern purposive approach to interpretation, 64
Monetary compensations, 210–212
adequacy, 163, 165
harm suffered, 165
number of victims, 165
obligation under customary international law, 166
Movement for Freedom and Justice, 50
Murder of three high court judges, 47

N
Names of perpetrators, 91
National Commission for Democracy, 49, 50
National Investigations Commissions, 47
National Liberation Council, 36, 37
National Liberation Movement, 30–33
National Reconciliation Commission (NRC)
features, 57, 66
legal factors, 60
reasons for the establishment, 60
transitional justice policy, 57, 62, 98
transitional provisions, 60–62
National Redemption Council
political trials, 40
Price Control Decree of 1974, 39
Subversion Decree, 40
Supreme Military Council, 39–41, 43, 45
Nature of human rights violations, 112
Needs of victims, 12
Newspaper Licensing Decree, 39, 48
Nigeria, 2, 17, 68, 69, 72–76, 78, 79, 84, 88–90, 93, 95, 97, 112, 114, 132, 139
Normative, 14, 15, 18
NRC's impact, 14, 18–20
NRC's mandate
controversy, 81, 83
door of opportunity, 83
limitations on the historical timeframe, 84
window of hope, 83

O
Objectives, 1, 14, 15, 20
Obligation by the state to investigate, 11
Obligations, 10, 11, 15, 16
Offences and penalties
safeguards, 97
One-party state, 34
Opposition, 116–121, 138

Origin of Truth Commissions
  first instance of using a truth commission, 7
  first truth commission, 9
  globalisation and its attendant effects, 7
  third wave of democratisation, 7
  truth during transition, 8
Overthrow of Nkrumah
  assassination attempts, 33, 35
  Coup d'état, 34
  Operation Cold Chop, 34
  reasons, 34

P

Palace coup, 40
Parties to armed conflicts, 10
Peace, 2, 3, 5, 7, 12, 17
  absence of conflict, 181
  crime rate, 183, 184
  pockets of violence, 151, 181, 184
  political instability, 151, 180, 184
Peace accord, 17
Peoples Defence Committees, 45
Peoples' National Party, 44
Perceptions, 146, 150, 153–157, 159, 161, 164, 165, 167, 168, 170, 171, 173, 175, 177–179, 181, 183, 185
Perceptions about the NRC, 20
Perpetrators, 105, 110, 111, 115, 117, 121–124, 126, 131–133, 135–137, 142
Peru, 118, 133
Police, 115, 125, 128, 132, 133, 140
Political environments, 118
Political instability, 28, 29, 53
Political prisoners, 36
Political resistance, 119
President's Own Guard Regiment, 34, 35
Preventive Detention Act of 1958, 32
Principle of legality, 57, 60, 63–65, 86, 98
Prisons services, 125, 128, 133, 140
Proceedings, 61, 69, 72, 76, 78, 85, 87, 90, 91, 93, 95, 98
Progress Party, 37–39
Property rights
  seizure, 47
Protection of witnesses, 86
Provisional National Defence Council, 27, 45–52
Publication of report, 96
Public officials, 38, 42
Public outreach, 113
Public tribunals, 45–47

Q

Qualitative and quantitative data, 18
Qualitative survey, 18, 156, 172, 183

R

Radbruch formula, 64
Re Akoto and Seven Others, 32
Recommendations, 224–226
  army, 126
  civil society bodies, 139
  human rights education, 127
  institutional reform, 127, 128, 132, 133, 141
  judiciary, 128
  role of religious bodies, 130
  traditional rulers, 130
  transitional provisions, 126
Reconciliation, 1–3, 5, 6, 9, 12
  ethnic intolerance, 179
  lack of consensus, 175
  national reconciliation, 145, 146, 151–153, 157, 158, 160, 161, 164, 166, 167, 173–175, 177–181
  political and ethnic differences, 178
  religious, 173, 179, 184
  indicators of, 178
Recurrence of human rights violations
  lapses, 171, 172, 185
  prevention, 160, 167, 168, 170, 173
  putting a closure on the past, 170, 172
Recurring questions that transitional societies have to deal with, 8
Referendum, 34, 40, 51
Rehabilitation of perpetrators, 12
Reparations
  apologies, 132
  compensation, 140
  memorials, 131
  reparations and rehabilitation fund, 131, 140
Report
  extent of truth, 136
  failure to name perpetrators, 137
  identify perpetrators, 135
  implementation, 139, 141
  merits, 133

publicity, 137–139, 141
soft recommendations, 132
weaknesses, 134
Reporting requirements of truth commissions, 95
Respondents, 18, 19
Restoration for victims, 12
Retribution, 12, 13
Retrospective jurisdiction, 42, 46
Right to an effective remedy, 196, 197, 205
Right to reparations
adequacy, 210–212
de-confiscation, 210
effectiveness, 211, 212
non-repetition, 209, 210, 213
promptness, 212
rehabilitation, 209, 210
restitution, 209, 210
satisfaction, 209, 210
Right to Truth
entitlement of victims, 9
erection of memorials, 11
full and complete truth, 11
memory, 11
need for truth, 9
relatives of disappeared individuals, 10
Roots of transitional justice, 4

S
Sallah v Attorney General, 38
Search and seizure powers, 85, 89, 90, 93
Second Republic, 37
Security threats, 118
Social division, 28, 29, 53
Source of funds, 94
South African Truth and Reconciliation Commission, 9
Special military tribunals, 46, 47
Special Tribunal, 44, 46
Standard of proof, 65
Statement-taking and processing, 109
States, 3, 5, 7, 8, 10–12, 15, 16
Structures and offices
counselling and support services, 106, 108
finance and administration directorate, 107
investigations and research, 106
investigations and research directorate, 107
legal directorate, 108
Public affairs and community liaison, 106, 107
secretariat, 106
thematic committees, 106, 108
Subpoena powers, 85–87, 89
Success, 145–148
Supreme Military Council, 39–41, 43, 45
Survey
Ghana Centre for Democratic Development, 152–154, 156, 161, 181
qualitative survey, 18, 156, 172, 183
quantitative, 170, 171, 175, 183

T
Third Republic, 43, 44
Timor Leste, 133, 139
Togoland, 31
Torture Convention, 193, 194, 196, 199, 201–203
Transition, 2–5, 8, 9, 14, 16, 17, 20
Transitional justice, 1–6, 9, 13–18, 20, 21
Transitional Justice Database Project, 9
Transitional justice mechanisms, 191, 192, 198
Transitional plan, 222, 224, 225
Transitional provisions, 43, 44
Transition to democracy
consultative assembly, 50
electoral process, 52
International Monetary Fund, 50
John Agyekum Kufuor, 52
New Patriotic Party, 51, 52
opposition, 50
World Bank, 50
Trials, 4, 6–8, 12, 13
Trust territory, 31
Truth
accurate and complete record, 154
Components of the right to truth, 159
limitations, 147, 153, 158, 160
moral right to know, 150
screening out exercise, 156, 158
truth finding mandate, 152, 153, 157, 158
versions of truth, 152, 153
Truth commissions, 1, 3, 6–9, 12–14, 16–18, 20, 145–149, 152, 153, 158, 160, 185
benefits, 12
shortcoming, 12
Tuffour v Attorney General, 64, 65

U
United Gold Coast Convention, 29–31, 37
United Nations War Crimes Commission, 7

Universal Declaration of Human Rights
customary international law status, 200
Universal of human rights
customary international law status, 200

V
Valech Commission, 224
Victims, 106, 108, 109, 111–113, 115, 122, 123, 126, 130, 131, 134, 136–138, 140–142
Victims' rights to remedies, 160, 161, 166
Volta, 31

W
War crime, 193, 198, 199, 203
Weaknesses, 16
West Africa, 2, 17
When the subject of transitional justice began to emerge, 4
Witch-hunt, 157, 159, 178
Witness-related powers, 86, 88, 98
Workers Brigade, 34
Work of the NRC, 104, 117, 121, 135

The manufacturer's authorised representative in the EU is Springer Nature Customer Service Centre GmbH, Europaplatz 3, 69115 Heidelberg, Germany. If you have any concerns regarding our products, please contact ProductSafety@springernature.com

Printed and bound by CPI Group (UK) Ltd, Croydon, CR0 4YY

05/10/2026

02228120-0005